Adobe® Illustrator® CS3

The Professional Portfolio

AGAINST THE CLOCK
mastering graphic technology

Managing Editor: Ellenn Behoriam
Cover & Interior Design: Erika Kendra
Copy Editor: Laurel Nelson-Cucchiara
Proofreader: Angelina Kendra
Printing/Bindery: Impact Media

10 9 8 7 6 5 4 3 2 1   978-0-9764324-6-3

PO Box 260092, Tampa, Florida 33685
800-256-4ATC • www.againsttheclock.com

Acknowledgements

About Against The Clock

Against The Clock has been publishing computer arts educational materials for more than 15 years, starting out as a Tampa, Florida-based systems integration firm whose primary focus was on skills development in high-volume, demanding commercial environments. Among the company's clients were LL Bean, The New England Journal of Medicine, the Smithsonian, and many others. Over the years, Against The Clock has developed a solid and widely-respected approach to teaching people how to effectively utilize graphics applications while maintaining a disciplined approach to real-world problems.

Against The Clock has been recognized as one of the nation's leaders in courseware development. Having developed the *Against The Clock* and the *Essentials for Design* series with Prentice Hall/Pearson Education, the firm works closely with all major software developers to ensure timely release of educational products aimed at new version releases.

About the Authors

Gary Poyssick, co-owner of Against The Clock, is a well-known and often controversial speaker, writer, and industry consultant who has been involved in professional graphics and communications for more than twenty years. He wrote the highly popular *Workflow Reengineering* (Adobe Press), *Teams and the Graphic Arts Service Provider* (Prentice Hall), *Creative Techniques: Adobe Illustrator*, and *Creative Techniques: Adobe Photoshop* (Hayden Books), and was the author or co-author of many application-specific training books from Against The Clock.

Erika Kendra holds a BA in History and a BA in English Literature from the University of Pittsburgh. She began her career in the graphic communications industry as an editor at Graphic Arts Technical Foundation before moving to Los Angeles in 2000. Erika is the author or co-author of more than fifteen books about graphic design software, including QuarkXPress, Adobe Photoshop, Adobe InDesign, and Adobe PageMaker. She has also written several books about graphic design concepts such as color reproduction and preflighting, and dozens of articles for online and print journals in the graphics industry. Working with Against The Clock for more than seven years, Erika was a key partner in developing the new Portfolio Series of software training books.

Contributing Authors, Artists, and Editors

A big thank you to the people whose comments and expertise contributed to the success of these books:

- **David McGill**, Azusa Pacific University
- **Debbie Davidson**, Sweet Dreams Designs
- **Dean Bagley**, Against The Clock, Inc.
- **Scott MacNeill,** MacNeill and Macintosh

Thanks also to Laurel Nelson-Cucchiara, editor, and Angelina Kendra, proofreader, for their help in making sure that we all said what we meant to say.

Walk-Through

PROJECT GOALS

Each project begins with a clear description of the overall concepts that are explained in the project; these goals closely match the different "stages" of the project workflow.

THE PROJECT MEETING

Each project includes the client's initial comments, which provide valuable information about the job. The Project Art Director, a vital part of any design workflow, also provides fundamental advice and production requirements.

PROJECT OBJECTIVES

Each Project Meeting includes a summary of the specific skills required to complete the project.

REAL-WORLD WORKFLOW

Projects are broken into logical lessons or "stages" of the workflow. Brief introductions at the beginning of each stage provide vital foundational material required to complete the task.

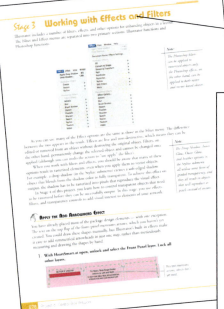

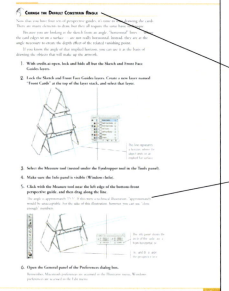

STEP-BY-STEP EXERCISES

Every stage of the workflow is broken into multiple hands-on, step-by-step exercises.

VISUAL EXPLANATIONS

Wherever possible, screen shots are annotated so students can quickly identify important information.

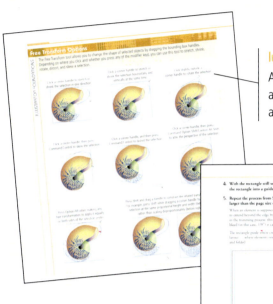

ILLUSTRATOR FOUNDATIONS

Additional functionality, related tools, and underlying graphic design concepts are included throughout the book.

ADVICE AND WARNINGS

Where appropriate, sidebars provide shortcuts, warnings, or tips about the topic at hand.

VISUAL SUMMARY

Using an annotated version of the finished project, students can quickly identify the skills used to complete different aspects of the job.

PORTFOLIO BUILDER PROJECTS

Each step-by-step project is accompanied by a related freeform project, allowing students to practice their skills and exercise creativity, resulting in an extensive and diverse portfolio of work.

The Against The Clock *Portfolio Series* teaches graphic design software tools and techniques entirely within the framework of real-world projects; we introduce and explain skills where they would naturally fall into a real project workflow. For example, rather than including an entire chapter about printing (which most students find boring), we teach printing where you naturally need to do so — when you complete a print-based project.

The project-based approach in the *Portfolio Series* allows you to get in depth with the software beginning in Project 1 — you don't have to read several chapters of introductory material before you can start creating finished artwork.

The project-based approach of the *Portfolio Series* also prevents "topic tedium" — in other words, we don't require you to read pages and pages of information about text (for example); instead, we explain text tools and options as part of a larger project (in this case, as part of a kitchen design guide).

Clear, easy-to-read, step-by-step instructions walk you through every phase of each job, from creating a new file to saving the finished piece. Wherever logical, we also offer practical advice and tips about underlying concepts and graphic design practices that will benefit students as they enter the job market.

The projects in this book reflect a range of different types of Illustrator jobs, from creating a series of icons to designing a kitchen planning guide to building a Web page. When you finish the eight projects in this book (and the accompanying Portfolio Builder exercises), you will have a substantial body of work that should impress any potential employer.

The eight Illustrator CS3 projects are described briefly here; more detail is provided in the full table of contents (beginning on Page viii).

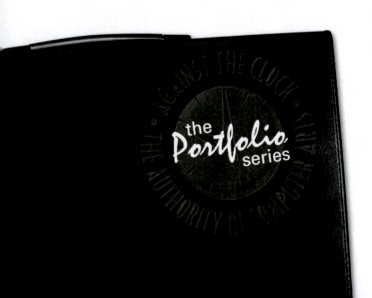

Project 1 — International Symbols

❏ Drawing Primitive Shapes

❏ Scaling, Cloning, and Alignment

❏ Controlling Fills and Strokes

❏ Drawing Other Simple Objects

❏ Drawing Complex Objects

Project 2 — Kitchen Planning Guide

❏ Align Text to Specific Objects

❏ Creating Technically Accurate Artwork

❏ Controlling Basic Type Attributes

❏ More Advanced Typesetting

❏ Placing Images and Outputting Files

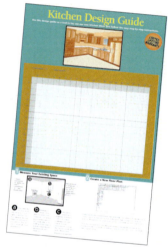

Project 3 — Identity Package

❏ Using Photographic Templates

❏ Using Color and Type for Logo Design

❏ Creating the Corporate Stationery

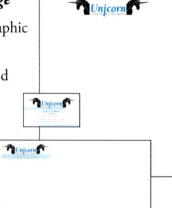

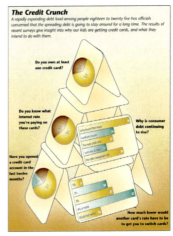

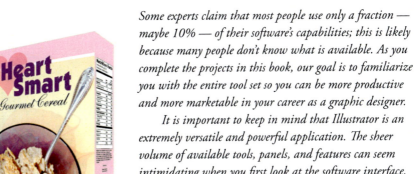
Some experts claim that most people use only a fraction — maybe 10% — of their software's capabilities; this is likely because many people don't know what is available. As you complete the projects in this book, our goal is to familiarize you with the entire tool set so you can be more productive and more marketable in your career as a graphic designer.

It is important to keep in mind that Illustrator is an extremely versatile and powerful application. The sheer volume of available tools, panels, and features can seem intimidating when you first look at the software interface. Most of these tools, however, are fairly simple to use with a bit of background information and a little practice.

Wherever necessary, we explain the underlying concepts and terms that are required for understanding the software. We're confident that these projects provide the practice you need to create sophisticated artwork by the end of the very first project.

Contents

PREREQUISITES

The entire Portfolio Series is based on the assumption that you have a basic understanding of how to use your computer. You should know how to use your mouse to point and click, as well as to drag items around the screen. You should be able to resize and arrange windows on your desktop to maximize your available space. You should know how to access drop-down menus, and understand how check boxes and radio buttons work. It also doesn't hurt to have a good understanding of how your operating system organizes files and folders, and how to navigate your way around them. If you're familiar with these fundamental skills, then you know all that's necessary to use the Portfolio Series.

RESOURCE FILES

All of the files that you need to complete the projects in this book are on the provided Resource CD in the RF_Illustrator folder. The main RF folder contains eight subfolders, one for each project in the book; you will be directed to the appropriate folder whenever you need to access a specific file. Files required to complete the related Portfolio Builder exercises are in the RF_Builders folder.

The Resource CD also includes a WIP folder, which also contains (mostly empty) subfolders for each project in the book. This is where you will save your work as you complete the various projects. In some cases, the location of a file will be extremely important for later steps in a project to work properly; that's why we've provided a specific set of folders with known file names.

Before you begin working on the projects in this book, you should copy the entire WIP folder to your hard drive or some other recordable media such as a flash drive; when we tell you to save a file, you should save it to the appropriate folder on the drive where you put that WIP folder.

ATC FONTS

You must install the ATC fonts from the Resource CD to ensure that your exercises and projects will work as described in the book; these fonts are provided on the Resource CD-ROM in the ATC Fonts folder. Specific instructions for installing fonts are provided in the documentation that came with your computer. You should replace older (pre-2004) ATC fonts with the ones on your Resource CD.

SYSTEM REQUIREMENTS

As software technology continues to mature, the differences in functionality from one platform to another continue to diminish. The Portfolio Series was designed to work on both Macintosh or Windows computers; where differences exist do from one platform to another, we include specific instructions relative to each platform.

One issue that remains constant from Macintosh to Windows is the use of different modifier keys (Control, Shift, etc.) to accomplish the same task. When we present key commands, we always follow the same Macintosh/Windows format — Macintosh keys are listed first, then a slash, followed by the Windows key command.

System Requirements for Adobe Illustrator CS3:

Windows®

- Intel® Pentium 4 or higher or equivalent
- Microsoft® Windows XP with Service Pack 2 or Windows Vista™ Home Premium, Business, Ultimate, or Enterprise
- 512MB of RAM
- 2 GB of available hard-disk space
- 1024×768 monitor resolution with 16-bit video card
- DVD-ROM drive
- QuickTime 7.1 required for multimedia features

Mac OS

- PowerPC® G4 or G5 or Intel-based Macintosh
- Mac OS X v.10.4.8
- 512MB of RAM
- 2.5 GB of available hard-disk space
- 1024×768 monitor resolution with 16-bit video card
- DVD-ROM drive
- QuickTime 7.1 required for multimedia features

The user interface (often referred to as the UI) is what you see when you first start the program. As is the case with all commercial applications, certain settings are already determined and set up by the software developer. These include variables such as the size of the "normal" page, whether your images are destined for the Web or paper, and many others.

Let's start with an overall look at what you see when you first start the program. The following illustration is a sample that comes with the program (a map of Yellowstone National Park), which we used to help identify the components of the application interface.

Note:

*Values set by the software manufacturer are called **default settings**.*

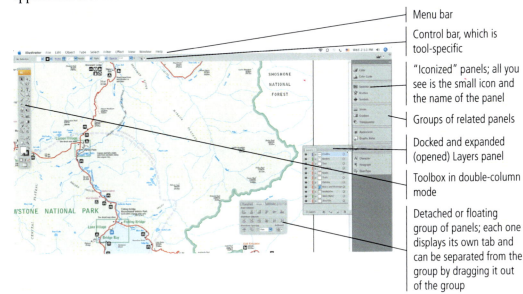

Menu bar

Control bar, which is tool-specific

"Iconized" panels; all you see is the small icon and the name of the panel

Groups of related panels

Docked and expanded (opened) Layers panel

Toolbox in double-column mode

Detached or floating group of panels; each one displays its own tab and can be separated from the group by dragging it out of the group

MENUS

Like most other applications, Illustrator has a menu bar across the top of the screen. If you've ever used a computer, you're probably familiar with navigating menus. In Illustrator, ten menus provide access to virtually all of the available options. (Macintosh users have two extra menus. The Apple menu provides access to system-specific commands. The Illustrator menu follows the Macintosh system-standard format introduced in OS X for all applications; this menu controls basic application operations such as About, Hide, Preferences, and Quit Illustrator.)

If a menu command isn't available for a specific image or selection, it appears grayed out. Some menu commands can be accessed using a keyboard shortcut. If a menu command has an associated shortcut, it is listed to the right of the specific command (such as the Group command in the image you see here).

Note:

The Tools panel you see in the main user interface screen shot displays the tools in two columns. All Creative Suite applications share the same interface, but you can change how the Tools panel appears in each application. You can see the two-column Tools panel shown in this image, or you can see the Tools panel in a single column.

Many of the commands in Illustrator are **toggles**, which means they're either on or off. You can identify toggles by their names. Look at the View menu in the following image and notice the Hide Edges selection. When you select an object on the page, and then click this command, the menu option will change to Show Edges. When you click Show Edges, it will return to the Hide Edges option. Show and Hide are the two key words to look for. Each Illustrator toggle can either show or hide, and each toggled selection has a keyboard equivalent, which we'll talk about in a moment.

THE DRAWING WINDOW

When you create a new drawing or open an existing illustration, it exists in its own window. By default, the drawing window will fill the screen space to the right of the Tools panel (called Standard Screen Mode); your desktop will be visible directly below the drawing window.

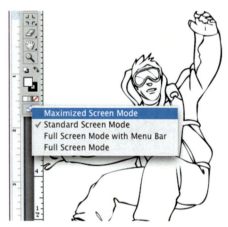

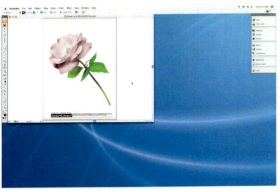

Standard Screen mode

Maximized Screen mode

Full Screen mode with menu bar

Full Screen mode

You can change the screen mode in two ways:

- Clicking the Screen Mode icon at the bottom of the Tools panel

- Pressing the F key (be aware, however that if you're entering text or working with the Type tool, pressing F will insert the letter F instead of changing the view of your screen)

In Standard and Maximized Screen modes, the bottom-left of the drawing space shows the current magnification level. Through the use of a pop-up list, you can change the view percentage to an incredible 6400%.

Note:

You can save custom workspaces by choosing Window>Workspace> Save Workspace. This option allows you to save specific collections of panels, tabs, and tool defaults — along with the screen mode — and then later select them to fit specific working requirements.

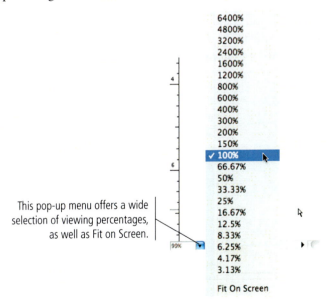

This pop-up menu offers a wide selection of viewing percentages, as well as Fit on Screen.

In addition to the view percentage, the bottom-left corner of the workspace also allows you to see five different attributes of the file you're working on.

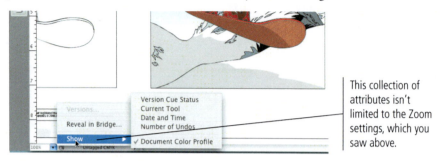

This collection of attributes isn't limited to the Zoom settings, which you saw above.

The following list shows the options in this pop-up menu.

- The **Version Cue Status** is a group or team file format and server management application; Version Cue Status is beyond the scope of this book.

- The **Current Tool** shows what tool you're using.

- The **Date and Time** shows when the file was last saved.

- The **Number of Undos** shows how many undos are left in the cache. (You'll learn more about the number of Undo commands you can use — or have left — in the Preferences section.)

- The **Document Color Profile** is a very important attribute because it allows you to see whether the document complies with standard printing color requirements (CMYK) or Web publishing standards (RGB).

Not every attribute will be important in every working environment, including workflow-oriented attributes such as the Version Cue Status. Other attributes are powerful and useful in virtually all projects, including the important Current Tool attribute, which identifies the tool currently active in your project.

THE CONTROL BAR

Regardless of the screen mode you use, Illustrator (and the other applications in the Adobe Creative Suite) displays a Control bar at the top of the screen. It's sometimes called the **Options bar** because it provides options relative to the tool you're using.

For example, if you were using the Type tool, you could use the Control bar to select different fonts, change the size of the text, and adjust the text's alignment — whether it's centered, aligned on the left, or aligned on the right of the text box in which it resides.

When the Type tool is in use, the Control bar shows options that affect the appearance of selected text objects.

If, on the other hand, you were using the Pen tool, the options available on the Control bar would change to reflect attributes specific to that tool.

When you change to the Pen tool, the Control bar displays completely different options that are specific to the Pen tool. The context-sensitive Control bar is a common component of all Adobe Creative Suite applications.

To the extreme right of the Control bar — regardless of the tool you're using or what options are available — you can jump to Adobe Bridge. Adobe Bridge is a companion program to the Suite programs (Adobe Illustrator included) that allows you to organize, assign, share, publish, and manage images.

From the right side of the Control bar, you can access Adobe Stock Photos, a service from Adobe that allows you to search through the libraries of some of the world's most renowned photographers and illustrators for artwork to use in your own projects.

Using Adobe Bridge

ILLUSTRATOR FOUNDATIONS

Adobe Bridge is a stand-alone application designed to assist in the sharing of projects and project components between different Creative Suite applications, including Adobe Photoshop, Adobe Illustrator, and Adobe InDesign, to name a few. But Bridge doesn't stop there; it can help you manage virtually any digital and graphic file.

Bridge includes a Favorites area, where you can save quick links to specific locations on your system. The center displays thumbnail images of all the files in the location you choose. File-specific information (such as Preview, Metadata, and Keywords) appears in the panes on the left and right sides of the window. You can customize Bridge however you prefer. To find out more, visit the Adobe site and search for Bridge tutorials.

If you have other Creative Suite applications, Bridge can be accessed from and share data between all of them. You can even drag Photoshop images into your Illustrator drawings, or drag Illustrator drawings into any other Creative Suite application.

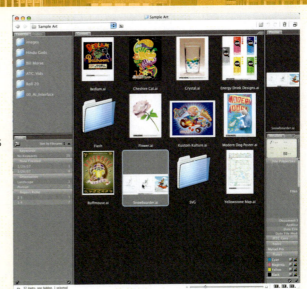

Tools

Similar to most industrial-strength programs — especially ones from Adobe — Illustrator has no shortage of tools. If you look at the Tools panel, it appears to contain 26 tools. That would be correct if each tool icon represented only one tool; but in fact, some of these icons are **nested**.

Because showing the 76 different tools that actually exist within the Illustrator Tools panel would be (to say the least) a bit overwhelming, Adobe uses **nested tool icons**. If a tool icon displays a small black mark in the lower-right corner, there are alternate tools available. You can click the small arrow icon on the right side of any nested tool and drag the entire set of tools off the Tools panel, making the entire group of tools visible on the workspace.

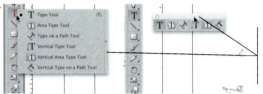

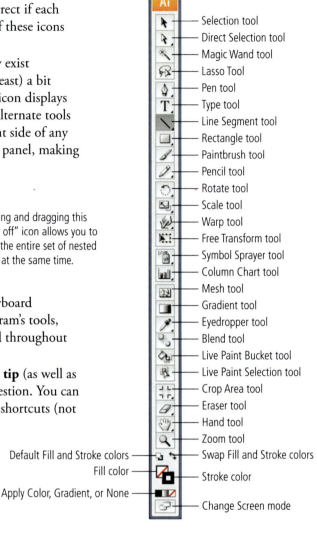

Clicking and dragging this "tear off" icon allows you to view the entire set of nested tools at the same time.

Each of the default tools can be accessed with a keyboard command. As you become more familiar with the program's tools, you'll see more of these **keyboard equivalents** scattered throughout the projects as sidebars.

If you hover your mouse over a tool, a pop-up **tool tip** (as well as a letter in parentheses) will appear above the tool in question. You can access certain tools by pressing the associated keyboard shortcuts (not all tools can be accessed by the keyboard). If you're working with the Type tool, pressing a letter key inserts that letter. You can't call a tool with the keyboard shortcut while an insertion point is flashing.

Tool Shortcuts

ILLUSTRATOR FOUNDATIONS

Use these keyboard shortcuts to access the different tools:

+	Add Anchor Point tool	H	Hand tool	O	Reflect tool
W	Blend tool	Q	Lasso tool	-	Remove Anchor Point tool
J	Column Graph tool	\	Line Segment tool	R	Rotate tool
Shift-C	Convert Anchor Point tool	K	Live Paint Bucket tool	S	Scale tool
Shift-O	Crop Area tool	Shift-L	Live Paint Selection tool	C	Scissors tool
A	Direct Selection tool	Y	Magic Wand tool	V	Selection tool
L	Ellipse tool	U	Mesh tool	Shift-K	Slice tool
Shift-E	Eraser tool	B	Paintbrush tool	Shift-S	Symbol Sprayer tool
I	Eyedropper tool	P	Pen tool	T	Type tool
E	Free Transform tool	N	Pencil tool	Shift-R	Warp tool
G	Gradient tool	M	Rectangle tool	Z	Zoom tool

One other thing to remember about the Tools panel is that it can be seen in one of two ways. By default, all of the tool icons appear in a single stack or column. At the top left of the Tools panel, however, is a double-arrow icon. When you click that icon, the Tools panel changes from a single column of tool icons to a double column. The bottom section of the Tools panel remains the same, but the individual icons stack in half the vertical space. Throughout the book, you'll see the Tools panel both ways.

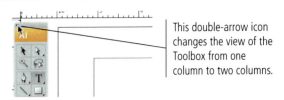

This double-arrow icon changes the view of the Toolbox from one column to two columns.

ILLUSTRATOR FOUNDATIONS

Nested Tools

You should explore which tools are available below the default tools. The following chart offers a quick reference.

Selection tool	**Paintbrush tool**	**Column Graph tool**
Direct Selection tool	**Pencil tool**	*Stacked Column Graph tool*
Group Selection tool	*Smooth tool*	*Bar Graph tool*
Magic Wand tool	*Path Erase tool*	*Stacked Bar Graph tool*
Lasso tool	**Rotate tool**	*Line Graph tool*
	Reflect tool	*Area Graph tool*
Pen tool		*Scatter Graph tool*
Add Anchor Point tool	**Scale tool**	*Pie Graph tool*
Delete Anchor Point tool	*Shear tool*	*Radar Graph tool*
Convert Anchor Point tool	*Reshape tool*	**Mesh tool**
Type tool	**Warp tool**	**Gradient tool**
Area Type tool	*Twirl tool*	**Eyedropper tool**
Type on a Path tool	*Pucker tool*	*Measurement tool*
Vertical Type tool	*Bloat tool*	**Blend tool**
Vertical Area Type tool	*Scallop tool*	**Live Paint Bucket**
Vertical Type on a Path tool	*Crystallize tool*	**Crop Area tool**
Line Segment tool	*Wrinkle tool*	*Slice tool*
Arc tool	**Free Transform tool**	*Slice Select tool*
Spiral tool	**Symbol Sprayer tool**	**Eraser tool**
Rectangular Grid tool	*Symbol Shifter tool*	*Scissors tool*
Polar Grid tool	*Symbol Scruncher tool*	*Knife tool*
Rectangle tool	*Symbol Sizer tool*	**Hand tool**
Rounded Rectangle tool	*Symbol Spinner tool*	*Page tool*
Ellipse tool	*Symbol Stainer tool*	**Zoom tool**
Polygon tool	*Symbol Screener tool*	
Star tool	*Symbol Styler tool*	
Flare tool		

PANELS

In addition to the many tools and ancillary functions found in Illustrator's drawing environment, the program also provides 34 different **panels** that can be either floating around the working space or locked into place in the **dock**, which appears by default on the right side of your monitor. The dock is an integral part of the user interface — and this is true for all Creative Suite applications. Items found under the Window menu can be activated and left floating or placed into the dock.

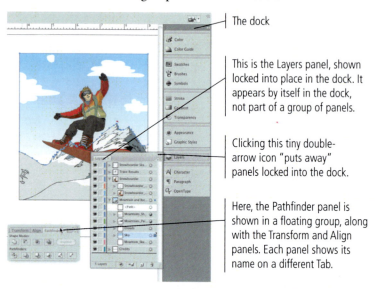

The dock

This is the Layers panel, shown locked into place in the dock. It appears by itself in the dock, not part of a group of panels.

Clicking this tiny double-arrow icon "puts away" panels locked into the dock.

Here, the Pathfinder panel is shown in a floating group, along with the Transform and Align panels. Each panel shows its name on a different Tab.

In the upper-right corner of the dock, you see a small double-arrow icon. Clicking it expands the dock from its iconized default view to an expanded version. If you're familiar with older versions of Illustrator, you will be familiar with these fully opened panels. You can also drag the left handle of the dock to shrink it down until all you see are the icons, without any labels indicating what each panel does.

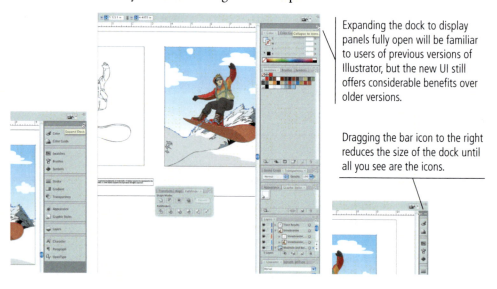

Expanding the dock to display panels fully open will be familiar to users of previous versions of Illustrator, but the new UI still offers considerable benefits over older versions.

Dragging the bar icon to the right reduces the size of the dock until all you see are the icons.

By default, any panels left open (visible) in the dock continue to be visible while you're working on your illustration. You can close them by clicking the small icon at the upper right of each panel. If you Control/right-click the top of the dock (where the tiny view icons are located), you can change this attribute so panels will automatically close when you click elsewhere on the document.

As we already mentioned, you have a great deal of control over Illustrator's user interface. To start with, you can toggle panels on and off using the Window menu. If you choose a panel that's already in an existing group, the entire group opens and the Tab displaying the name of that (chosen) panel rises to the top of the group.

If a panel is selected while it or its group is within the dock, the panel appears hanging to the left or right and connected to its icon, depending on where you position the dock on your monitor. If you close a panel, and then reactivate it from the Window menu, the panel will reappear wherever it was when you closed it — whether floating or connected to the dock, and whether alone or part of a group.

When you activate an as-yet unused panel or panel group from the Window menu, by default it's a floating panel or panel group. You can drag a floating panel into the dock by simply clicking the panel or group at the top and dragging it into the dock until you see a bright blue line indicating where the panel or group will be located. You can place a panel or group at the top of any panel already there, in between any two panels, or at the bottom of the stack.

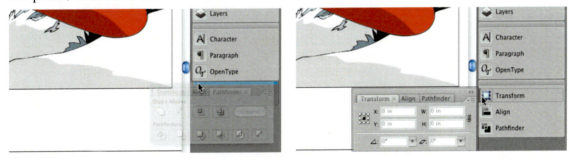

Every panel contains submenus, which provide panel-specific functionality and can be accessed by clicking the submenu icon in the top-right corner of the panel.

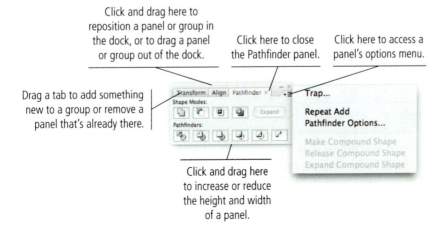

Click and drag here to
reposition a panel or group in
the dock, or to drag a panel
or group out of the dock.

Click here to close
the Pathfinder panel.

Click here to access a
panel's options menu.

Drag a tab to add something
new to a group or remove a
panel that's already there.

Click and drag here
to increase or reduce
the height and width
of a panel.

Customizing the Workspace

Different people use Adobe Illustrator for various types of jobs, often making use of unique, very personalized collections of tools, panel groups, View modes. Each professional designer or illustrator can create projects in his or her own way.

You have the ability to add or modify the keyboard commands that are defined when the application is first installed, and you can also modify how the program's menus appear. Each unique combination of keyboard commands can be saved for use on similar jobs. For example, if you want to use a tool that has multiple options (such as the Symbol Sprayer tool), rather than toggle through five or six alternate tools, you can assign each tool an individual keyboard equivalent, allowing you to access each tool with a single click instead of five clicks.

To change keyboard commands, choose Keyboard Commands from the Edit menu. The default dialog box that appears can be used to modify Menu commands. You can use the icons on the left side of the list to open menu commands.

You can also change the default keyboard commands for accessing specific tools by choosing Tools from the pop-up menu at the top of the Keyboard Shortcuts dialog box.

Note:

While you might think this is a minor issue, when you're working on real jobs, saving five mouse clicks every time you do something can quickly add up to a day off.

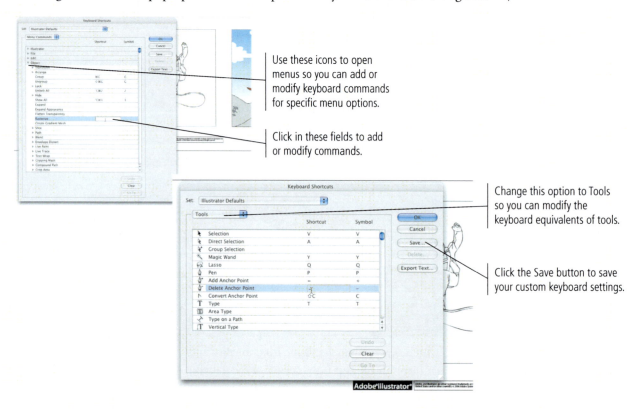

Use these icons to open menus so you can add or modify keyboard commands for specific menu options.

Click in these fields to add or modify commands.

Change this option to Tools so you can modify the keyboard equivalents of tools.

Click the Save button to save your custom keyboard settings.

You can also customize the entire workspace, as we mentioned previously. The best way to understand how workspaces operate is to experiment with them as you learn more about the program. Under the Window menu, you'll find several options related to default and custom workspaces. In the image to the right, you see one custom workspace (the one being used to write this book), three default workspaces, an option for saving the workspace you're working with at an exact moment in time, and an option that accesses a workspace management dialog box.

Selecting workspaces — such as the Type workspace, for example — changes everything to meet the requirements of the artist who created the workspace. For example, the Type workspace shows panels that definitely weren't in the default workspace — including Character and Paragraph Styles.

The best thing about managing workspaces is that you can keep Illustrator and any of the Creative Suite applications in any number of different forms — and you can switch back and forth as dictated by the requirements of the moment. Choosing the Manage Workspaces option allows you to create copies of existing workspaces and delete workspaces that you don't need anymore. Changes to your workspaces appear in the menu as soon as you click OK and close the Manage Workspaces dialog box.

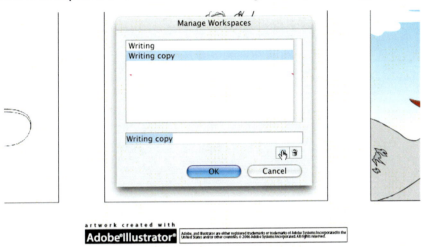

Switching workspaces changes not only the Viewing mode, keyboard commands and current font, but it also remembers to replace your panels — whether opened, closed, or in-between — exactly as you left them the last time you worked on the file.

Preferences

In addition to customizing the interface, you can also customize the way many of the program's options function. The right side of the Preferences dialog box (Illustrator>Preferences on Macintosh or Edit>Preferences on Windows) allows you to move forward and backward through the various Preferences dialog boxes (there are 11 different sets of Preferences available in Illustrator). As you work your way through the projects in this book, you'll learn not only what you can do with these different Preferences collections, but also *why* you would want to use them and when it makes sense to use them.

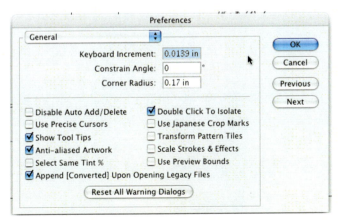

International Symbols

Biotech Services manages large-scale manufacturing facilities specializing in everything from digital photographic equipment to machines used to drill for oil. The company builds plants all over world that in many cases handle dangerous chemicals and undertake dangerous tasks — which means they must prominently display danger warnings. Biotech Services hired you to create a digital collection of universal symbols they can use to create signs, print on the side of large machines, place as icons on their Web sites, and embroider onto employee uniforms.

This project incorporates the following skills:

❑ Placing raster images into an Illustrator file to use as drawing templates

❑ Creating and managing simple shapes and lines

❑ Using various tools and panels to transform objects' color, position, and shape

❑ Cloning objects to minimize repetitive tasks

❑ Using layers to organize and manage complex artwork

❑ Drawing complex shapes by combining simple shapes and using Bezier curves

The Project Meeting

Client Comments

We have a set of universal warning symbols on our Web site, but we need to use those same icons in other places as well. Our printer told us that the symbols on our Web site are "low res," which can't be used for print projects. The printer also said he needs vector graphics that will scale larger and still look good. The printer suggested we hire a designer to create digital versions of the icons so we can use them for a wide variety of purposes, from large machinery signs to small plastic cards to anything else that might come up. We need you to help us figure out exactly what we need and then create the icons for us.

Art Director Comments

Basically, we have the icons, but they're low-resolution raster images, so they only work for the Web, and they can't be enlarged. The good news is that you can use the existing icons as templates and more or less trace them to create the new icons.

The client needs files that can be printed cleanly and scaled from a couple of inches up to several feet. Illustrator vector files are perfect for this type of job. In fact, vector graphics get their resolution from the printer being used for a specific job, so you can scale them to any size you want without losing quality.

Project Objectives

To complete this project, you will:

- ❏ Create a grid that will eventually hold all fourteen icons in one document
- ❏ Control objects' stroke, fill, and transparency attributes
- ❏ Import and use the client's raster images as templates, which you can then trace
- ❏ Use the Line tool to create a complex object from a set of straight lines
- ❏ Lock, unlock, hide, and show objects to navigate the object stacking order
- ❏ Scale, rotate, and reflect objects to create complex artwork from simple shapes
- ❏ Use Layers to manage complex artwork
- ❏ Use Live Trace to automatically create a vector outline of a raster image
- ❏ Use the Pathfinder to combine simple shapes into a single complex object
- ❏ Use the Pen tool to manually draw complex shapes

Stage 1 Drawing Primitive Shapes

This lesson focuses on the real basics: creating **primitive** objects — such as circles, ovals, squares, stars, and rectangles. Shapes that you draw in Illustrator are fairly simple to understand once you know how they're built. In this project, you draw with Illustrator's primitive tools, which allow you to draw ovals, rectangles, spirals, and polygons, as well as perfect squares and circles.

Whatever Illustrator tool you use to draw, doing so creates anchored points — appropriately called **anchor points** — and connects them with mathematically accurate lines known as **paths** or **segments**. All anchor points contain information for controlling the shape of curves (which you learn about later in this project).

Note:

We call circles, squares, rectangles, stars, and other basic shapes "primitive shapes"; Adobe, however, calls them "geometric shapes," so you might see some discrepancy between our terminology and Adobe's.

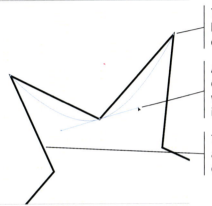

These solid and hollow squares are called anchor points.

Anchor points can contain curve handles, which we talk about later in this project.

These lines connecting anchor points are called paths.

Raster vs. Pixel Artwork

ILLUSTRATOR FOUNDATIONS

There are two primary types of artwork: vector graphics and raster images. (Line art, sometimes categorized as a third type of image, is actually a type of raster image.) Adobe Photoshop is what some people call a "paint" program; it is primarily used to create and manipulate pixel-based or **raster images**.

Vector graphics are composed of mathematical descriptions of a series of lines and geometric shapes. These files are commonly created in illustration ("drawing") applications such as Adobe Illustrator or in page-layout applications such as Adobe InDesign. Vector graphics are **resolution independent**; they can be freely scaled and are automatically output at the resolution of the output device.

Raster images are made up of a grid of individual **pixels** (**rasters** or **bits**) in rows and columns (called a **bitmap**). Raster files are **resolution dependent**; their resolution is determined when you scan, photograph, or create the file.

Why is it important for you to know the difference between rasters and vectors? Many of the files that you build in Illustrator will be placed in various print projects, so you have to build the files with the appropriate settings for commercial printing.

- **Pixels per inch (ppi)** is the number of pixels in one horizontal or vertical inch of a digital raster file.
- **Lines per inch (lpi)** is the number of halftone dots produced in a horizontal or vertical linear inch by a high-resolution imagesetter in order to simulate the appearance of continuous-tone color.
- **Dots per inch (dpi)** or **spots per inch (spi)** is the number of dots produced by an output device in a single line of output. DPI is sometimes used interchangeably with pixels per inch.

When reproducing a photograph on a printing press, the image must be converted into a set of different-sized dots that fool the eye into believing that it sees continuous tones. The result of this conversion process is a halftone image; the dots used to simulate continuous tone are called **halftone dots**. Light tones in a photograph are represented as small halftone dots; dark tones become large halftone dots. Prior to image-editing software, photos were converted to halftones with a large graphic arts camera and screens. The picture was photographed through the screen to create halftone dots, and different screens produced different numbers of dots in an inch — hence the term dots per inch.

CREATE A NEW DOCUMENT

In this project, you will draw a variety of international warning symbols. For now, however, all you need is one new document to complete all of your preliminary work.

1. **Start Illustrator.**

   When you launch Illustrator, the Welcome screen appears. If you don't see the Welcome screen, someone has stopped this feature from appearing when the program starts.

2. **If you can't see the Welcome screen, choose Help>Welcome Screen.**

   The Open a Recent Item column on the left of the Welcome screen displays the last eight or ten images you worked on, along with an Open icon that allows you to browse around until you find the file you need. Different categories of new file types are available on the right side of the dialog box.

This column lists files you've been working on and allows you to browse around to find a specific file.

Start a new print document by clicking this icon.

This list offers interactive help and links to external resources.

You can prevent the Welcome screen from opening by clicking this check box.

Note:

Before completing this project, copy the Symbols folder from the WIP folder on your Resource CD to your WIP folder wherever you are saving your work. When you save files for this project, you will save them in your WIP>Symbols folder.

3. **Click Print Document in the Create New column on the right side of the Welcome screen.**

4. **In the resulting New Document dialog box, type "Symbols" in the Name field. Make sure the Portrait orientation option is selected, and then click the Advanced button on the lower left.**

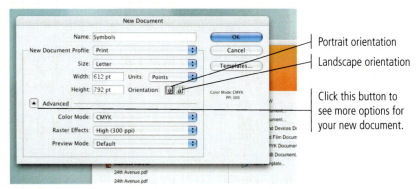

Portrait orientation

Landscape orientation

Click this button to see more options for your new document.

When you first look at the New Document dialog box, it appears in Standard view. Clicking the Advanced button expands the dialog box, allowing you to change color mode (RGB for the Web or CMYK for print jobs) and resolution, which determines the number of pixels in a square inch of an image; higher resolution numbers are used for print jobs and lower numbers are used for Web distribution. The default setting is 300 dpi — the standard resolution used to print color magazines. If your artwork is destined for the Internet, 72 dpi is the preferred setting.

Note:

It's always a good idea to keep high-resolution copies of the files that you show on the Web; if you ever need to print that file, you'll already have the data you need. It's much easier to reduce a file from 300 dpi to 72 dpi than to increase from 72 dpi to 300 dpi.

5. **Click OK to create the new, blank document named Symbols.**

6. **Choose Window>Workspace>[Basic].**

   We want to ensure that what you see on your screen is the same as what we show you in this exercise; starting from a basic workspace is the first step in that process.

7. **On the right side of the monitor you see a stack of icons. Drag the left edge of the stack until you can see the panels' names.**

   This stack is called the dock, and it contains active panels. This user interface appeared with the Creative Suite 3 applications. It is a significant improvement over older versions of Illustrator, in which panels had fixed minimum widths and couldn't be grouped.

   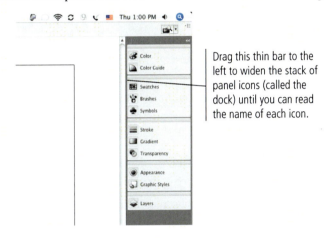

   Drag this thin bar to the left to widen the stack of panel icons (called the dock) until you can read the name of each icon.

8. **Choose File>Save As (or press Command/Control-S) and navigate to your WIP>Symbols folder.**

   When you save an Adobe Illustrator file for the first time, you encounter the Save As dialog box. It gives a number of options, including the ability to save a file using a different name.

   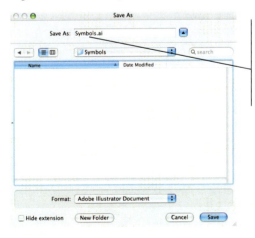

   This name defaults to Symbols.ai since you named the file Symbols when you first created it. If you hadn't named the file when you first created it, the default name would be Untitled.ai.

9. **Click Save, and then click OK in the Illustrator Options dialog box.**

These options determine what will be stored in the file. In most cases, you can simply leave these options at their default values.

10. **Leave the file open for the next exercise.**

 ## Draw Squares and Circles

The best place to start is at the beginning, and that holds true for learning how to use Illustrator. Before you can create award-winning illustrations, you have to learn the basics, such as drawing squares and circles.

1. **Continue working in the open file. In the Tools panel, click the Rectangle tool and hold down the mouse button.**

As you may remember from reading the chapter about the Illustrator user interface, many tools have alternate or nested tools, and the Rectangle tool is one such tool.

Any tool that displays these tiny black icons in the lower-right corner comes in several different varieties. These sets of tools are called nested tools.

Select the Rectangle tool from the Toolbox. If you hold down the mouse button, you'll see the alternate (nested) tools.

What are Default Values?

ILLUSTRATOR FOUNDATIONS

A **default value** is a setting that was either originally set up by the manufacturer or (in many cases) was the last setting entered by the last person using the program. Default values (also called simply "defaults") are related to such settings as the size of your document, how Illustrator interprets and translates colors (Web or print), and a host of other conditions. Almost every tool and function in the program has default parameters: How thick is a line? What color fills a circle? What is the transparency of the edge?

If you change a value that was originally set by Adobe, it's likely the change will remain in place until you change it again. Almost all default settings work that way — they can be modified and customized by the user. As you expand your knowledge of the Illustrator program, you'll become familiar with each of the default settings, and you'll know which ones you need to modify to better suit your unique workflow.

2. Click the Default Fill and Stroke button at the bottom of the Tools panel.

Clicking this button restores the fill to white and the stroke to black.

 Default Fill and Stroke button

3. Option/Alt-click the Rectangle tool anywhere on the empty page.

The resulting dialog box asks you how big you want the rectangle to be. The default measurement system is pixels, but if the machine you're working on has been used before, the dialog could show any of Illustrator's measurement units.

You can enter a number and type a different unit of measurement ("pt" for points, "i" for inches, "mm" for millimeters, and a few others that are rarely used) in these fields.

4. Type "2 in" into the Width field and press Tab to move to the Height field.

When you move to the next field, Illustrator calculates the conversion of inches (the "in" you put in the Width field) to points (the 144 pt that appears in the Width field after you moved to the Height field).

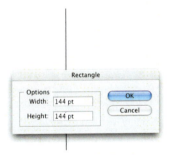

5. Type "2 in" into the Height field and click OK.

A box appears with its center exactly where you clicked the Rectangle tool. You now know one way to draw a box (or circle, or almost any other basic shape) that's exactly 2 inches square.

Key Command:

*Press Command/ Control-H to show or hide the bounding box of any selected objects. Objects or functions that turn on and off by pressing the same key command are said to be **toggled functions** or simply **toggles**.*

Note:

*A **point** is a unit of measurement that comes from the traditional typesetting industry; there are 72 point in an inch.*

6. **Now choose the Ellipse tool from the nested tools under the Rectangle tool.**

Ellipse is another name for oval. The Ellipse tool can draw ellipses or perfect circles if you hold down the Shift key while you draw the shape. Similarly, the Rectangle tool can draw perfect squares if you hold the Shift key while you draw or simple rectangles if you use only the mouse when you create the shape.

Key Command:

Press the L key to access the Ellipse tool.

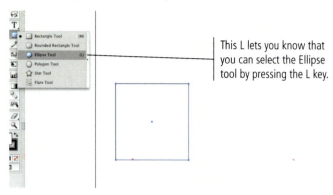

This L lets you know that you can select the Ellipse tool by pressing the L key.

7. **Click the upper-left corner of the square that's already there and drag to the right and down.**

The circle begins to appear in the square you already drew. Press the Shift key to keep the circle perfectly round.

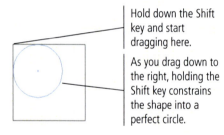

Hold down the Shift key and start dragging here.

As you drag down to the right, holding the Shift key constrains the shape into a perfect circle.

Drawing Primitive Shapes

If you simply Option/Alt-click a shape tool in the drawing window, you can determine the width and height of the shape by entering the appropriate values in the dialog box that appears. The center of the shape will be positioned exactly where you clicked, which is what you did in Step 3 of this exercise.

Second, you can click and drag immediately (which keeps the dialog box from appearing) and simply release the mouse button where you want to end the shape. If you hold the Option/Alt key while drawing a primitive shape, it grows outward from where you first click, with the exact center of the object as its starting or **origin** point.

Lastly, if you press the Shift key while drawing any of these primitive objects, the height and width will remain equal, and the shape will be a perfect circle, square, star, or polygon. A primitive object drawn while pressing the Shift key, and thus with equal heights and widths, is said to be **constrained.**

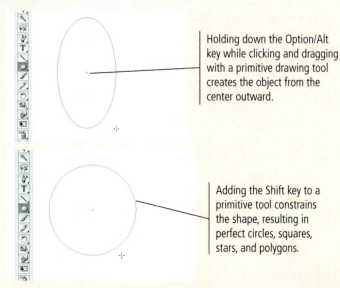

Holding down the Option/Alt key while clicking and dragging with a primitive drawing tool creates the object from the center outward.

Adding the Shift key to a primitive tool constrains the shape, resulting in perfect circles, squares, stars, and polygons.

8. **Release the mouse button to create the shape.**

9. **Select the two objects on the page (Edit>Select All) and press Delete/Backspace to delete them.**

Key Command:

Press Command/Control-A to select all the objects on the page.

10. **Select the Rounded Rectangle tool.**

    A rectangle or square can either have regular (square) corners or rounded corners. A rounded rectangle is the same as placing one-quarter of a circle in the corner of a regular square.

11. **Click the tool cursor on the page and create a 2″ rounded square with a 12-pt corner radius.**

    This will become the frame for all the symbols you create in this project.

    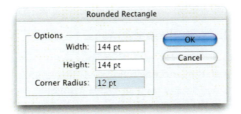

Note:

A rounded-corner rectangle is a square with the corners cut at a specific distance from the end, and the two resultant edges connected with part of a circle whose radius is equal to the amount of the rounding.

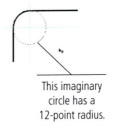

This imaginary circle has a 12-point radius.

12. **Save the file and keep it open for the next exercise.**

EDIT ANCHORS AND PATHS

As we mentioned earlier, all objects you create contain two basic building blocks: anchor points, which appear any time you click the Pen tool (and other tools) on the page, and paths, which are lines that connect anchor points. In this exercise, you learn to work with these primary components of an Illustrator drawing.

1. **If it's not already open, open the Symbols.ai file you created earlier.**

2. **Choose the Selection tool (the solid arrow) and select the square you created in the previous exercise.**

    The hollow squares you see around the main object are the corners of the **bounding box** — the visual border around an object. The bounding box makes it easier to stretch, rotate, and scale objects.

Key Command:

Press Command/Control-Shift-H to show or hide the bounding box.

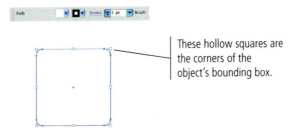

These hollow squares are the corners of the object's bounding box.

3. Choose Hide Bounding Box from the View Menu.

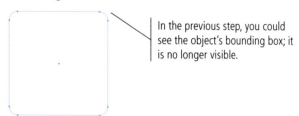

In the previous step, you could see the object's bounding box; it is no longer visible.

4. Use the Zoom tool to enlarge the upper-right corner of the box.

To zoom in this manner, simple draw a marquee with the Zoom tool. If you draw a three-inch marquee, those three inches of your page will expand to fill the screen.

Zoom tool

Key Command:

Pressing the Option/Alt key when you click with the Zoom tool zooms out, or reduces your view percentage.

5. Using the Direct Selection tool (the hollow arrow), click anywhere on the blank drawing window outside the shape.

This action deselects the square so you can select part of it.

6. Click the round corner to select its path. Do not release the mouse button.

When you draw primitive shapes, Illustrator creates the necessary anchor points automatically. Clicking between anchor points with the Direct Selection tool allows you to select individual paths (the lines that connects two anchor points). Curve handles come out of anchor points on either side of a curve. By pulling curve handles in one direction or another, you can bend and shape a curve — another foundational aspect of drawing with Illustrator.

Direct Selection tool

Curve handles

Path (connections between anchors)

Anchor point

Zooming In and Out

ILLUSTRATOR FOUNDATIONS

While creating a drawing, you will undoubtedly zoom in and out many times. At one moment, you may want to look at your drawing as if it were across the room; at another moment, you may want to look at the tiniest detail at very close range. There are a number of ways to step back from your drawing or move in closer for a detailed examination.

First, you can press the Plus (+) key to zoom in to a maximum of 6400%, or press the Minus (-) key to zoom out to the minimum of a little more than 4%.

You can fit a drawing into the available space by pressing Command/Control-0, or you can look at a drawing in the actual (100%) size by pressing Command/Control-1.

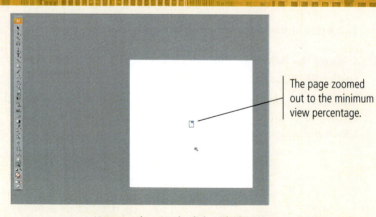

The page zoomed out to the minimum view percentage.

You can also simply click with the Zoom tool. Using only the Zoom tool zooms in; holding down the Option/Alt key with the Zoom tool zooms out (also referred to as "stepping back"). Finally, you can drag a marquee with the Zoom tool to zoom in on a specific area.

7. Pull the path (the curved part of the line) slightly up and to the right.

You see the curve handles move a bit, and you see the path — or at least a very thin version of the path — move as you pull on it.

8. Press Command/Control-Z to undo the shape change.

9. Save the file and keep it open for the next exercise.

Stage 2 Scaling, Cloning, and Alignment

Before learning how shapes and objects are filled and stroked, let's look at how objects interact. You'll do this by temporarily creating an object and moving it on top of and underneath another object (called **stacking**). At the same time, you can learn about **cloning**, or creating an exact duplicate of an existing object; **aligning** objects, which is lining up objects' tops, centers, bottoms, or sides; as well as **distributing** space between objects.

 ## SCALE AN OBJECT

Scaling refers to re-sizing an object. You can scale an object in several different ways. For example, you can make an object smaller (*scale it down*) while maintaining the same proportion (height and width) of the original object. You can also make an object larger (*scale it up*), stretch an object, and make an object wider than higher or vice versa. To become familiar with scaling, let's make the rounded rectangle you created earlier a bit smaller so you have more room to work.

1. With Symbols.ai open, use the Selection tool (solid arrow) to select the rounded rectangle.

You'll know when an object is selected when you can see its anchor points and connecting paths.

2. Choose View>Show Bounding Box.

The bounding box shows the outer parameters of an object. Bounding boxes don't look like normal anchor/path objects; you only see eight anchors or handles regardless of the shape of the object — one on each corner and one on each side (top, bottom, right, and left). You can view the bounding box of any irregular-shaped object and still see the same eight handles.

3. **Select the Scale tool in the Tools panel.**

   Take a moment to look at the two alternate tools under the Scale tool. The first one is a **Shear tool**, which is used to distort and skew objects; the second is the **Reshape tool**, which is used to pull and push on the paths that connect anchor points.

4. **With the Scale tool active, click once on the anchor point (not the bounding box handle) on the upper-left side, then click the bottom-right handle of the object and drag to resize it.**

   Clicking the upper-left anchor point establishes the origin point of the scaling process. The object is stuck to the page at the point you clicked the Scale tool. The rest of the object, however, is pliable, stretching horizontally and vertically, as you prefer.

   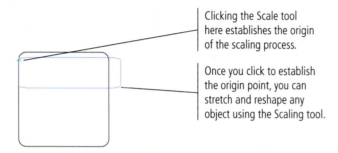

   Clicking the Scale tool here establishes the origin of the scaling process.

   Once you click to establish the origin point, you can stretch and reshape any object using the Scaling tool.

5. **Press Command/Control-Z to undo the scaling of the object.**

6. **Still using the Scale tool, hold down the Option/Alt Key and click the center of the object.**

   The Scale dialog box that appears provides a variety of options relative to resizing a selected object: Uniform and Non-Uniform (whether the object retains its shape or is stretched differently on its horizontal and vertical axes), and whether you want to scale an object's strokes, effects, and patterns when you resize it.

7. **Type "50" in the Scale field and click OK.**

   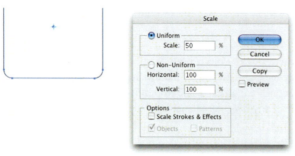

8. **Save the file and keep it open for the next exercise.**

The Scale function — and many other Illustrator functions — are better understood when you have some idea of what will happen when you click OK. That's where the Preview function comes in. Most (but not all) of the dialog boxes associated with visual-altering functions in Illustrator have Preview check boxes.

For functions such as scaling — particularly when you're changing scale non-uniformly (the horizontal and vertical scales are different from one another) — the Preview function can be invaluable.

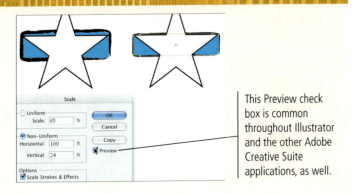

This Preview check box is common throughout Illustrator and the other Adobe Creative Suite applications, as well.

 ## CLONE AND ALIGN OBJECTS

Cloning is another way of saying, "make an absolutely perfect duplicate of this object." In this exercise, you make clones of the rectangle.

Once you have more than one object (cloned or not), you can use the Align panel not only to ensure perfect alignment of many object attributes (tops, sides, centers, bottoms, etc.), but also to distribute objects evenly — using the edges (tops, sides, or bottoms) and an average space, or using precise values.

1. **With the Symbols.ai file open, choose the Selection tool (solid arrow).**

2. **Press the Option/Alt key, and then click and drag the rectangle down and to the right.**

   Dragging an object while holding down the Option/Alt key clones the object. The copy appears where you release the mouse button.

   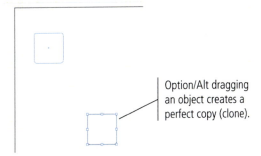

   Option/Alt dragging an object creates a perfect copy (clone).

3. **Use the Selection tool to draw a marquee that touches both rectangles.**

   When you use the Selection tool, you don't have to entirely surround an object to select it. Any object even partially within the selection marquee is selected.

    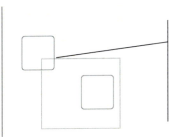

   When you're selecting multiple objects with the Selection tool, you only have to touch them to select the entire object. If you were using the Direct Select tool here, only the lower right of this rectangle would be selected.

Aligning and Distributing Objects

Drawings often require that you accurately distrubute objects on the page. For example, you may need to align a company logo on a business card; or you may need to distribute a row of stars in a variety of ways on different-shaped paths. All this and more can be accomplished using the Align panel, which you use extensively in the remainder of this project.

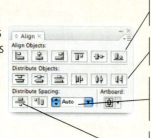

These buttons align objects to each other or to the page on which they're located.

These buttons distribute objects, either relative to each other or to the page.

This button aligns selected objects to the page instead of to each other. (The small arrow allows you to align objects to a cropped area).

These buttons distribute selected objects relative to their horizontal or vertical spacing; the field allows you to enter exact values for the spacing.

4. **With both rectangles selected, choose Align from the Window menu.**

The Align panel appears as a floating panel. It's not connected to the various panels in the dock.

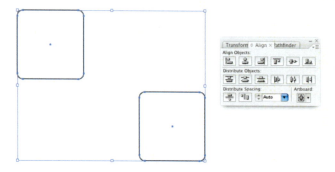

5. **Align the tops of both rectangles by clicking the Vertical Align Top button on the Align panel.**

The buttons in the Align panel can be used to align and distribute objects in a wide variety of ways.

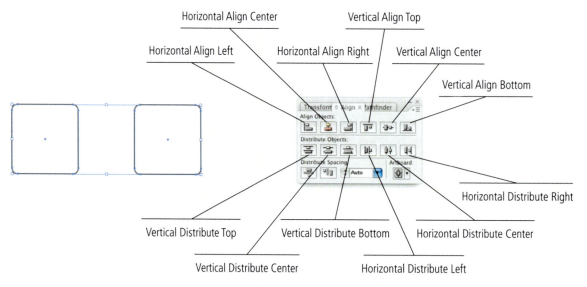

6. Press Shift, and then Option/Alt drag the two selected objects to the right.

This command clones both rectangles. Pressing the Shift key constrains the movement of the duplicate to 90° or 45° angles.

7. Select all four rectangles and click the Horizontal Distribute Center button on the Align panel.

This is a very efficient way to align and then instantly space/distribute a number of different objects, using only two clicks to accomplish the task.

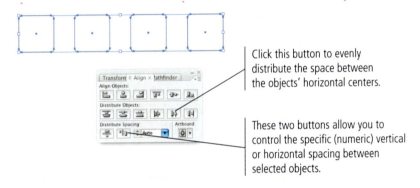

Click this button to evenly distribute the space between the objects' horizontal centers.

These two buttons allow you to control the specific (numeric) vertical or horizontal spacing between selected objects.

8. Save the file and keep it open for the next exercise.

Selecting Objects and Anchor Points

A marquee created with the Direct Selection tool (the hollow arrow) selects only those anchor points and/or paths that the marquee touches. In the image on the left, you can see the marquee drawn with the Direct Selection tool. In the image on the right, you can see that only those anchors surrounded by the marquee are selected; the other ones are hollow and are therefore unselected.

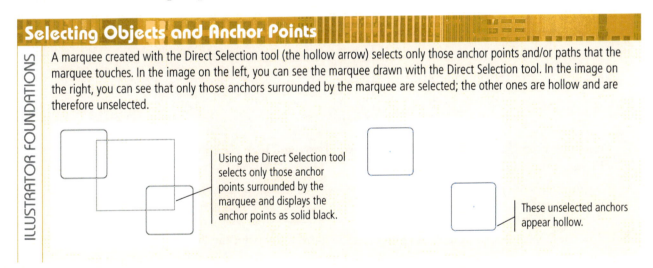

Using the Direct Selection tool selects only those anchor points surrounded by the marquee and displays the anchor points as solid black.

These unselected anchors appear hollow.

ILLUSTRATOR FOUNDATIONS

Stage 3 Controlling Fills and Strokes

The rounded squares you created in the previous lesson have two primary components. The first is the stroke, or the border that delineates the edges. The second component is what fills the square. Both attributes — stroke and fill — can either be invisible (with a value of None) or they can have color.

 ## CONTROL OBJECTS' FILL AND POSITION

In this exercise, you create a few temporary rectangles, and then use them to learn how to manage fills and strokes. When you're done, you'll simply delete the rectangles. Creating temporary objects to test a color, effect, or pattern before applying it to an actual document is a tried-and-true method that digital artists use every day in on-the-job situations.

1. **With Symbols.ai open, select the two objects in the middle of the row and clone them so you have two copies.**

   Drag the two clones while holding the Shift key so they align perfectly below the two originals. At this point, you should see six rounded rectangles; four on one row and two underneath.

   You should also be able to see the dock, which should contain 11 **iconized** panels. These panels were positioned when you called the default workspace in the first part of this project. If you see something different on your screen, simply choose Window>Workspace>[Basic] to restore the Adobe-defined default settings.

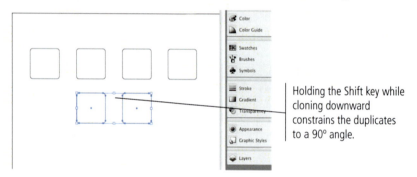

Holding the Shift key while cloning downward constrains the duplicates to a 90° angle.

2. **Select the rectangle on the right side of the second row, and then click the Fill box at the bottom of the Tools panel.**

   Now that you have a couple of extra rectangles on the page, you can use them to experiment with changing the color of paths and fills.

3. **Click the Swatches icon in the dock and drag the panel away from the dock.**

4. **Click the first red swatch in the first row of swatches.**

   When the Fill box is active in the Tools panel, clicking a swatch fills the selected object with that color.

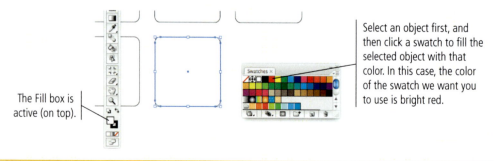

The Fill box is active (on top).

Select an object first, and then click a swatch to fill the selected object with that color. In this case, the color of the swatch we want you to use is bright red.

5. Using the Zoom tool, zoom in on the two lower objects until they fill the drawing window.

Without zooming in, you could easily see that picking the red swatch filled the selected rectangle with red. Looking closer, however, you can also see that a black stroke (outline) surrounds the red fill.

Key Command:

Stacking order *refers to which object is on top and which is below. It's a good idea to learn the key commands associated with stacking and moving stacked objects:*

Bring to Front: Command/Control-Shift-]

Bring Forward: Command/Control-]

Send Backward: Command/Control-[

Send to Back: Command/Control-Shift-[

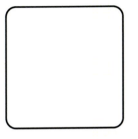

6. Use the Selection tool (the solid arrow) to drag the left rectangle underneath the rectangle on the right.

The lower left of the red object covers most of the right side of the white object. The position of an object, whether one is on top of or underneath another, is determined by the order in which the objects are created — unless you manually move an object up (higher) or down (lower) in the stack.

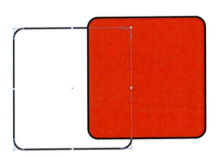

7. With the white-filled rectangle selected, choose Object>Arrange>Bring to Front.

With an object selected on the drawing page, you can use the Arrange menu options to bring that object forward to the top, to place it underneath another object, or to send it to the bottom of a stack.

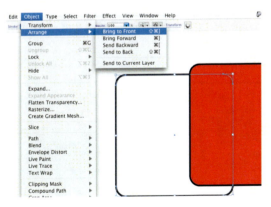

8. **Click the Swap Stroke and Fill button at the bottom of the Tools panel.**

The red object remains unchanged, but the top rectangle is now quite different. The stroke color swapped with the fill color, so the fill is now black and the stroke white.

Note:

If you want to change an object's fill color, bring the Fill swatch to the front in the Tools panel. If you want to change an object's stroke color, bring the Stroke swatch to the front.

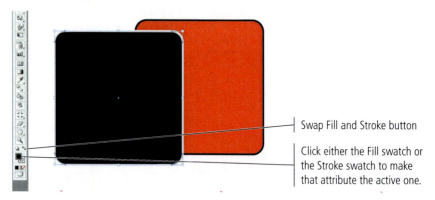

Swap Fill and Stroke button

Click either the Fill swatch or the Stroke swatch to make that attribute the active one.

9. **Save the file and keep it open for the next exercise.**

 ## ALTER STROKE ATTRIBUTES AND OBJECT TRANSPARENCY

By default, an object's fill is solid; if it's on top of another object, the underlying object is covered completely. Objects also possess an attribute known as **opacity,** which refers to an object's **transparency** or how much an underlying object "shows through." In this exercise, you change the transparency of the black rectangle you created earlier.

1. **With Symbols.ai open, zoom in so the two rectangles fill your monitor.**

You can use the Zoom tool or another method of zooming in.

2. **Click the Transparency icon in the dock.**

The Transparency panel opens on your screen.

3. **Make sure the black-filled shape is selected. In the Transparency panel, drag the Opacity slider (the small triangle) until the Opacity field says 50%, or enter the number manually.**

While both methods are equally effective, the field works best for entering specific values (for example, 42%), whereas the slider makes it easier to experiment with different effects.

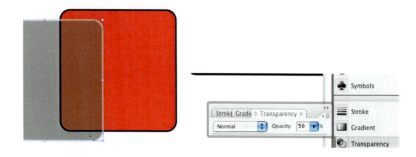

4. Access the Stroke panel in the dock and change the weight of the stroke to 9 pt.

The new Stroke value — combined with the Transparency values, the visibility of the paths and anchor points, and the visibility of the bounding box — allows you to see how Illustrator handles individual vector objects, regardless of their complexity.

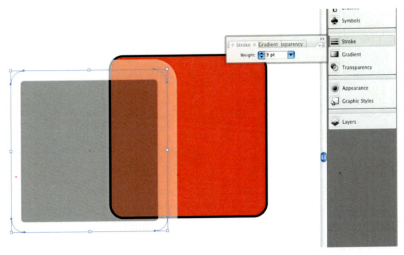

Note:

The View>Hide Edges command turns off the visible nature of paths. If the edges were hidden, the screen image in Step 4 wouldn't look the same; you would see the thicker stroke but not the actual paths.

5. On the Stroke panel, click the small button on the upper-right corner and choose Show Options from the panel options menu.

By default, the thin path of the shape is in the exact center of the thicker stroke. The stroke and the path are connected, but they are separate, individual attributes. You can change a number of stroke attributes using the stroke options.

6. Click the Align Stroke to Inside button (the center button) in the Stroke Options area.

Using the stroke options, you can determine where the stroke ends relative to the path, how the path is aligned to the stroke, and more.

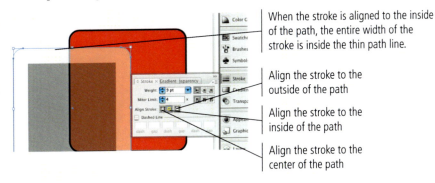

When the stroke is aligned to the inside of the path, the entire width of the stroke is inside the thin path line.

Align the stroke to the outside of the path

Align the stroke to the inside of the path

Align the stroke to the center of the path

7. **Click the Align Stroke to Center button to return the stroke to its original position.**

8. **Swap the stroke and fill colors for the black rectangle.**

   The rectangle again has a white fill and a black stroke (the default settings).

9. **Change the Weight field (thickness) to 3 pt, and change the Miter Length field (the width of the stroke's edge) to 3.**

10. **Click the Dashed Line check box and enter "1 pt" for the first dash and gap of the dashed line.**

    The Dash value defines how big each "stretch" of the line will appear. The gap is the space between each dash.

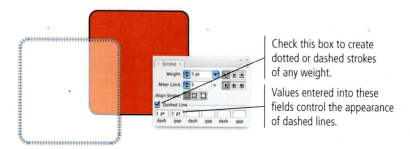

Check this box to create dotted or dashed strokes of any weight.

Values entered into these fields control the appearance of dashed lines.

11. **Delete the two temporary objects, save the file, and keep it open for the next exercise.**

Bridging the Space Between Adobe Applications

The screen image shown here came from Adobe Bridge, an application that came with Adobe Illustrator. Bridge is designed to server as a centralized repository for "all things Adobe." You can store, organize, and manage the multiple file types and media formats supported by the various families of Adobe applications — everything from EPS illustrations to native Adobe Illustrator, Photoshop, InDesign, Flash, and Dreamweaver files, as well as Premiere, Fireworks, and more. For more information, visit Adobe.com and search for "Bridge."

Stage 4   Drawing Other Simple Objects

At this early stage of the project, you've already developed many of the necessary skills for creating Illustrator drawings. The next step is to draw something meaningful, such as a snowflake or a skull.

To complete this project, you must draw 4 different international warning symbols. Drawing these objects — within the confines of your already-perfect frames — will teach you a great deal about drawing complex illustrations.

If you remember from the client meeting, the client's bitmap icons work fine on the Web, but they look terrible in print. After you redraw the icons in Illustrator, the client will be able to print the icons anywhere, with no loss in quality — which is the primary advantage of vector-based artwork vs. raster-based images.

USE GROUPS TO DEVELOP ARTWORK

1. **In Symbols.ai, select the four rectangles on the page.**

2. **Display the Align panel (if it's not already open) and click the Horizontal Align Center button.**

Horizontal Align Center

> **Key Command:**
>
> *Press Command/Control-G to group selected objects. Press Command/Control-Shift-G to ungroup grouped objects.*

That's not at all what you need to do. Instead, you want to center the row of four squares to the **artboard** (another word for the page you're working on). To do that, you first need to group the row of four rectangles.

3. **Press Command/Control-Z to undo the error.**

4. **Choose Object>Group to group the four rectangles.**

   A **group** is a set of individual objects connected together so they behave as a single, discrete object (or a component of a larger, more complex object).

5. **Click the Artboard button on the Align panel, and then click the Horizontal Align Center button to align the entire row on the artboard.**

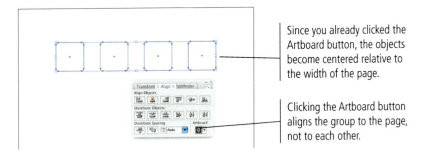

Since you already clicked the Artboard button, the objects become centered relative to the width of the page.

Clicking the Artboard button aligns the group to the page, not to each other.

6. Clone the row so there are two rows of rectangles on the page.

Make sure there's a good amount of space between each row, as shown below.

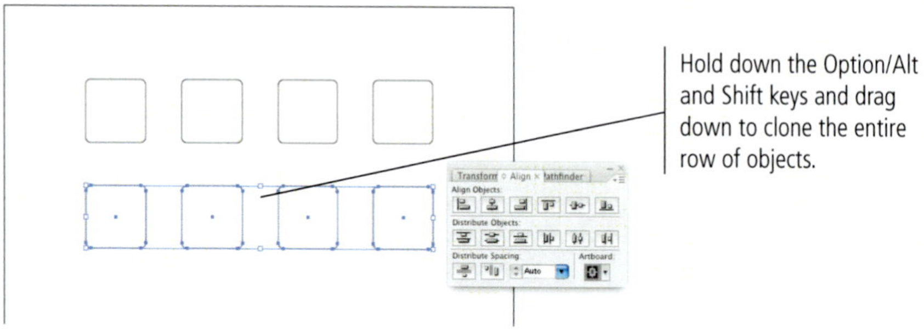

Hold down the Option/Alt and Shift keys and drag down to clone the entire row of objects.

7. Choose Object>Transform>Transform Again.

This command duplicates the last transformation you applied, whether on the artboard or in a dialog box. For example, if you used the Move dialog box to both move and rotate an object at the same time, the Transform Again command would both move and rotate the current selection.

Key Command:

Press Command/ Control-D to apply the Transform Again command.

8. Transform the selection again to make another copy of the selected row.

9. Try using the Selection tool to select and delete the last two rectangles in the bottom row.

Each row is a group, and the Selection tool can't select individual pieces of a group. To delete individual pieces of a group, you must use the Direct Selection tool.

10. Press Command/Control-Z to restore the fourth group.

11. Using the Direct Selection tool (hollow arrow), drag a marquee around the last two objects on the bottom row.

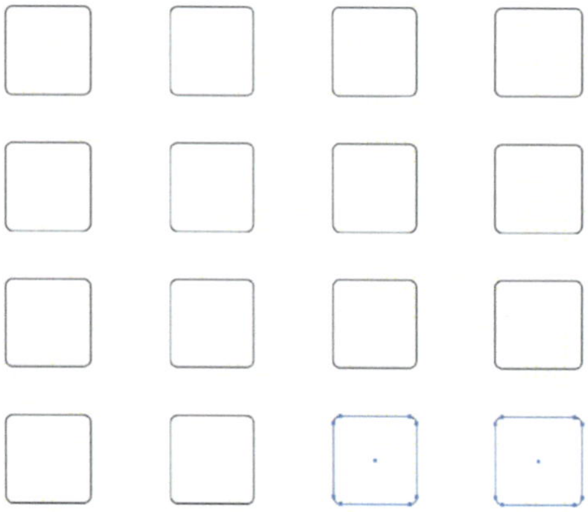

12. Delete the two selected rectangles.

13. Select all objects on the page and turn all fourteen objects into a single group.

14. Save the file and keep it open for the next exercise.

Now you have everything you need to create the international warning signs: you have the page to draw on, and you have 14 borders in which to place the graphics. The graphics will act as templates that you can trace to create the symbols.

IMPORT TEMPLATES AND PLACE GUIDES

Many of your projects will require you to start with something outside the realm of computer graphics. It's possible that some of your best illustrations will start with old drawings or photographs. Many award-winning designs started out with very humble beginnings, such as a quick sketch on a napkin at a roadside café.

In this exercise, you bring an existing piece of art into your project and transform it into perfect Illustrator artwork. You start the process by importing your template, which is a pre-existing object supplied by your client.

1. **In Symbols.ai, zoom in to the upper-left corner of the 14-rectangle grid.**

   When we say "grid," we're not talking about the actual Adobe Illustrator grid; we're referring to the 14 rectangles that look like a grid on your screen. You'll learn more about the Illustrator grid later in this book.

2. **If you can't see rulers on the left and top of the document window, choose View>Show Rulers.**

3. **Choose File>Place and double-click the file named Cold.tif from the RF_Illustrator>Symbols folder.**

   The image appears in the center of your monitor, but that's not where we want it to be. We want it to be perfectly centered inside the first rectangle on the first row.

Key Command:

Press Command/Control-R to toggle rulers on and off.

Using Templates

Templates are Illustrator files that are saved in such a manner that they can't be altered, but they can be saved as all-new documents. Templates contain information, illustrations, layouts, backgrounds, and workspaces that you can use to create other projects. For example, if you create a template for your company's business card, you can use that template to create business cards for your clients as well — all you need to do is save the template under a unique file name and make the necessary changes. You will save hours of development time using templates. The hard work is done once, and then all you need to do is "tweak" (make minor changes) the template to create new files.

When you first start Illustrator, the Welcome screen provides a number of different categories of new drawings such as Print projects, Web projects, Devices (such as telephones), and more. At the bottom of the list on the right is a folder icon named Templates, which is where you'll find the templates the artists at Adobe supplied for you.

The images to the right show two examples of the many templates that come with Illustrator. Artists working on these types of projects could save hours of development time if they used the guides, shapes, type positions, font selections, and general production information contained in the templates. It would be easy to change client logos, copy, and typefaces without having to re-invent the entire document from scratch.

The use of templates differs widely from one user to the next. Some people make their own templates, choosing not to rely on the dozens of templates that ship and install with Illustrator. Other people — particularly those in corporate environments where they need a flyer today and a Web site tomorrow — use the pre-built Adobe templates with excellent results. And then there are certain people who have been using Illustrator for decades but don't realize that the program includes templates.

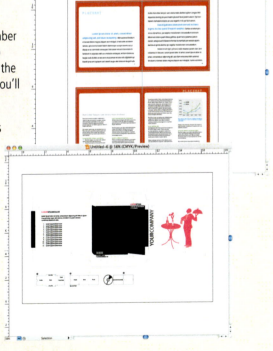

4. Drag the imported Cold.tif image into the center of the first rectangle. Use the Arrow keys to fine-tune its position.

The Arrow keys move selected objects by 1 pixel at a time. Pressing Shift with any of the Arrow keys moves the selection by 10 pixels at a time.

5. Using the Transparency panel, lower the Opacity value of the object to 20%.

Reducing the opacity of an imported template image is quite common. Illustrator can automatically identify something as a template and reduce its opacity, but it's best to learn how to do it done manually.

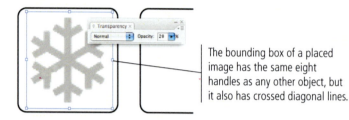

The bounding box of a placed image has the same eight handles as any other object, but it also has crossed diagonal lines.

6. Click within the horizontal (top) ruler and drag down until you see a guide on the exact center of the bounding box.

Remember, the bounding box is the external border of any object or group of objects, including placed images. In addition to a bounding box, placed images also have crossed diagonal lines. You can use the bounding box handles and the crossed lines to identify the vertical and horizontal centers of an object.

Placing Images

ILLUSTRATOR FOUNDATIONS

There are many cases where Illustrator projects require pieces from other Illustrator documents or entire documents from other programs such as Photoshop, InDesign, Flash, or Dreamweaver. (Extended functionalities, which are outside the realm of this book, actually provide the ability to work with video formats.)

When you place files into Illustrator, you can either **embed** them (make them part of the document you're working on) or you can **link** them (to print or publish your drawing, you need the placed files, as well as the file itself, available to the program). Embedding is the default condition for placed files. If you want to link a file, you can make that selection in the Place dialog box.

You can also automatically place a file as a template object (which is different than the page templates we discussed earlier). The first image to the right shows one TIFF file already placed on the page. When we placed a second image, we checked the Template option in the Place dialog box. In the layout, the second image is placed on its own locked and dimmed layer, which allows you to trace the template image without moving it.

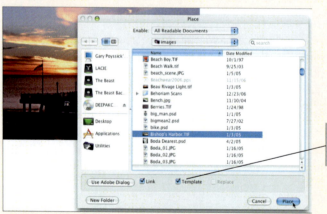

This image is going to serve as a template.

You can see how dim the second image is compared to the first one. The Dim Images To field in the Layer Options dialog shows that the layer is set to 50%.

7. **Drag from the vertical (left) ruler onto the center of the image's bounding box.**

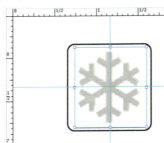

8. **Using the Selection tool, click the group of rectangles to select them and show the center points of the rectangle shapes.**

9. **Drop vertical ruler guides on the centers of the remaining rectangles in the first row.**

   You're now ready for the remaining graphics that must be converted from bitmaps to vectors. These guides will come in handy as you move forward.

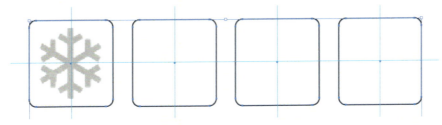

10. **Use the Selection tool to select both the rectangle group and the snowflake graphic, and then choose Object>Lock>Selection.**

    The two selected objects (the group that makes up the first row of rectangles and the snowflake) no longer display their bounding boxes, anchor points, or paths. They're locked to the page and can't be touched unless you unlock them.

    For more complex locking requirements, you can use layers — which you'll do in virtually every Illustrator project you develop. For now, though, this method works fine: selecting and locking the objects to the page and leaving non-printing guides in place.

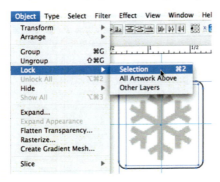

Key Command:

Press Command/ Control-2 to lock a selected object.

Press Command- Option-2/Control-Alt-2 to unlock all locked objects.

11. **Save the file and continue to the next exercise.**

Managing Guides

Guides are visible on the artboard but do not appear in print or in exported files. You use guides to position objects, to mark edges, and for a host of other tasks. In addition to simply dragging horizontal or vertical guides onto the page, you have a number of other options for working with guides. Most guide controls are available in the View>Guides menu.

Hide Guides toggles guides off temporarily. When guides are hidden, you can turn them back on again by choosing View>Guides>**Show Guides**.

Lock Guides prevents you from selecting or moving guides already placed on the page. By default, guides are not locked; you can select and move placed guides by simply clicking and dragging in the document window. If you drag a selection marquee around an area that includes a guide, you will also select the guide — meaning you would move the guide if you moved the selection, and that would be an error. The Lock Guides command prevents this frequent mistake. When guides are locked, you can unlock them again by choosing View>Guides>**Unlock Guides**.

Make Guides allows you to convert a selected object into a guide. This means you can create a guide in any shape that you can draw — round, square, star, or freeform. When you convert an object to a guide, you effectively hide the stroke and fill attributes of the object.

Release Guides allows you to convert a guide object into a regular object; the object's original fill and stroke (before you converted it to a guide) are restored.

Clear Guides removes all guides from the page. If you want to remove only a single guide, you can select it (as long as it's unlocked) and press Delete.

The **Smart Guides** command, which maintains its own position in the main View menu, effectively allows you to use existing objects as guides without physically converting those objects to guides, providing valuable feedback about the location of the cursor in relation to other object on the page.

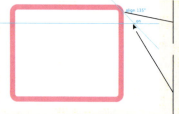

The anchor point of an unselected object is addressed by the Smart Guide feature.

Using Smart Guides, dragging the guide near the existing object shows the position (align 135°) of the cursor relative to the anchor point of the object.

You can control the appearance and behavior of guides in the Preferences dialog box. The **Guides & Grid** pane defines the color and style of guides, frequency of lines in the Illustrator grid, and the position of guides (front or back) relative to existing artwork

The **Smart Guides & Slices** pane defines which hints display in the cursor, which angles are recognized by the Smart Guide feature, and how close the cursor can be to an object before that object is recognized (called the **Snapping Tolerance**).

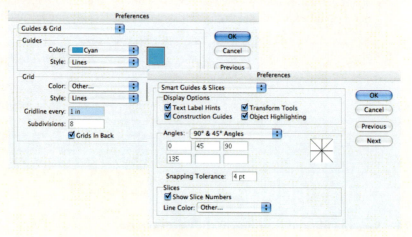

DRAW STRAIGHT LINES

Using a combination of simple, straight lines, you can create some very intricate objects. In this exercise, you practice the technique by creating a relatively complex snowflake out of only straight lines.

1. **Continue working in the open file. Select the Line tool from the Tools panel.**

2. **Click at the top of the center snowflake branch, hold down the mouse button, press the Shift key, and drag to the junction of the vertical and horizontal guides.**

   The line stays at a 90° angle because the Shift key is constraining the drag.

   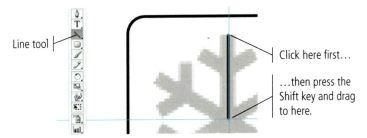

   Line tool

   Click here first...

   ...then press the Shift key and drag to here.

3. **On the Stroke panel (in the dock), change the Weight value to 5 pt.**

   A range of typical stroke weights is built into the pop-up menu — everything from 1/4 (0.25) of a point to 100 points. In fact, you might consider trying several different weights, such as 3 point or 8 point, to see why we used 5 point as the best stroke width for this assignment.

   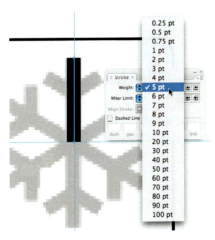

4. **Using the Line tool, click the upper center of the left angled line and drag to where that branch meets the vertical guide.**

This creates the left side of the first "branch" of the snowflake. It's starting to take shape.

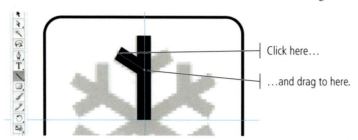

Click here...

...and drag to here.

5. **Choose the Reflect tool in the Tools panel (it might be nested under the Rotate tool).**

6. **Click the junction of the angle and straight lines to move the origin point of the angled line you just drew.**

The **origin point** is the point from which something grows, shrinks, spins (rotates), stretches, or reflects during a **transformation**. You'll set the origin point for a number of different transformation tools, including the Rotate tool that you use in the next exercise.

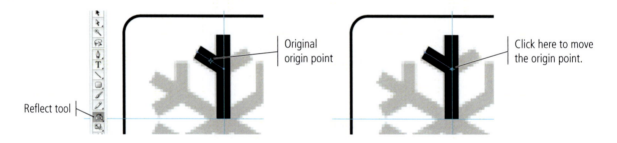

Reflect tool

Original origin point

Click here to move the origin point.

7. **Hold down the Option/Alt key and drag the angled line from the upper left to the upper right of the image.**

It might take a few tries to get this right. Don't forget that Command/Control-Z will undo almost any action (or mistake). When you get it right, the clone will be an exact reflection of the line you started with.

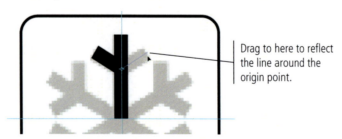

Drag to here to reflect the line around the origin point.

Note:

Clicking once with a transformation tool such as the Reflect tool places the origin point. If the origin point is already in the correct place, you can simply click and drag to apply the transformation you want.

8. **Select all three line segments and group them.**

Now you see the value of locking the row of rectangles and the placed Cold.tif file — you can create anything you want on top of the objects without moving them.

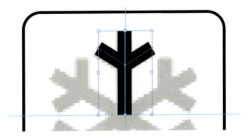

9. **Save the file and keep it open for the next exercise.**

 ## ROTATE AND MIRROR OBJECTS

In this exercise, you rotate, flip, and reflect copies of the set of lines you created earlier to complete the snowflake. Using these transformation techniques, you can use existing design elements (such as three straight lines) to create a complete drawing (such as a snowflake with eighteen separate and manageable components).

1. **In the open Symbols.ai file, zoom into the upper-left side of the first row of rectangles.**

2. **Select the grouped lines on the page, and then select the Rotate tool in the Tools panel (nested under the Reflect tool).**

3. **Click where the two guides meet to position the origin point for the rotation.**

You did this earlier when you cloned the angled portions of the first stroke of the snowflake. You must do it again here. This origin point is also known as the **transform point**, meaning it's the spot from which objects rotate, mirror, grow, shrink, and morph (short for metamorphose).

4. **Press the Option/Alt key, and then drag left to rotate a clone of the branch around the origin point.**

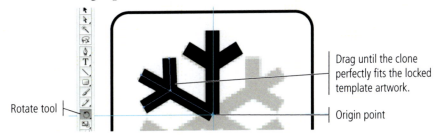

Rotate tool

Drag until the clone perfectly fits the locked template artwork.

Origin point

5. **With the rotated clone selected, switch back to the Reflect tool. Option/Alt-click-drag to create a clone that fits the right side of the original.**

Since the origin point is already in place (at the intersection of the guides), you don't have to reposition the origin point before using the Reflect tool.

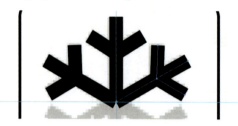

6. **Select all three of the branches and reflect a clone to complete the lower half of the original snowflake.**

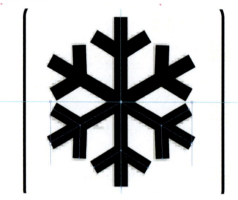

7. **Select all the branches and choose Object>Path>Outline Stroke.**

The Outline Stroke command converts strokes to discrete objects. The new objects have a fill (which is the same color as the original stroke) but no stroke.

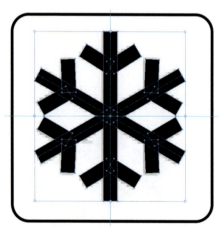

8. **Select the paths and use the Object>Group command to create a single object from several components.**

The Cold.tif file is now re-created as a grouped and structured collection of organized rectangles, filled with black. This image can be printed on golf balls or the side of a twenty-story building without losing a single pixel of accuracy or resolution.

9. **With the entire snowflake group selected, choose Object>Hide>Selection.**

   Similar to the Lock command you used earlier, you can hide selected objects on the artboard. When objects are hidden, they are effectively locked as well, since you can't select or change a hidden object.

   Also similar to locking objects, hiding and showing selections in this way can be complicated because you can only show *all* hidden objects, not just certain ones. For better control of specific objects' visibility, you should use layers.

10. **Choose Object>Unlock All to unlock the rounded rectangles and the placed snowflake image.**

11. **Select and delete the now-unlocked original snowflake image.**

12. **Choose Object>Show All to re-show the snowflake icon you created.**

   When you show a hidden object, it is automatically selected.

Key Commands:

Press Command/Control-3 to hide the current selection. Press Command-Option-3/Control-Alt-3 to show all hidden objects.

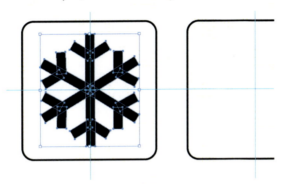

13. **Save the file and keep it open for the next exercise.**

More On Transformations

ILLUSTRATOR FOUNDATIONS

You've already had some experience with transformation: you've rotated objects while cloning them, you've changed their size, and you've reflected them. (The fourth of the major transformations is shearing, which is a form of distortion.)

It's important to consider where Illustrator considers an object to be located when you apply a transformation. You can use the Reference Point icon in the Transform panel to determine where the measurement or transformation begins. This is particularly important when you need to work on more than one object at a time, or (for example) when you need to position an object a specific distance from the center of another object.

To understand the reference point, think of the object's bounding box. The points on the Reference Point icon correspond to the object's bounding box handles and center point. Whichever point is selected in the Reference Point icon determines which bounding box handle is being measured and reflected in the Transform panel fields.

If you move the reference point from the center (top image) to the lower right (bottom image), the x-y values change to show the location of the new reference point (bounding box handle), but the height and width of the object remain the same.

Stage 5   Drawing Complex Objects

You have learned about drawing primitive shapes, manipulating their anchor points and path components, and placing them appropriately. Now it's time to expand that core knowledge and skill set.

You learned that you can use the Object>Lock command to lock a specific object on the page. But when it comes to locking 14 objects, the Object>Lock command can be somewhat clumsy. It locks and unlocks all objects at the same time. You don't have the option of locking or unlocking individual objects. Layers, however, provide much more flexibility in locking and unlocking individual objects on the page.

 ## USE LAYERS TO LOCK INDIVIDUAL OBJECTS

In this exercise, you use the Layers panel for the first time, create a new layer, and move your 14 rectangular frames onto the new layer. This way, as we move forward, you can lock imported template graphics without bothering with the frames in which they reside.

1. **In the open Symbols.ai file, select the group of rounded rectangles. Don't select the snowflake icon you already drew.**

   You're going to lock all of the rectangles at once by dragging them to their own layer, and locking that layer instead of the individual rows of rectangles.

2. **Click the Layers icon on the dock to access the Layers panel.**

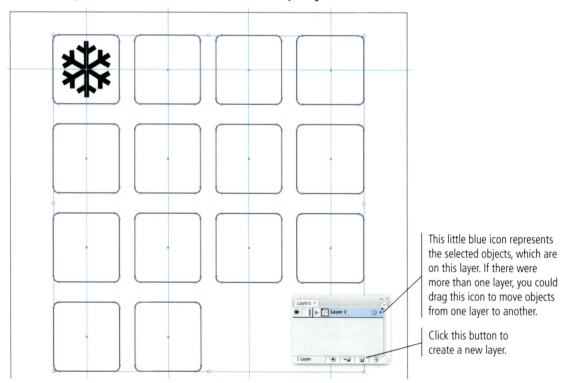

This little blue icon represents the selected objects, which are on this layer. If there were more than one layer, you could drag this icon to move objects from one layer to another.

Click this button to create a new layer.

3. **Click the New Layer button at the bottom of the Layers panel, and then double-click Layer 2 to open the Layer Options dialog box.**

4. In the Layer Options dialog box, type "Borders" in the Name field.

This color swatch matches the one in the Layers panel. The paths and bounding boxes of objects match the color of the layer on which they reside.

5. Click OK to close the Layer Options dialog box.

6. Drag the blue square icon from Layer 1 to the Borders layer.

When you release the mouse button, the icon turns red to match the layer color defined in the Layer Options dialog box. In the document window, the bounding box handles of the selected objects are also red to reflect the layer on which they now reside.

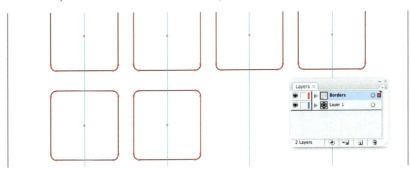

In the document, notice that you can't see the snowflake anymore; it's completely hidden by the rectangle. (If you remember, that rectangle is filled with solid white, so you can't see through it.) Dragging the rows of rectangles onto the new layer — which is on top of the old Layer 1 — covers anything on the underlying layer with solid white.

7. Drag the Borders layer to the bottom of the stack in the Layers panel.

You can change the stacking order of layers by dragging them up and down.

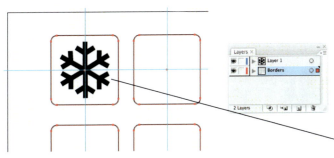

The layer with the rounded rectangles is now below the layer with the snowflake, so you can see the snowflake again.

Note:

Moving objects from one layer to another is as simple as selecting the objects and dragging the little square in the Layers panel to wherever you want to relocate them.

8. **On the left side of the Layers panel, click the empty square to the right of the eyeball icon to lock all the rows at once.**

   Locking a layer locks all objects on that layer. When objects are locked — either individually or by locking the layer — the bounding boxes are no longer visible. The ruler guides remain visible even when a layer is locked.

Click this space to lock a layer. If the layer is locked, click the Lock icon to unlock the layer.

9. **Save the file and keep it open for the next exercise.**

 ## LIVE TRACE AN OBJECT

The **Live Trace** tool is a quick and easy way to draw a simple object, an object comprised of only one or two elements, or an object that is otherwise relatively easy to trace. In the following exercise, you import another template image, lock it, use the Live Trace tool to trace it automatically, and then manually refine the trace until it's perfect.

1. **In the open Symbols.ai file, double-click Layer 1 in the Layers panel and rename it "Icons". Click OK.**

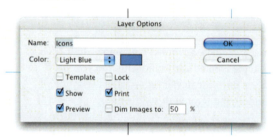

2. **Choose File>Place and double-click the Fire.tif file in the RF_Illustrator>Symbols folder.**

3. **Zoom into the second rectangle. Use the guides to position the Fire.tif object in the second rectangle in the first row.**

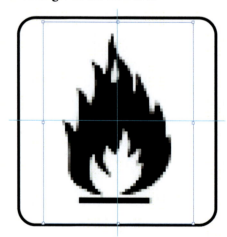

4. **With the placed object selected, choose Object>Live Trace>Make.**

   The Live Trace tool draws the entire flame with a single click. Drawing these flames using the Pen tool (which you'll learn about soon) could take 20 minutes or more to complete — even for an experienced illustrator.

5. **If necessary, move the artwork up or down slightly so its white fill covers none of the border.**

6. **Use the Rectangle tool to draw a thin, black-filled rectangle to cover the rounded base of the Fire icon.**

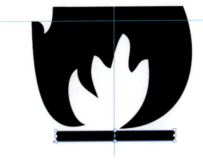

7. **Select both sections of the illustration and group them.**

   When using the Live Trace tool, the placed image you used as the template is automatically deleted from the document.

8. **Save the file and keep it open for the next exercise.**

The Pathfinder allows you to combine multiple shapes into one object, use one object as a "cookie cutter" to remove a shape from another object, and many other combination and merge functions. Again, you will learn more about the Pathfinder as you work with the toolset. In the meantime, it's a good idea to experiment with the Pathfinder panel to get a better idea of what it does.

In this exercise, you use a small circle to cut its shape from a larger circle to create an entirely different shape for your third icon.

1. **In the open file, import Biohazard.tif and position it in the third rectangle on the first row.**

2. **Set the transparency of the object to 20% and lock it in place.**

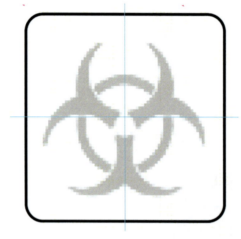

3. **Select the Ellipse tool, set the fill color to black and the stroke color to none, and then draw a circle by pressing the Shift key while you drag.**

4. **Using the Selection tool, drag the circle into place over the top "horn" shape in the template image.**

5. **Change the transparency of the object to 50% so you can see the artwork below.**

6. **Choose Select>Deselect so nothing is selected on the artboard, and then change the fill color to white and the stroke to None.**

    If something is selected when you change the fill and stroke colors, the fill and stroke of the selected object will change — which isn't what you want in this case.

7. **Draw a smaller white circle and drag it onto the inside area of the "horn" shape, overlapping the first circle you drew.**

8. **Use the top, bottom, left, and right bounding box handles to resize the smaller circle until it matches the template image.**

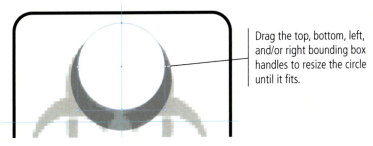

Drag the top, bottom, left, and/or right bounding box handles to resize the circle until it fits.

9. **Choose Window>Pathfinder to open the Pathfinder panel.**

10. **Select both circles, and then click the second button on the top row of the Pathfinder panel.**

   This is the "cookie-cutter" we mentioned earlier. When you select two objects and click this button, Pathfinder cuts the bottom shape out, using the upper shape as the guide.

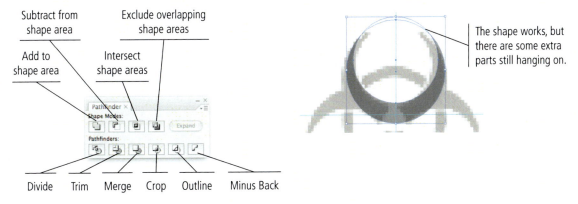

Subtract from shape area

Exclude overlapping shape areas

Add to shape area

Intersect shape areas

Divide   Trim   Merge   Crop   Outline   Minus Back

The shape works, but there are some extra parts still hanging on.

11. **Click the Expand button to simplify the shape.**

   Clicking the Expand button removes those portions of the circles that the Pathfinder function left behind. In this situation, the artwork would have worked without expanding, but that's seldom the case. It's always a good idea to expand Pathfinder objects that display extraneous (unwanted) fragments.

12. **Select the Rotate tool. Click where the guides intersect to place the origin point for the rotation, and then Option/Alt-drag to clone-rotate the horns to the lower-left side of the original template image.**

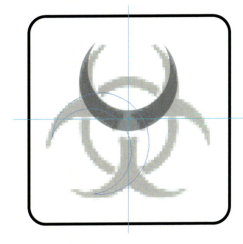

13. Use the same technique to create the last (lower-right) set of horns.

14. Select all three sets of horns, return their opacity to 100%, and group them.

15. Using the Ellipse tool with a fill of none and a 3-pt. black stroke, draw the black circle part of the template shape.

16. Draw a second circle, with a white fill with no stroke, in the area where the three sets of horns overlap.

    Use the template image as a guide. You're creating the white space in the center of the image.

17. Unlock the template image (Object>Unlock All) and delete it.

18. Select all the pieces of the icon and group them.

19. Save the file and leave it open for the next exercise.

 ## USE THE PEN TOOL

As you've already seen, many objects can be drawn without ever picking up the Pen tool. That being said, however, there are numerous objects you can't draw without considerable effort unless you use the Pen tool. Some artists will argue that the Pen tool is the most important tool in the Illustrator Tools panel.

When you draw with the Pen tool, an anchor point marks the end of a line segment, and the point handles determine the shape of that segment. That's the basic definition of a vector, but there is a bit more to it than that.

Each segment in a path has two anchoring end points and two associated handles. In the following image, we first clicked to create Point A and dragged (without releasing the mouse button) to create Handle A. We then clicked and dragged to create Point B and Handle B1; Handle B2 is automatically created as a reflection of B1 (Point B is a **symmetrical point**).

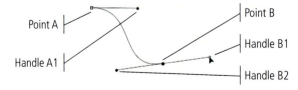

The next image shows the result of dragging Handle B1 to the left instead of to the right. Notice the difference in the curve, as compared to the curve above. When you drag the handle, the segment arcs away from the direction of the handle.

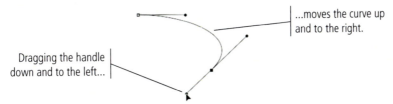

It's important to understand that a segment is connected to two handles. In the next image, dragging the handle to the right pulls out the arc of the connected segment. You could change the shape of Segment A by dragging either Handle A1 or A2.

The final concept you should understand about anchors and handles (for now, at least) is that clicking and dragging a point creates a symmetrical point. Dragging one handle of a symmetrical point also changes the other handle of that point. In the next image, dragging Handle B also moves Handle A, which affects the shape of Segment A.

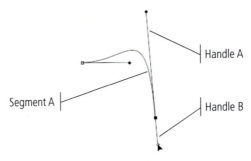

You can create corner points by simply clicking with the Pen tool instead of clicking and dragging. **Corner points** do not have their own handles; the connected segments are controlled by the handles of the other associated points.

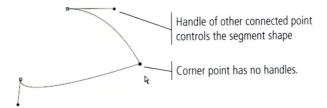

You can convert a symmetrical point into a corner point by clicking the point with the Convert Point tool (nested under the Pen tool). You can also add a handle to only one side of an anchor point by Option/Alt-clicking a point with the Pen tool and dragging.

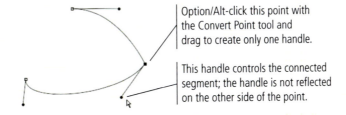

1. **In the open Symbols.ai file, place the Fingers.tif file into the last rectangle in the first row.**

2. **Change the Opacity value of the placed file to 20% and lock the template image.**

3. **Change the fill to None and the stroke to black.**

   Use the Stroke panel to make sure the stroke weight is set to 1 pt.

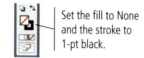

   Set the fill to None and the stroke to 1-pt black.

4. **Zoom in so the Fingers image fills the workspace.**

   The exact zoom percentage you're using may be slightly different than ours. Get close enough so you can see the jagged edges around the fingers.

5. **Select the Pen tool in the Tools panel.**

6. **Click in the upper-left corner of the Fingers image, and then click slightly down the hand, just before the bend in the wrist.**

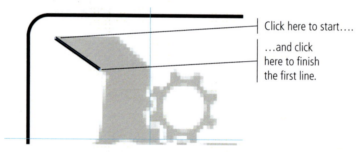

   Click here to start....

   ...and click here to finish the first line.

7. **Click just below the lower curve in the wrist and pull down and to the left to create a curved segment between the two anchor points.**

   Without releasing the mouse button, drag the handle until the curve fits the template image. If you released the mouse button before the curve fit perfectly, you can select the point with the Direct Selection tool and drag the associated handle to reshape the curve.

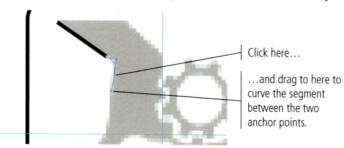

   Click here...

   ...and drag to here to curve the segment between the two anchor points.

Note:

If you don't change the fill to None before you start using the Pen tool, whatever shape you create by adding anchor points and pulling the handles will instantly fill with the color set for the Fill value.

8. **Click near the point of the thumb and again pull down and left to create the handle. Pull the handle until the curve matches the template image.**

It takes time and practice to get used to the Pen tool. Don't get frustrated as you pull and bend these curves. There are other ways of doing this – such as drawing all straight lines, and then pulling and stretching them till they fit. This is the best way we've found, however, and the way most professional designers and illustrators accomplish the task.

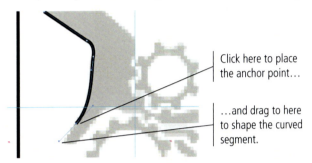

Click here to place the anchor point…

…and drag to here to shape the curved segment.

9. **Click the Pen tool to create a new anchor point on the other side of the tip of the thumb. Pull the handles until the object fits.**

10. **Continue adding curved anchor points to complete the shape to the beginning of the lower gear.**

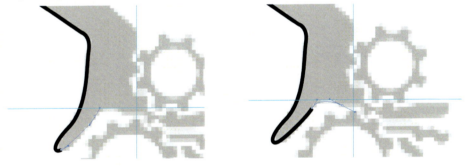

11. **Click to add another anchor point to the right of the lower gear.**

You can use a straight line here. When you draw the gear later, it will cover part of the hand and create the "crushed" appearance.

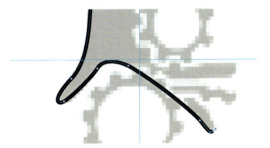

12. **Continue adding anchor points to complete the tip of the first finger. When you get to the crotch of the two fingers, click to create a corner point.**

13. **Using the same techniques, continue clicking and dragging to outline the second and third fingers. Use a corner point where the second and third fingers meet.**

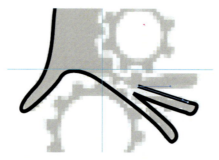

14. **Work your way around the rest of the hand shape. Ignore the right gear shape, as you did the one on the left. End your drawing by single-clicking to place a point at the top-right edge of the arm.**

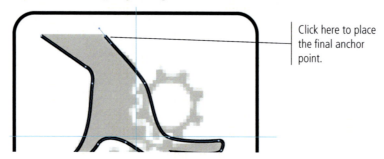

Click here to place the final anchor point.

15. **Save the file and continue to the next exercise.**

CLOSE OPEN PATHS

You're almost done. All that's left to do is connect the two anchor points at the top of the arm and straighten out the top line on the hand. Illustrator includes tools that make these two operations very simple. Then you can move on to creating the gears.

1. **In the open file, zoom into the top of the hand. Using the Direct Selection tool, draw a marquee around the two top anchor points.**

The selected anchor points are solid.

Unselected anchor points are hollow.

2. **Choose Objects>Path>Join to connect the selected anchor points with a path.**

3. **Choose Objects>Path>Average. In the Average dialog box, click the Horizontal radio button, and then click OK.**

   This command aligns the two selected anchor points on the horizontal axis.

4. **Swap the fill and stroke colors to fill the hand with black and turn off the stroke.**

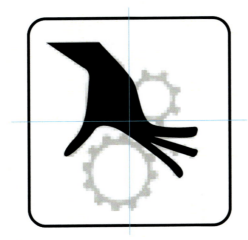

5. **Hide the hand shape (Object>Hide>Selection).**

6. **Save the file and keep it open for the next exercise.**

 ## USE MATH TO STRUCTURE OBJECTS

In this exercise, you use mathematics to calculate the specific distance you need to clone each of the teeth on the two gears. The smaller gear has 8 teeth, and the larger gear has 12. Since a complete circle has 360 degrees, all you have to do is divide 360 by the number of gears (either 8 or 12) to arrive at the amount you need to rotate a clone to end up with the proper amount of teeth on each of the gears. Sound complicated? It's actually quite easy using Illustrator's built-in tools.

360 degrees / 8 teeth on the small gear	=	45° per tooth
360 degrees / 12 teeth on the bigger gear	=	30° per tooth

1. **In the open file, make sure nothing is selected. Set the fill to black and the stroke to white.**

   You should always check your Fill and Stroke values before you start to draw an object. Just as a solid fill can be distracting when you use the Pen tool, so can applying a heavy stroke when all you need is the fill.

2. **Using the Ellipse tool, draw a circle to fit the smaller of the two gears (on the right).**

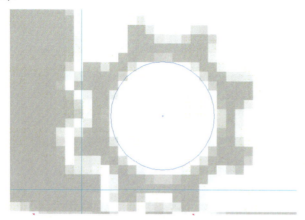

3. **Draw a rounded rectangle approximately the size of one of the teeth. Change the shape's fill to black and the stroke to none.**

   The exact size and shape of the first cog doesn't have to be perfect. As with any object you draw in Illustrator, you can change and modify the cogs after you create the basic shape.

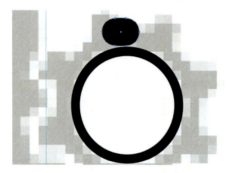

4. **Using the Direct Selection tool, select the two bottom anchors on the cog shape.**

   Be sure to select only the two bottom anchors.

5. **Press Delete/Backspace to delete the bottom anchors and the paths connected to them.**

   You could connect the two remaining anchors using the Join command, but there's no need to do so. The join area is going to end up underneath the gear.

6. **Using the Direct Selection tool, pull the top of the cog up a little.**

   Select the two top anchor points and drag them up and right to "angle" the cog.

Note:

We know you can't see the original perfectly. If you had a 300-dpi original bitmap that measured 8 × 10 ", you could have traced the image perfectly — but you don't. What you're doing in this exercise is a fairly accurate reflection of what actually happens in on-the-job assignments.

7. **Use the Stroke panel to change the circle's stroke to 2 pt. and align the stroke to the outside of the path.**

Click here to align the stroke to the outside of the path.

8. **Drag the cog until the bottom of the shape touches the circle's stroke. Use the Align panel to center the cog on top of the circle.**

9. **Select the circle and choose View>Guides>Make Guides.**

   This command changes the stroked path into a guide so you can see the center point even when the circle isn't selected. The 2-pt. black stroke is now gone (but only temporarily).

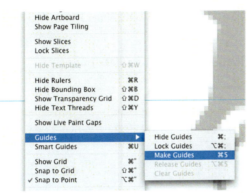

Key Command:

To make a guide from a regular object, first select the object, and then press Command/Control-5. To turn a guide object back into the regular object (with its same stroke weight, color, and other attributes), add the Option/Alt key to the Command/Control-5 combination.

10. **Select the cog with the Selection tool, and then choose the Rotate tool in the Tools panel.**

11. **Option/Alt-click the Rotate tool on the center of the circle guide.**

    Remember, clicking the first time places the origin point for the transformation. Option/Alt-clicking places the origin point and opens the related dialog box where you can make specific numeric transformations and copies.

12. **Type "45" in the Angle field and click the Copy button.**

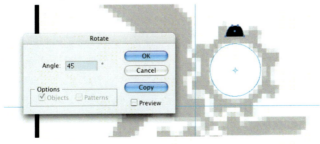

13. **Choose Object>Transform>Transform Again (Command/Control-D) to make six more copies of the gear tooth.**

14. **Select all of the cogs at once and apply a 0.5-pt. white stroke to all of them.**

15. **Group the eight cog shapes.**

16. **Rotate the grouped cogs around the gear center until the gears you drew match the position of the cogs in the template image.**

17. **Choose View>Guides>Release Guides to return the circle guide to a regular object.**

18. **Select all the pieces of the gear and group them.**

19. **Using the same process we outlined in the preceding steps, create the larger gear on the left side of the hand. When you clone/rotate the cogs, use a 30° angle for 12 total cogs.**

20. **Show the hidden hand artwork, unlock and delete the template image**

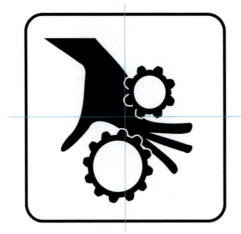

21. **Save the file and close it.**

Summary

The skills you used to complete these four icons will be the foundation for most work you do in Illustrator. You learned how to draw primitive shapes and transform them by scaling, rotating, cloning and aligning objects to meet specific needs. You also learned how to place raster images as templates, from which you created scalable vector graphics that will work for virtually any printed application.

Creating the individual icons required a number of different techniques and skills: transforming simple lines (for the snowflake), Live Tracing a bitmap image (for the fire), combining simple shapes into complex artwork (for the radioactive icon), and creating custom Bezier lines with the Pen tool (for the crushed hand).

As you move forward through the projects in this book, you'll build on the basic skills that you learned in this project.

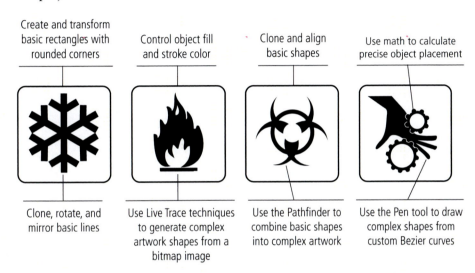

Create and transform basic rectangles with rounded corners

Control object fill and stroke color

Clone and align basic shapes

Use math to calculate precise object placement

Clone, rotate, and mirror basic lines

Use Live Trace techniques to generate complex artwork shapes from a bitmap image

Use the Pathfinder to combine basic shapes into complex artwork

Use the Pen tool to draw complex shapes from custom Bezier curves

Portfolio Builder Project 1

The client is pleased with the first four icons, and they want you to complete the rest of the warning icons. They also want you to create an additional set of icons for travel and outdoor activities that they offer as benefits during their international corporate conferences.

To complete this project, you should:

❏ Complete the remaining international warning icons. The bitmap versions are in your RF_Illustrator>Symbols folder.

❏ Carefully consider the best approach for each icon and use whichever tool (or tools) you feel is most appropriate.

❏ Create a second Illustrator file for the six new recreation icons.

"We host a number of large, international conventions and conferences every year, and many attendees bring their families along for a working vacation. To keep everyone happy, we've started offering different outdoor activities for the families while their spouses are atending sessions, but the international nature means that a lot of people need visual help getting to the right place.

"Since you did such a good job on the first four icons, we'd like you to finish those. But first, we want you to create icons for horseback riding, sailing, swimming, hiking, rock climbing, and nature walks.

"We don't have the images for these ones. Can you find something on the Internet to use as a guide? Remember, icons need to be easily recognizable in any language, so they should very clearly convey visually what each one is for."

Kitchen Planning Guide

Your client is a local cabinet maker. In the past, he designed and built each box from scratch, but demand has become so high that he's going to start selling cabinets that have already been constructed. He needs to print a large, empty grid that his customers can use to determine how many cabinets they need. The grid must also contain the measurements for each individual cabinet, as well as measurements for the combined units. The client would like to have a large grid area for drawing, and instructions must appear on the page, as well.

This project incorporates the following skills:

❑ Creating a custom color scheme using saved swatches

❑ Creating a precise scale grid using accurate measurement and placement tools

❑ Creating and controlling point type using different character formatting attributes

❑ Importing text from external word-processing files

❑ Creating area type and controlling different paragraph formatting attributes

❑ Incorporating artwork from other applications and file types

❑ Exporting artwork as a PDF file

Client Comments

I've been making custom cabinets for 12 years. Generally speaking, I use four different sized cabinets — combined properly and planned accurately — to create kitchens of virtually all sizes and configurations.

My business is thriving, and I'm getting so many calls that I can't keep up with the estimates. As it stands right now, I get one sale for every ten times I pull a tape at a client site. I could service many more clients — and make more money — if my clients knew what kind of cabinets they want, how many, how wide, and how deep before calling me.

Can you help me create some kind of planning sheet that I can send to my clients? It would be great if clients could take measurements and record them on the sheet, as well as draw overhead views of their kitchens, and then send the completed planning sheets back to me. Most kitchens are smaller than 14′ × 20′, so I don't need anything bigger than that. I also need a "wall" row and column on the grid so that clients can show me where outlets, gas lines, and windows are located.

Art Director Comments

We're going to create this document on an 11″ × 17″ (tabloid) page. That's a standard paper size, so the client can get copies at the local quick printer whenever he needs them. For that kind of printing, the job can't bleed (run off the page edge) because bleeding requires printing on a larger size paper and then cutting it down to 11 × 17 inches.

The tabloid page gives us enough room to create a large grid, similar to graph paper but a little more detailed. I want heavy grid lines to mark every 1 foot and lighter lines to mark every 3 inches. You'll have to calculate how big each grid square needs to be and where the three-inch markers belong. You must be precise — this kind of technical job requires extreme accuracy.

The client sent the text he wants to use. I've already had some illustrations created, which you need to incorporate. The final job has to look like a cross between a drawing/ design sheet for our client's customers and a set of instructions on how to use the sheet.

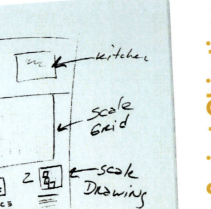

Project Objectives

To complete this project, you will:

❏ Design an 11″ × 17″ sheet with space for a number of different design elements

❏ Develop a custom color scheme and save the colors as swatches for quick access

❏ Calculate the spacing and measurements for a scale grid and create it using precise measurements and the Illustrator transformation tools

❏ Create and format headlines and text "bugs"

❏ Place and break up text from a Microsoft Word file

❏ Manage long blocks of text using area type

❏ Import illustrations from EPS files, Photoshop files, and other Illustrator files

Stage 1 Align Text to Specific Objects

As was the case in the first project you completed, this and subsequent projects will begin with a "foundational" exercise — one where you create the file, make sure the color mode is correct, check the sizes to ensure they meet production requirements, and save the file so it remains separate from all other projects.

 CREATE THE GUIDE DOCUMENT

In this exercise, you create the new document with the appropriate production size and color mode.

1. **Choose File>New (or click Print Document in the Welcome screen).**

2. **Name the new file "Kitchen Design Guide", choose Tabloid from the Size menu, and make sure the Units menu is set to Inches.**

   Make sure you select the Portrait Orientation button. This project must be 11″ wide by 17″ high. If you applied landscape orientation, the values would be reversed, and the file would be 17″ wide by 11″ tall.

3. **In the Advanced options, make sure the Color Mode menu is set to CMYK and the Raster Effects menu is set to High (300 ppi). Click OK to create your new document.**

Make sure you select portrait orientation.

4. **Make sure the page rulers are visible (press Command/Control-R). Choose View>Fit in Window so you can see the entire page.**

   Rulers are invaluable, especially when creating technical drawings that require precise measurements.

5. **Drag ruler guides onto the page to create a 0.5″ margin.**

   By placing guides 0.5″ from each edge, you leave a 10″ live area (11″ page minus 0.5″ margins on two sides equals 10″). The **live area** is where the important elements of a job are placed, far enough away from the page edge to avoid problems in the mechanical printing and trimming processess.

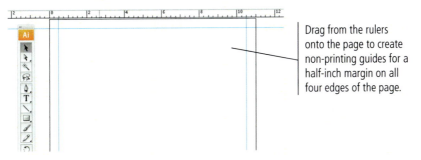

Drag from the rulers onto the page to create non-printing guides for a half-inch margin on all four edges of the page.

> **Note:**
>
> *Before completing this project, copy the Kitchen folder from the WIP folder on your Resource CD to your WIP folder wherever you are saving your work. When you save files for this project, you will save them in your WIP>Kitchen folder.*

6. **Zoom in and make sure the guides are exactly one-half inch from each edge. Align the guides to the half-inch mark on the rulers.**

If the placement isn't perfect (and it usually isn't the first time), simply click the guide and drag it into place with the Selection tool or Direct Selection tool.

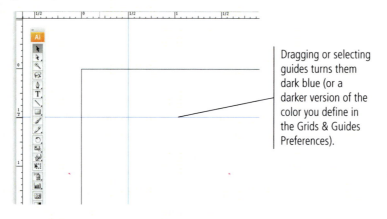

Dragging or selecting guides turns them dark blue (or a darker version of the color you define in the Grids & Guides Preferences).

Key Command:

To hide guides, press Command/Control-Semicolon.

To show hidden guides, press Command-Option-Semicolon/Control-Alt-Semicolon.

7. **Click the point where the two rulers meet (called the zero point) and drag it to the intersection of the top and left guides.**

The **zero point** is the origin of the rulers — where both horizontal and vertical measurements are 0. When developing technical illustrations such as this one, you'll find it very useful to be able to change the zero point of the page.

Key Command:

To make a guide from an existing object, first select it and then press Command/Control-5.

To convert a guide object back to a regular object, press Command/Control-Shift-5.

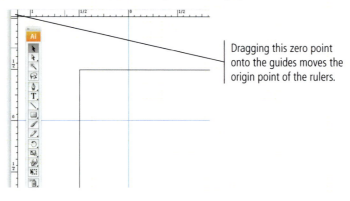

Dragging this zero point onto the guides moves the origin point of the rulers.

Note:

Double-click the zero point crosshairs to return the zero point to its original position. Illustrator uses the bottom-left corner of the page as the original zero point, as does the PostScript language, which is the core language that underlies Illustrator drawing capabilities.

8. **Save the file as "Kitchen Design Guide.ai" in your WIP>Kitchen folder and keep it open for the next exercise.**

We've already discussed views in several locations, but there's still more to learn. The first set of View controls can be found in the View menu or by using the related keyboard shortcuts:

Command/Control-0	Fit to Screen	Command/Control-Plus (+) key	Enlarge/Zoom in
Command/Control-1	Actual Size	Command/Control-Minus (-) key	Zoom out

You can also determine the exact percentage at which you want to view the illustration by using the View Percentage field in the lower-left corner of the workspace. You can type a number in this field, press the Return/Enter key, and the view will assume that percentage value; enter 200 and you'll see the image at twice actual size; enter 50 and you'll see it in half size.

Enter a value in the field and press Return/Enter to change the percentage view.

The Navigator panel, accessed in the Window menu and grouped with the Info panel by default, is another method of adjusting what you're looking at, how close your viewpoint is, and what part of the page you're currently viewing (if you're zoomed in close enough so you can't see the whole page).

The Navigator panel shows a thumbnail of the page you're looking at; a red rectangle represents exactly how much of the document you can see on your monitor. In the image to the right, we zoomed in on the north side of Yellowstone Lake. The Navigator panel shows a red rectangle around the equivalent area in the thumbnail. You can drag the red rectangle within the panel thumbnail to change what displays in the document window.

The slider and field at the bottom of the Navigator panel can be used to change the view percentage.

You can also save named views, which can prove very helpful if you must repeatedly return to the same area and view. A simple and easy-to-understand example would be a close-up view of a particular area of every file you create where you place company information, your personal copyright data, or other information common to all images. In other cases (especially technical drawings), you might need to frequently refer to a specific portion of a particular image as you develop the overall project. By choosing View>New View, you can save the current view with a specific name. Once you've saved a specific view, you can call it again by choosing that option from the bottom of the View menu.

You can add as many views as you need; you can then change view names or delete views you no longer need by choosing View>Edit Views.

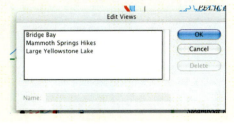

USE THE COLOR PANEL

Color is one of the "foundational" aspects of learning to use a software application. It is one of those things you continue to learn for as long as you draw. Understanding color is truly a process, not an event. For this project, you begin to learn about color using Illustrator's Color panel, and you use the Swatches panel to save the results of your work.

The first place to begin exploring color is in the Color panel itself. By default, and using the Basic workspace (Window>Workspace>Basic), the Color panel and the Color Guide panel are grouped together. The Swatches panel, which is related to color — especially custom colors you create using the Color and Color Guide panels — is grouped with the Brushes and Symbols panels.

1. **In the open file, set your stroke color to black and the fill to white.**

   These are the default stroke and fill settings, so clicking the Default Fill and Stroke button at the bottom of the Tools panel will accomplish this task with a single click.

2. **Draw a 0.5″ rectangle in the upper-right corner of the page and click the Color panel icon on the dock.**

   If your workspace doesn't match ours, set yours to the default Basic workspace (Window>Workspace>Basic).

3. **If the Stroke icon (black and hollow) is on top and the Fill icon (white and solid) is in the back, click the solid white icon to activate the Fill function.**

   Whichever of these icons is on top of the stack is the one that will be affected or modified by changes you make inside the Color panel. Always check which icon is active before adjusting colors to ensure correct results.

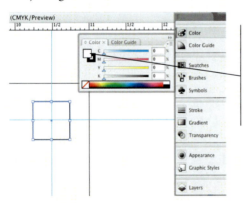

Press the X key or click here to make sure the changes you're making will affect the correct part of the selected object. In this case, you need to work on the fill, so make sure the Fill icon is on top of the stack.

Key Command:

Press the X key to swap back and forth between the stroke and fill while you work in any of the Color panels. Always check to make sure you're changing colors on the correct components for the currently selected object.

4. **Click the rainbow color bar at the bottom and find a brown color.**

These are the Stroke and Fill icons.

This icon tells you that the color you selected is out of range and will be adjusted to display properly on the media you're using.

Click this button to set the stroke or fill to None.

Drag around this color bar to search for the correct color.

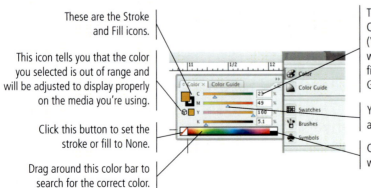

These are the value fields for Cyan (C), Magenta (M), Yellow (Y) and Black (K). If this file were in RGB color mode, the fields would be for Red (R), Green (G), and Blue (B).

You can use these sliders to adjust individual ink colors.

Click here to apply solid white or solid black.

5. **Change the value for the C, M, Y, and K components to C=20, M=50, Y=100, and K=8.**

   Colors for printed jobs are defined as relative percentages of Cyan, Magenta, Yellow, and Black. Changing these values modifies the "feel" of the brown color — shifting it more toward a camel color.

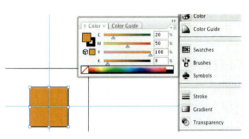

Note:

Black is called "K" in CMYK color to prevent it from being confused with Blue, which is referred to as "B" in RGB color. Black is also the "Key" color, to which other colors are registered

6. **Clone the brown rectangle to the left so you have a second brown square.**

7. **Change the color of the new cloned rectangle to C=30, M=2, Y=7, K=0.**

   Remember that you have to use the Tab key to move through the CMYK fields, and you have to press Return/Enter after you enter the last number to see the results.

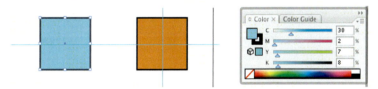

8. **Delete the two rectangles you created for this exercise.**

9. **Save the file and keep it open for the next exercise.**

Create Custom Swatches Using the Swatches Panel

The Swatches panel allows you to select colors from a relatively organized and structured collection of **color swatches**. Click a swatch, and you can change either the stroke or fill of a selected object; with nothing selected, clicking a swatch changes the fill or stroke icon (whichever is on top of the stack) in the Tools panel.

The Swatches panel resides in the default dock below the Color panel, in the same panel group as the Brushes and Symbols panels.

Accessing Built-In Swatch Libraries

ILLUSTRATOR FOUNDATIONS

The Swatches panel provides access to existing swatch libraries that install when you install Illustrator. These libraries include every color you can imagine, from fruits and landscaping to metals. You can access any of these built-in libraries by clicking and holding the first button in the bottom-left corner of the Swatches panel.

The Swatches panel is popular with some artists, and others use it very infrequently. There are a number of tasks you can accomplish using the features on the panel, which you'll learn about in this and later projects.

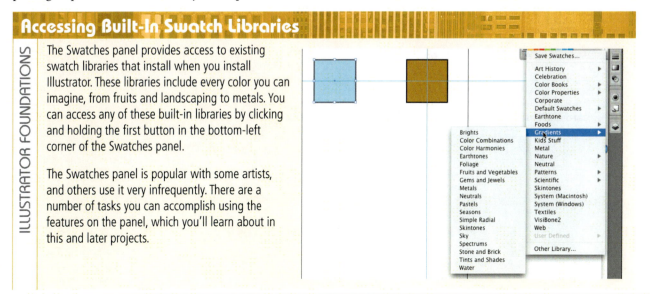

1. **In the open file, click the New Swatch button on the Swatches panel.**

New Swatch button

2. **Name the new swatch "Kitchen Blue" and change the individual ink colors to C=30, M=2, Y=7, K=0.**

3. **Make sure the Global option is checked.**

If you create a swatch as a global color, it is treated as a single color value instead of a component color. This has two very real benefits:

- You can apply a percentage or **tint** of the swatch by dragging one slider. If you don't check the Global option, clicking the swatch applies the correct color to the object, but the Color panel shows the different percentages of CMYK ink components. To change to a tint of the swatch, you have to manually figure out the percentage for each of the CMYK values.

- Changing the definition of the swatch will affect any object colored with that swatch. If Global is not checked, changing the swatch value will have no effect on existing objects.

Note:

If you check the Global option, changing the swatch definition later will apply the changed color values to objects on the page that use that swatch.

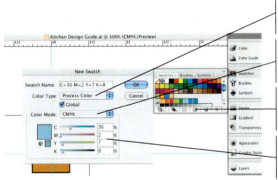

You can define a color as Process or Spot — which you'll learn more about in Project 3.

You can select a different color mode if you're designing for a different medium.

Click this icon to create custom groups (libraries) of specific color swatches.

Field values work the same for global swatches as they do for specific object colors.

4. **Click OK to create the swatch.**

Notice that the swatch you created displays a tiny white marker on its lower-right corner. This tells you that you have a custom and global swatch on the default library panel.

This white corner indicates that this blue swatch is a global color.

5. **Create another global swatch using the brown color you defined earlier (C=20, M=50, Y=100, K=8).**

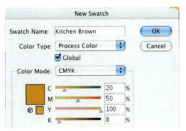

6. **Add a third global color and name it "Kitchen Green". Use C=70, M=6, Y=40, and K=6.**

7. **Save the file and keep it open for the next exercise.**

Stage 2 Creating Technically Accurate Artwork

The first part of this project requires creating a scale grid where customers can draw their own kitchen floor plans, complete with pencil drawings of the tops of their cabinets, sinks, and appliances.

The grid needs to be big enough to represent a 14 × 20-foot kitchen, including an extra row on the grid that represents "walls" to mark where windows, electrical outlets, and other important objects are located. The grid also needs a legend on the top and left edges to mark each foot of space.

 ## ESTABLISH THE SCALE

Since this type of project visually represents square feet, the grid lines will be spaced the same in both directions. You have all the information you need to figure out what that spacing should be:

- Your maximum horizontal width is 10″.

- You need to leave room for the legend on the left edge. We'll leave 1.25″ for that, which leaves 8.75″ of space available for the grid.

- You need 21 spaces in each row of the grid (20 feet plus 1 square for the "wall" area).

    8.75 / 21 = 0.41666…

- Round that number up to 0.417, and now you know how big each square in the grid should be.

- Each column in the grid needs 15 spaces (14 feet plus 1 square for the "wall" area.)

    15 × 0.417 = 6.255

    So your vertical gridlines need to be 6.26″ long.

1. **In the open file, zoom out so you can see the entire top of the page.**

2. **Select the Line tool in the Tools panel and click to the right and below the top-left margin guide.**

Note:

If you're wondering why the math doesn't work (the number 6.255 is mentioned as being 6.26 inches), it's because Illustrator can't do the .255 calculation; it rounds up to .26.

3. **In the resulting dialog box, type "8.75" in the Length field and change the Angle field to 180°. Click OK.**

Depending on the technical nature of your drawing, being able to create lines with exact measurements and angles — as you can when you single-click the Line tool — can be very useful.

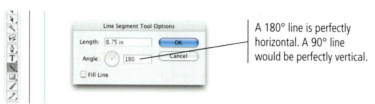

A 180° line is perfectly horizontal. A 90° line would be perfectly vertical.

4. **Drag the line so it is roughly positioned in the upper middle of the page. Set the stroke to 0.5-pt black.**

This is the first horizontal line in the grid. Right now, placing it roughly at the top of the page is fine. Before you're done, however, you will create a single unified grid object, which will allow you to perfectly position the entire grid at one time.

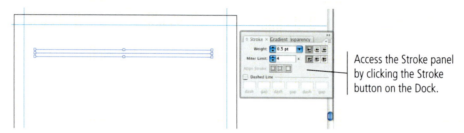

Access the Stroke panel by clicking the Stroke button on the Dock.

5. **Select the Type tool and click to the left of the line. DO NOT click the line itself.**

When you single-click with the Type tool, you create **point type** (sometimes also called **path type**). You'll see a flashing insertion point where text will appear when you begin typing.

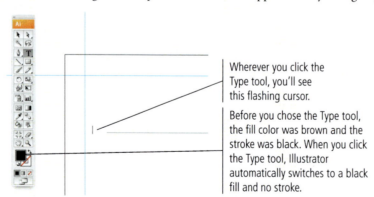

Wherever you click the Type tool, you'll see this flashing cursor.

Before you chose the Type tool, the fill color was brown and the stroke was black. When you click the Type tool, Illustrator automatically switches to a black fill and no stroke.

There are two basic kinds of type (or text) objects you can create in Illustrator: **point type** (also called **path type**), which usually resides on a single line or path; and **area type,** which is text that fills a shape, usually a rectangle. You'll learn more about type objects and how they behave as you move forward in this project.

Note:

If you click the line, the text will "stick" to it. It will turn the line into a text path instead of just a line, and that's not what you want to do. If the cursor appears to be stuck to the line, use the Undo feature (Command/Control-Z) and click again with the Type tool.

6. **While the insertion point is flashing, type "0′ ".**

When you add a new type object (whether point type or area type) without changing anything in the application, the type is automatically set in the last-used font and type settings, which will probably be different from one computer to another.

7. **In the Control bar, change the font to 12-pt. ATC Oak Normal.**

8. **Using the Selection tool, drag the text so the foot mark (′) is about 0.625″ (1/16″) from the end of the line.**

9. **Select the point type and the line and use the Align panel to vertically align the centers of the type and line.**

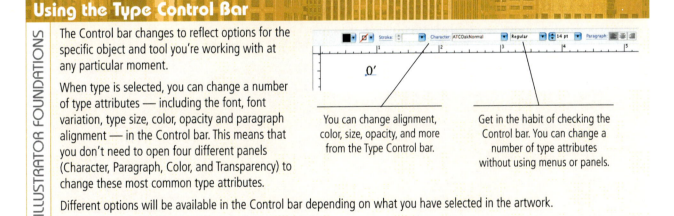

Note:

If the Align panel isn't in the Dock, choose Window>Align.

10. **Group the selected objects, save the file, and keep it open for the next exercise.**

The Control bar changes to reflect options for the specific object and tool you're working with at any particular moment.

When type is selected, you can change a number of type attributes — including the font, font variation, type size, color, opacity and paragraph alignment — in the Control bar. This means that you don't need to open four different panels (Character, Paragraph, Color, and Transparency) to change these most common type attributes.

You can change alignment, color, size, opacity, and more from the Type Control bar.

Get in the habit of checking the Control bar. You can change a number of type attributes without using menus or panels.

Different options will be available in the Control bar depending on what you have selected in the artwork.

 DUPLICATE ELEMENTS TO IMPROVE EFFICIENCY

You started this project by creating one line, placing text to the left of it, and then aligning the centers of both objects. You need a lot of these lines and text elements, and creating each of them with exact measurements would be tedious at best. You already know that you can clone objects by Option/Alt-dragging. Fortunately, Illustrator also includes tools that allow you to clone objects using precise measurements.

1. **Continue working in the open file. With the grouped objects selected, choose Objects>Transform>Move.**

   The Move dialog box defaults to the last settings used for moving an object. Even if you moved something by dragging it, the distance and angle you dragged would be reflected in this dialog.

2. Change the Horizontal field to 0 and change the Vertical field to –0.417.

You want to copy the group directly below the original; you don't want the copy to move left or right.

Remember, each square in the grid needs to be 0.417″ square — so you're moving the copy by 0.417″.

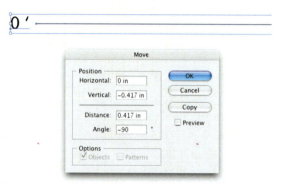

Note:

Using negative values in the Position fields moves the object left or down. Positive values move the object right or up.

3. Click the Copy button.

4. Choose Object>Transform>Transform Again (Command/Control-D) 14 times.

You now have the magic number:16 horizontal lines, equally and precisely placed, to create the scale grid. The text elements are already in place for each line. All that's left is to change the measurement associated with each line.

Note:

If you're wondering why you have 16 lines for a 15-square grid, remember that the bottom square in the grid needs to have a bottom line to "close" it. Any time you draw a grid, add one line more than the number of squares you need in the grid.

5. Using the Type tool, click the text to the left of the third line.

Clicking an existing text object with the Type tool places the insertion point in the text.

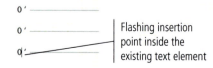

Flashing insertion point inside the existing text element

6. Highlight the 0 in this text element (leave the foot mark alone) and type "1".

```
0 ' _____
0 ' _____
1| ' _____
```

7. Using the same method as in Steps 5–6, change the number for each line so the lines (beginning with the second one) are numbered from 0 to 14.

The first line is the top of the "wall" square, which isn't part of the "floor" plan. You're going to delete the text element from the first line next.

When you reached the number 10, you might have noticed that the design didn't look as good as when every number was one digit. You'll fix that problem shortly.

```
0 '
0 '
1 '
2 '
3 '
4 '
5 '
6 '
7 '
8 '
9 '
10 '
11 '
12 '
13 '
14 '
```

8. Using the Selection tool, click the text element of the first line.

Remember, you grouped the text and the line; selecting with the Selection tool selects the entire group.

```
0 '  _____
```

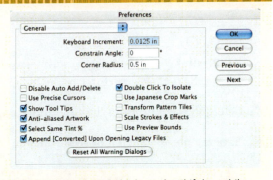

9. **Choose the Direct Selection tool, click off the group to deselect it, and then click only the text element of the first line.**

   Using the Direct Selection tool, you can select part of a group — as you used it to select part of an object in Project 1. Using the Direct Selection tool, you can also move or delete a specific part of a group.

   0 ' ————————————————————————

   0 ' ————————————————————————

10. **Press Delete/Backspace to delete the text element to the left of the first line.**

11. **Using the Direct Selection tool, drag a marquee that selects all the text elements but not the related lines.**

12. **In the Control bar, click the Align Right button to realign the text.**

    You can change some text formatting options without highlighting the actual type. In this case, all characters in the selected text object will be affected by your changes.

    By right-aligning the text, the numbers look better in relation to each other, but now they're too far from the end of the lines.

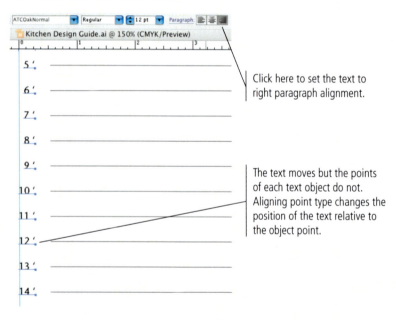

Click here to set the text to right paragraph alignment.

The text moves but the points of each text object do not. Aligning point type changes the position of the text relative to the object point.

Note:

Align text from the keyboard:

Command/Control-Shift-L for left justified

Command/Control-Shift-C for centered

Command/Control-Shift-R for right justified,

Command/Control-Shift-F for fully justified

13. **While all the text elements are still selected, press the Right Arrow key to nudge the text objects closer to the lines.**

14. **Select all the objects on the page and group them.**

15. **Save the file and keep it open for the next exercise.**

USE THE TRANSFORM PANEL

To create the vertical gridlines, you use the same basic techniques that you used to create the horizontal lines.

1. **In the open file, select the Line tool and set the stroke color to black.**

2. **Click an empty space on the page. In the resulting dialog box, type "6.255" in the Length field and change the Angle value to 90°. Click OK.**

   By changing the angle to 90 degrees, you create a vertical line instead of a horizontal line. You can enter any specific angle in this field, depending on what you want to create on the page.

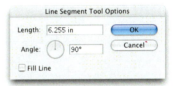

3. **Using the Direct Selection tool, click the first horizontal line to select it. Open the Transform panel.**

4. **Click the top-left reference point button and note the X and Y values.**

   The reference point buttons determine the origin of measurements for the selected object. If the top-middle point were selected, for example, the X and Y fields would show the location of the selection's top-center bounding box handle.

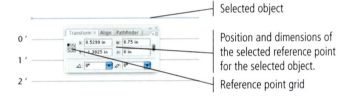

5. **Select the vertical line you drew in Step 1. In the Transform panel, make sure the top-left reference point is still selected and change the X and Y fields to match those that you noted for the left end of the vertical line.**

   Using the specific numeric values, the vertical line is now exactly aligned with the top horizontal line.

   The Transform panel is an easy way to make exact changes to selected objects. You can enter specific X and Y positions, height, and width; link the height and width to constrain the object's proportions; and rotate or skew an object using a specific angle. All of these transformations can be applied around any of the nine reference points for a selected object.

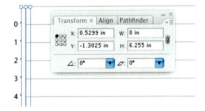

6. **Create a text element above the vertical line and type "0′ ".**

7. **Using the Control bar, apply the same font and type size that you used for the horizontal line labels, and then apply centered paragraph alignment.**

8. **In the Transform panel, choose the bottom-center reference point and apply the same X and Y values that you used in Step 5.**

   This step aligns the bottom-center point of the text element to the top of the vertical line. Obviously, however, you don't want the text to be immediately on top of the line.

9. **Press the Up Arrow key three times to move the text off the line.**

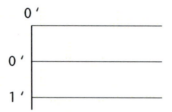

10. **Select the Vertical line and its related text and group the two objects.**

11. **Using the methods you learned in the previous exercise, make copies of the vertical group at 0.417″ horizontal intervals until the last vertical line meets the right end of the horizontal lines.**

12. **Change the text on the vertical lines from 0 to 20, and remove the text from above the first vertical line.**

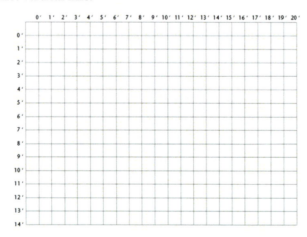

13. **Select all the vertical line groups and group them into a single unit.**

14. **Select both groups of lines, group them all together, and then lock the entire group.**

15. **Save the file and continue to the next exercise.**

Point Type vs. Area Type

Point type (or path type) starts at a single point and extends along or follows a single path. Area type fills up an area (normally a rectangle). The following images show point type on the top and area type on the bottom. In the image on the right, bounding boxes have been turned off in the View menu. (When you're working on type, it's usually easier — at least at first — to work with bounding boxes turned off.)

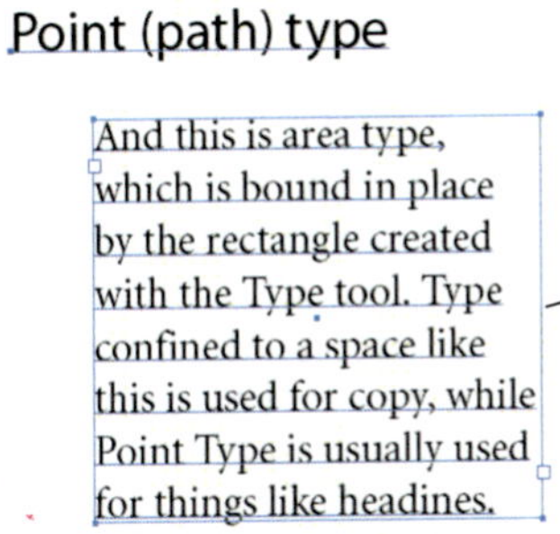

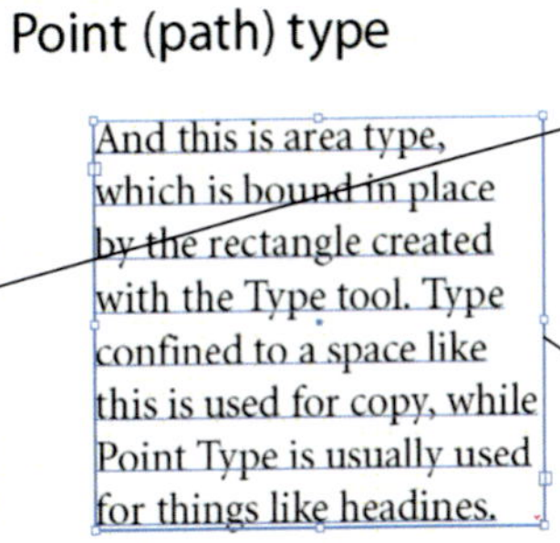

Point (path) type

And this is area type, which is bound in place by the rectangle created with the Type tool. Type confined to a space like this is used for copy, while Point Type is usually used for things like headines.

Point (path) type

And this is area type, which is bound in place by the rectangle created with the Type tool. Type confined to a space like this is used for copy, while Point Type is usually used for things like headines.

When bounding boxes are hidden, type shows no bounding box handles.

This is the text area boundary, as well as the bounding box boundary.

The difference between the two kinds of type becomes obvious when you try to resize them or otherwise modify their shape using the Selection tool.

If you scale or resize point type by dragging a bounding box handle, the type in that object resizes according to what you do to the object's handles. Because it's point type, it retains the shape you create.

Area type is in an area. If you resize that area, the type doesn't resize; it remains in the area and simply flows (or wraps) differently, based on what you do to the area.

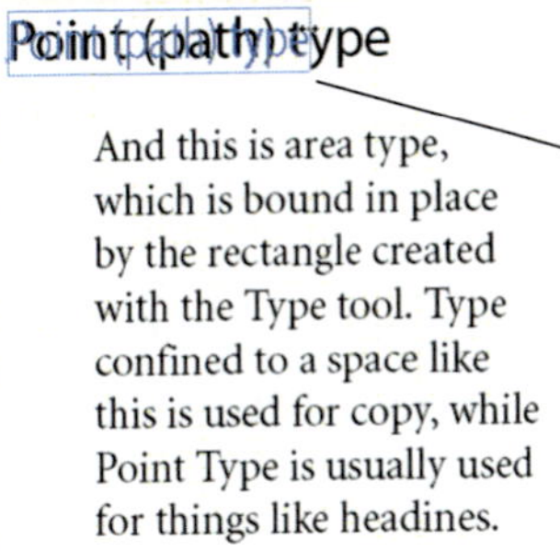

Point (path) type

And this is area type, which is bound in place by the rectangle created with the Type tool. Type confined to a space like this is used for copy, while Point Type is usually used for things like headines.

Resizing the bounding box resizes the text on that point-type object.

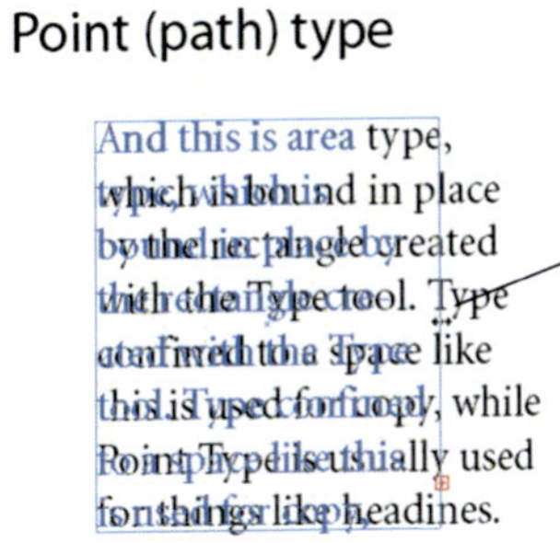

Point (path) type

And this is area type, which is bound in place by the rectangle created with the Type tool. Type confined to a space like this is used for copy, while Point Type is usually used for things like headines.

Drag the right edge of the text area to make the area narrower; the type simply rewraps inside the adjusted area.

Another consideration is where the "point" sits on the type path. When you change the paragraph alignment of point type, the point itself does not change position; instead, the text on the point moves to the appropriate position relative to the fixed point.

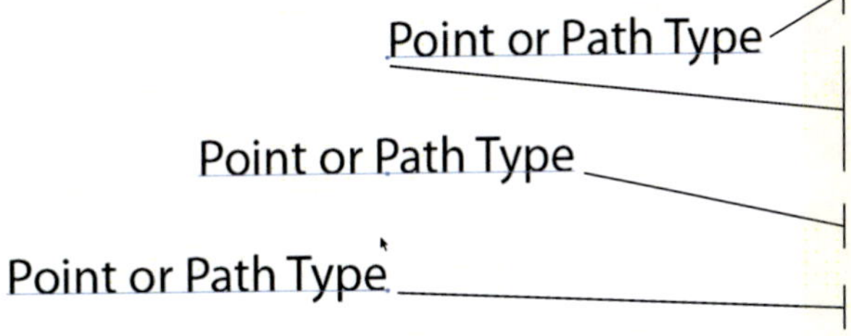

Point or Path Type

Left-aligned text

The point for path type is determined by where you align the type.

Point or Path Type

Center-aligned text

Point or Path Type

Right-aligned text

USE DIVISION TO FINISH THE GRID

The grid marking the 1-foot lines is complete, but the final grid requires lighter dotted lines to represent three-inch intervals. You could use a calculator to figure out one-quarter of 0.417, and then start placing the lines, but that isn't necessary. Instead, you can use a trick that's been working since the first version of Illustrator: using objects to accurately divide spaces.

You need to split each one-inch square into four quarters, so you need to first split a square in half, and then in half again. Each time you split a square, you need to drag a ruler guide into place to mark the spot.

1. **Continue working in the open file. Make sure nothing is selected on the page, and then set the Fill and Stroke values to None.**

2. **Select the Rectangle tool. Click once and create a rectangle that is exactly 0.417" square.**

3. **In the Transform panel, select the top-left reference point and enter the same X and Y positions that you used to place the top of the vertical line in the previous exercise.**

   This places the square in the exact location as the first spot on the grid. Now you can use this square to easily and quickly — using no mathematics whatsoever — place all the guides you need.

4. **Drag a vertical ruler guide to mark the center point of the invisible square.**

   We call it invisible because if you deselected it now, you would see nothing because the square has no fill or stroke attributes.

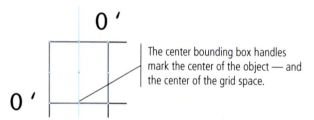

The center bounding box handles mark the center of the object — and the center of the grid space.

5. **Drag the right handle of the square's bounding box until it touches the center guide you just created.**

   If you can't see the bounding box, turn it on by choosing View>Show Bounding Box.

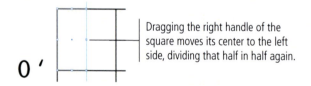

Dragging the right handle of the square moves its center to the left side, dividing that half in half again.

Key Command:

Command/Control-Shift-B toggles bounding boxes on and off.

6. **Drag another vertical guide to mark the center of the new box, and thus the 3" mark in the grid.**

7. **Move the box until the left edge meets the center guide, and then drag a third guide to mark the 9″ mark of the grid.**

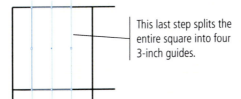

This last step splits the entire square into four 3-inch guides.

8. **Delete the square you used to mark the guides.**

   We often forget to delete these temporary dividers — and if you do, it could lead to trouble later on. This file isn't so complex that forgetting to remove the square would destroy anything important; but nonetheless, it's a good habit to delete temporary objects whenever possible.

9. **Save the file and keep it open for the next exercise.**

 ## FINISH THE ALIGNED TEXT GRID

At this point, each of the text elements is properly positioned relative to its measurement lines, and the client's customers now have a scaled grid they can use to draw kitchen designs. But you still need to add a few things to the document. First, you need to create the lines that mark 3″ intervals. Then you need to group the 100+ elements that comprise the grid so it's easier to manage as a single unit.

1. **In the open document, create a 6.255″ vertical line.**

2. **Drag the line on top of the guide that marks the 3″ point of the grid, and position the line so the top edge aligns with the top horizontal line.**

3. **In the Stroke panel, change the line to 1 pt. and apply a dashed stroke with a 2-pt. dash value.**

4. **Using the Swatches panel, change the stroke color to the Kitchen Blue swatch you defined at the beginning of this project.**

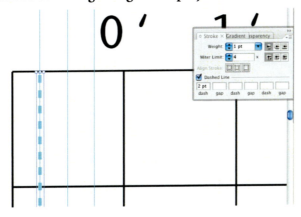

5. **Using the Selection tool, Option/Alt-Shift-click the line you just drew and drag right to the 6″ guide.**

6. **Repeat Step 5 to add a dashed line at the 9″ mark.**

7. **Select all three dashed lines and group them.**

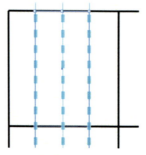

8. **With the group selected, choose Object>Transform>Move and make a copy of the group at a 0.417″ horizontal offset.**

   Remember, 0.417″ is the magic number for building this grid.

9. **Use the Transform Again command (Command/Control-D) to fill the rest of the grid with the vertical lines.**

10. **Use the Selection tool to select all the dashed lines and group them.**

11. **Repeat this entire process to create the 3″ horizontal markers. Start by creating a 0.417″ invisible square. Use the square to drag three horizontal guides that split the first grid square into four pieces. Create a 1-pt. light-blue dashed line that fills the horizontal width of the grid. Clone the line to fill the entire grid.**

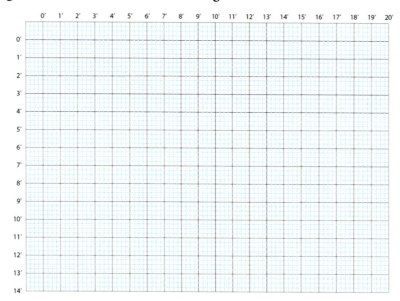

12. **Group all the dashed lines (horizontal and vertical) together.**

13. **Choose View>Guide>Lock Guide to unlock guides. Drag a selection marquee that selects only the horizontal guides that you created in this exercise and press Delete/Backspace.**

14. **Delete the three extra vertical guides as well.**

   If you used the Clear Guides command, you would also delete the margin guides that you created at the beginning of this project. That's not what you want to do, so you need to manually delete the extra guides.

15. Unlock the main grid.

Because you created the dashed line on top of the primary grid, the ends of the dashed lines are currently on top of the black lines in the main grid.

16. With the main grid still selected, choose Object>Arrange>Bring to Front.

Note:

You could also accomplish this task by cutting the main grid and choosing Paste in Front to move the grid to the front of the stacking order.

You can use any of the Arrange options to change the stacking order of objects on the page. You can move an object to the very front or very back of the stacking order, or move an object one level up or back.

The last step to creating this grid is to add shading behind the "wall" squares.

17. Using your new skills, create a rectangle that is 0.417″ high by 8.75″ wide with a 25% black fill and no stroke. Align the rectangle in the top row of grid squares and send it to the back of the stacking order.

18. Add a second 25% black rectangle behind the first column of the grid.

19. Add a white-filled rectangle that exactly matches the outside boundaries of the gridlines, and then send it to the back of the stacking order.

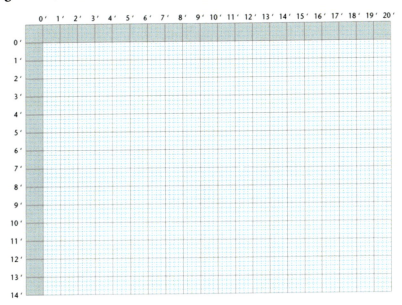

20. Group everything on the page. Center the group horizontally and vertically on the artboard.

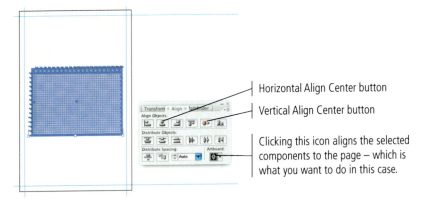

Horizontal Align Center button

Vertical Align Center button

Clicking this icon aligns the selected components to the page – which is what you want to do in this case.

21. Save the file and keep it open for the next exercise.

Stage 3 Controlling Basic Type Attributes

Fonts come in two primary **styles** — serif and sans serif. The font you're reading right now is a serif font. **Serif** fonts have little decorative bumps, curves, circles, or handles on them, as shown in the image on the right. **Sans serif** fonts do not have any of those extra little decorations, as shown in the image on the left. (The **sans** in "sans serif" means *without*.)

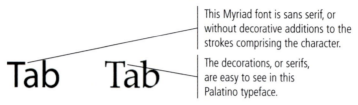

This Myriad font is sans serif, or without decorative additions to the strokes comprising the character.

The decorations, or serifs, are easy to see in this Palatino typeface.

In the following series of exercises, you learn to control a number of attributes that affect how type appears. You import, modify, and manage copy intended for headlines (or **banner text**), as well as copy intended for simple instructions (commonly called **body copy**).

 ## CREATE COLORED BACKGROUND ELEMENTS

Before you create your first headline, you need to do a little mechanical work on the layout. Specifically, you need to create a few colored objects that will allow you to create bright type that will stand out (often called **reverse type**, especially when using white type on a colored background) when users look at the Kitchen Design Guide.

1. **Continue working in the open file. In the Layers panel, double-click Layer 1 and rename it "Scale Grid". Lock that layer.**

2. **Create a new layer named "Colored Objects".**

3. **Draw a rectangle, set the Stroke value to None, and fill it with Kitchen Green from the Swatches panel.**

   It's important that you get used to using the Swatches panel and controlling the stroke and fill of objects you create.

4. **In the Transform panel, select the top-left reference point. Change the X position to –0.25″ and the Y position to 0.25″. Change the box width to 10.5″ and the box height to 12″.**

   This positions the green rectangle perfectly within the top two-thirds of the page. The negative X position moves the left edge of the rectangle to the left of the zero point at the top-left margin guide. The positive Y value moves the top edge above the zero point.

You should be able to spot the custom global swatches you created earlier by the white icons in their lower-right corners.

5. **Move the Colored Objects layer to the bottom of the layer stack.**

When you drag a layer up or down, a Hand icon appears and you can see the outline of the layer you're moving. A dark line shows you where the layer will be positioned when you release the mouse button.

6. **Draw another rectangle that's 10″ wide and 7.5″ high, with its top-left point positioned at X=0″ and Y=−4″. Apply the Kitchen Brown color to the rectangle.**

You will place explanatory text in the brown rectangle above the grid.

7. **Lock the Colored Objects layer. Create another layer called "Main Text Layer".**

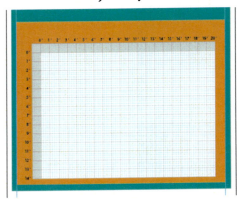

8. **Save the file and keep it open for the next exercise.**

 CREATE AREA TYPE

The next task is to create a large, brightly colored headline for the guide. To start, you need to draw a text region using the Type tool. This is called working with area type.

1. **Continue working in the open file. Select the Type tool and use it to draw a rectangle across the top of the page.**

Click on the left margin and drag to the right and down, releasing the mouse button when the cursor hits the margin guide on the right side of the page.

2. **Display the Character panel and set the font to 12-pt. ATC Laurel Bold.**

If you don't see the Character panel, access it by choosing Window>Type>Character.

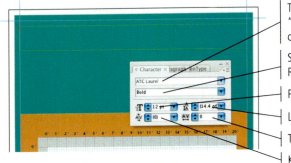

The "family" of fonts, also called the "typeface" or simply "font"; families can include a dozen different fonts.

Style of the font, such as Regular, Bold, or Italic.

Point size of the font

Leading, or the space between lines

Tracking, or the space between multiple characters

Kerning, or the space between two characters

3. Type "Kitchen Design Guide".

4. In the Options bar (Control bar), click the Align Center button.

5. With the insertion point flashing in the text, choose Select>All.

When you're working in a text element, Select All selects all the text in the element instead of selecting all objects on the page.

6. In the Character panel, change the type size to 60 pt.

7. Change the text fill color to any of the yellows from the Swatches panel.

The text is still selected, so you can't actually see the color change to yellow.

8. Deselect the type by clicking the Selection tool anywhere on the page.

9. Save the file and keep it open for the next exercise.

Key Command:

Press Command/ Control-C to center text.

Key Command:

Press Command/ Control-A to select all (text or objects).

Key Command:

Press Command/Control-Shift-> to enlarge type size by 2 points. Press Command/Control-Shift-< to reduce type size by 2 points.

Add the Option/Alt key to these commands to change the type size by 10 points.

ADJUST TRACKING AND KERNING

Tracking and kerning are two terms related to the horizontal spacing between the characters on a line of text. **Tracking** refers to the spacing of the entire line (or **track**). **Kerning** is the spacing between two specific characters.

Tracking and kerning are more important for headlines than for regular body copy. Most industrial-quality font families come with built-in kern and track values. Smaller type does not usually pose tracking and kerning problems; when type is very large, however, spacing often becomes an issue. To fix the problem, you need to adjust the kerning and/or tracking values.

1. **Continue working in the open file. Select the entire line of text and display the Character panel.**

   Note that there are two value fields at the bottom of the panel. The one with the AV label and the two tiny arrows is the Kerning (pair) value; the one with the wide arrows at the bottom of the icon is the Tracking (line) value.

These two fields at the bottom of the Character panel control character kerning and tracking.

2. **Change the Tracking field to –40 to tighten the space between the selected letters.**

   You can change the field manually, choose a pre-defined value from the pop-up menu, or click the up- or down-arrow buttons to change the tracking by 1 unit with each click.

The spacing has tightened considerably.

The Kern (Pair) value will remain set to "Auto", which is the default setting build into this particular typeface.

Key Command:

Press Option/Alt-Left Arrow or Right Arrow to change tracking or kerning by 20 units. Add the Command/Control key to change the tracking or kerning units by 100 units.

3. **Click the Type tool to place the insertion point between the "G" and the "u" in the word Guide.**

   This is a good example of a **kern pair** that needs adjustment. The Auto setting built into the font leaves a little too much space between the two characters — even after you've tightened the tracking considerably.

4. **Change the Kern field to –60.**

   Similar to tracking, you can change the field manually, choose a value from the pop-up menu, or use the field buttons to change tracking by 1 unit.

5. **Change the Kern values for the D/e pair to –20.**

   The rest of the line looks pretty good now. These slight modifications to tracking and kerning improve the overall appearance and readability of the headline. Get used to making minor adjustments such as these to large type, which can usually use it.

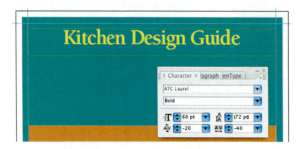

6. **Using the Selection tool, reduce the height of the headline rectangle by dragging the bottom-center handle up a little.**

   Adjusting the vertical size of the entire rectangle doesn't resize the type — it reduces the size of the rectangle *containing* the text.

Reducing the height of the rectangle doesn't alter the size of the text.

7. **Save the file and keep it open for the next exercise.**

CHANGE VARIOUS TYPE ATTRIBUTES

You've created a headline as area type, resized it, and adjusted the character and horizontal line spacing. In this exercise, you create a subhead (or **deck**) and practice working with character formatting.

1. **Continue working in the open document. Using the Selection tool, Option/ Alt-Shift-drag the headline text area to create a clone directly below the original.**

2. **In the Character panel, type "ATCOakNormal" into the top (Font) field and use the pop-up menu to choose Regular as the style.**

   You could also click the arrow to the right of the field and scroll through the list of fonts available on your system.

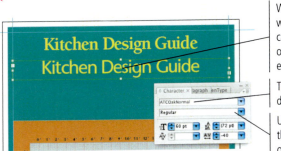

When a text object is selected with the Selection tool, you can still change the character or paragraph attributes of the entire object.

Type "ATCOakNormal" directly into the Font field.

Use the pop-up menu to set the style of the new type object to Regular.

3. **Using the Type tool, select all of the second line of text.**

4. **Choose Auto from the Kerning pop-up menu and 0 from the Tracking pop-up.**

   These values return the horizontal spacing to the factory default that was built into the now-changed font. ATC Oak is a sans-serif font. The sans-serif family will work better for this secondary headline.

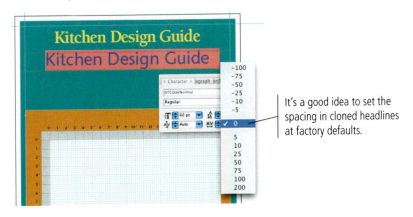

It's a good idea to set the spacing in cloned headlines at factory defaults.

5. **Change the deck copy to 12-pt ATC Oak Bold and change the type fill color to white.**

6. **Replace the selected text with the following paragraph:**

> **Use this design guide as a tool to lay out your new kitchen ideas. Just follow the easy step-by-step instructions.**

7. **Adjust the position and sizes of the two text elements.**

The top of the headline should touch the top margin; the deck copy should be just below the descender on the "g" in Design. (A **descender** is the part hanging below the baseline on letters such as g, y, and j.)

8. **Lock the Main Text Layer and unlock the Scale Grid layer.**

9. **Create point type as 10-pt ATC Oak Normal on the Scale Grid layer that reads "Small squares = 3"".**

10. **Clone the line to the right and change the copy to read "Large squares = 1'".**

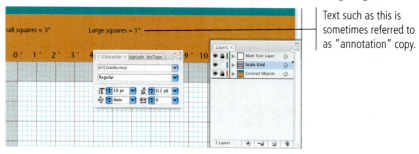

Text such as this is sometimes referred to as "annotation" copy.

11. **Save the file and keep it open for the next exercise.**

Stage 4 More Advanced Typesetting

By this point you know how to create type objects, how to change the font and type size of text, how to tighten and loosen the space between words and letters, and how to clone and replace one piece of text with another. There's much more to learn about how text looks and acts on the page. In the following series of exercises, you learn about working with longer text elements (body copy), including how to import text from other programs.

CONTROL LEADING

When you work with more than a single line of text, you will often need to change the vertical spacing between lines, which is called **leading**. (The word "leading" refers to the days when the space between lines of lead type blocks was controlled with long, 1-point thick lines of lead.)

The term **bugs** is used in ad agencies to refer to floating banners, characters, signs, "special sale" graphics, and other objects that are not actually connected to the artwork in question, but used to gain the reader's attention. You make just such an attention-grabbing bug in this exercise.

1. **Continue working in the open file. Lock the Scale Grid layer and the Main Text Layer, and then create a new Layer named "Bugs" at the top of the layer stack.**

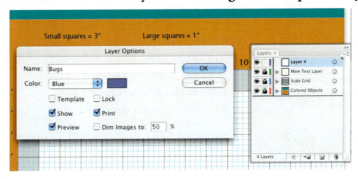

2. **Using the Type tool, click to create a point text element and type "LIMITED".**

3. **Press Shift-Return/Enter, and then type "LIFETIME".**

4. **Press Shift-Return/Enter, and then type "WARRANTY".**

    Pressing Shift-Return/Enter places **soft returns** at the end of each line. A soft return allows you to end a line in a specific place without starting a new formal paragraph.

    This command is important when you want to change a paragraph formatting attribute such as line spacing or alignment. If you ended each line in this bug with a hard return (pressing Return/Enter), you could apply different paragraph attributes to each line — accidentally or intentionally.

5. **Change the type to 24-pt ATC Oak Bold and apply centered paragraph alignment.**

6. **In the Character panel, change the Leading field to 19.**

You can change leading manually by typing in the Leading field, you can use the field arrow buttons to change the value 1 point at a time, you can use the field pop-up menu to apply a predefined value, or you can use the keyboard shortcuts.

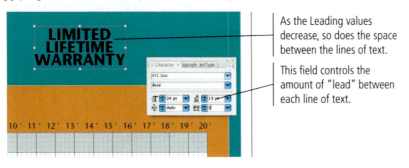

As the Leading values decrease, so does the space between the lines of text.

This field controls the amount of "lead" between each line of text.

A leading amount equal to the size of the font would be 24 points of lead. You've reduced the leading to less than 19 points, creating very tight spacing between each line of text. This is commonly done when creating signs, banners, and other kinds of bugs.

7. **Using the Selection tool, drag the right-center handle to the left to squeeze the text.**

8. **If you don't see the Horizontal Scale field in the Character panel, click the options button in the top-right corner of the panel and choose Show Options from the pop-up menu.**

In the Character panel, look at the Horizontal Scale field. Squeezing the left or right handle changes the horizontal scale of the text. This is a good way to create condensed type from just about any font you have. Be careful using it, however, because it can ruin the shape of your letters if it's overused. (This method does not work with area type.)

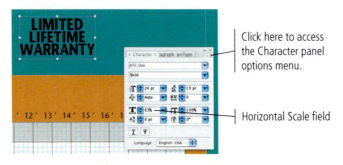

Click here to access the Character panel options menu.

Horizontal Scale field

Note:

By default, Illustrator sets the Leading value to 120% of the point size so there's always a small space between lines in a paragraph. Auto is one of the selections in the pop-up menu beside the Leading field.

If you set the Leading to Auto, the figure in the field will show a decimal value and be displayed in parentheses.

Key Command:

Press Option/Alt-Up or Down Arrow to change the Leading value by 2 points at a time. If you add the Command/Control key, you change the Leading value by 10 points at a time.

The Paragraph Panel

ILLUSTRATOR FOUNDATIONS

The Paragraph panel includes options for aligning and justifying text in various ways. The indent fields move text in from the sides of the type area. You can set the left and right indents separately, or define a unique indent for the first line of the paragraph. In the extended options, you can define a specific amount of space above and below the paragraph.

Area type is copy that resides in a given area — most often, but certainly not always a rectangle.

You can also put type in any shape you can imagine.

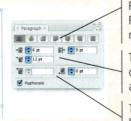

These icons represent various justification options (from left to right): Left, Center, Right, Full with left-justified last line, Full with centered last line, Full with right-justified last line, and Forced-full.

This portion of the panel has options for changing the left, right, and first-line indent values.

These two fields control the space before and space after a paragraph.

9. **Use the Ellipse tool to create one 1.5″ perfect circle, and use the Swatches panel to fill it with the yellow-to-orange radial gradient swatch.**

We haven't covered gradients yet, but that won't stop you from applying one of the few that come as part of the default Swatches panel. Since you do know how to use swatches, simply do the same thing with the yellow-to-orange gradient swatch.

10. **Center align the circle and the text element relative to each other.**

The circle appears on top of the text since you created the circle after you created the text.

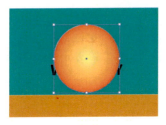

11. **Select only the circle and choose Object>Arrange>Send Backward.**

This command moves the circle back one step in the stacking order. The circle should now be behind the text.

12. **Use the Selection tool again to squeeze the text object to fit inside the gradient circle.**

Option/Alt-drag one of the side-center handles to resize the text object around the object center.

13. **Group, rotate, resize, and reposition the bug, using the following screen shot as a guide.**

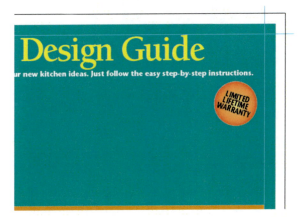

14. **Lock the Bugs layer, save the file, and keep it open for the next exercise.**

Note:

*Traditional typographers called the density of type its **color**. That term is still used among artists and designers schooled by more traditional professors and instructors. "Dense" type is considered darker then a lighter typeface, but color goes far beyond the bold character attribute; it goes to the visual impact on the eye. A 12-point Helvetica paragraph looks much lighter than a 12-point Eras paragraph.*

Most people — especially your clients — won't use Adobe Illustrator to create the text elements and components that you'll ultimately need to complete your part of a project. This project is a perfect example; there are a number of places where more than a single line of text is required — such as the instructions section at the bottom of the page. This copy has been entered, proofread, spell-checked, and saved using Microsoft Word, arguably the most popular and widely used word-processing program in the marketplace today.

The word "copy" is often used as a label for text intended for ads, instructional material, books, magazines, and other publications. This includes copy written for the Web, advertisements, packaging, or newspapers. In short, "copy" doesn't mean "a" copy of anything; it refers to original text.

1. **In the open file, make sure the Main Text Layer is unlocked and selected, and all other layers are locked.**

2. **Choose File>Place and to navigate the RF_Illustrator>Kitchen folder.**

3. **Double-click the Measure Copy.doc file to see the options related to placing Microsoft Word files.**

   These options allow you to import entire documents created in Word — including documents that have their own tables of contents, foot- and endnotes, and indices — as well as disable any formatting contained in the original.

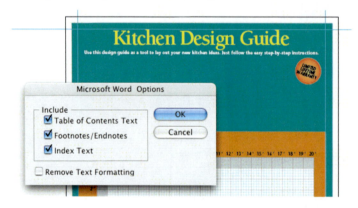

4. **Check the Remove Text Formatting box, and then click OK. Zoom out if necessary so you can see the entire imported text block.**

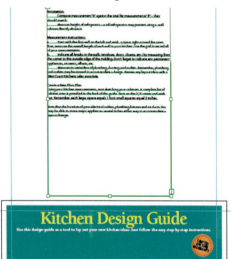

Note:

Press Command/Control-0 (zero) to show the entire page in the document window.

5. Zoom in and review the text you just imported.

You're not going to use this text exactly as it is now. Instead, you're going to cut it up, paste it back in, and generally massage its appearance to suit your needs.

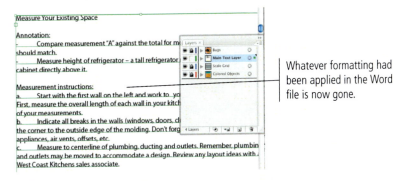

Whatever formatting had been applied in the Word file is now gone.

6. Save the file and keep it open for the next exercise.

 ## CREATE AREA TYPE

So far you've created both point type and area type. You know how to exercise quite a bit of control over type that sits on a single line, such as a headline or a deck, and you can control the spacing between lines of a paragraph. Now it's time to learn about controlling area type that includes more than one line — which is the most common type of text element you'll work with on projects such as this one, where text is a sizeable percentage of the job's components.

Look at the hand-drawn comp that the client provided to your agency at the start of the project. (The term **comp** comes from the days when designers physically glued things together to show a client what the job was going to look like.) At the bottom of the client's drawing, the instructions appear on the left side of the page, and a scale drawing and copy appear on the right. You'll need to create and control area type to fulfill the requirements of the project.

Note:

A text area is often a rectangle, but in certain conditions it might be a circle, an oval, an angled rectangle, or a shape of any kind. If a shape is filled with copy, it's called area type.

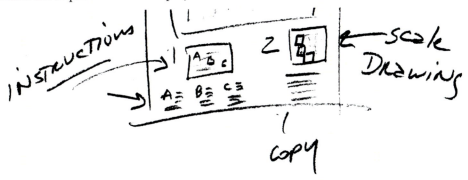

The headline you created earlier is technically area type since you created a rectangle (type area) with the Type tool before typing. But that headline is only one line of text; there are many other issues involved when working with longer bodies of text in a text area.

Positioning copy in columns is a very common practice. You see it in newsletters, magazines, ads, the Web, and even billboards. In the case of the instructions you've imported for this project, the lettered "A-B-C" text is a prime candidate for a text area that contains three columns. This three-column text content needs to occupy only the left side of the page. Let's start by splitting the page in two pieces — left and right.

1. **In the open document, pull the zero-point crosshairs to the exact upper-left corner of the artboard.**

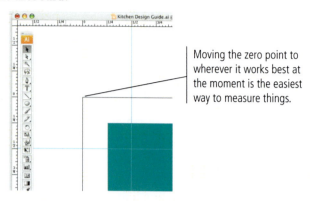

Moving the zero point to wherever it works best at the moment is the easiest way to measure things.

2. **Drag the imported Microsoft Word file to the lower-right side of the document (outside the paper edge).**

3. **Drag a ruler guide to 5.5″ to mark the center (the paper is 11″ wide), and then drag two more guides at 0.25″ on either side of the center guide.**

The end result will be three guides splitting the page in half and leaving a small margin on both sides of the center of the page. You're going to use the left side of the page for one part of the text and the right side for the other.

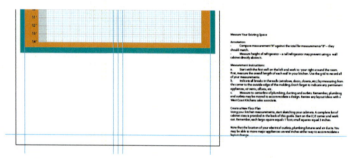

4. **Using the Type tool, highlight the Measurement instructions copy, starting in front of the letter "a." and ending with the words "sales associate" (as you can see below).**

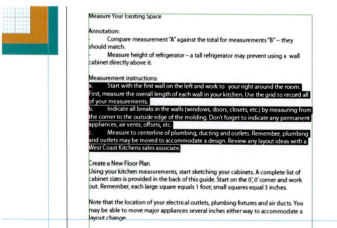

5. **Cut (Edit>Cut or Command/Control-X) the copy from the block of text.**

6. **Using the Type tool, draw a rectangle on the lower-left side of the page.**

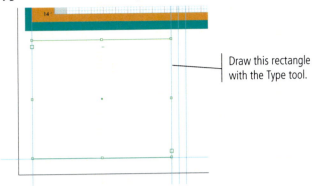

Draw this rectangle with the Type tool.

7. **Paste (Edit>Paste or Command/Control-V) the copy into the shape.**

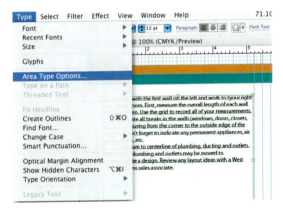

8. **With the area type object selected, choose Type>Area Type Options.**

   If the type object isn't selected, the Area Type Options command will be grayed out in the Type menu.

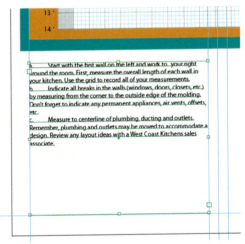

9. **Change the number of columns to 3 with a 0.25″ gutter. Check the Preview box to see what's going to happen when you click OK.**

   Controlling the number of columns and the distance between them — and a host of other visual features — makes the Area Type Options dialog box one of the most important type tools you can learn to use.

Note:

*The **gutter** value refers to the gap between the columns within the area type object.*

This dialog box offers control over not only the number of columns, but rows as well. As you become increasingly familiar with the many aspects of area type (and what can be accomplished using Area Type Options), you'll discover how to set tab spaces and the heights of rows, as well as use Illustrator to execute some outstanding financial and scientific data in the form of tables, graphs, and charts.

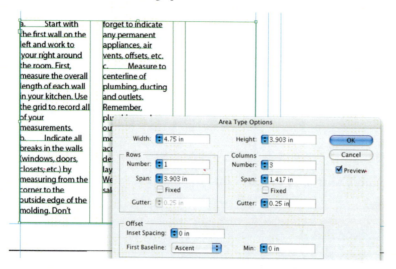

10. **Using the Character panel, change the font to ATC Laurel Book and increase the size to 14 pt.**

In body copy, serif fonts are easier to read than sans-serif faces. Fonts such as Helvetica aren't impossible to read, but they tire the eyes much faster than sans serif fonts.

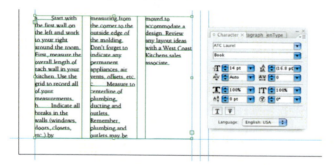

11. **Place extra returns after each section of copy to break the text into three appropriate columns — one for a, b, and c.**

Each column should begin the next lettered section, as shown below. Don't worry that the bottoms of the columns aren't exactly even. You'll work on that shortly.

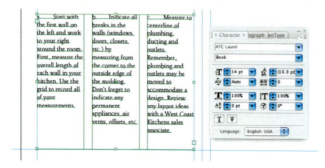

12. **Save the file and keep it open for the next exercise.**

The lower case "a," "b," and "c" are specifically required to ensure this block of instructional copy matches the illustration you will add later. Rather than leave these letters as regular text, you need to create bugs for each lowercase letter, and then use those bugs to point out exactly what and how the user needs to measure.

1. **In the open file, delete the lowercase letters (a, b, and c) and their following periods and tabs from the beginning of each column.**

   You're going to replace these letters with floating bugs that will serve as wrapping objects for each column of text.

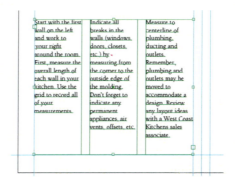

2. **Using either selection tool, click anywhere on the page to deselect the copy object.**

   Deselecting text elements is an important and arguably annoying task — but it will soon become second nature. Failure to deselect text objects such as this can easily result in the object changing color, getting too big, or simply disappearing. To ensure successful results, always remember to deselect text elements before applying any new attributes.

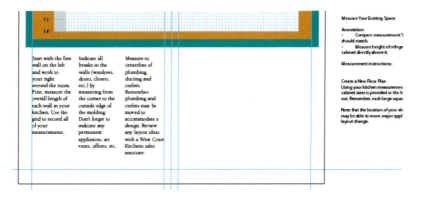

Key Command:

Press Command/Control while using the Type tool to temporarily switch to the Direct Selection tool, and then click away from the text to deselect it.

3. **Using the Ellipse tool, create a 0.5″ black circle with no stroke.**

   To accomplish this, set the Fill and Stroke values first, and then select the tool and click the empty workspace to the left of the existing area type object.

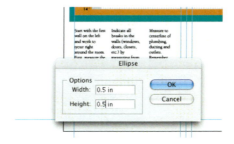

4. **Apply ATC Maple Medium (a display font) to create a white-filled, non-stroked letter "a" as point type. Align the letter and size it to the black circle you created in Step 3.**

   You have all the skills you need to complete this action without step-by-step instructions.

5. **Group the letter and the circle, and then make two cloned copies of the group.**

   When a single design element such as this is made up of multiple objects, it's always a good idea to group the objects. You can still change the type even after the objects have been grouped.

6. **Use the Type tool to change the second letter to "b" and the third to "c".**

   Remember to deselect and select appropriately as you complete this step.

   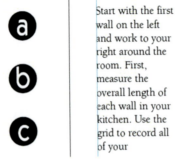

   Start with the first wall on the left and work to your right around the room. First, measure the overall length of each wall in your kitchen. Use the grid to record all of your

7. **Make a copy of the three objects, and then move the copies off the page to the left.**

8. **Select the first three objects and choose Type>Create Outlines.**

   Turning text elements into regular, path-based elements is another one of those "always-use" techniques. It's particularly important when you're creating large, high-resolution artwork and outputting it on a device that doesn't have the same fonts that you have on your computer.

   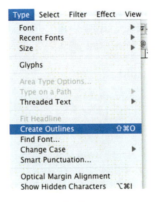

9. Place the "a" bug at the top of the first column, the "b" bug at the top of the second column, and the "c" bug at the top of the third column. Align the bottom edges of the three bugs.

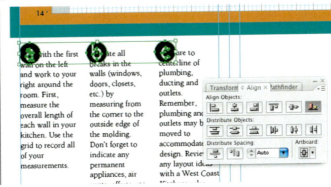

10. Choose Object>Text Wrap>Make to wrap the text around each of the three bugs.

Even though it's a type-related command, wrapping type around objects is found under the Object menu — you're affecting the type by changing the *object's* wrap attributes.

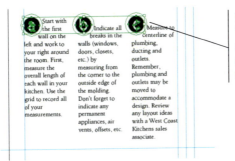

When you choose Object>Text Wrap>Make, the application creates non-printing borders around the copy. The surrounding text "bounces off" those borders.

11. Resize the type and bugs so they better fit the space:

   – Select the text in the three-column area and change it to 10 pt.

   – Resize each bug to be 0.4 in high and wide (80%).

   – Align the bugs so they affect only the first two lines of text in each column.

   – Drag up the bottom edge of the text area until it is just high enough for the longest column.

   – Delete any unnecessary paragraph returns that you added earlier to move the columns.

12. Group the bugs and the text area, and then drag the group down until it snaps to the bottom and left margin guides.

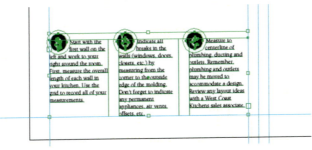

13. Save the file and keep it open for the next exercise.

Stage 5 Placing Images and Outputting Files

You're almost finished with the project. All that's left is to move some text around, place a couple of images, and save the file as a PDF document so you can show it to the client.

It is common practice to place external files into an Illustrator document. In Project 1, you placed low-resolution raster images to use as drawing templates. In the following exercises, you place several images to complete the design and planning sheet for your client .

INCORPORATE IMAGES OF VARIOUS FILE TYPES

To complete the annotations, you will cut and paste two annotations (each in an independent text area), and then position the annotations and copies of the lowercase "bugs" on top of an imported Encapsulated PostScript (EPS) drawing. EPS is a long-standing file format used to create illustrations and other visual components that are meant to be used in other drawings (as is the case in this project) or by other applications (such as Adobe InDesign).

1. **In the open file, create a new layer named "Placed Pictures" at the top of the layer stack.**

2. **Choose File>Place. Navigate to the file measure_room.ai (in the RF_Illustrator>Kitchen folder). Make sure the Link check box is not selected in the bottom-left corner of the dialog box and click Place.**

   In this step you're using a native .ai file, but you can place virtually any type of file, including an image file created in Adobe Photoshop.

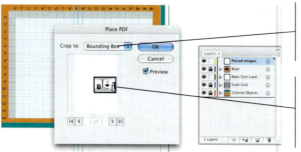

Whenever you place an AI or PDF file, make sure you select the correct crop value — in this case the Bounding Box value.

This ensures that the incoming AI file is cropped to the correct size. You can see the dotted marquee defining the region that will import.

3. **Choose Art in the Crop To menu and click OK to place the file into the Kitchen Design Guide file.**

4. **Zoom out so you can see the entire page.**

   Depending on how files are created, placing an AI file into another document might also place some extra bits that can cause problems.

   If you look at the current selection in the placed file, you see a large rectangle outlined with a yellow bounding box. That rectangle marks the page edge of the original placed file, but it has no use in this layout. You should delete the rectangle.

5. **Using the Direct Selection tool, drag a marquee around the bottom-right corner point of the outer bounding box.**

   When you place illustration files, all elements in the placed file are grouped together. By using the Direct Selection tool, you can select and delete part of the group without affecting (or ungrouping) the other elements in the group.

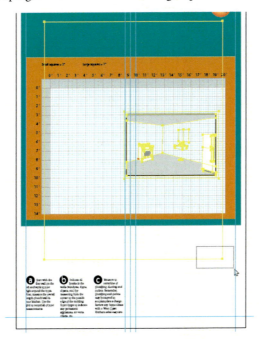

6. **Press Delete/Backspace to delete the selected anchor point.**

   It appears that part of the illustration is gone, but don't worry — it's not. This is one of the quirks to working with placed files in Illustrator.

Understanding Placed-Image Bounding Boxes

The **Crop To** option determines exactly what will be placed:

- The **Bounding Box** option places the page's bounding box, or the minimum area that encloses the objects on the page, including that page area that is displayed or printed by Adobe Acrobat.

- The **Art** option crops incoming files relative to the size and position of any objects selected at the time of the cropping. For example, you can create a frame and use it to crop an incoming piece of artwork.

- The **Crop** option places the artwork based on a defined crop area; you can use the the Crop Area tool to define a custom crop area.

If you define a custom crop area using the Crop Area tool, you can use that area as the basis for placing the file into another file.

- The **Trim** option identifies the place where the final page will be physically cut in the production process, if trim marks are present.

- The **Bleed** option places only the area that represents where all page content should be clipped, if a bleed area is present. This information is useful if the page is being output in a production environment. (The printed page might include page marks that fall outside the bleed area.)

- The **Media** option places the area that represents the physical paper size of the original document (for example, the dimensions of an A4 sheet of paper), including page marks.

The outer rectangle that you're deleting is treated as a clipping mask, which marks the boundaries of the visible content. When you delete the bottom-right anchor point, Illustrator automatically "connects" the top-right and bottom-left corners as the new edges of the clipping mask shape. (You'll learn more about clipping masks later in this book.)

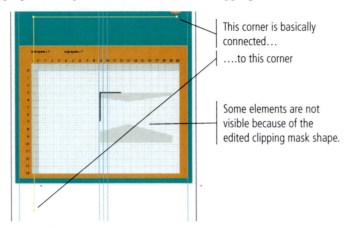

This corner is basically connected...

....to this corner

Some elements are not visible because of the edited clipping mask shape.

7. **Press Delete/Backspace again to remove the remaining points of the selected box.**

8. **Use the Selection tool to select the placed image.**

   The outer bounding box is now gone, making it easier to work with only the actual image.

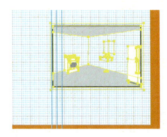

Note:

If you select a single anchor point on a shape and delete it, all the remaining anchor points on the shape become automatically selected, so you can delete the rest of the shape with one click. This is a very common technique for removing objects in complex Illustrator files.

9. **Using the Transform panel, scale the placed image until it's about 2.5″ wide by 1.7″ high, and then center the placed image above the three-column text area.**

   These are approximate sizes; use your judgment on the actual sizes you apply.

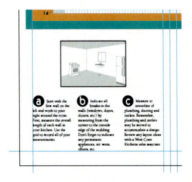

10. **Move the clones of the lowercase bugs (the ones you created earlier) from the Main Text layer to the Placed Pictures layer.**

ILLUSTRATOR FOUNDATIONS

Many Illustrator projects require more than just drawing. You often need to import or **place** images that were created or modified in Illustrator or other applications. File names and file formats are good indicators of a placed file's origin (although not 100% accurate). You can, for example, save an Illustrator file as:

- **Native (.ai)** is the default file format for images you create in Illustrator. Native Illustrator files are useable in other applications in Adobe's Creative Suite, but cannot be placed in other programs such as QuarkXPress.

- **Adobe PDF** (or simply PDF) stands for Portable Document Format. This format has become a universal method of moving files to virtually any digital destination. One of the most important uses for the PDF format is the ability to create perfectly formatted digital documents, exactly as they would look if they were printed on paper. You can embed fonts, images, drawings, and other elements into the file so that all the required bits are available on any computer. The PDF format can be used to move your artwork to the Web as a low-resolution RGB file or to a commercial printer as a high-resolution CMYK file.

- **Illustrator Template (.ait)** is a good choice when you need to use a specific file in numerous forms or iterations. Remember that when you open an Illustrator template to start a new version of the design, you must save the file under a new name; you cannot modify the template itself.

- **Illustrator EPS (.eps)** is short for **Encapsulated PostScript**. This format provides a very useful method of moving Illustrator files into other programs — especially programs that don't support native AI files.

- **SVG** (and **SVGZ**) is sometimes used for publishing vector graphics on the Web. The format is not widely used today, but it is gaining popularity is some small market segments.

This menu controls the format of the placement preview that will appear in other applications. If there is even the slightest chance that the file will cross platforms (Macintosh to Windows or vice versa), use one of the TIFF options. (The Macintosh formats cannot be read on a Windows computer.)

11. **Reduce the clones to about 50% of their current size, and then place the clones to mark the left wall, window on the right wall, and the plumbing/sink location in the placed image, as shown below.**

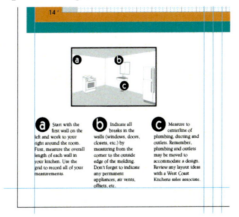

12. **Cut the first paragraph of annotation copy from the text you imported, and then paste it into a small rectangular text area to the left of the placed picture. Format the text as 8-pt ATC Laurel Book.**

13. **Repeat Step 12 to paste the second annotation paragraph to the right of the placed picture, and then align the top edges of the two text areas.**

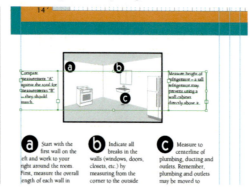

14. **Place the file named Hand-drawn Grid.psd (from the RF_Illustrator> Kitchen folder) into the layout.**

    This is a raster image file created in Adobe Photoshop CS3. This type of file does not have the bounding box problems associated with placing AI or PDF files.

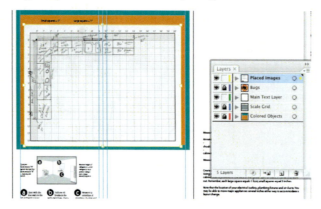

15. **Scale the placed file to closely match the image on the left, and then place it at the top of the empty space in the lower-right corner.**

16. **Cut the instructional copy from the imported text, and then paste it into a text area below the grid you placed in Step 15.**

17. **Format the pasted text with the same font and type size you applied to the body text on the left, and then adjust the top edge of the right text area to the same Y position as the top edge of the left text area.**

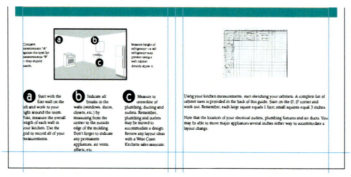

18. **Create a rounded rectangle, about 0.4″ wide by 0.6″ high, with a 60% Kitchen Green fill. Add a point text element with the number "1" at 30-pt., filled white, set in ATC Oak Bold.**

19. Center align the rounded rectangle and large number 1, group the two elements, and then place the group above the left column on the lower part of the page.

20. Clone the group, and then place the clone over the right side of the page. Change the number in the clone to "2".

21. Cut the two headlines from the imported text and paste each as a point type element over the appropriate side of the page. Format these elements however you prefer. (We used 14-pt. ATC Oak Bold.)

If necessary, move the placed pictures and instructional text elements down to allow enough space for the headlines.

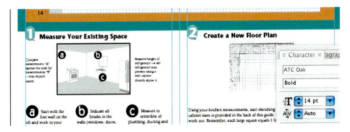

22. Place the file cabinets.ai (From the RF_Illustrator>Kitchen folder), and then scale and align the placed file to fit the center of the green space at the top of the page.

23. Delete the text area that was created when you imported the Microsoft Word file.

24. Save the file and continue to the next exercise.

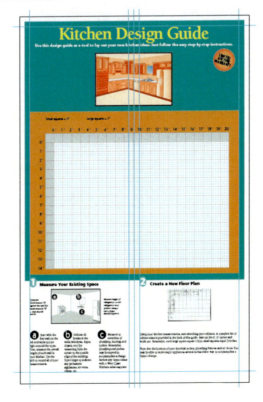

Save a File as PDF

Your final task is to prepare the file for digital delivery to your client. This is a common step in nearly every workflow, so you should become familiar with saving PDF files from Adobe Illustrator.

1. **In the open file, Choose File>Save As.**

2. **Navigate to your WIP>Kitchen folder, choose Adobe PDF in the Format/ Save As Type menu, and click Save.**

Click here to see the options for saving a PDF file.

3. **Review the options in the General pane.**

   Read the description area to see what Adobe has to say about these options.

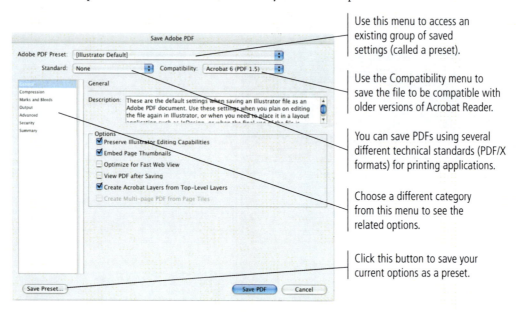

Use this menu to access an existing group of saved settings (called a preset).

Use the Compatibility menu to save the file to be compatible with older versions of Acrobat Reader.

You can save PDFs using several different technical standards (PDF/X formats) for printing applications.

Choose a different category from this menu to see the related options.

Click this button to save your current options as a preset.

4. **Click Compression in the list of categories on the left and review the options.**

   These options allow you to reduce the resulting file size by compressing color, grayscale, and/or monochrome bitmap (raster) images. You can also compress text and line art by clicking the check box at the bottom.

5. **Review the Marks and Bleeds options.**

   These options add different types of marks to the output page:

   - **Trim marks** indicate the edge of the page where a page printed on a larger sheet will be cut down to its final size. You can also define the thickness (weight) of the trim marks, as well as how far from the page edge the lines should appear (offset).

   - **Registration marks** resemble a small crosshair. These marks are added to each ink unit on a printing press to make sure the different inks are properly aligned to one another.

   - **Color bars** are rows of small squares across the sheet, used to verify press settings for accurate color reproduction.

   - **Page information** adds the file name, date, and time of output. You can also define what font to use for page information

   - **Bleeds** define how much of elements outside the page boundaries will be included in the final output. Most printers require at least a 0.125″ bleed on each side, but you should always ask before you create the final file.

Note:

Most printers require trim marks to be created outside of the bleed area. Always check with your service provider when saving a PDF for commercial output.

   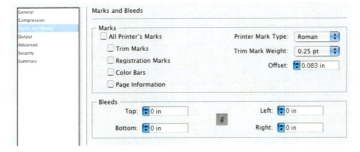

6. **Choose Acrobat 4 in the Compatibility menu.**

Note:

The Output, Advanced, and Security options are explained in later projects that discuss transparency and color management.

   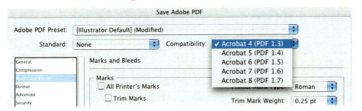

7. **Leave all other options at their default values and click Save PDF.**

8. **Close the Illustrator file.**

Summary

This kitchen design guide is a good example of a project that combines form and functionality. You created an accurate scale drawing space, then added and formatted client-supplied text to create a complete piece that meets the client's needs. The end result is both easy to read and easy to understand, including graphics and graphic elements that will help your client's customers to draw their new kitchen plans.

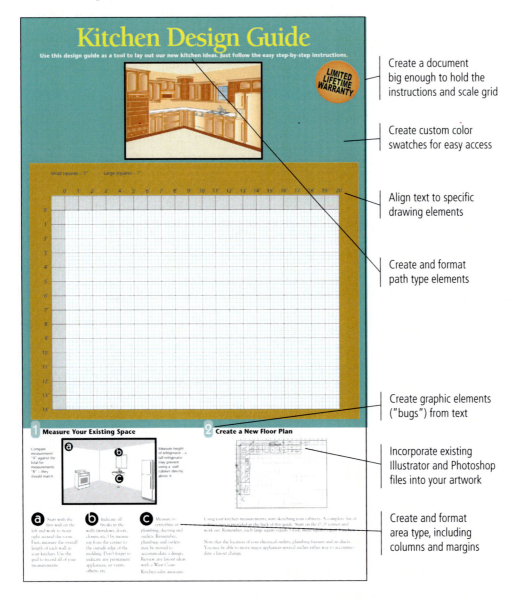

Create a document big enough to hold the instructions and scale grid

Create custom color swatches for easy access

Align text to specific drawing elements

Create and format path type elements

Create graphic elements ("bugs") from text

Incorporate existing Illustrator and Photoshop files into your artwork

Create and format area type, including columns and margins

✍ Portfolio Builder Project 2

The owner of your agency is very happy with the scale drawing you did for the Kitchen Guide. Now he wants you to design a layout for the agency's new offices. The new space is 1,200 square feet overall, and needs to include space for a foyer, offices, bathroom, and kitchen area.

❑ Draw a scale grid that will accommodate the new 1,200 square foot space.

❑ Include an office for the owner, offices for two salespeople, and offices for four designers.

❑ Include wall thickness (6″) and door width (30″) when you plan the office layout.

"The overall space in the new office is 30 feet by 40 feet. Create a scale grid that will be big enough to read once you're finished; I'd suggest using a tabloid-size page. Make sure you include text that shows the scale on the grid so our contractors will be able to translate it.

"When you're finished with the new scale grid, create a second copy of the file with an actual plan for our new offices.

"Add text to indicate which rooms will do what, as well as door and hallway locations. Remember to align the text with the objects they're related to; there's nothing more confusing than explanatory text just floating around the page."

"I also want to see some suggestions for placement of desks and other furniture. Measure some standard office furniture (desks, chairs, tables, etc.) so you know whether your plans will be feasible. The more detailed this drawing is, the better it's going to be."

Identity Package

Your client is starting a spiritual retreat in the Northern California mountains. He hired you to create a corporate identity package so he can begin marketing the resort through regional and national travel boards. He asked you to first develop a logo, and then create the standard identity pieces (letterhead, envelope, and business card) that he will use for business promotion and correspondence.

This project incorporates the following skills:

❏ Developing custom logo artwork based on an object in a photograph

❏ Using layers to easily manage complex artwork

❏ Building various logo versions to meet specific output requirements

❏ Saving EPS files for maximum flexibility

❏ Defining a crop area and printing a proof

❏ Building a complete logotype by converting type to outlines

❏ Creating new documents in various sizes to meet the project needs

Client Comments

The name of our resort is "Unicorn: A Retreat for the Spirit." I have a unicorn statue on my desk from a company called *Schleich* in Germany that would be the perfect logo. If I give you a photograph of the statue, can you convert it into a drawing that we can use for our branding? For the full logotype, I'm actually thinking of the resort name surrounded by two unicorns facing out.

Then I want you to use the logo on business cards, letterhead, and envelopes that I will have preprinted; I want a more professional feel than I can create using my laser printer. The printer I spoke with said I could do this for less money if I go "4-color" for the business card and letterhead, but "2-color" for the envelope; I really don't know what that means — I'm hoping you do.

Art Director Comments

The logo is the first part of this project because you'll use it on the other three pieces. The client told you exactly what he wants, so that part is taken care of. Since logos are used on far more than just these three jobs in this one application, you'll save the final logo in a file format that can be used in different ways, and then place that file into the other three pieces.

The client wants to print the card and letterhead in 4-color and the envelope in 2-color, so you'll have to create two different versions of the logo. One of the colors will be black in this case, because most of the text on the letterhead and envelope should be black. We have to pick one other spot ink color; I think we should use some shade of blue.

Project Objectives

To complete this project, you will:

❑ Draw the logo artwork using the Pen tool to trace the outline in a photograph

❑ Create versions of the artwork for 1-color, 2-color, and 4-color printing

❑ Print a composite proof of your completed artwork

❑ Save files as EPS so they can be accessed in all common page-layout applications

❑ Build a complete logotype by combining the logo artwork with the company name and tagline

❑ Build letterhead, business card, and envelope layouts to meet a printer's stated output requirements

Stage 1 Using Photographic Templates

The first part of this project is to create the client's logo. There are several important points to keep in mind when you design a logo.

First, logos need to be scalable. A company might place its logo on the head of a golf tee or on the side of a building. (This is a strong argument for the simpler line art approach instead of photography.) Vector graphics — the kind you typically create in Illustrator — can be scaled as large or small as necessary without losing quality; photographs are raster images, and they can't be greatly enlarged or reduced without losing quality. That's why you're converting the client's photograph into a vector graphic.

Second, you will almost certainly need more than one version of any given logo — and possibly in more than one file format. Different kinds of output require different formats (specifically, one set of files for print and one for the Web), and some types of jobs might require special options saved in the files (such as the 4-color and 2-color versions of the logo you will create in this project). After you draw the unicorn graphic, you'll save both 4-color and 2-color versions of the file.

Understanding CMYK Colors

ILLUSTRATOR FOUNDATIONS

The CMYK color model, also called "process color," recreates the range of printable colors by overlapping layers of cyan, magenta, yellow, and black inks in varying percentages from 0–100.

Using theoretically pure pigments, a mixture of equal parts of cyan, magenta, and yellow would produce black. Real pigments, however, are not pure; the actual result of mixing these three colors usually appears as a muddy brown. The fourth color, black (K), is added to the three subtractive primaries to extend the range of printable colors and to allow much purer blacks to be printed than is possible with only the three primaries. Black is abbreviated as "K" because it is the "key" color to which others are aligned on the printing press. Using K for black also avoids confusion with blue in the RGB color model. In the image to the right, the left block is printed with 100% black ink. The right block is a combination of 100% cyan, 100% magenta, and 100% yellow inks.

In process color printing, the four process colors — cyan, magenta, yellow, and black (CMYK) — are imaged (also referred to as separated) onto individual printing plates. Each color separation is printed on a separate unit of a printing press. The semi-transparent inks, when printed on top of each other in varying percentages, produce the range of colors in the CMYK gamut. Special (spot) colors are printed using specifically formulated inks as additional color separations.

Different color models have different ranges or **gamuts** of possible colors. A normal human visual system is capable of distinguishing approximately 16.7 million different colors; color reproduction systems, however, are far more limited. The RGB model has the largest gamut of the output models. The CMYK gamut is far more limited; many of the brightest and most saturated colors that can be reproduced using light (in the RGB model) cannot be reproduced using CMYK inks.

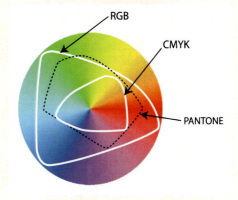

PREPARE THE LOGO DRAWING WORKSPACE

This project ultimately requires four files: one for creating the logo, one for the business card, one for the letterhead, and one for the envelope. The logo file is basically freeform, since it's essentially an artboard on which to draw. The other three files have specific size and output requirements, which you can define when you create the files.

1. **Create a new file using the default size. Assign the name "Unicorn" to the new file, make sure Inches is selected in the Units menu, and then click OK.**

2. **Choose File>Place. Navigate to the file Unicorn.jpg in the RF_Illustrator>Identity folder and place the image. Make sure the Link check box is not selected before you click Place.**

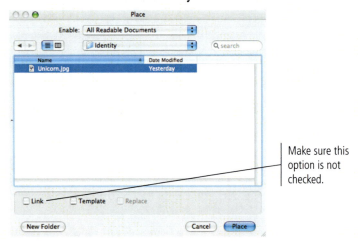

Make sure this option is not checked.

Note:

Before completing this project, copy the Unicorn folder from the WIP folder on your Resource CD to the WIP folder where you are saving your work. When you save files for this project, you will save them in your WIP>Unicorn folder.

Understanding Spot Colors

ILLUSTRATOR FOUNDATIONS

Spot colors are reproduced with special premixed inks that will produce a certain color with one ink layer — not built from the standard process inks used in CMYK printing. When you output a job with spot colors, each spot color appears on its own separation. Spot inks are commonly used to reproduce colors that you can't get from a CMYK build, in two- and three-color documents, and as additional separations in a process color job when an exact color (such as a corporate color) is needed.

Even though you can choose a spot color directly from the library on your screen, you should look at a swatch book to

verify that you're using the color you intend. Special inks exist because many of the colors can't be reproduced with process inks, nor can they be accurately represented on a computer monitor. If you specify special colors and then convert them to process colors later, your job probably won't look exactly as you expect.

In the United States, the most popular collections of spot colors are the Pantone Matching System (PMS) libraries. TruMatch and Focoltone are also used in the United States. Toyo and DICColor (Dainippon Ink & Chemicals) are used primarily in Japan.

3. **With the placed file selected on the page, look at the W and H fields in the Transform panel.**

   These fields show you the width and height of the selected object(s). If more than one object is selected, you'll see the outermost dimensions of the entire selection.

4. **Choose File>Document Setup.**

5. **With Artboard showing in the menu, change the Width and Height fields to be 1″ larger than the width and height of the placed unicorn image, and then click OK.**

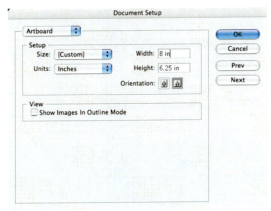

   Using the Document Setup options, you can change the size of your page at any point in a project. In the case of this logo, it's a good idea to have a workspace that is just slightly bigger than the artwork you're creating.

6. **Choose File>Document Color Mode>CMYK Color.**

   As with the document size, you can change the document color mode at any time in the process. Your menu might already show CMYK Color selected; since we can't know everyone's default settings, we're including this step to be sure your file is in the CMYK mode.

Note:

Some raster effects, which you will learn about in Project 6, can only be applied in RGB color mode.

7. **Center the placed image vertically and horizontally on the artboard.**

Align the placed image to the resized artboard.

8. **In the Layers panel, double-click the existing layer to open the Layer Options dialog box.**

9. **Change the layer name to "Template Photo". Activate the Template check box and make sure the Dim Images To field is set to 50%. Click OK to apply your choices.**

Note:

The default color of new layers is based on the order in the Color list of the Layer Options dialog box. The first layer in a file is Light Blue, the second layer is Red, the third layer is Green, and so on.

10. **In the Layers panel, click the Create New Layer button.**

11. **Double-click the new Layer 2 to access the layer options. Change the layer name to "Unicorn Drawing" and click OK.**

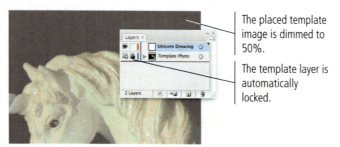

The placed template image is dimmed to 50%.

The template layer is automatically locked.

12. **Save the file in your WIP>Identity folder using the default file name (Unicorn.ai) and options, and then continue to the next exercise.**

USE THE PEN TOOL TO TRACE PHOTOGRAPHS

In Project 1, you used the Pen tool to trace a black-and-white bitmap graphic of a hand being crushed between two gears. That exercise introduced a number of concepts that you will expand on in this project as you draw a complex graphic based on a full-color photograph.

1. **With Unicorn.ai open, choose the Pen tool in the Tools panel.**

2. **Set the stroke to 0.5-pt black and the fill to None.**

3. **Click once where the unicorn's jaw meets its neck to place the first anchor point.**

   This is your starting point.

4. **Click and pull again where the jaw meets the nose, and then pull handles so the connecting line segment fits the curve of the animal's jaw.**

   If necessary, use the Direct Selection tool to modify the anchor points or handles until the curve exactly matches the photograph.

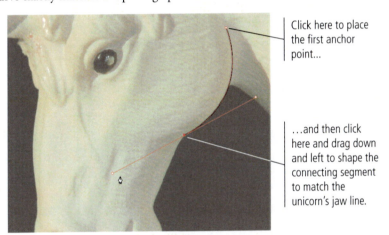

Click here to place the first anchor point...

...and then click here and drag down and left to shape the connecting segment to match the unicorn's jaw line.

5. **Option/Alt-click the second anchor point and pull slightly down and left to generate a new handle for the left side of the anchor point.**

   Pulling the new handle determines the direction of the next segment you create. If you pull too far to the left or right, the curve will billow out in that direction. To make this work, you have to pull in the direction you want the path to follow.

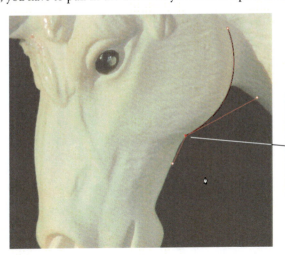

Option/Alt-clicking an anchor point converts the smooth point to a corner point, allowing you to change direction along the path.

Note:

If you're editing an existing path, you can click a point with the Convert Anchor Point tool (nested under the Pen tool) to change a smooth point to a corner point. You can also click and drag to change an existing corner point to a smooth point.

6. **Continue adding anchor points around the animal's nose, converting smooth points to corner points whenever you need to change direction.**

7. **Use the Direct Selection tool as necessary to adjust each anchor point and handle until your shape exactly matches the shape of the unicorn's head.**

    While using the Pen tool, you can press Command/Control to temporarily switch to the last-used selection tool (Selection tool or Direct Selection tool).

    This option allows you to drag points and handles without manually switching to the Direct Selection tool, and then switching back to the Pen tool when you want to continue drawing a path.

8. **When you get to the forelock and horn, draw a curve that skips those parts of the photograph, slightly inset from the edges.**

9. **Draw additional curves that skip over the ear and extend roughly into the unicorn's mane.**

10. **Click without dragging inside the mane near the right edge of the photograph.**

    Clicking without dragging creates a corner point so you can change directions. The previous curve will still be defined by handles, but the next segment will be a straight line unless you drag handles from the next point.

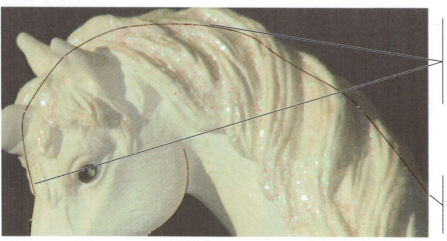

Beginning with the forelock, the path should be inset from the edges in the photograph. Objects on other layers will cover these lines.

Click here without dragging to add a corner point at the edge of the photo.

As we've already said, layers can be extremely helpful when you're constructing complex drawings such as this unicorn. You'll be drawing the horn, ears, and mane on separate layers to help simplify the artwork structure, so the body shape doesn't need to be perfect where those elements will be drawn.

11. Press the Shift key, and then click at the bottom-right corner.

Pressing Shift when you click adds a point at an exact angle (in 45° increments) from the last anchor point. This option allows you to create perfectly vertical, horizontal, or diagonal lines away from an anchor point.

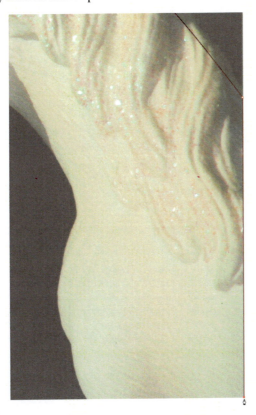

12. Press Shift again and click where the unicorn's chest meets the bottom of the photograph.

Again, the connecting line is perfectly straight — in this case, horizontal.

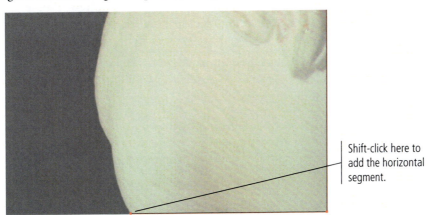

Shift-click here to add the horizontal segment.

13. Save the file and continue to the next exercise.

Selection and Anchor Display Preferences

To more easily manage and control individual anchor points and handles, you can control their behavior and appearance in the Selection & Anchor Display preferences.

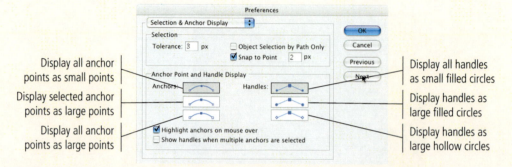

In the Selection area, you can specify the tolerance for pixel selection and choose other options that can make selection easier for a particular document.

Tolerance defines the pixel range for selecting anchor points; higher values mean you can click farther away from an anchor point to select it.

Object Selection by Path Only determines whether you can select a filled object by clicking anywhere in the object, or whether you must click the object's path.

Snap to Point snaps objects to anchor points and guides within the defined distance (default to 2 pixels).

In the Anchor Point and Handle Display area, you can change the appearance of anchors and handles to make them easier to select. If the **Highlight Anchors on Mouse Over** option is checked, moving the cursor over an anchor point will cause the anchor point to temporarily appear larger.

The last option (**Show Handles When Multiple Anchors Are Selected**) is unchecked by default. You can turn on this option to see the handles of more than one anchor point at once.

CONTINUE BUILDING AN EXISTING PATH

As you develop complex objects, the number of layers you need changes – it might go up or down depending on the stage of the project. As this Unicorn grows, the number of layers will also grow accordingly.

There are many times when pen paths work just fine, but the vast majority of professional designers and illustrators make it standard practice to never leave a path open — especially if the path has one end placed on top of the other.

1. **With Unicorn.ai open, click the existing path with the Direct Selection tool to show the anchor points.**

   If you continued straight from the previous exercise to this one, these first few steps won't be technically necessary. We're including these steps to show that you can continue building on an existing open path at any time.

2. **Choose the Pen tool from the Tools panel and place the cursor over the last point you added to the path.**

   When the Pen tool cursor is over the end point of an open path, the icon shows a diagonal line, indicating that clicking will connect to the existing path so you can continue drawing.

3. **Click the last point with the Pen tool, and then continue adding anchor points and adjusting handles to exactly match the shape of the unicorn's chest.**

4. **Add the last anchor point near — but not quite touching — the curve of the animal's jaw.**

5. **Zoom in close to the point you added in Step 4.**

6. **Choose the Scissors tool (nested under the Eraser tool) from the Tools panel.**

Scissors tool

7. **Using the Scissors tool, click the path along the jaw line near the open end of the path.**

   As you might have guessed, clicking with the Scissors tool cuts the path. As soon as you cut the path, a curved anchor point appears where you clicked. Illustrator assumes you want curved handles whenever you cut a curved path.

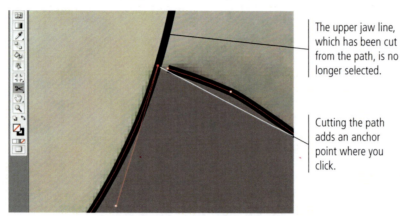

The upper jaw line, which has been cut from the path, is no longer selected.

Cutting the path adds an anchor point where you click.

8. **Using either selection tool, click the path above the point where you cut and choose Object>Hide>Selection.**

   By hiding the top half of the jaw line, you can more easily see (and select) the end point of the remaining path.

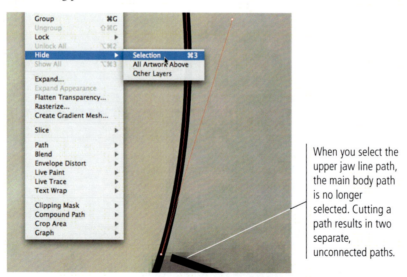

When you select the upper jaw line path, the main body path is no longer selected. Cutting a path results in two separate, unconnected paths.

9. **Choose View>Snap to Point to make sure this option is toggled on (it should be checked in the menu).**

10. **Using the Direct Selection tool, drag the right end point on top of the left end point.**

    When Snap to Point is active, dragging one point close to another point causes the second point (the one you're dragging toward) to act like a magnet. The point you're dragging will snap to the exact same position as the point you're dragging toward.

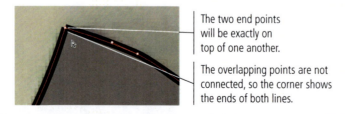

The two end points will be exactly on top of one another.

The overlapping points are not connected, so the corner shows the ends of both lines.

11. Still using the Direct Selection tool, drag a selection marquee around both points to select them, and then choose Object>Path>Join.

12. Choose the Corner option in the Join dialog box and click OK.

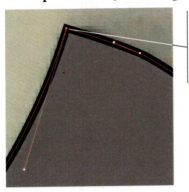

The joined corner now appears properly; you can't see the line ends from each point.

13. Choose Object>Show All to re-show the hidden segment that forms the top of the jaw line.

14. Select the closed path and change the fill to white.

Refer to Projects 1 or 2 for detailed instructions on changing the fill and stroke colors.

15. In the Layers panel, double-click the Unicorn layer and rename it "Unicorn Body". Activate the Lock check box and click OK to return to the document.

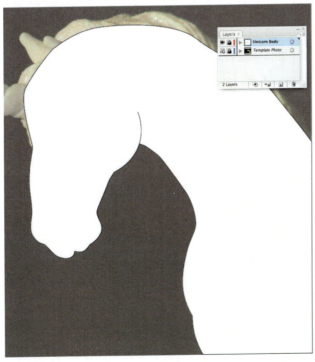

Note:

You could achieve the same result by selecting the upper jaw line, cutting it, and then pasting it back in place (Edit>Paste in Front or Command/Control-F). The Paste in Front command pastes the cut object in exactly the same place as when you cut it, but in the front of the stacking order on the selected layer. (Edit>Paste in Back or Command/Control-B pastes the object in the same position in the back of the stacking order on the selected layer). Regular pasting (Edit>Paste or Command/Control-V) pastes the object in the center of the document window.

16. Hide the Unicorn Body layer, save the file, then continue to the next exercise.

FINE-TUNE COMPLEX PATHS

Tracing the unicorn's horn is a good way to practice working with the Pen tool. To achieve the best results, you have to:

a. Create anchor points at specific spots on the photograph so the curves perfectly fit the image.

b. Use a combination of smooth and corner points to create the appropriate shapes.

c. Accept that you don't have to perfectly match the shape as you draw. You can (and often will) adjust curve handles to make the curves fit the figure's outline.

This shape (the horn as a single shape) also highlights some of the issues associated with creating a line drawing from a photograph. The horn in the photograph is a single shape, but to successfully reproduce the curves with line art will require a series of connected shapes.

1. **With Unicorn.ai open, create a new layer named "Horn".**

2. **Make sure the Pen tool is active, the fill is set to None, and the stroke is set to 0.5-pt black.**

3. **Using the Pen tool, click at the upper-right corner of the horn, where the top of the horn meets the unicorn's head.**

4. **Draw curves that match the shape of the first horn segment, using corner points and adjusting handles where necessary to fit the shape in the photograph.**

    In some areas of the photograph — such as the lower edge of the first full horn segment — the shape edge is not as clearly defined as the shadows in the photo. In these cases, use your best judgment to create the shape outline.

5. **To close the shape, place the Pen tool cursor over the first anchor point until you see a small circle in the tool icon. Click to close the shape.**

    You can close shapes while drawing by simply clicking the first anchor point of the path.

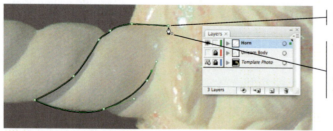

Start the path here.

The small circle indicates that clicking will close the path.

6. **With the closed shape selected, choose Object>Lock>Selection to lock the shape in place.**

Key Command:

Press Command/ Control-2 to lock the current selection.

7. **With the Pen tool still selected, begin drawing the second horn segment by clicking where the top of the first segment meets the second segment.**

   Because the first segment is locked, you can click directly on top of the existing path without affecting the first shape. If you didn't lock the first shape, clicking with the Pen tool would add an anchor point to that shape instead of starting a new shape.

   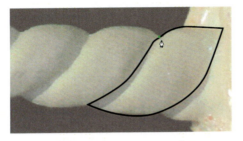

8. **Click again and drag where the second horn segment meets the third segment. Drag to create handles to shape the connecting segment.**

   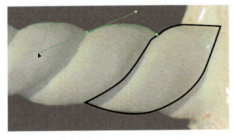

9. **Option/Alt-click the second point to change direction, click the bottom-left corner of the horn segment, and then drag handles to shape the connecting curve.**

10. **Option/Alt-click the third point to change direction again, and then click and drag to create a smooth point where the second segment meets the first segment.**

11. **Click the first anchor point of the path to close the shape.**

    As you can see, the curves do not exactly match the horn segment. When you're drawing complex shapes such as these, it's usually a better idea to create the basic shape first, and then edit the path as necessary to fit the curves to the shape.

    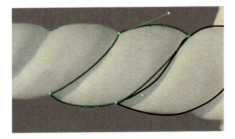

12. **Choose the Add Anchor Point tool (nested under the Pen tool) in the Tools panel.**

    If you look closely at this shape, you can see that the edge curves outward and inward along the same path. To achieve this effect, you have to add an anchor point along the path so you can change the curve's direction along the same smooth curve.

13. **On the top edge of the shape, click near the left side of the line to add a point to the existing segment.**

    As soon as you click, a new anchor point is added to the path; handles are automatically added to maintain the current shape of the path where you added the point.

    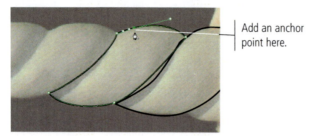

    Add an anchor point here.

14. **Press Command/Control to temporarily access the Direct Selection tool.**

    If pressing Command/Control gives you the Selection tool instead of the Direct Selection tool, click the Direct Selection tool in the Tools panel and then switch back to the Pen tool.

15. **Click the handle of the left corner point on the top edge, and then drag down to change the direction of the connecting path.**

16. **Add two anchor points along the shape's right edge. Adjust the points and handles to match the shape in the photograph.**

    Again, some edges are not perfectly defined in the photograph. Use your best judgment when refining the shape.

    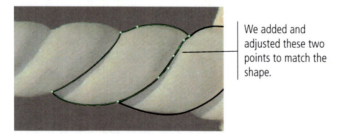

    We added and adjusted these two points to match the shape.

17. **Fill the second segment with white. Make sure the right edge of the second segment completely covers the left edge of the first segment. Adjust the points and handles of the second segment as necessary so no gaps exist between the two lines.**

    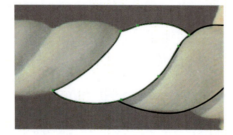

18. **Return the second segment's fill to None, and then lock the second shape in place.**

Note:

Because you created the second segment after creating the first segment, the second segment is on top of the stacking order. That's why the fill obscures the stroke of the first shape.

19. **Using the techniques you have learned, create the remaining horn segments, working right to left.**

   - Place smooth and corner points and adjust the handles as necessary to fit the curves in the photograph.

   - Make sure no gaps exist between the different segments.

   - As you complete each horn segment, lock it in place before moving to the next segment.

20. **Create a final shape for the small triangle on the bottom-right side of the horn.**

   When you started drawing the first section of the curved horn, it made more sense to start with the first full piece; this is common in many illustration projects. You start with what makes best sense to you visually, keep working until the drawing is close to what you want it to be, and then fix the details.

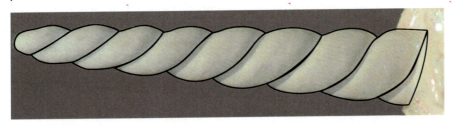

21. **Unlock all the locked shapes (Object>Unlock All), select all objects on the Horn layer, and change the fill to white.**

22. **Select the triangle shape you created in Step 20 and choose Object>Arrange>Send to Back.**

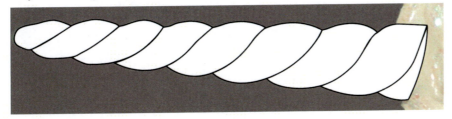

23. **Lock and hide the Horn layer, save the file, and then continue to the next exercise.**

 FINISH THE DRAWING

At this point, you have all the tools you need to create the remaining pieces of the logo. For the best results, you should create each component on a separate layer so you can turn off and rearrange layers as necessary to complete the final unicorn drawing.

1. **With Unicorn.ai open, create a new layer named "Mane".**

   As with the horn, the edges of the mane are not entirely distinguishable in the photograph. In fact, the photograph has far more "pieces" than you need to create the desired effect in your logo artwork.

2. **Using the Pen tool with a fill of None and a 0.5-pt black stroke, draw shapes however you prefer to produce the effect of the animal's mane. Adjust anchor points and handles as necessary, using the techniques you learned in previous exercises.**

Note:

Make sure you change the fills and lock these pieces as you shape them; this is a complex object, which can be difficult to manage if you're not careful.

Note:

The options in the Object>Arrange menu affect the stacking order of objects on a single layer. They will not move an object below objects on other layers that are lower in the stacking order.

3. **When you're finished, fill all the pieces of the mane with white.**

4. **Adjust the stacking order of each shape you created on the Mane layer until you're satisfied with the result.**

   This is our solution; you might have fewer or more pieces, depending on what you decided would create the best result.

Note:

The Send and Bring commands in the Object>Arrange menu can be very helpful when you're drawing something like this mane.

5. **Lock and hide the Mane layer.**

6. **Add a new layer named "Front Ear" and draw both ear shapes with the Pen tool. Apply a white fill and 0.5-pt black stroke to the shapes of the ears.**

   Draw both ear shapes (front and back) now; you'll move the back ear to its own layer shortly.

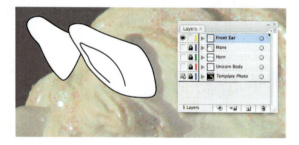

7. **Show (but don't unlock) the Unicorn Body and Mane layers.**

8. **Add a new layer named "Back Ear" and move it under the Unicorn Body layer in the Layers panel.**

9. **Select the back ear shape with the Selection tool. In the Layers panel, drag the Selected Object icon from the Front Ear layer to the Back Ear layer.**

Drag this icon…

…to the Back Ear layer

10. Adjust the curves and anchor points on the back ear shape as necessary until there are no gaps between the bottom edge of the back ear and the top edge of the unicorn body and/or mane.

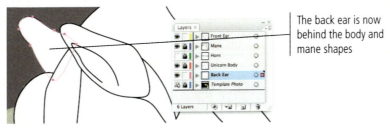

The back ear is now behind the body and mane shapes

11. Lock all layers, hide all layers but the Template Photo, then add a new layer named "Eye" at the top of the layer stack.

12. Build the eye from a rotated black ellipse with no stroke. Add a second white ellipse on top of the first one (for the iris).

Make sure the Eye layer is on top of the Front Ear layer.

13. Lock and hide the Eye layer, and then add a new layer named "Mouth" at the top of the layer stack.

14. Use the Pen tool with a black fill and no stroke to create the mouth and nostril shapes.

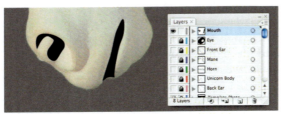

15. Show and unlock all layers.

16. Delete the Template Photo layer, save the file, and continue to the next stage.

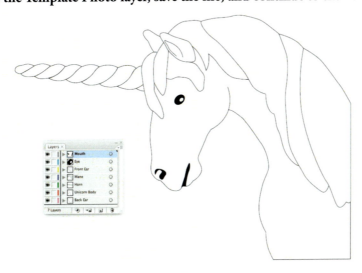

Stage 2 Using Color and Type for Logo Design

After completing Stage 1, you have a perfectly workable black-and-white version of the unicorn artwork. As you already know, you need two different versions of the logo to complete the different identity pieces: one for 4-color printing and one for 2-color printing. Other versions might be necessary later for other applications (such as an RGB version for the Web).

Print the Logo Artwork

Before you create the alternate versions of the logo, it's a good idea to print a sample to see how the artwork looks on paper. Illustrator gives you a large number of options for outputting files, including the ability to define the area that makes up the actual artwork.

There are two important points to remember about using inkjet and laser proofs. First, inkjet printers are usually not PostScript driven. Because the commercial output process revolves around the PostScript language, proofs should always be created using a PostScript-compatible printer. If not, the proofs will not accurately represent what will be output in final production. Second, inkjet and laser printers do not accurately represent color.

Note:

You can purchase a software RIP (such as the one we use from Birmy Graphics) that will allow you to print PostScript information to some inkjet printers. Consult the documentation that came with your printer to see if this option is available.

1. **With Unicorn.ai open, choose the Crop Area tool in the Tools panel.**

2. **Click in the page and drag to draw a marquee that surrounds the artwork you created.**

   By default, Illustrator crops artwork to the size you define in the New Document or Document Setup dialog box. You can change that setting by drawing a new shape with the Crop Area tool. You can drag any of the bounding box handles to resize the crop area, or click inside the crop area boundaries to drag the current area to a new position.

   Crop areas are bordered by a heavy dashed line when the Crop Area tool is active; areas outside the crop area appear dimmed while the Crop Area tool is active. The black lines outside the crop area boundary are **trim marks** (also called **crop marks**), which are printer's marks that define where a page should be cut from an oversized press sheet.

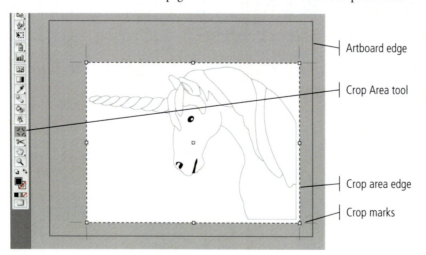

Artboard edge

Crop Area tool

Crop area edge

Crop marks

Note:

The Crop Area tool sets the position of printer's marks on your document and defines the boundaries of the artwork.

Note:

In Project 2 you saw the option to place an EPS file based on one of several bounding boxes, including Crop. This is the area you are defining now.

When you draw a crop area, you can define a number of options in the Control bar. Specifically, you can choose one of the preset sizes, or you can define a custom height and width of the area. The X and Y fields define the crop area's center location relative to the bottom-left corner of the artboard. (Repositioning the ruler's zero point has no effect on this option; the crop area position is always shown relative to the bottom-left corner of the artboard.)

Additional options are available in the Crop Area Options dialog box, which you can open from the Control bar. (Some of these are only relevant if you're designing artwork that will be included in a video.)

- **Preset, Width, Height, X, and Y** have the same function as the associated options on the Control bar.
- **Constrain Proportions** maintains a consistent aspect ratio (height to width) if you manually resize the crop area.
- **Show Center Mark** displays a point in the center of the crop area.
- **Show Cross Hairs** displays lines that extend into the artwork from the center of each edge of the crop area.
- **Show Video Safe Areas** displays guides that represent the areas that fall inside the viewable area of video.
- **Show Screen Edge** displays guides that represent the edge of a video screen.
- **Show Crop Area Rulers** displays rulers around the crop area, with the zero point in the upper-left corner.
- **Ruler Pixel Aspect Ratio** specifies the pixel aspect ratio used for the rulers.
- **Fade Region Outside Crop Area** displays the area outside the crop area in a darker shade when the Crop Area tool is active.
- **Update While Dragging** keeps the area outside the crop area darker as you drag to resize the crop area.
- **Crop Areas** indicates how many crop areas exist (if more than one).

3. **Choose File>Print.**

   The Print dialog box is divided into eight sections or categories, which display in the window on the left side of the dialog box. Clicking one of the categories in the list shows the associated options in the right side of the dialog box.

   The most important options you'll select are the Printer and PPD (PostScript printer description) at the top of the dialog box. Illustrator reads the information in the PPD to determine which of the specific print options are available for the current output.

4. **In the Printer menu, choose the printer you want to use, and then choose the PPD for that printer in the PPD menu (if possible).**

5. **In the Media Size menu, choose whatever size paper your printer can output (letter is large enough for this job) and make sure the Do Not Scale option is selected.**

Note:

A print preset is a way to store many different settings in a single menu choice. You can create a print preset by making your choices in the Print dialog box, and then clicking the Save Preset button.

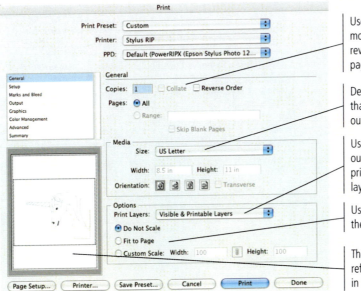

Use these options to print more than one copy and reverse the output order of pages (last to first).

Define the size of paper that will be used for the output.

Use this menu to output visible and printable layers, visible layers, or all layers.

Use these options to scale the output (if necessary).

The dynamic preview reflects different settings in the Print dialog box.

6. **Click the Setup option in the list of categories in the left pane. In the Crop Artwork To menu, choose Crop Area.**

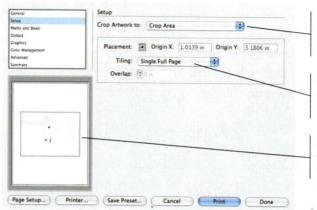

Use this menu to access the crop area you defined in the first part of this exercise.

Use these options to print a single file to multiple pages (called tiling).

The preview now shows the crop area instead of the Artboard edge.

7. **Click the Marks and Bleed option in the list of categories on the left. Activate the All Printer's Marks option.**

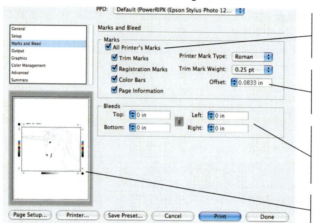

Use these options to select individual printer's marks or simply print them all.

The offset determines how far from the page edge the printer's marks will be placed.

Use these fields to include a specific amount of space beyond the defined crop area in the output.

The preview now includes all the selected printer's marks.

Note:

Some printers require printer's marks to stay outside the bleed area, which means the offset should be at least the same as or greater than the defined bleed area.

8. **Click the Output option in the list of categories on the left. Choose Composite in the Mode menu.**

You can print all colors to a single sheet by choosing Composite, or you can print each color to an individual sheet by choosing Separations (Host-based). The third option — In-RIP Separation — allows data to be separated by the output device.

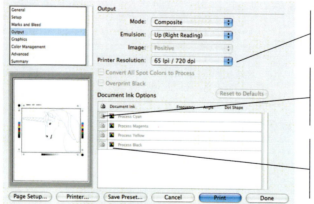

When printing separations, choose the line screen and resolution for the output.

When printing separations, click any of these icons to stop that ink separation from outputting.

If a job includes spot colors, click the icon in this column to convert the spot color to process color for the output.

Note:

The other options in this dialog box (Emulsion and Image) are reserved for high-end commercial output to a filmsetter or imagesetter.

9. **Click Print to output the artwork.**

10. **Keep the file open and continue to the next exercise.**

 **SAVE AN EPS FILE**

EPS, or Encapsulated PostScript, is a file format designed for high-quality print applications. The format can store both raster and vector elements, and it also supports transparency. You could simply save this file as a native Illustrator file, but not all applications can read or import .ai files. As logos need to be versatile, and all print applications can import EPS files, EPS is the best choice.

1. **In the open file, choose File>Save As and navigate to your WIP>Identity folder as the target location.**

   Since a black-only version might be useful at some point, you might as well save it now so you won't have to change it from the color version later.

2. **Choose Illustrator EPS in the Format/Save As Type menu.**

   The file name automatically changes to show the correct extension (.eps).

3. **Add "_black" to the file name before the extension and click Save.**

4. **In the EPS Options dialog box, choose TIFF (8-bit Color) in the Format menu and click the Transparent radio button. Make sure Embed Fonts is checked, and then click OK**

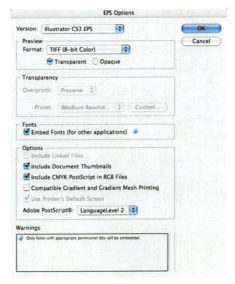

5. **Close the file and continue to the next exercise.**

When you save a file in the EPS format, you can define a number of format-specific options.

Version allows you to save a file to be compatible with earlier versions of Illustrator. Be aware that features not available in earlier versions will be lost in the saved file.

Format defines the type of preview that will be saved in the file (these previews are used for applications that can't directly read the EPS file format). Be aware that Windows users cannot access Macintosh-format previews; if you're working in a Windows-based or cross-platform environment, use one of the TIFF preview options.

The background of a TIFF preview can be transparent or opaque. When you choose TIFF (8-bit Color) in the Preview menu, you can choose the **Transparent** option to save a preview that will show background objects through the empty areas of the artwork; the **Opaque** option creates the preview with a solid white background.

Transparency options control the output settings for transparent and semi-transparent objects, including drop shadows and other effects (see Project 6).

Embed Fonts (for other applications) embeds used fonts into the EPS file. This option ensures that the type displays and prints properly when the file is placed into another application such as Adobe InDesign or QuarkXPress.

Include Linked Files embeds files linked to the artwork.

Include Document Thumbnails creates a thumbnail image of the artwork that displays in the Illustrator Open and Place dialog boxes.

Include CMYK PostScript in RGB Files allows RGB color documents to be printed from applications that do not support RGB output. When the EPS file is reopened in Illustrator, the RGB colors are preserved.

Compatible Gradient and Gradient Mesh Printing is necessary for older printers and PostScript devices to print gradients and gradient meshes; those elements (explained in Project 8) are converted to JPEG format.

Adobe PostScript® determines what level of PostScript is used to save the artwork. PostScript Level 2 represents color and grayscale vector and bitmap images. PostScript Level 3 allows printing mesh objects on a PostScript 3 printer.

CREATE COLOR LOGO VERSIONS

In this exercise, you make two additional versions of the logo — one that prints with two colors of ink and one that prints with four colors (CMYK).

1. **Open Unicorn.ai from your WIP>Identity folder and lock all but the Eye layer.**

2. **Show the Swatches panel (Window>Swatches).**

3. **Using the Selection tool, click the black ellipse that forms the eye. At the bottom of the Tools panel, make sure the Fill swatch is active.**

4. **Choose Window>Swatch Libraries>Color Books>Pantone Solid Coated.**

   Illustrator offers a number of pre-defined swatch libraries, including collections of swatches based on color schemes, artistic methods, or other logical groupings. When designing with spot colors, the most important sets of color swatches are found in the Color Books submenu. These libraries include swatches of special inks that print specific colors without relying on CMYK ink percentages.

Note:

When choosing special colors, ask your printer which ink system they support. If you designate TruMatch and they use Pantone inks, you won't get the colors you expect.

Note:

Spot colors are generally chosen from a swatch book — a book of colors printed with different inks, similar to the paint chip cards used in home decorating.

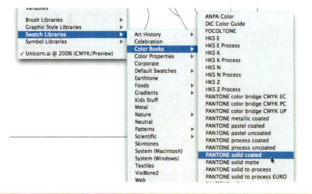

5. **In the Pantone Solid Coated panel options menu, choose Small List View.**

Each swatch library opens in a separate panel (possibly grouped with other open swatch library panels). The list view, which is available for any swatch panel, helps if you are looking for a specific Pantone color based on something you selected from a swatch book.

6. **Scroll through the swatch list. When you find Pantone 313 C, click the color name in the panel to change the color of the selected object.**

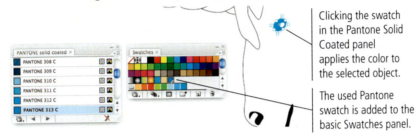

Clicking the swatch in the Pantone Solid Coated panel applies the color to the selected object.

The used Pantone swatch is added to the basic Swatches panel.

7. **In the regular Swatches panel, choose Select All Unused from the panel options menu, and then click the panel Delete button.**

As you know, the Illustrator Swatches panel includes a number of default swatches. These can clutter your workspace, so it's a good idea to remove unused swatches for better organization.

8. **Click Yes to the resulting warning, which asks you to confirm the deletion.**

Not much is left after you delete the unused swatches.

Delete button

9. **Save the file as an EPS file named "Unicorn_2c.eps" in your WIP>Identity folder, using the same options you used for the black-only version.**

10. **Make sure nothing is selected in the layout.**

11. **Double-click the Pantone swatch in the Swatches panel.**

12. **In the Swatch Options dialog box, choose Process Color in the Color Type menu and choose CMYK in the Color Mode menu.**

Notice that the Global option is checked by default. When this option is checked, anything colored with that swatch will change when you change the swatch definition.

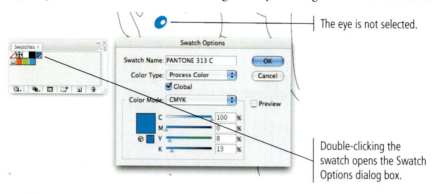

The eye is not selected.

Double-clicking the swatch opens the Swatch Options dialog box.

Note:

Although the actual process of changing spot colors to process is easy, be careful when you do so. Special inks often exist to reproduce colors that can't be printed with only CMYK; converting those inks to process builds can result in significant color shift.

13. **Save the file as an EPS file named "Unicorn_4c.eps" in your WIP>Identity folder, using the same options you used for the other versions.**

14. **Close the file and continue to the next exercise.**

INVERT THE LOGO

Your client decided that printing a white unicorn on white paper is too stark. He asked you to invert the colors of the body strokes and fills so the fills are black and the strokes are white.

You already created three different versions of this file, and now you have to repeat the process three more times (once for each file). You'll end up with six different versions of the logo — the three you already created plus the three inverted versions.

1. **Open the file Unicorn_black.eps from your WIP>Identity folder and make sure all layers are unlocked.**

2. **Using the Selection tool, click one of the objects that make up the mane.**

This artwork includes many objects on multiple layers. Reversing the colors requires several steps.

3. **Choose Select>Same>Stroke Color.**

You know you want all black strokes to become white strokes. This command provides an easy way to affect all those strokes at once.

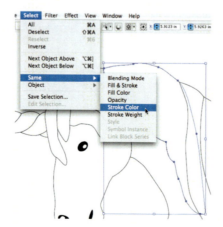

Look carefully at what is currently selected. The mouth, nostril, and eye objects have no stroke value, so those aren't selected.

At the bottom of the Tools panel, a question mark shows in the Fill icon because more than one fill option is applied to the selected objects (remember, the upper edge of the jaw line has a fill value of None).

4. Change the stroke color to white for the selected objects.

5. Using the Selection tool, Shift-click the upper part of the jaw line to remove that object from the current selection.

When this object is deselected, the Fill icon in the Tools panel changes to white.

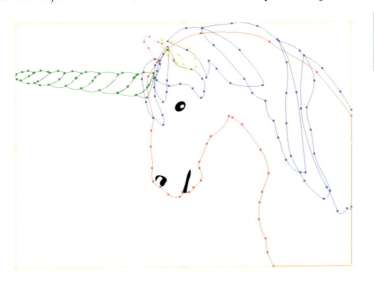

Note:

Depending on how you created the ear shapes, you might also have to deselect unfilled paths on the Ears layer.

6. **Change the fill color of the current selection to black.**

7. **Hide all but the Mouth layer. Select both objects on the layer and change the fill to white.**

   Because you used clearly organized layers to create the different pieces, it's easy to find and change specific elements.

8. **Hide the Mouth layer and show the Eye layer.**

9. **Change the black shape to a white fill and change the white-filled shape to a black-filled shape.**

10. **Show all the layers.**

11. **Save the file as an EPS file named "unicorn_inverse_black.eps" in your WIP>Identity folder, and then close it.**

12. **Repeat this process for the other two versions of the logo. Open each EPS file and invert the black and white fills and strokes. For the inverted color versions, leave the eyes alone (filled with a variant of blue, with a black iris).**

    Save the new versions of the files as "Unicorn_inverse_2c.ai" and "Unicorn_inverse_4c.ai".

CREATE THE FINAL LOGOTYPE

The last part of building the logo is creating the complete logotype — that is, the artwork paired with the text that makes up the corporate brand (the company name and, if there is one, the tagline).

You already have six versions of the artwork — three of the white-filled, black-stroked unicorn and three of the black-filled, white-stroked unicorn. When you finish this exercise, you will have three additional files: a black-only version, a 2-color version, and a 4-color version of the complete logotype. There is no need to create the logotype with the black-stroke/white-fill versions since the client wasn't happy with that version.

Having to build three new files raises a workflow question: Should you open each of the existing versions and make the necessary changes to all three files, or should you make the changes to the black-only version of the file and save three different versions (black, 2-color, and 4-color) from the one revised file?

We prefer the second method, since most of the work can be done once, and the variations require only a few extra clicks. Any time you can remove steps from a process, you improve productivity.

1. **Create a new letter-size document named "logotype" using landscape orientation and the CMYK color mode.**

2. **Save the new file as a native Illustrator file named "logotype.ai" in your WIP>Identity folder.**

3. **Place the file Unicorn_inverse_black.eps into the file as an embedded object.**

   Because you are placing the logo artwork into another file, you won't affect the original artwork.

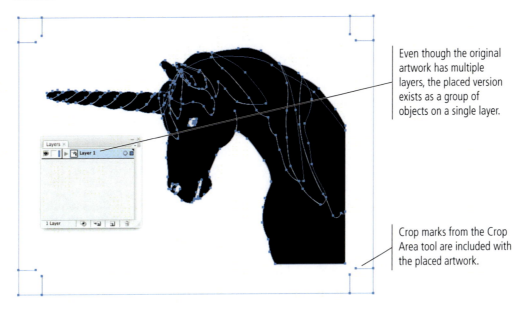

Even though the original artwork has multiple layers, the placed version exists as a group of objects on a single layer.

Crop marks from the Crop Area tool are included with the placed artwork.

4. **Using the Direct Selection tool, draw marquees around the placed crop marks and delete them from the file.**

   By drawing a selection marquee to select the crop marks, you might notice that you have also selected a rectangle shape around the outside edges of the crop marks. This shape, which has no fill or stroke color, was automatically created when you defined the crop area.

5. Select the placed group with the Selection tool. In the Transform panel, make sure the Constrain Proportions icon is active and change the W field to 2.75".

Activating the Constrain Proportions option scales the height and width values proportionally.

6. Click the Type tool to the right of the placed graphic to create a point type object, and then type the word "Unicorn".

7. Select the entire word and change the font to 48-pt ATC Laurel Black Italic.

8. Clone the type object, and then change the cloned text to "a retreat".

9. Format the second type object as 24-pt ATC Laurel Book.

10. Hide the "retreat" type object.

11. Place the first type object (Unicorn) about one-eighth inch to the right of the placed artwork, aligning the top edge of the type with the corner on the right edge of the artwork.

12. Using the Selection tool, Shift-drag the bottom-right handle of the type object's bounding box until the type is about three-quarters of the vertical line on the placed artwork.

Note:

Shift-clicking keeps the type proportional as you scale it.

When you resize the text, you'll probably notice that the top edge of the letters moves even though you are dragging the bottom-right handle. This is a quirk of the application. You might need to reposition the type object and resize it a couple of times to get everything right. Guides can be very helpful in this process.

Original text object

Text being resized

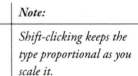

13. Drag the right-center handle of the type bounding box until the horizontal scale is about 90% of the original size.

Drag this handle to resize only the horizontal scale.

14. Save the file and continue to the next exercise.

 ## CREATE OUTLINES FROM TYPE OBJECTS

In Illustrator, fonts — and the characters that comprise them — are like any other vector object. They are made up of anchors and paths, which you can modify just as you modify any other vector object. To access the anchor points, however, you have to first convert the text to outlines.

1. In the open file, drag a horizontal page guide to align with the bottom edge of the unicorn artwork.

2. Select the type object with the word "Unicorn", then choose Type>Create Outlines.

When you convert the type to outlines, the anchor points and paths that comprise the letter shapes appear. All the letters are in one group, which you can break apart by choosing Object>Ungroup.

3. Using the Direct Selection tool, draw a marquee around the bottom of the "i" shape to select only the lower half of the shape.

Only the solid anchor points are selected.

4. Pull the selected anchor points down and to the left, so the shape of the serif is just below the horizontal guide.

When you drag the selected anchors, the blue lines indicate the new shape when you release the mouse button.

5. Show the "retreat" type object (Object>Show All), and then position it below the "Un" in Unicorn and aligned with the horizontal guide.

6. **Scale the type object to fit entirely under the "Un" (to the left of the reshaped "i").**

7. **Press Option/Alt-Shift, and clone the type object to the right of the reshaped "i."**

   Pressing Shift while cloning keeps the copy perfectly aligned with the original.

8. **Change the text in the cloned type object to "for the spirit".**

9. **Using the Selection tool, drag the right-center handle of the type object until the three words fill the space to the right of the stylized "i."**

   If you drag the corner handle, the right half of the tagline might become higher than the left half. By dragging the center handle, you stretch the type horizontally so both halves of the tagline remain at the same height.

10. **Convert the two type objects in the tagline to outlines.**

    Since this is a logotype, you want it to be as versatile as possible. Converting the second type object to outlines means the fonts don't need to be embedded in the file.

11. **Make a clone of the placed unicorn artwork. Use the Reflect tool to make the clone face to the right.**

12. **Place the clone about one-eighth inch to the right of the company name and tagline.**

13. **Save the file as an EPS file named "logotype_black.eps" in your WIP>Identity folder.**

14. **Change the eye on each unicorn and the word "Unicorn" to Pantone 313 C.**

15. **Save the file as an EPS file named "logotype_2c.eps" in your WIP>Identity folder.**

16. **Convert the Pantone 313 C swatch to a CMYK process color.**

17. **Save the file as an EPS file named "logotype_4c.eps" in your WIP>Identity folder.**

18. **Close the file.**

Stage 3 Creating the Corporate Stationery

The final stage of this project requires three additional files: one for the letterhead, one for the envelope, and one for the business card. Each of these files has specific size and output requirements, which you should consider when you create the files.

 ## CREATE THE LETTERHEAD DOCUMENT

The most important aspect of a letterhead is to clearly and unobtrusively present the sender's contact information. The content on the letterhead — meaning the actual letter being sent — should be the main focus when someone receives a piece of your client's (or your) letterhead. You can certainly be creative in the design, but you should use restraint (don't get carried away with huge, overbearing design elements that take away from the contents of the letter).

Some production-related concerns dictate how you design your letterhead. In general, there are two ways to print a letterhead: commercially in large quantities or one-offs on your desktop laser or inkjet printer. (The second method involves a letterhead template, which you can use to write and print your letters from directly within a page-layout program. While this method is quite common among designers, it is rarely done using Illustrator.)

If your letterhead is being printed commercially, it is probably being printed with multiple copies on a large press sheet, from which the individual letterhead sheets will be cut. (In fact, most commercial printing happens this way.) This type of printing means design elements can run right off the edge of the sheet, called **bleeding**.

If you're designing for a printer that can only run letter-size paper, you have to allow enough of a margin area for your printer to hold the paper as it moves through the device (called the **gripper margin**); in this case, you can't design with bleeds.

The letterhead for this project will be printed commercially. The printer said that the design should not bleed since the job is being printed on a letter-size digital press that requires a 0.375″ gripper margin.

1. **Create a new letter-size document; use portrait orientation and CMYK mode.**

2. **Drag guides to 0.375″ from each edge of the artboard (these will serve as margin guides, keeping objects out of the gripper area.)**

3. **Open the General pane of the Preferences dialog box. Make sure the option to Scale Strokes & Effects is checked and click OK.**

   If this option is checked, scaling an object also scales the strokes proportionally to the new object size. For example, reducing an object by 50% will change a 1-pt. stroke to a 0.5-pt. stroke. If this option is not checked, a 1-pt. stroke will always be a 1-pt. stroke, regardless of how much you reduce or enlarge the object.

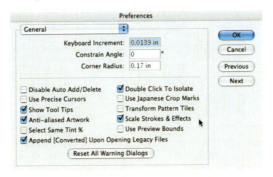

Note:

These are only general rules. If you're using a commercial printer, always ask the output provider whether it's safe (and cost-effective) to design with bleeds, and find out how much allowance to include.

Note:

Older desktop printers typically have a different minimum margin at the page edges. You're usually safe with 3/8″. Newer inkjet printers might have the capability to print 8.5 × 11″ with full bleed. In either case, consult your printer documentation to be sure.

4. **Place the file logotype_4c.eps onto the letterhead and scale it proportionally to 5″ wide.**

   Remember from the production meeting that the letterhead and business card will be printed 4-color; the envelope will be printed 2-color.

5. **Align the placed logotype to the horizontal center of the artboard, with its top edge aligned to the top margin guide.**

6. **Create an area type object at the bottom of the artboard that extends from one side margin guide to the other.**

7. **In the type area, enter:**

   Unicorn Spa and Health Facility
   321 Anadima Circle, Houston, California 99012
   unicorn321.com
   800.555.7823

8. **Format the type however you prefer.**

   We used 10-pt ATC Laurel Book with 12.5-pt leading, centered horizontally and aligned so the bottom line meets the bottom margin guide.

9. **Save the file as an Illustrator file named "letterhead.ai" in your WIP>Identity folder, and then close the file.**

CREATE THE BUSINESS CARD DOCUMENT

When business cards are printed, they are almost always printed as multiple copies on a single sheet, and then trimmed from the sheet to the standard 3.5 × 2″ size. Not long ago, printers asked for business cards to be submitted already **imposed multiple-up** (the term for printing more than one copy of an item on the same page). This practice has largely fallen out of use, partly because software makes it easier for the printer to impose the cards, and partly because the small cards are often **ganged** on a press sheet with other jobs (printed on the sheet outside the main job margins, making efficient use of what would otherwise be wasted paper).

According to the printer, the Unicorn business cards will be printed on their own press sheets. The design can safely bleed on the top, left, and right, and requires a 1/8″ bleed allowance. The printer also said you should allow a 1/8″ live area margin to avoid important elements being cut off when the cards are cut from the press sheet.

1. **Create a new file that is 3.5″ wide by 2″ high.**

2. **Drag guides to 0.125″ (1/8″) from each edge of the artboard.**

3. **Place the file logotype_4c.eps onto the artboard and scale it to fit between the margin guides.**

4. **Use the same text you added to the letterhead as the contact information, and include your client's name (James R. Harris) and title (President).**

5. **Format the text however you prefer.**

6. **Experiment with shapes and lines to create an interesting, attractive business card layout.**

7. **Save the file as an Illustrator file named "card.ai" in your WIP>Identity folder, and then close the file.**

CREATE THE ENVELOPE DOCUMENT

In general, printed envelopes can be created in two ways. You can create and print the design on a flat sheet, which will be specially **die cut** (stamped out of the press sheet), and then folded and glued into the shape of the finished envelope. Alternatively (and usually at less expense), you can print on pre-folded and -glued envelopes.

Both of these methods for envelope design have special printing requirements, such as ensuring no ink is placed where glue will be applied (if you're printing on flat sheets), or printing far enough away from the edge (if you're printing on pre-formed envelopes). Whenever you design an envelope, consult with the output provider that will print the job before you get too far into the project.

In this case, the design will be output on pre-folded #10 business-size envelopes (4.125 × 9.5″). The printer requires a 0.25″ gripper margin around the edge of the envelope where you cannot include any ink coverage.

1. **Create a new file that is 9.5″ wide by 4.125″ high.**

2. **Drag guides to 0.25″ from each edge of the artboard.**

3. **Place the file logotype_2c.eps onto the artboard and scale it as appropriate for the return address area of an envelope.**

4. **Use the same address you added to the letterhead as the return address. Leave off the phone number and Web site address.**

5. **Format the text however you prefer.**

6. **Save the file as an Illustrator file named "envelope.ai" in your WIP>Identity folder, and then close the file.**

Standard Envelope Sizes

When designing envelopes, it is usually a good idea to stick with standard sizes. Non-standard sizes can result in extra printing and custom die-cut costs, as well as additional postage costs. (There are several thousand pages of rules about mailing in the United States; go to www.usps.gov for more information.)

The following tables include the most common sizes of two envelope styles, as well as the standard enclosure size that fits inside the envelope. (All measurements are shown in inches.)

A-Style Envelopes

Type	Size	Enclosure size
A-1	3.625 × 5.125	
A-2	4.375 × 5.75	4.25 × 5.5
A-6	4.75 × 6.5	4.5 × 6.25
A-7	5.25 × 7.25	5 × 6.875
A-8	5.5 × 8.125	5.25 × 7.75
A-Long	3.875 × 8.875	3.75 × 8.625
A-10	6 × 9.5	5.75 × 9.125

Standard Business & Correspondence Envelopes

Type	Size	Enclosure size
6 1/4	3.5 × 6	3.25 × 5.75
6 3/4	3.625 × 6.5	3.5 × 6.25
8 5/8	3.625 × 8.625	3.5 × 8.375
7	3.75 × 6.75	3.5 × 6.5
Monarch (7 3/4)	3.875 × 7.5	3.75 × 7.25
9	3.875 × 8.875	3.75 × 8.675
9 (policy)	4 × 9	3.75 × 8.5
10	4.125 × 9.5	4 × 9.25
DL	4.313 × 8.625	4.125 × 8.375
11	4.5 × 10.375	4.25 × 10.125
12	4.75 × 11	4.5 × 10.75
14	5 × 11.5	4.75 × 11.25
16	6 × 12	5.75 × 11.75

Standard Booklet Envelopes

Type	Size	Enclosure size
3	4.75 × 6.5	4.5 × 6
4 1/2	5.5 × 7.5	5.25 × 7
5	5.5 × 8.125	5.25 × 7.625
6	5.75 × 8.875	5.5 × 8.375
6 1/2	6 × 9	5.75 × 9
6 5/8	6 × 9.5	5.75 × 9
6 3/4	6.5 × 9.5	6.25 × 9
7 1/4	7 × 10	6.75 × 9.5
7 1/2	7.5 × 10.5	7.25 × 10
9	8.75 × 11.5	8.5 × 11
9 1/2	9 × 12	8.75 × 11.5
10	9.5 × 12.625	9.25 × 12.125
13	10 × 13	9.75 × 12.5

Summary

Logos are one of the most common types of artwork that you will create in Illustrator. These can be as simple as text converted to outlines, or as complex as a line drawing based on an object in a photograph. Most logos will actually be some combination of drawing and text-based elements. As you learned throughout this project, one of the most important qualities of a logo is versatility — the ability to use it in many different types of projects and output it in many different types of print processes. To accomplish this goal, logos should work equally well in grayscale, four-color, and spot-color printing.

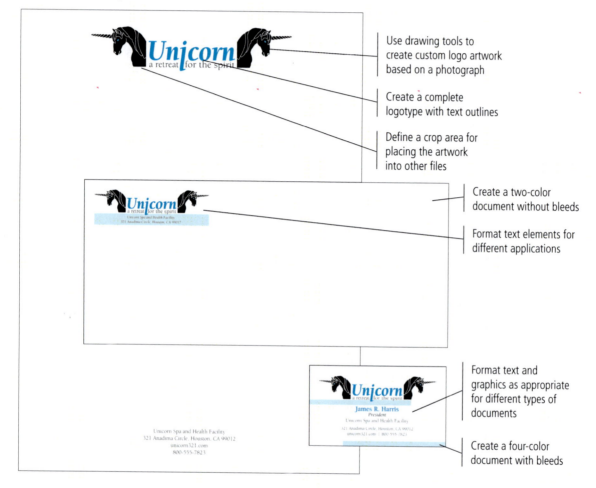

Use drawing tools to create custom logo artwork based on a photograph

Create a complete logotype with text outlines

Define a crop area for placing the artwork into other files

Create a two-color document without bleeds

Format text elements for different applications

Format text and graphics as appropriate for different types of documents

Create a four-color document with bleeds

Portfolio Builder Project 3

Your client, Tracey Dillon, is a local architect. She has hired you to create a corporate identity package so she can begin marketing her services to local land development companies. She has asked you first to develop a logo, and then to create the standard identity pieces that she can use for business promotion and correspondence.

To complete this project, you should:

❑ Develop a compelling logo that suggests the agency's purpose (architectural services).

❑ Incorporate the agency's name (TD Associates) into the logo.

❑ Build the letterhead, envelope, and business cards with the same technical specs that you used to design the Unicorn Retreat pieces.

"I've decided to open my own architectural services firm, and I need to start advertising. That means I need to brand my business so that companies who need an architect will recognize and remember my name. I'm calling my business TD Associates.

"I want a logo that really says 'architect', and I want the central color in my logo to be blue — like the blue you'd see on a blueprint.

"Once the logo is finished, I need you to use the logo on business cards, letterhead, and envelopes that I will have preprinted; I want a more professional feel than I can create using my laser printer. The printer I spoke with said I could do this for less money if I go 4-color for the business card and letterhead, but 2-color for the envelope.

"Eventually, I'll be incorporating my logo into all kinds of advertising — newspaper, local magazines, and even the Internet; I'd like you to create whatever versions you think I'll need for any purpose."

Realty Development Map

Your client is a real estate developer who needs an illustrated map of a new community development. Phase I of the development is already complete; Phase II is just getting underway. The developer wants a map to show the overall property, available and sold homes in Phase I, and available and sold home sites in Phase II.

This project incorporates the following skills:

❑ Accessing and managing built-in libraries of swatches, brushes, and symbols

❑ Defining custom art and pattern brushes for specific applications

❑ Applying and controlling brush strokes in relation to paths

❑ Saving user-defined libraries of custom assets

❑ Opening and using symbol libraries created by other users

❑ Understanding and creating symbols and symbol instances

❑ Transforming symbol instances and editing symbol artwork

❑ Swapping symbols in placed instances

❑ Creating a clipping mask

The Project Meeting

Client Comments

We're starting to make a big marketing push on Phase II of the new development, and we want to include an illustrated map in marketing materials and newspaper advertisements. I've sent a sketch of the property to your art director, and I've already approved the icons she showed me when we first met about this project.

I want to be able to change the map every time we sell a home in Phase I and reserve a lot or complete a construction in Phase II. I forgot to bring the current sale information, but I will send it to you as soon as I get back to my home office next week.

Finally, we advertise in a lot of places and we never know what formats they require. We need you to create different types of files that can be used by anyone doing print design work.

Art Director Comments

When I first met with the client about this project, I showed him some ideas for icons we can use for the map. We also discussed the importance of creating a legend for the finished map so potential buyers can make sense of the different icons.

The client approved the icons I suggested, so I created the legend with those, and I created a library you can use to pull the different elements instead of reinventing the proverbial wheel. I also created the artwork for the lot spaces because I needed to include "Standard Lot" and "Premium Lot" identifiers in the legend. That artwork is in the same library.

The most important feature of this project, from our point of view as the people who create and manage the files, is versatility. The client needs to be able to make changes frequently — as soon as a home is sold, a home site is reserved, or a new house is built in Phase II. As the client said, he didn't bring the current status report, so you can't mark the sold spaces right away. You can build the file, however, and mark the sales as soon as you have that information.

Anything you can do to make revisions easier will be worth the effort later.

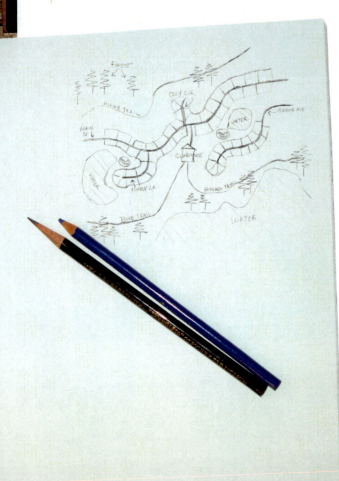

Project Objectives

To complete this project, you will:

- ❏ Open and use built-in swatch libraries
- ❏ Define custom gradient swatches
- ❏ Create a new pattern swatch based on a built-in pattern
- ❏ Define custom art brushes to paint roads and paths
- ❏ Define a pattern brush to paint roads with cul de sac endings
- ❏ Save a custom brush library so it can be accessed again later
- ❏ Open a symbol library created by another user
- ❏ Place and control symbol instances
- ❏ Edit symbol artwork to change all placed instances
- ❏ Break the link from placed instances to the original symbols
- ❏ Swap symbols in placed instances
- ❏ Create a clipping mask to hide unwanted parts of the artwork

Stage 1 Swatches, Gradients, and Patterns

The default Swatches panel (Window>Swatches) includes a seemingly random collection of swatches from the different built-in libraries.

Swatch Libraries menu

Default Swatches panel

Illustrator also includes a large number of built-in swatch libraries, many of which contain thematic color schemes (such as Earthtone, Metal, and Nature). These libraries are accessed by choosing Window>Swatch Libraries or by clicking the Swatch Libraries menu button at the bottom of the Swatches panel.

If you open more than one swatch library from the Window>Swatch Libraries menu, each library opens as a new panel, grouped by default with other open swatch libraries. If you open a different library using the menu at the bottom of an open library panel, the new library replaces the one that was active when you opened the new library.

Note:

You can drag any library panel out of the group to manage it independently.

Opening the Neutral library from the Window>Swatch Libraries menu adds the Neutral library to the panel group with the Metal library.

Opening the Skintones library using the panel's Swatch Libraries menu replaces the Neutral library.

The Swatches panel appears by default in Thumbnail mode. If you choose List View from the panel options menu, you will see the name of the color, as well as an icon that indicates the type of the color. Viewing swatches by name can be useful because the swatch names indicate the components of each color.

Note:

When a library is showing in Thumbnail mode, you can roll the mouse over a specific swatch to see the swatch name in a tool tip. The same option is available for brush libraries, graphic style libraries, and symbol libraries.

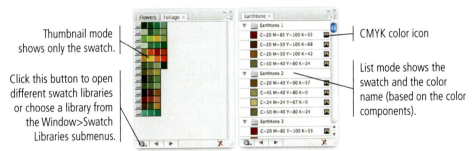

Thumbnail mode shows only the swatch.

Click this button to open different swatch libraries or choose a library from the Window>Swatch Libraries submenus.

CMYK color icon

List mode shows the swatch and the color name (based on the color components).

OPEN BUILT-IN SWATCH LIBRARIES

Before you begin drawing and painting, you need to prepare the workspace and import the client's sketch to use as a template. You'll use the sketch to create the shape of the roads, the location of the water, and the position of the different amenities available in the development. The sketch also shows the location of the clubhouse and other amenities, which you will create using symbols in the second stage of this project.

1. **Create a new letter-size CMYK document using landscape orientation; type "map" in the Name field before clicking OK.**

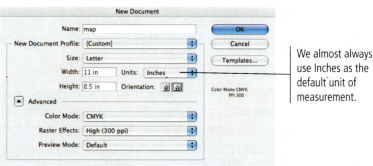

We almost always use Inches as the default unit of measurement.

Note sidebar*Note:*

Before completing this project, copy the Realty folder from the WIP folder on your Resource CD to your WIP folder where you are saving your work. When you save files for this project, you will save them in your WIP>Realty folder.

2. **Place the file Sketch.jpg from the RF_Illustrator>Realty folder. Make sure the file is not linked when you place it.**

3. **Using the Align panel, align the sketch horizontally and vertically to the center of the artboard.**

4. **Rename the default layer "Sketch" and convert it to a template layer.**

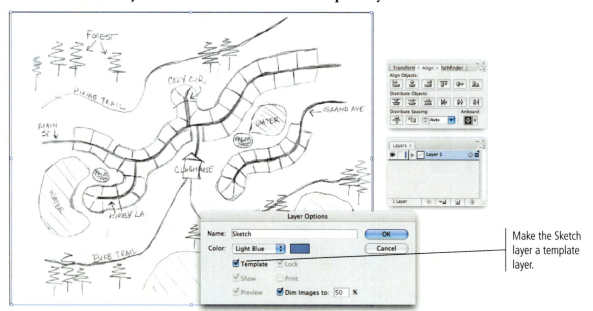

Make the Sketch layer a template layer.

5. **Choose Window>Swatch Libraries>Nature>Landscape.**

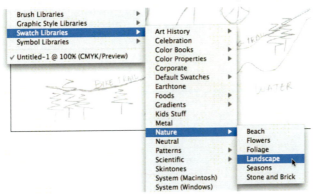

When you open the first swatch library, the library appears in its own panel.

Note:

Library panels open in the same location and state as the last time they were used. If a panel is not automatically grouped with other library panels, it was already used and repositioned.

6. **Repeat Step 5 to open the Stone and Brick swatch library from the Nature collection.**

   Don't click the button at the bottom of the library panel to open the new library. Doing so would replace the Landscape library with the Stone and Brick library.

The Stone and Brick library is added to the panel group with the Landscape library.

Note:

You might want to drag this panel group to the dock and save a custom workspace so that you can easily access the same libraries later.

7. **Save the file as a native Illustrator file named "map.ai" in your WIP>Realty folder and continue to the next exercise.**

DEFINE GRADIENT SWATCHES

A **gradient** smoothly merges one color into another color. Illustrator supports both **linear gradients**, which move in a line from one color to another, and **radial gradients**, which move from one color at the center of a circle to another color at the outer edges.

Illustrator also includes a number of built-in pattern and gradient swatches, several of which are available in the default Swatches panel; you can even use the panel to display only swatches of a specific kind.

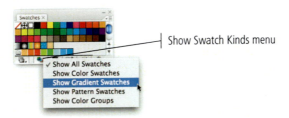

Show Swatch Kinds menu

Of course, the few options in the default Swatches panel are probably not sufficient for most jobs. You can open other gradient or pattern swatch libraries using the Swatch Libraries menu (or using the Window>Swatch Libraries submenus).

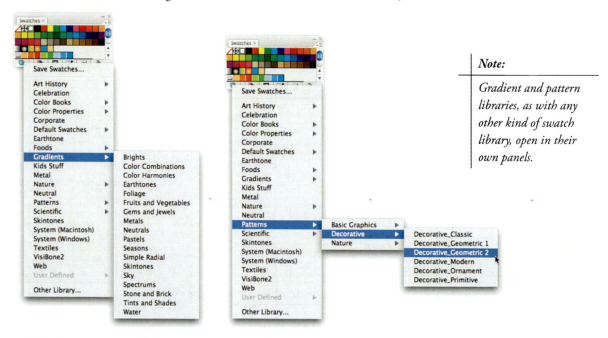

Note:

Gradient and pattern libraries, as with any other kind of swatch library, open in their own panels.

You're going to create two custom gradient swatches to fill the major areas of the map (the lake and ponds, and the grass surrounding the houses).

1. **With map.ai open, create two new layers named "Water" and "Grass".**

2. **Make sure the Landscape swatch library is visible. If not, choose Window>Swatch Libraries>Nature>Landscape.**

3. **Open the Gradient panel (Window>Gradient).**

4. **If you see only a gradient sample in the panel, open the panel options menu and choose Show Options.**

5. **Choose Radial in the Type menu.**

Note:

You can use the Gradient panel to define a gradient, save a specific gradient by dragging the gradient into the Swatches panel, and use the Gradient tool to apply a gradient swatch to an object on the artboard.

6. **Drag a medium-blue swatch from the Landscape swatch library onto the right stop of the gradient ramp (in the Gradient panel).**

The stop color changes from black to blue, and the sample swatch now shows the effect of the new stop color.

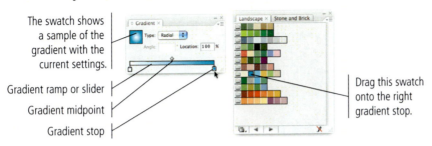

The swatch shows a sample of the gradient with the current settings.

Gradient ramp or slider

Gradient midpoint

Gradient stop

Drag this swatch onto the right gradient stop.

7. **Drag the gradient midpoint left until the Location field shows approximately 30%.**

This point indicates where the colors of the two surrounding stops are equally mixed. Dragging the point extends and compresses the gradient on either side of the point.

8. **Open the main Swatches panel (Window>Swatches).**

9. **Click the sample swatch in the Gradient panel and drag it into the main Swatches panel.**

10. **Double-click the new swatch in the Swatches panel to open the Swatch Options dialog box. Change the swatch name to "Water Gradient" and click OK.**

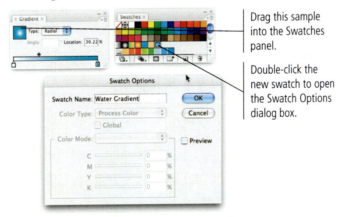

Drag this sample into the Swatches panel.

Double-click the new swatch to open the Swatch Options dialog box.

11. **In the Gradient panel, change the Type menu to Linear.**

12. Drag a light green color to the left gradient stop, and drag a dark green color to the right gradient stop.

We used this swatch for the left gradient stop...

...and this swatch for the right gradient stop.

By default, the midpoint retains the location from the last gradient you created.

13. Drag the gradient midpoint back to 50%.

14. Drag the left gradient stop until the Location field shows approximately 60%.

As you can see in the gradient ramp, most of the gradient (left of the leftmost stop) will be filled with the lighter green color.

15. Click below the gradient ramp near the left end of the ramp.

You can create additional stops on the gradient, each of which can have a different color.

16. Drag the dark green swatch onto the new leftmost gradient stop.

Your gradient should now go from dark to light and back to dark.

Note:

Delete specific stops from the gradient by dragging them away from the panel.

17. Create a new swatch from this linear gradient, and name the swatch "Grass Gradient".

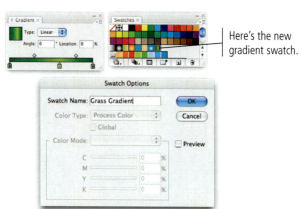

Here's the new gradient swatch.

18. Save the file and continue to the next exercise.

APPLY AND CONTROL GRADIENTS

Once you have created gradient swatches, you can apply them by simply selecting an object and clicking the appropriate swatch. You can also use the Gradient tool to control the position of a gradient.

1. **With the Grass layer of the map.ai file selected, change the Fill to None and the Stroke to 0.5-pt black.**

2. **Use the Pen tool to create a shape for the grass. Use the following image as a rough guide for where to create the shape's edges.**

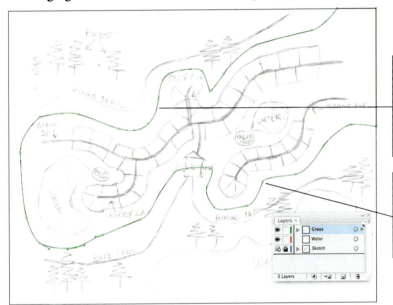

The grass line you're drawing here is not on the sketch. We're shaping the grass based on the outline of the entire community.

The grass should surround the houses and roads, as well as the two ponds within the community.

3. **Make sure the shape you just drew is selected, then click the Grass Gradient swatch in the Swatches panel to fill the shape with the defined gradient.**

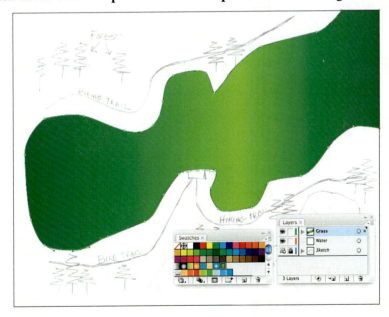

4. **Choose the Gradient tool in the Tools panel.**

5. **Click in the left side of the shape and drag up and right toward the right edge.**

When working with a linear gradient, the first place you click with the Gradient tool defines the location for the starting color of the gradient; where you drag to marks the location for the ending color of the gradient. Any areas beyond the two ends will be filled with the end-stop colors of the gradient.

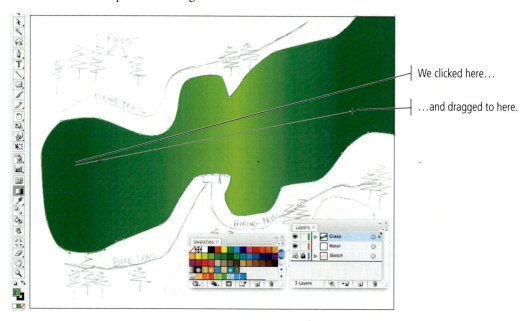

We clicked here...

...and dragged to here.

Dragging with the Gradient tool defines the direction and position of gradient.

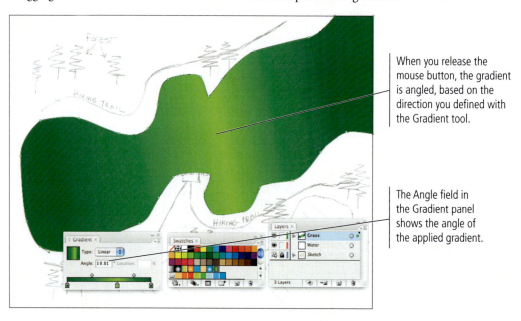

When you release the mouse button, the gradient is angled, based on the direction you defined with the Gradient tool.

The Angle field in the Gradient panel shows the angle of the applied gradient.

6. **In the Layers panel, drag the Grass layer to the bottom of the layer stack (directly above the Sketch layer). Hide and lock the Grass layer.**

7. **With the Water layer selected, use the Pen tool with a black stroke and no fill to draw the three shapes for the lake and ponds.**

8. **Apply the Water Gradient swatch to all three of the water shapes.**

9. **Use the Gradient tool to determine the position of the gradient center for each body of water.**

To modify each body of water separately, you have to first deselect all three objects and then select the one you want to modify with the Gradient tool. If you leave all three objects selected when you drag with the Gradient tool, the single gradient will extend across all three selected objects.

When working with a radial gradient, the first place you click with the Gradient tool defines the center point (the starting color) of the applied gradient. The location where you drag marks the outer edge of the radial gradient; any areas beyond the outer edge of the gradient will be filled with the end-stop color of the gradient.

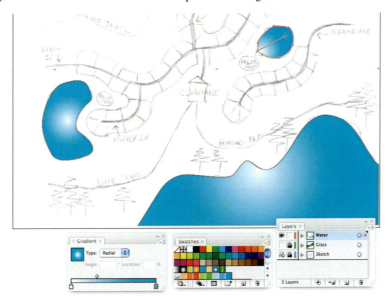

10. **Create a new layer named "Undeveloped".**

11. **Draw a rectangle that covers the entire artboard and fill it with an olive green swatch from the Landscape swatch library.**

12. **In the Layers panel, drag the Undeveloped layer below the Grass layer.**

13. **Show all layers and unlock all but the Sketch layer.**

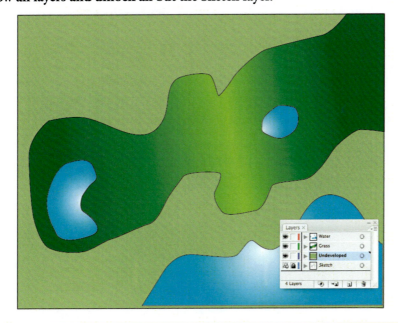

14. **Choose Select>All.**

15. **Change the stroke for all selected objects to None.**

16. **Deselect all objects and review your results.**

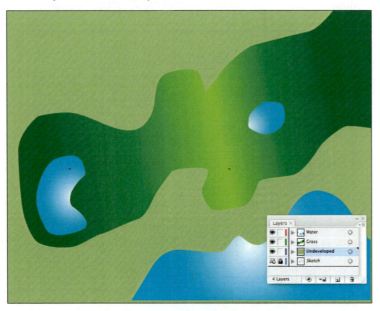

17. **Save the file and continue to the next exercise.**

Using Spot Colors in Gradients

ILLUSTRATOR FOUNDATIONS

Gradients are simple in one way and complex in others, especially when you work with spot colors (such as Pantone swatches) in addition to CMYK colors. If you create a gradient that blends a spot color into a process color build, the results will be unpredictable at best and disastrous at worst. In short, we highly recommend that you do not do this.

It is fairly common to create a gradient that blends from a spot color to white. This can be problematic too, but there is an easy solution for this type of gradient.

The image here shows a basic linear gradient that blends from white to Pantone 1375. When you click a gradient stop, the Color panel shows the color values of the selected stop.

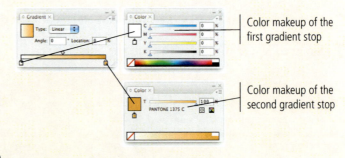

Color makeup of the first gradient stop

Color makeup of the second gradient stop

The White stop is actually a CMYK build, even though all four inks are set to zero. When the Pantone color blends into the CMYK color, the intermediate steps of the gradient will actually be created with CMYK builds instead of shades of the Pantone color — resulting in extra separations for a job that might not allow for more than one or two.

To solve the problem, you can apply the same spot color to both stops, and use the Color panel to apply 0% of the spot color for the stop where you want the gradient to be white. When both stops in the gradient are colored with a Pantone color (regardless of the defined tint for the stop), the intermediate shades of the gradient will be created as shades of the Pantone color instead of CMYK percentages.

CREATE PATTERNS

The final step in creating the background artwork is to add texture to the grassy areas in the main community. This will clearly differentiate the grass from the surrounding "land" area and the individual properties.

1. **With map.ai open, duplicate the Grass layer and name the duplicate "Grassy Texture". Hide all but the Sketch and Grassy Texture layers, and lock all but the Grassy Texture layer.**

2. **Choose Windows>Swatch Libraries>Patterns>Basic Graphics>Basic Graphics_Textures. Change the panel display to one of the List views (small or large, whichever you prefer).**

3. **With nothing selected in the file, click the Burlap swatch and drag it onto the empty area right of the artboard.**

   When you drag a pattern or brush from a library panel, you place a copy of the artwork that is used to make that pattern or brush.

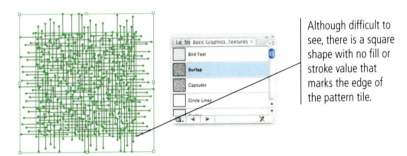

Although difficult to see, there is a square shape with no fill or stroke value that marks the edge of the pattern tile.

4. **Deselect all the pattern elements, and then use the Direct Selection tool to select only one of the interior lines.**

   It doesn't matter which line you select, as long as it's not the square tile shape.

5. **Choose Select>Same>Fill & Stroke.**

   Because all other layers are locked and the grass shape on this layer has a gradient fill, this command will select all of the lines in the pattern artwork, but nothing else.

6. **With all of these lines selected, change the stroke color to a light green from the Landscape swatch library.**

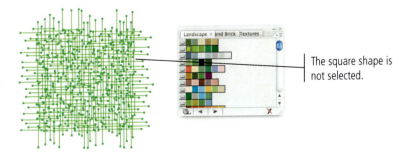

The square shape is not selected.

7. **Using the Selection tool, drag a marquee to select the entire pattern artwork — including the square tile shape.**

8. **Drag the selected art into the Swatches panel to create a new pattern swatch.**

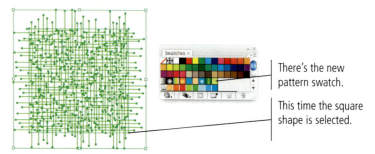

There's the new pattern swatch.

This time the square shape is selected.

9. **Double-click the new pattern swatch to open the Swatch Options dialog box. Name the pattern "Grassy Texture", and then click OK.**

10. **On the artboard, delete the objects that you used to create the Pattern.**

11. **Select the grass area shape on the artboard. Change the shape's fill to the new Grassy Texture pattern.**

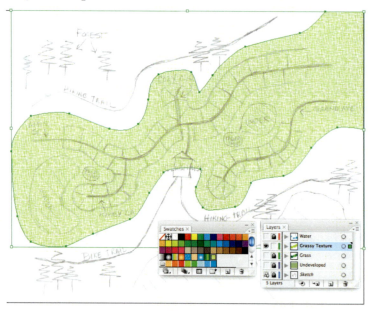

12. Show the Grass layer.

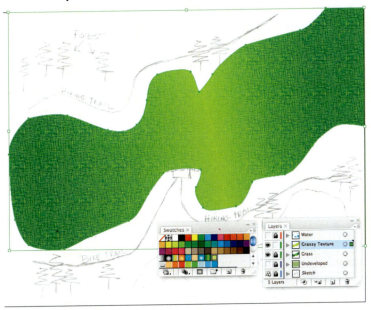

13. Save the file and continue to the next stage of the project.

Stage 2 Using Brushes and Brush Libraries

Brushes enhance or (as Adobe puts it) decorate paths. The default Brushes panel (Window>Brushes) includes several basic brushes of different types. You can use the Brushes panel options menu to change the panel display, manage brushes, and load different brush libraries.

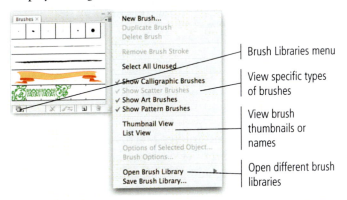

Illustrator includes a number of different brushes for various purposes, broken into four categories:

- **Calligraphic brushes** create strokes that resemble what you would draw with the angled tip of a calligraphic pen.

- **Scatter brushes** scatter copies of an object along a path.

- **Art brushes** stretch a brush or object shape across the length of a path.

- **Pattern brushes** paint a pattern of defined tiles along the length of a path. You can define different tiles for straight edges, inner and outer corners, and the beginning and end of a path.

The Brushes panel appears by default in Thumbnail mode. If you choose List View from the panel options menu, you will see the name of the brush, as well as an icon that indicates the type of the brush. Viewing brushes by name can be useful — especially when working with the built-in brushes — because the brush names indicate what each brush will create.

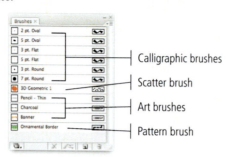

Calligraphic brushes

Scatter brush

Art brushes

Pattern brush

Note:

We added the 3D Geometric 1 brush to the default panel so we could show you the icon for a scatter brush. This brush is not included in the default Brushes panel.

Beyond the few brushes in the default Brushes panel, you can also open a number of built-in brush libraries using the Brush Libraries menu at the bottom of the Brushes panel or at the bottom of the Window menu.

When you open the first brush library, the library appears in its own panel. If you open more than one brush library using the Window>Brush Libraries menu, each library opens as a new panel, grouped by default with other open brush libraries. You can drag any library panel out of the group to manage it independently.

If you open a different library using the menu at the bottom of an open library panel, the new library replaces the one that was active when you opened the new library.

Note:

Library panels open in the same location and state as the last time they were used. If a panel is not automatically grouped with other library panels, it was already repositioned at an earlier time.

Multiple brush libraries are automatically combined into a single panel group when you open them from the Window>Brush Libraries menu.

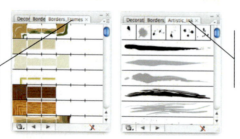

Opening a new library from the menu at the bottom of the Brushes panel replaces the active panel with the new one.

CREATE A NEW ART BRUSH

To complete this project, you're going to create two custom art brushes: one to make the main roads in the development resemble brick with darker brick edges, and one to paint the hiking and bike trails. As we explained at the beginning of this stage, an art brush stretches an object across the length of a path. So, to create an art brush, you have to first create the object that you want to use as the brush stroke.

1. **With map.ai open, lock all layers and then hide all but the Sketch layer. Create a new layer at the top of the stack named "Roads".**

All the Layers should be locked at this point except for the Roads layer.

2. **With the Roads layer selected, create a rectangle that is 1″ wide by 0.5″ high.**

3. **Change the rectangle's stroke to None. Use one of the dark red swatches from the Stone and Brick Swatch library as the rectangle's fill color.**

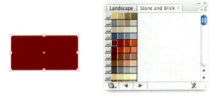

4. **Select the rectangle with the Selection tool, and then copy the rectangle.**

5. **Choose Edit>Paste in Front to paste a copy of the rectangle directly on top of the original.**

6. **In the Transform panel, make sure the Constrain option is turned off. Select the center reference point and change the object height to 0.45".**

7. **Change the fill color of the top rectangle to one of the lighter brick colors.**

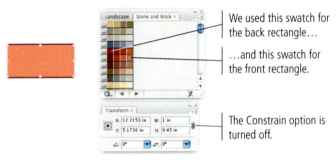

We used this swatch for the back rectangle…

…and this swatch for the front rectangle.

The Constrain option is turned off.

Key Command:

Press Command/ Control-F to apply the Paste in Front command.

Press Command/ Control-B to apply the Paste in Back command.

8. **Select both rectangles and group them (Object>Group or Command/ Control-G).**

9. **Make sure the basic Brushes panel is open (Window>Brushes).**

10. **Drag the grouped rectangles into the Brushes panel.**

Note:

You can't create an art brush from objects that use gradients, meshes, bitmap elements, masks, or type.

11. **In the New Brush dialog box, select the New Art Brush option and click OK.**

12. **Type "Road" in the Name field of the Brush Options dialog box, and then click OK.**

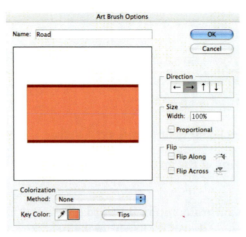

After you click OK in the Art Brush Options dialog box, the new brush appears in the Brushes panel.

There's the new art brush.

13. **Using the Direct Selection tool, drag the top edge of the top rectangle down so that it occupies less than half the height of the back rectangle.**

14. **Change the fill color of the front rectangle to a light gray, and change the fill color of the back rectangle to a light brown.**

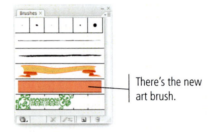

We used this swatch for the front rectangle…

…and this swatch for the back rectangle.

Note:

We're still using the Stone and Brick swatches that we loaded in the first part of this project.

15. **Create a new art brush named "Hike and Bike" from the group of two modified rectangles.**

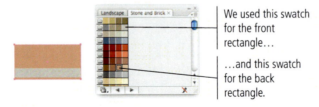

16. **Delete the grouped rectangles from the artboard.**

17. **Save your work and continue to the next exercise.**

ILLUSTRATOR FOUNDATIONS

Art brush options control how the object will be applied as a brush stroke. This dialog box opens automatically when you create a new art brush. You can also double-click any existing art brush to change the options for that brush.

The **Direction** options control the direction of the artwork in relation to the path. The direction of the active button matches the direction of the arrow in the preview; both of these indicate which side of the original artwork will be the end of the stroke.

The **Width** field adjusts the width of the applied brush stroke relative to the width of the original art. The **Proportional** option preserves proportions in scaled art.

Flip Along and **Flip Across** reverse the orientation of the art in relation to the path.

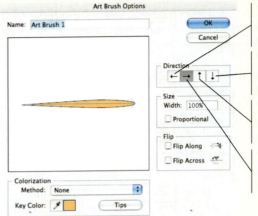

The left side of the artwork is the end of the stroke.

The bottom of the artwork is the end of the stroke.

The top of the artwork is the end of the stroke.

The right side of the artwork is the end of the stroke.

Brush Colorization

The **Colorization** menu allows you to control how the colors in a brush (art, scatter, or pattern) interact with the currently defined stroke color.

Select **None** to use only the colors as defined in the brush.

Select **Tints** to apply the brush stroke in tints of the current stroke color. (Black areas of the brush become the stroke color, other areas become tints of the stroke color, and white remains white.)

Select **Tints and Shades** to apply the brush stroke in tints and shades of the stroke color. Black and white areas of the brush are not affected; all other areas are painted as a blend from black to white through the stroke color.

Select **Hue Shift** to change the defined key color in the brush artwork to the defined stroke color when the brush is applied; other colors in the brush are adjusted to be similar to the stroke color. (Black, white, and gray areas are not affected). The key color defaults to the most prominent color in the brush art. To change the key color, click the eyedropper in the brush preview to select a different key color.

Click the Tips button to see a preview of the different colorization options.

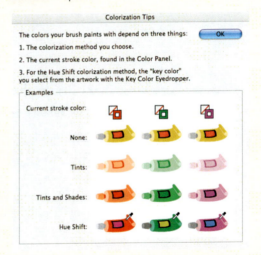

CONTROL AN ART BRUSH STROKE

Applying a brush stroke is simple — draw a path (or select an object) and click the brush you want to apply. Once a brush stroke is applied, however, you should also understand how to control it.

1. **With map.ai open and nothing selected, change the fill to None and the stroke to 1-pt. Black.**

2. **Using the Pen tool, draw a path that follows Main Street in the map sketch.**

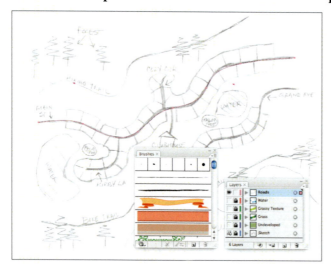

3. **Click the Road brush in the Brushes panel.**

   The road immediately takes on the appearance of the brush you created earlier.

   You created the original rectangle with a height of 0.5″. When you created a brush from the grouped rectangles, you left the Size Width field (in the Brush Options dialog box) at the default 100%.

   The width of the path stroke is also important when using brushes. When you apply artistic brush strokes, the width of the path's stroke actually defines the percentage of the brush width that will be applied.

   In this case, the width of the path stroke is 1 pt., so the applied brush stroke is 100% of the brush size. In other words, applying the brush to a 1-pt. path results in a brush stroke with a 0.5″ width.

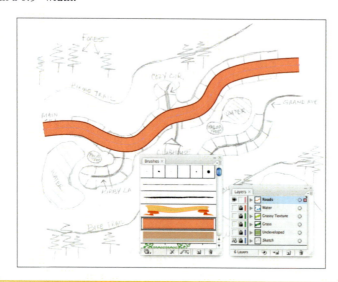

Note:

Changing the path width to 0.5 pt. would reduce the brush stroke to 50% of the brush size; changing the path width to 2 pt. would enlarge the brush stroke to 200% of the brush size.

4. **With the brushed path selected, click the Options of Selected Object button at the bottom of the Brushes panel.**

5. **In the Stroke Options (Art Brush) dialog box, change the Size field to 50% and click OK.**

Note:

You could have accomplished the same result by changing the path stroke to 0.5 pt. Every job has different requirements, so it is important to understand your options.

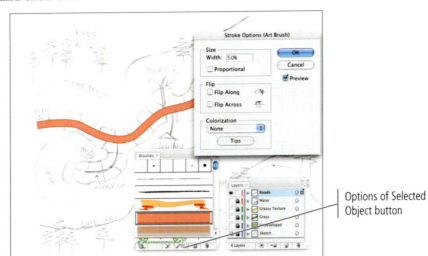

Options of Selected Object button

Changing Brush Options

ILLUSTRATOR FOUNDATIONS

You could have changed the size for the entire brush by double-clicking the Road brush in the Brushes panel. When you change the options for a specific brush, you can determine what to do for strokes where the brush has already been applied.

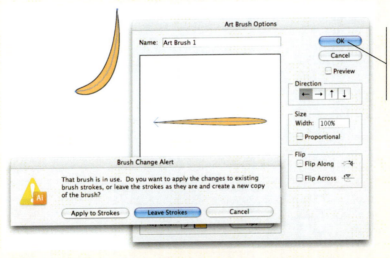

Clicking OK opens the Brush Change Alert if the brush has already been applied in the artwork.

If you click **Apply to Strokes**, the changes will be applied to any path where the brush has been applied.

If you click **Leave Strokes**, existing paths are unaffected; a copy of the brush (with changes) is added to the Brushes panel.

If you click **Cancel**, the Brush Options dialog box closes without applying the new brush options.

6. Create another new layer named "Bike Paths".

7. Use the Pen tool to draw the hiking trails and bike path with a 1-pt. black stroke and no fill.

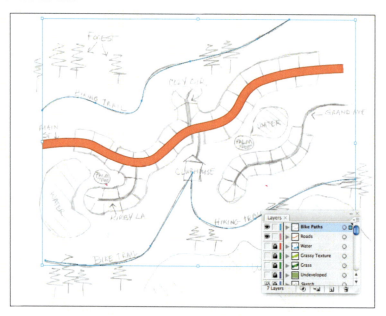

8. Apply the Hike and Bike art brush to the paths you drew in Step 7.

9. Adjust the paths' stroke width so the trails seem proportionate to the roads.

We changed the strokes to 35% of the brush size.

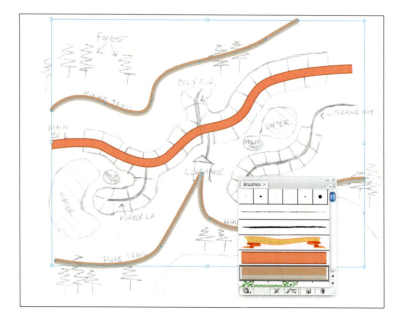

10. Save the file and continue to the next exercise.

CREATE PATTERN BRUSH TILES

The art brush you created earlier is basic, but it suits its purpose — painting the main road. According to the client, the side roads (Cozy Circle, Kirby Lane, and Grand Avenue) are actually cul de sacs with circles at the ends of the roads.

You could manually create and align these "lollipop" road endings, but you can use a pattern brush to more easily complete the task. Before you can create a pattern brush, however, you need to first create the pattern tiles that will be used in the brush.

1. **With map.ai open, make sure nothing is selected on the artboard.**

2. **Drag the Road brush from the Brushes panel onto the artboard outside of the main map area.**

   You can always access the basic brush art by dragging the brush onto the artboard.

   Dragging the brush from the panel onto the artboard creates a group with the basic brush art.

3. **Choose the Ellipse tool from the Tools panel. Click once on the artboard and define a circle with a 0.8″ diameter.**

4. **Copy the circle and paste a copy in front of the original.**

5. **Change the diameter of the pasted circle to 0.75″, based on the center reference point.**

6. **Fill the top circle with the same color as the center road color, and fill the back circle with the same color as the road edges.**

7. **Select the two circles and group them.**

   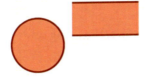

8. **Align the vertical centers of the grouped circles and the grouped rectangles.**

9. **Using the Selection tool, Shift-drag the grouped circles until they obscure the right end of the grouped rectangles.**

   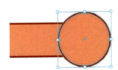

10. **Ungroup both groups of objects.**

11. **Select only the back rectangle and back circle. In the Pathfinder panel, click the Add to Shape Area button, and then click Expand.**

Using the Pathfinder panel can have unexpected effects on object stacking order. Because you created both circles after the two rectangles, the back circle lies in front of the top rectangle. When the two darker objects are united by the Pahfinder operation, the back rectangle is brought forward to the same stacking level as the darker circle — in front of the lighter rectangle.

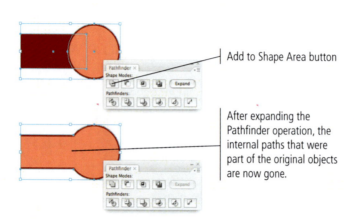

Add to Shape Area button

After expanding the Pathfinder operation, the internal paths that were part of the original objects are now gone.

Note:

Option/Alt click the Pathfinder buttons to automatically expand the operation.

12. **Send the new combined shape to the back of the stacking order.**

13. **Repeat this process to create a single shape for the inner road area (the two lighter shapes).**

When you create pattern brush elements, you should simplify the shapes as much as possible. Using the Pathfinder options, you have simplified the overall shape from four objects to two.

14. **Group the two pieces of the road ending (cul de sac).**

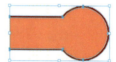

15. **Drag the Road brush from the Brushes panel to the artboard again.**

These two groups (the cul de sac ending segment and the rectangle segment) will be the tiles for your pattern brush.

16. **Save the file and continue to the next exercise.**

CREATE A NEW PATTERN BRUSH

Now that you have the two objects you need to create the pattern brush, you have to convert those objects to patterns, and then define the pattern brush.

Note:

1. With map.ai open, open the Swatches panel. Use the Show Swatch Kinds menu at the bottom of the panel to show only pattern swatches.

2. Using the Selection tool, click the cul de sac group and drag it into the Swatches panel.

3. Deselect the group on the artboard.

   If you don't deselect the group, double-clicking the swatch in the next step will fill the selected object with the pattern.

Note:

If the roads in this project had sharp corners, you would also need to define shapes for both inside and outside corners.

4. Double-click the swatch in the panel, name it "Cul De Sac", and then click OK.

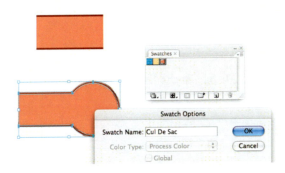

5. Drag the straight road segment into the Swatches panel, then deselect the group on the artboard.

6. Double-click the new swatch in the panel; name it "Straight Road" and click OK.

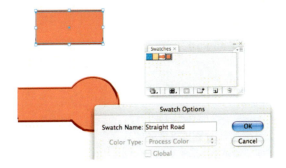

7. Delete the two grouped elements from the artboard, and make sure nothing is selected.

8. In the Brushes panel, click the New Brush button at the bottom of the panel.

9. Select the New Pattern Brush option and click OK.

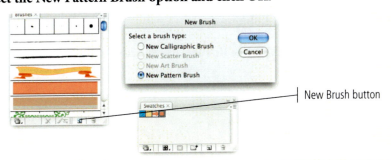

Note:

If anything had been selected when you clicked the New Brush button, Illustrator would have tried to create a new brush based on the current selection.

10. **In the Pattern Brush Options dialog box, name the brush "Cul De Sac Roads".**

11. **Click the Side Tile icon, and then choose Straight Road from the list of available pattern swatches.**

   Pattern brush tiles must be saved as patterns so you can access them in the Pattern Brush Options dialog box.

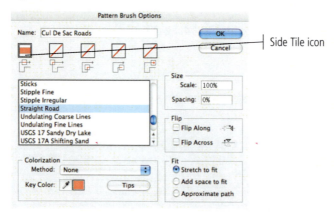

Side Tile icon

Note:

Pattern brushes can consist of five possible tiles: side, outer corner, inner corner, start, and end. You can define different patterns for any or all of these tiles.

12. **Click the End Tile icon, and then click Cul De Sac in the list of patterns.**

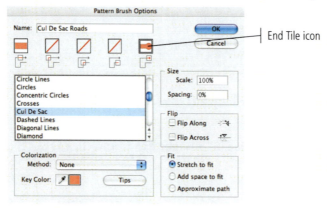

End Tile icon

Note:

The arrow in the End Tile icon shows why you moved the circle group to the right side instead of the left side of the rectangle group.

The end tile of a pattern brush should always be created with the path end pointing to the right. If the "end" of the end tile points to the left, you could end up with unexpected results:

This direction has no effect on the stroke that will be applied in the artwork; if you draw a path from right to left, the end tile of the applied pattern brush will point to the left:

13. **Click OK to create the brush.**

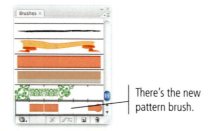

There's the new pattern brush.

14. **Select the Roads layer as the active layer.**

15. **Using the Pen tool with a fill of None and a 1-pt. black stroke, draw the four side roads (including the one that leads to the clubhouse).**

16. **Select all four of these paths and click the Cul De Sac Roads pattern brush in the Brushes panel.**

17. With all four paths selected, change the Stroke value to 0.5 pt.

As we mentioned earlier, you can change the stroke size for the applied art brush, or you can achieve the same result by changing the stroke width of the path. The half-point (0.5) stroke width means the applied stroke is half the width of the defined brush.

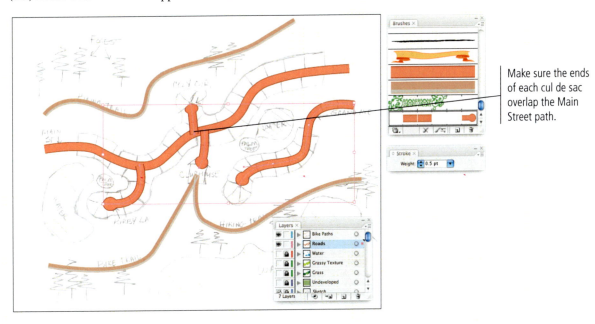

Make sure the ends of each cul de sac overlap the Main Street path.

18. Send the four selected paths to the back of the stacking order.

The main road should appear in front of the other roads.

19. Save the file and continue to the next exercise.

Pattern Brush Options

As with art brushes, you can control the settings for pattern brushes when you first create them or by double-clicking an existing pattern brush in the Brushes panel.

The **Tile buttons** allow you to apply different patterns to different parts of the line.

The **Scale** option adjusts the size of tiles relative to their original size.

The **Spacing** option adjusts the space between tiles in the applied stroke.

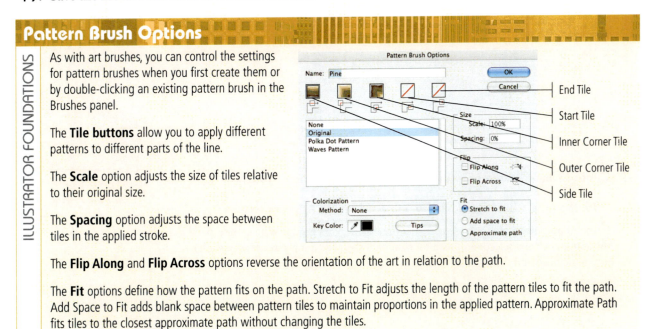

The **Flip Along** and **Flip Across** options reverse the orientation of the art in relation to the path.

The **Fit** options define how the pattern fits on the path. Stretch to Fit adjusts the length of the pattern tiles to fit the path. Add Space to Fit adds blank space between pattern tiles to maintain proportions in the applied pattern. Approximate Path fits tiles to the closest approximate path without changing the tiles.

The **Colorization** options are the same here as for art brushes.

EXPAND BRUSH STROKES INTO OBJECTS

If you look at the map as it is now, you might notice a problem where the different road paths connect — actual intersections don't have curbs running through them. You need to fix these path intersections to more accurately reflect the appearance of real road intersections. To solve this problem, you have to convert the road path strokes to regular objects so you can manipulate selected parts of the roads (i.e., where the paths intersect).

1. **With map.ai open, select the Main Street road path.**

2. **Open the Appearance panel.**

   The Appearance panel shows the properties of the selected objects, including the applied stroke and fill attributes. You can see here that the stroke attribute is "Road".

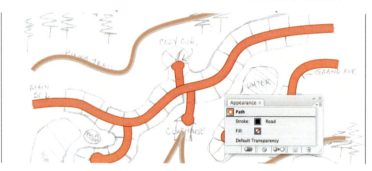

3. **Choose View>Outline.**

   In Outline mode, you can see the basic paths without the applied stroke.

Key Command:

Press Command/Control-Y to switch to Outline viewing mode.

4. **Choose View>Preview to return to the full-color version of your work.**

5. **With the path still selected, choose Object>Expand Appearance.**

   In the Appearance panel, you now see that the selection is a group. When you expand the appearance of a selection, Illustrator simplifies the selection (as much as possible) into basic filled and stroked shapes; the resulting shapes are grouped.

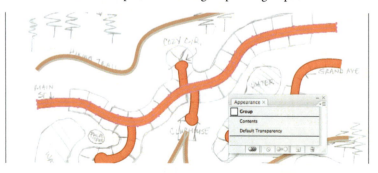

Note:

Note: Art brushes can produce unexpected results on sharp corners and closed paths.

Pattern brushes are the best choices for creating borders on closed paths or for other paths that have sharp corners.

The Appearance panel (Window>Appearance) allows you to review and change appearance attributes of objects, including stroke, fill, transparency, and applied effects.

When you create new objects, the last-used appearance attributes (including fill, stroke, applied effects, etc.) are automatically applied to the new object. You can change this behavior by toggling off the **New Art Maintains Appearance** option at the bottom of the Appearance panel. When the button is dark gray, new objects will maintain the same basic attributes (fill and stroke) but applied effects and other attributes will not be applied to the new object.

Clicking the **Clear Appearance** button reduces the selected object to a fill and stroke of None. You can also reduce an object to its basic fill and stroke attributes by clicking the **Reduce to Basic Attributes** button; fill color and stroke weight and color are maintained, but all other attributes will be removed.

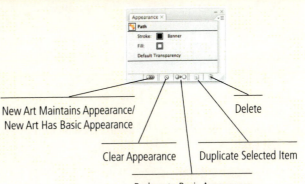

New Art Maintains Appearance/
New Art Has Basic Appearance

Delete

Clear Appearance

Duplicate Selected Item

Reduce to Basic Appearance

You can also use the **Duplicate Selected Item** button to create multiple versions of the same attribute for a single object, such as two different stroke weights and colors. This allows you to compound the effect of different attributes without layering multiple objects on top of each other. If you want to remove a specific attribute from an object, select that item in the panel and click the panel **Delete** button.

6. **Choose View>Outline.**

   In this case, expanding the stroked path results in two filled objects — the inner road bed (with the lighter fill color) and the outer road bed (with the darker fill). The original path is also maintained, with a fill and stroke of None.

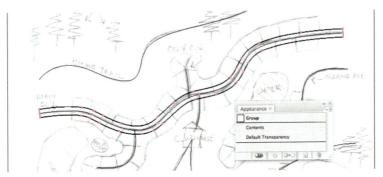

7. **Return to Preview mode and select the three road paths that intersect Main Street.**

8. **With all three paths selected, choose Object>Expand Appearance.**

9. **Shift-click to select the expanded Main Street group.**

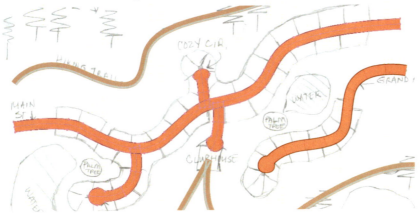

10. **Choose Object>Ungroup two times.**

You have to ungroup twice to remove the different groupings created by the Expand Appearance command.

11. **Deselect everything, and then select one of the dark-red-filled objects.**

You might have to zoom in to select the dark-red objects. Watch the Appearance panel to make sure your selection is the correct color.

12. **Choose Select>Same>Fill Color to select all the objects that have the dark-red fill.**

Notice the Grand Avenue path is not affected because you did not expand the appearance of that path.

13. **In the Pathfinder panel, click the Add to Shape Area button, and then click the Expand button.**

All the selected shapes are now a single object filled with the dark-red color.

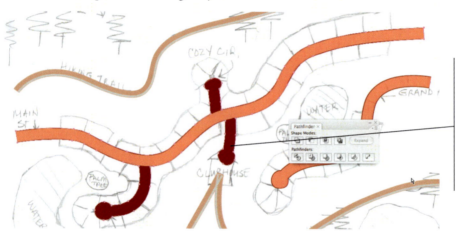

As mentioned previously, using the Pathfinder panel can have unexpected effects on stacking order. The dark-red areas of the three cul de sacs are brought to the front of the stacking order within their groups.

14. **Send the selected object to the back of the stacking order.**

15. **Repeat Steps 11–13 to combine all the light-red-filled objects into a single shape at the top of the stacking order.**

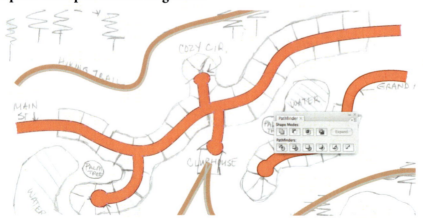

16. **Save the file and continue to the next exercise.**

SAVE CUSTOM BRUSHES

When you create custom brushes, swatches, or other elements, they are only available in the file where you create them. To access those assets in other files, you have to save your own custom libraries.

1. **With map.ai open, show the Brushes panel.**

2. **Open the panel options menu and choose Select All Unused.**

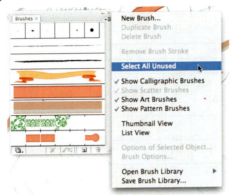

Everything but the Hike and Bike art brush and the Cul De Sac Roads pattern brush should be selected. (Remember, you expanded the appearance of Main Street, so the Road art brush is not currently applied in the file.)

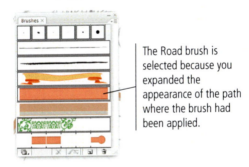

The Road brush is selected because you expanded the appearance of the path where the brush had been applied.

3. **Command/Control-click the Road art brush to deselect it, and then click the panel's Delete button.**

   You are not permanently deleting the brushes from the application; you are only deleting them from the Brushes panel for this file.

4. **Click the Expand Strokes button in the Delete Brush Alert dialog box.**

   Even though you used the panel options menu to select unused brushes, you still see this warning. This is a quirk of the software.

   In this case, you know the selected brushes haven't been used, so you can safely click either Expand Strokes or Remove Strokes.

5. **Open the panel options menu and choose Save Brush Library.**

6. **In the resulting dialog box, name the library "map brushes.ai" and click Save.**

   The extension ".ai" is automatically added for you.

7. **Close the Brushes panel.**

8. **Create a new document using the default settings, and then open the Brushes panel.**

9. **Choose Window>Brush Libraries>User Defined>map brushes.**

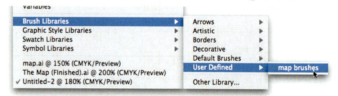

   The map brushes panel opens, grouped with the other open brush libraries. The panel contains only the three brushes that were available when you saved the library.

10. **Close the new file without saving.**

11. **Save the map.ai file and continue to the next stage of the project.**

Drawing Unique Custom Brushes

As you learned in the previous exercise, you can create custom brushes using objects you draw in Illustrator. You can also combine Illustrator's tracing functions with raster images (scans, photographs, or artwork created in Photoshop, for example) to create truly unique custom brushes.

In the example shown here, we scanned a line drawn on paper with a thick, red marker. We placed the scanned file into Illustrator and used the Live Tracing options (Object>Live Trace>Tracing Options) to change the scan into vector objects. (You will learn more about the Live Trace options in Project 8.) After the scanned object was converted to vectors, we dragged the vectors into the Brushes panel to create a new art brush.

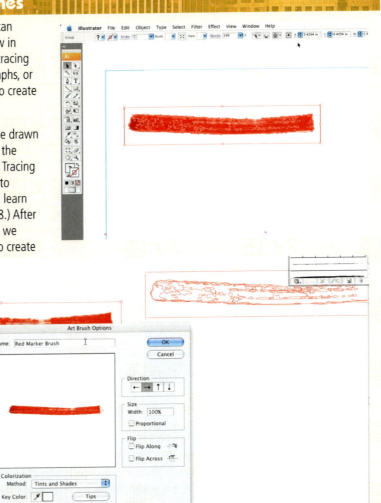

Stage 3   Using Symbols for Repetitive Graphics

Symbols are graphic elements that you draw once, and then use as many times as necessary in a drawing. The advantage to using symbols is that if you change the symbol, all placed instances of that symbol can reflect the same changes. You can also isolate specific instances of a symbol, which separates them and breaks the link to the main symbol (and other instances). Once the link is broken, changes to the main symbol have no effect on the isolated instances.

Like brushes and swatches, symbols are managed in panels. The default Symbols panel (Window> Symbols) has a few randomly selected symbols from the various built-in symbol libraries. You can also open different symbol libraries by choosing from the menu at the bottom of the Window menu.

Default Symbols panel

If you open a symbol library from the Window menu, the first library opens in its own panel. Successive panels open in separate panels that are automatically grouped with other open symbol libraries. If you open a symbol library using the Symbol Libraries menu at the bottom of a library panel, the active library is replaced with the new one you choose.

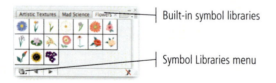

Built-in symbol libraries

Symbol Libraries menu

OPEN CUSTOM SYMBOL LIBRARIES

Several elements of this project will benefit from the use of symbols. Many of the symbols for this project have already been created and saved in a custom library. You can easily load that custom library so you don't have to recreate work that has already been completed.

1. **With map.ai open, open the Symbols panel (Window>Symbols).**

2. **Click the Symbol Libraries Menu button at the bottom of the default Symbols panel.**

3. **Choose Other Library at the bottom of the menu.**

   You can load custom symbol libraries that were created on another computer by choosing Other Library from the menu and navigating to the file that contains the library you want to use.

Note:

If you create a custom library on your computer, it appears in the User Defined submenu of the main Libraries menu. If a custom library was created on another computer, you have to use the Other Library option to load the new custom library on your computer.

4. **Navigate to the file named Map Symbols.ai in the RF_Illustrator>Realty folder and click Open.**

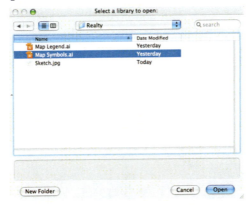

Note:

The same options are also available for loading swatch libraries and brush libraries that were created on another computer.

   The new symbol library appears in its own panel (possibly grouped with other library panels if other symbol libraries are also open).

5. **Open the options menu for the Map Symbols library panel and choose Large List View.**

6. **Continue to the next exercise.**

Note:

Symbols in loaded libraries are not connected to the current file unless you place an instance of a symbol from the loaded library into the file. When you place a symbol instance from a loaded library, the symbol is added to the default Symbol library for the file. (The same is true when working with brush libraries.)

CONTROL SYMBOL INSTANCES

In addition to loading built-in or custom symbol libraries, you can also create new symbols by drawing the art and dragging it into the default Symbols panel. You are going to create a custom symbol to identify the roads on the map; you ultimately need four different signs for the various roads.

1. **With map.ai open, lock and hide all layers. Create a new layer named "Street Signs" at the top of the layer stack.**

2. **Using the Rounded Rectangle tool, create a rounded rectangle 2″ wide and 0.75″ high with a medium-blue fill and a 3-pt. white stroke.**

3. **Deselect the rounded rectangle, then click the Default Fill and Stroke button in the Tools panel.**

4. **Using the Rectangle tool, draw a post for the sign, and arrange the post behind the blue rounded rectangle.**

5. **Click the Grass symbol in the Map Symbols panel and drag it onto the artboard.**

   You're going to use several of these symbols to add decorative elements to the road sign.

6. **Using the Selection tool, drag the instance in front of the signpost.**

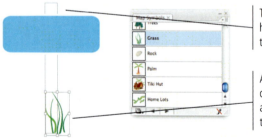

Take note that the post has square corners and the sign rounded.

A symbol instance is a single object. You can't directly access the individual shapes that make up the symbol.

7. **Drag the bounding box handles to resize the grass instance so it is appropriately sized in relation to the sign.**

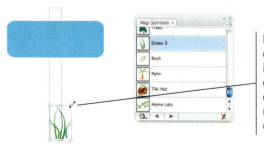

Because an instance is an object, you can transform the instance as you would any other object. This has no effect on the original symbol, nor on other placed instances of the same symbol.

8. **Clone (Option/Alt-drag) the Grass instance several times. Resize and arrange the instances to create a thick cluster of grass around the base of the post.**

   Each symbol instance is an object, which means they can be modified — transformed, rotated, stretched, etc. — as you would modify any other object. Transforming a placed instance has no effect on other placed instances.

9. **Drag an instance of the Rock symbol onto the artboard.**

10. **Use the Selection tool to resize and rotate the instance as appropriate for the surrounding artwork.**

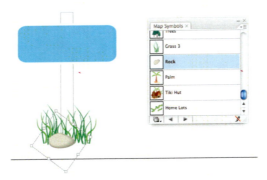

11. **Select the placed rock instance and click the Break Link to Symbol button at the bottom of the main Symbols panel.**

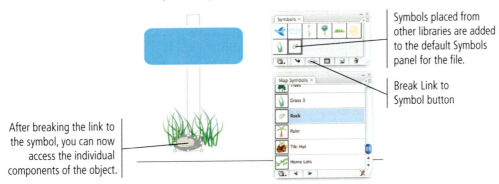

Symbols placed from other libraries are added to the default Symbols panel for the file.

Break Link to Symbol button

After breaking the link to the symbol, you can now access the individual components of the object.

12. **Break the links of all placed symbol instances.**

   In this case, you're only using the symbols to access the artwork; you don't need to maintain the links to the original symbols.

13. **Select all the objects on the Street Signs layer and group them.**

14. **Drag the grouped road sign onto the main Symbols panel.**

15. **In the resulting dialog box, name the symbol "Street Signs" and click OK.**

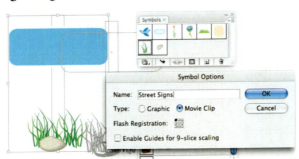

Note:

The Movie Clip option is used for symbols that will be exported to Adobe Flash. If your symbols will remain in Illustrator, you can use either the Graphic or Movie Clip option.

When you create a symbol from objects on the artboard, the original objects are automatically converted to an instance of the new symbol.

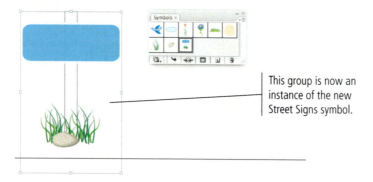

This group is now an instance of the new Street Signs symbol.

16. **Save the file and continue to the next exercise.**

 PLACE SYMBOL INSTANCES

Now that you've created the custom symbol, it will be fairly easy to place instances where you need them.

1. **With map.ai open, show the Sketch and Roads layers. Make sure the Street Signs layer is selected as the active layer.**

2. **Resize the existing instance of the Street Signs symbol so it is an appropriate size for the overall map.**

   We used the Transform panel to scale the instance to 25% of its original size.

3. **Drag the instance onto the left end of Main Street (where the street name is already sketched).**

4. **Clone three instances of the scaled instance. Place an instance where each street name is indicated on the sketch.**

   Cloning an instance results in an additional instance of the symbol. All instances are linked to the original symbol.

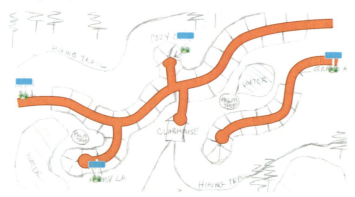

5. **In the Symbols panel, double-click the Street Signs symbol.**

   This opens a new artboard, called **symbol-editing mode**. The symbol artwork is the only thing visible.

6. **Create a point-type element with the text "Street Name", using 24-pt. ATC Maple Medium colored white, with centered paragraph alignment.**

7. **Position the type object directly over the rounded rectangle of the sign artwork.**

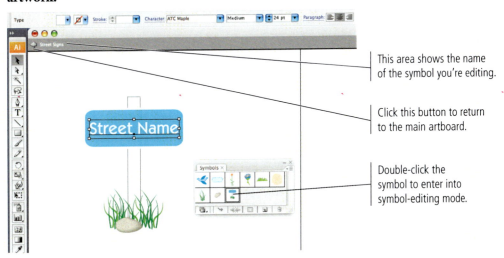

This area shows the name of the symbol you're editing.

Click this button to return to the main artboard.

Double-click the symbol to enter into symbol-editing mode.

8. **In the top-left corner of the screen, click the left arrow button to exit symbol-editing mode and return to the main artboard.**

   Notice that the new text element has been added to all four placed instances. As we mentioned, the advantage to using symbols is that all instances — whether 4 or 400 — reflect changes that you make only once.

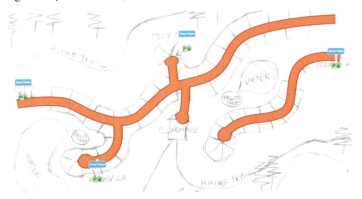

   The problem, of course, is that the streets are not all named "Street Name". To change the text on each individual road sign, you have to break the link from each instance to the symbol.

9. **Break the link between the main Street Signs symbol and each placed instance.**

   Once the links are broken, all the elements of the symbol artwork become a group in the main file.

10. **Change the text of each former symbol instance to identify the names of the roads in the map.**

   Abbreviate the name if necessary ("Ave." instead of "Avenue", for example) to make the road names fit on the signs.

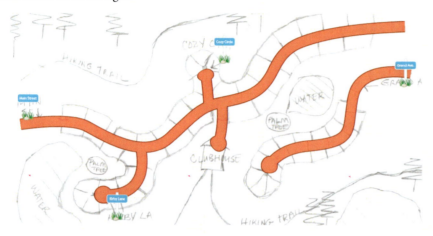

11. **Save the file and continue to the next exercise.**

Editing Symbols in Place

You can double-click any placed instance to enter a modified symbol-editing mode, called **editing in place**. Instead of seeing only the symbol artwork, you can see the entire file behind the instance you are editing. Changing an instance in this manner has the same effect as changing the main symbol — all other linked instances are also changed when you return to the main artboard.

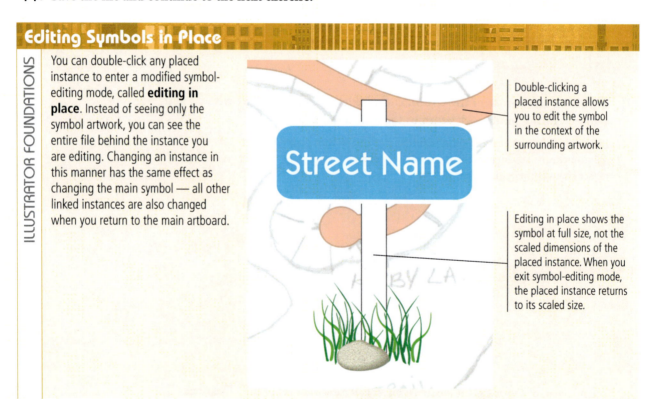

Double-clicking a placed instance allows you to edit the symbol in the context of the surrounding artwork.

Editing in place shows the symbol at full size, not the scaled dimensions of the placed instance. When you exit symbol-editing mode, the placed instance returns to its scaled size.

SPRAY SYMBOLS

The next part of this project is to create the hiking path and surrounding forest. The path requires another custom brush. Once the path is finished, you can use built-in nature symbols to create a nearly instant forest.

1. **With map.ai open, lock the Street Signs layer. Create a new layer named "Forest" at the top of the layer stack.**

2. **Choose the Symbol Sprayer tool from the Tools panel.**

   The Symbol Sprayer tool is used to spray multiple symbol instances onto the artboard. Other tools, nested under the Symbol Sprayer in the Tools panel, can be used to squeeze, spread, pinch, and otherwise modify the sprayed symbol instances.

3. **Click the Trees symbol in the Map Symbols library panel.**

4. **Press [to decrease or] to increase the size of the tool (and its cursor).**

   Brush size affects the Symbol Sprayer tool just as it does anything else — larger brush size results in larger symbol instances. We're using a large brush size to create the forest.

Note:

The Symbol Sprayer tool defaults to the last-used size.

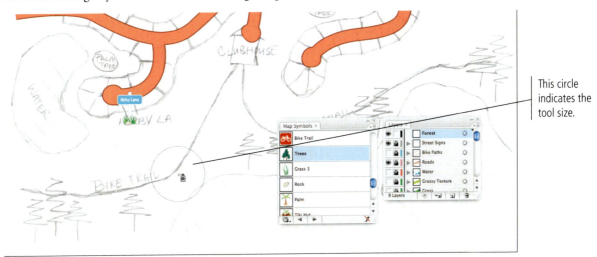

This circle indicates the tool size.

5. **Click directly above the top hiking trail and drag right, roughly following the shape of the hiking trail.**

   When you click and drag with the Symbol Sprayer tool, you create a **symbol set** — multiple instances of a single symbol that are treated as a single, cohesive unit.

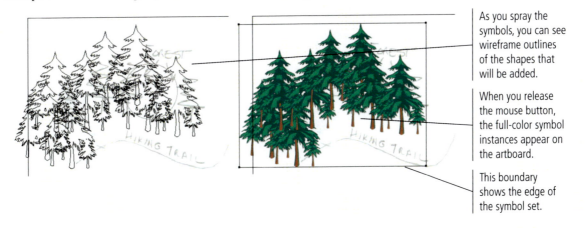

As you spray the symbols, you can see wireframe outlines of the shapes that will be added.

When you release the mouse button, the full-color symbol instances appear on the artboard.

This boundary shows the edge of the symbol set.

6. **Without deselecting the symbol set, add a few instances near the right side of the path.**

   By leaving the set selected, the new instances are added to the existing set.

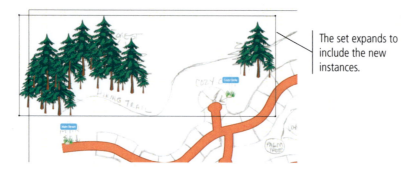

The set expands to include the new instances.

7. **Deselect the current symbol set.**

   If you don't deselect the active symbol set, clicking again will add more instances to the selected symbol set. You want to create a second symbol set, so you have to deselect the first set before clicking again with the Symbol Sprayer tool.

8. **Click below the lower bike path and drag right to the lake area of the sketch.**

9. **Without deselecting the set, add several additional instances in front of the lower path.**

10. **If necessary, use the Symbol Shifter tool (under the Symbol Sprayer tool) to move the instances within the sets. Make sure no trees are sprouting from the water.**

Note:

Press Option/Alt and drag with the Symbol Sprayer tool to delete symbol instances from a symbol set.

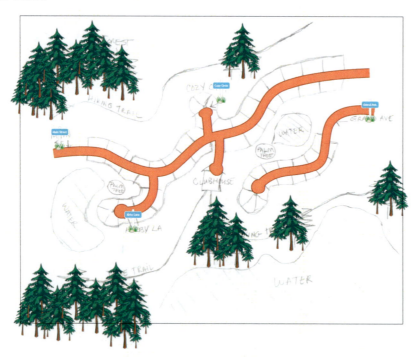

11. **Save the file and continue to the next exercise.**

Modifying Symbol Sets

When using sprayed symbols, many designs call for adjustments to individual components or instances within a symbol set. Without breaking the links between individual instances and the main symbol, a number of tools can be used to modify symbols within a set.

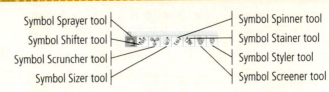

Symbol Sprayer tool	Symbol Spinner tool
Symbol Shifter tool	Symbol Stainer tool
Symbol Scruncher tool	Symbol Styler tool
Symbol Sizer tool	Symbol Screener tool

The **Symbol Shifter** tool pushes instances around the artboard. The tool only affects instances touched by the tool cursor.

The **Symbol Scruncher** tool causes the cursor to act as a magnet; all instances in the set are drawn toward the cursor when you click. Pressing Option/Alt reverses the effect, pushing instances away from the cursor.

The **Symbol Sizer** tool changes the size of instances within a set. Clicking causes instances under the cursor to grow. Option/Alt-clicking causes instances under the cursor to shrink.

The **Symbol Spinner** tool rotates instances under the cursor where you click. Dragging indicates the direction of the rotation.

The **Symbol Stainer** tool changes the hue of instances under the cursor using the defined fill color.

The **Symbol Screener** tool increases the opacity of instances under the cursor. Press Option/Alt to decrease instance opacity.

The **Symbol Style** tool allows you to apply a graphic style to symbol instances.

Symbolism Tool Options

Double-clicking any of the symbolism tools in the Tools panel opens the Symbolism Tools Options dialog box.

Diameter reflects the tool's current brush size.

Intensity determines the rate of change when modifying symbol instances.

Symbol Set Density creates more tightly packed (higher values) or loosely packed (lower values) instances in the symbol set.

Method determines how the symbol modifier tools (all but the Symbol Sprayer and Symbol Shifter) adjust symbol instances.

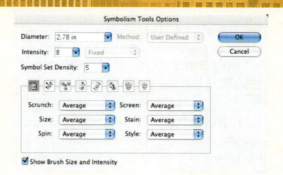

- Average smoothes out values in symbol instances.
- User Defined adjusts instances in relation to the position of the cursor.
- Random modifies instances randomly under the cursor.

If the Symbol Sprayer tool is selected in the middle of the dialog box, you can control a variety of options related to how new symbol instances are added to symbol sets; each option has two possible choices:

- **Average** adds new symbols with the average value of existing symbol instances within the brush radius. For example, in an area where the average existing instance is rotated by 10°, new instances will be rotated by 10°.
- **User Defined** applies specific values for each parameter, primarily based on the original symbol size, mouse direction, and current color settings.

If the Symbol Sizer is selected, you have two additional options.

- Proportional Resizing keeps the shape of each symbol instance uniform as you resize.
- Resizing Affects Density moves symbol instances away from each other when they are scaled up and moves them toward each other when they are scaled down.

If the **Show Brush Size and Intensity** option is checked, the cursor reflects the tool diameter.

 ADD THE REMAINING SYMBOLS

Much of the remaining artwork can be created using symbols. After you place these components, you can move on to the next stage and finish the artwork.

1. **With map.ai open, lock and hide the Forest layer. Create a new layer named "Amenities" at the top of the layer stack.**

2. **Using the symbols in the Map Symbols library:**
   - **Place an instance of the Tiki Hut symbol where the sketch indicates the club house.**
   - **Place instances of the Palm symbol where the sketch indicates.**
   - **Place an instance of the Playground symbol to the immediate right of the clubhouse.**
   - **Place an instance of the Swimming symbol near the smallest pond.**
   - **Place instances of the Hiking Trail symbol on the upper and lower trails.**
   - **Place an instance of the Bike Trail symbol somewhere along the lower trail.**
   - **Place instances of the Picnic Area symbol near the two ponds.**

3. Create another new layer named "Properties" and position the layer below the Roads layer in the layer stack.

4. Place an instance of the Home Lots symbol on the Properties layer. Use the Sketch layer as a guide for correctly positioning the symbol.

5. Create a new layer named "Houses" at the top of the layer stack.

6. Place an instance of the House Blue Roof symbol on each lot along Grand Avenue (as indicated on the "Properties" layer).

7. Place instances of the Red Flag symbol on each lot along Main Street and the connecting roads.

Note:

You might want to lock the Properties layer while you place the house and flag instances.

8. Save the file and continue to the next exercise.

 **REPLACE SYMBOLS**

Your clients stated that they want to be able to easily update the map to reflect houses that have been sold and properties that have already been reserved. Symbols make this task easy because you can quickly change the symbol associated with individual placed instances.

1. **With map.ai open, make sure nothing is selected in the layout.**

2. **Using either selection tool, Shift-click to select the Red Flag instances on the four lots nearest the clubhouse and the three lots at the end of Kirby Lane.**

3. **In the Map Symbols panel, click the Yellow Flag symbol once to copy it into the Symbols panel for the map file.**

4. **Click the House Red Roof symbol in the Map Symbols panel to add it to the main Symbols panel.**

5. **In the Control bar, open the Replace menu and click the Yellow Flag symbol.**

    As soon as you select the new symbol, the selected instances change to the new symbol.

Note:

The Replace menu only shows symbols in the current file's symbol library.

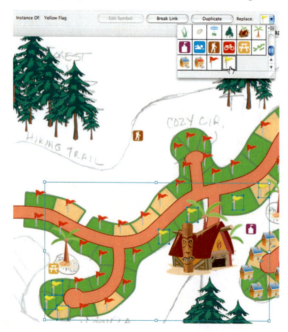

6. **Select the first five house symbols on the north end of Grand Avenue and the two instances on the tan lots on the south side of the road.**

7. In the Replace menu on the Control bar, choose the House Red Roof symbol.

Again, the selected symbol instances immediately change to reflect the new symbol you chose in the Replace menu. If you have multiple variations of an object — such as houses available and houses sold — the ability to replace symbol instances is a tremendous time saver, enabling you revise the file quickly and easily.

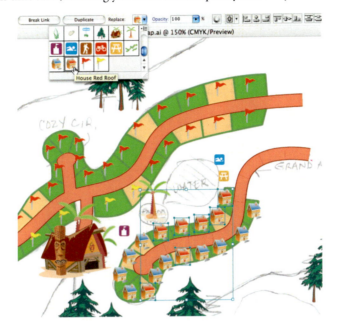

8. Save the file and continue to the final exercise.

 CREATE A CLIPPING MASK

For the last step of this project, you need to save the file so it can be used in other applications. Part of this process requires "finishing off" the edges so that no pieces — such as the trees or the road ends — hang past the edges. Rather than manually cutting your artwork to pieces, you can square off the artwork by creating a mask to hide the elements you don't want to see. Once you've created the mask, you need to save the file in several different formats so it can be used in a variety of applications.

A **clipping mask** is an object that masks other artwork; only those areas within the clipping mask shape remain visible. To create a clipping mask, however, all of the objects that you want to clip should to be part of the same layer as the masking object. Before you flatten the artwork, however, you should make all necessary final changes, and save an archive copy of the layered file so you can more easily make changes later.

1. **With map.ai open, delete the Sketch layer. Make sure all other layers are unlocked and visible.**

2. **Create a new layer named "Mask" at the top of the layer stack.**

3. **Draw a rectangle that is 7″ high by 9″ wide with a black stroke and no fill.**

Note:

*The clipping mask and the masked objects are called a **clipping set**.*

Note:

*You can create a clipping mask for objects on different layers, as long as the layers are visible and unlocked. When you apply the Clipping Mask>Create command, however, all affected objects are automatically copied to the layer that contains the mask object (called **flattening**).*

4. **Align the rectangle to the horizontal and vertical centers of the artboard.**

After you create a clipping mask with this rectangle, objects outside the rectangle's edges will no longer be visible.

5. **Make sure all of your artwork is positioned correctly:**

- If necessary, extend the ends of the road and path artwork so all paths and roads end outside the rectangle edges.

- Make sure the street signs fall entirely within the boundaries of the rectangle on the Mask layer.

- Make sure none of the red or yellow flag instances obscures a street sign.

- Make sure enough trees fall inside the rectangle's edge to create the illusion of a forest. If not, use the Symbol Sprayer tool to add more instances of the Trees symbol to the existing symbol sets.

- If any trees appear to be growing out of the water, use the Symbol Shifter tool to move them.

6. **Create another layer named "Legend" at the top of the layer stack (above the Mask layer).**

7. **Place the file Map Legend.eps (from the RF_Illustrator>Realty folder) onto the layer. Center the artwork horizontally to the artboard, and align the vertical center of the placed artwork to the rectangle on the Mask layer.**

8. **Save the file as "map_final_layered.ai" in your WIP>Realty folder.**

   If you see a message asking you about saving spot colors containing transparencies, click OK and accept the default settings. You'll learn about transparency in Project 6.

9. **In the Layers panel, select all but the Legend layer.**

   The map legend is not going to be clipped by the mask, so it can remain on its own layer.

10. **In the Layers panel options menu, choose Merge Selected.**

    You can merge only selected layers, or you can use the Flatten Artwork command to combine all layers in the selected file.

11. **Lock the Legend layer, and then choose Select>All.**

    When you create a clipping mask, the topmost selected object will be the masking shape; all selected objects below the mask shape will be masked.

    When you merge (or flatten) layers, the objects on each layer are combined into a single layer; the relative stacking order from the previous layer stack is maintained. In this case, the Mask layer was at the top of the layer stack, so the rectangle that was on the previous Mask layer is still the topmost object on the combined layer.

12. Choose Object>Clipping Mask>Make.

When you make a clipping mask, the masking object automatically converts to having no fill and no stroke. You can change these attributes after making the mask; if you apply a fill to a masking shape, the fill is added behind the objects that are masked.

Note:

Clipping masks do not permanently affect the artwork. You can remove the mask by selecting the mask shape and choosing Object>Clipping Mask>Release.

13. Save the file as "map_final_flat.ai" in your WIP>Realty folder.

Native Illustrator files can be placed into Adobe InDesign layouts, as well as other Illustrator files.

14. Choose File>Save As. Save another version of the map file using the Illustrator EPS format. Name this file "map_final_flat.eps".

Some applications — specifically QuarkXPress — can't import native Illustrator files. To make the map available for QuarkXPress users, you have to save a version in the EPS format.

Note:

Refer to Project 3 for information on the options in the EPS Options and PDF Options dialog boxes.

15. Choose File>Save As. Save another version of the map file using the Illustrator PDF format for high-resolution printing requirements. Name this file "map_final_flat.pdf".

In case you run into an application that can't manage native Illustrator or EPS files, PDF is almost universally accepted.

16. Close the file.

Summary

This project incorporated skills that will be useful in many different types of Illustrator projects — specifically, managing different types of assets (swatches, patterns, and brushes), as well as accessing built-in and custom libraries and creating your own custom assets. When you think through a project and plan your work in advance, these skills can save significant amounts of time and effort.

Some of the planning work for this project had been completed by the art director — including creating the icons for different elements of the development — and approved by the client in an earlier project meeting. Rather than taking the time to recreate those elements, or even to copy and paste the different pieces into your map file, saving the artwork as symbols made the entire process much faster and cleaner; as you might have realized, it's nearly impossible to *accidentally* edit the shapes that make up a symbol instance.

Using symbols, you have effectively solved your client's problem by creating a map that can be easily modified to indicate new sales and reservations. When Phase 2 of the development begins, you can even convert the "Homesite" symbols (the flags) to "Home" symbols to show where houses have already been built.

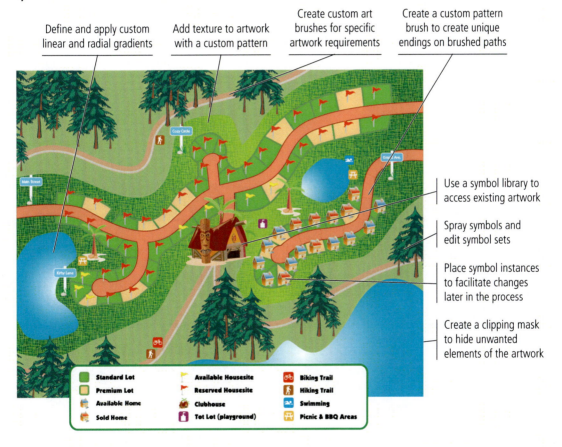

Define and apply custom linear and radial gradients

Add texture to artwork with a custom pattern

Create custom art brushes for specific artwork requirements

Create a custom pattern brush to create unique endings on brushed paths

Use a symbol library to access existing artwork

Spray symbols and edit symbol sets

Place symbol instances to facilitate changes later in the process

Create a clipping mask to hide unwanted elements of the artwork

Portfolio Builder Project 4

The Los Angeles parks and recreation director has hired you to create an illustrated, user-friendly map of the Griffith Park recreation complex.

❏ Download the park map from the master plan document (see the client's comments to the right) to use as a template.

❏ Use drawing techniques to create the basic park layout, including roads, trails, and defined paths.

❏ Create or find symbols to identify the different facilities and services.

❏ Add artwork, images, and color however you prefer to identify the different venues and attractions throughout the park.

"Griffith Park is one of the largest public green spaces in the Western United States. The park is home to a number of famous attractions, including the Griffith Observatory, Greek Theater, and the L.A. Zoo. It also offers equestrian trails, bike and hiking trails, and golf courses, as well as swimming, camping, concerts, and a host of other activities.

"As you can guess from all of these available activities and attractions, the park is a very large place. We currently have a detailed topographical map from our master plan document, but I'd like something that is more attractive to tourists. I want to create an attractive, colorful, printed brochure that visitors can purchase for a nominal fee at park entrances and facilities, so they can easily find what they're looking for.

"I don't have the actual map file. Can you access it on the Internet? I can't remember the address, but if you do a Google search on 'Griffith Park Map', it comes up as one of the first results."

Letterfold Brochure

Your client is a real estate developer specializing in affordable homes in gated suburban communities. The developer wants to create a mailing brochure that can be sent to real estate agents and prospective buyers, announcing a new community being built in central Florida.

This project incorporates the following skills:

❏ Creating templates for a letterfold brochure that meet production requirements for folds

❏ Importing client-supplied text and controlling the flow of text across multiple frames

❏ Working with styles to automate repetitive text formatting tasks

❏ Correcting typographic problems such as baseline alignment, smart punctuation, orphans, and widows

❏ Checking for and correcting spelling errors in the context of a specific layout

❏ Placing images to suit the unique needs and possibilities of a folding brochure

I really don't have that much input on what the flyer should look like — you know better then I what an effective brochure should look like. I have the text and a few pictures that I want to include; you can modify those pictures as necessary to better fit the overall project.

A lot of people design folding documents incorrectly. Some people use a six-page layout with each page the size of the final folded job; other people use two pages, each one divided into three equal "columns." In both cases, all the panels on the job are the exact same width — which is wrong.

Paper has inherent thickness; any panel that folds "in" to the other panels needs to be smaller than the other panels. In the case of a letterfold brochure such as the one you're designing here, the inside panel needs to be 1/16″ smaller than the other panels.

Different types of folding documents also have different facing- or non-facing-page requirements. For a letterfold, the job needs to be set up on two separate documents with guides and margins that mirror each other. One page has the front panel, back panel, and the outside of the folding flap; the other page has the three inside panels.

The last item to remember is that the brochure will be a self-mailer; the back panel needs to be left blank, with only the return address in the upper-left corner.

To complete this project, you will:

- ❑ Define folding guides and margins as required for a folding document

- ❑ Create Illustrator template files so you can access common layouts again later

- ❑ Import client-supplied copy into an existing text area

- ❑ Define paragraph and character styles to simplify formatting across multiple text elements and files

- ❑ Manage the flow of copy across multiple text frames

- ❑ Replace standard punctuation with smart punctuation

- ❑ Control hyphenation and line spacing

- ❑ Check spelling in a layout

- ❑ Place images based on the panel position in the final folded piece

Stage 1 Creating Documents that Fold

When working with folding (multi-panel) documents, many people mistakenly assume that the trim size of the job is the size it appears after folding. In fact, the trim size of a folded document is actually the size of the sheet before it's folded. In this section, you learn how to properly set up multi-panel documents that fold in a variety of ways.

There are two basic principles to remember when dealing with documents that fold:

- Paper has thickness. The thicker the paper, the more allowance you need to plan for the fold.

- Folding machines are mechanical devices. They process large amounts of material and are accurate to about 0.0125 inch. Paper sometimes shifts as it flows through the machine's paper path, just as it can in a laser printer or photocopier.

In the following illustration, a document has one fold — a smaller panel that folds over to cover half of the inside of the brochure. Fold marks on the outside layout have to mirror the inside of the brochure so that, when folded, the two sides line up properly.

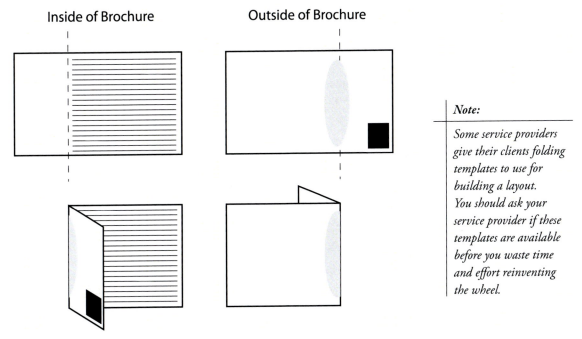

Inside of Brochure   **Outside of Brochure**

Note:

Some service providers give their clients folding templates to use for building a layout. You should ask your service provider if these templates are available before you waste time and effort reinventing the wheel.

It is important to consider the output process when planning a job with documents that are not just a single sheet of standard-size paper, including documents with multiple pages folded one or more times, or other non-standard page sizes. The mechanics of commercial printing require specific allowances for cutting, folding, and other finishing processes.

You should note that the issues presented here have little to do with the subjective elements of design. Layout and page geometry are governed by specific variables, including mechanical limitations in the production process. These principles are rules, not suggestions. If you don't leave adequate margins, for example, elements of your design will be cut off or won't align properly from one page to the next. It really won't matter how good a design looks on your monitor if it's cut off the edge of a printed page.

Basic Types of Folds

There are several standard types of folded documents, each with specific formulas for setting up the layout.

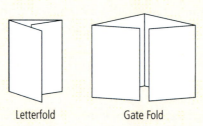

Letterfold   Gate Fold

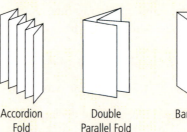

Accordion   Double   Barrel Fold
Fold   Parallel Fold

Letterfold (often incorrectly called "trifold" because it results in three panels) brochures can be printed at any size. There are three panels to a side and two folds; letterfold brochures should be created with facing pages because the two sides of the sheet need to mirror each other.

The formula for creating a letterfold brochure typically requires the panel that folds in to be 1/16" narrower than the two outside panels. (Ask your service provider if 1/16" allowance is enough based on the type of paper you're using.) Half of the area removed from the inside panel (1/32") is added to each of the outside two panels.

Trim size ÷ 3 = Starting panel size

Fold-in panel = Starting panel size – 1/16"

Outside panels = Starting panel size + 1/32"

Gate folds result in a four-panel document. The paper is folded in half, and then each half is folded in half toward the center so the two ends of the paper meet at the center fold. The formula for creating a gate fold is similar to the formula for the letterfold brochure; the panels that fold in are 1/16" narrower than the two outside panels. Gate-fold brochures can be created with non-facing pages.

Trim size ÷ 4 = Starting panel size

Fold-in panels = Starting panel size – 1/32"

Outside panels = Starting panel size + 1/32"

Accordion folds — a comparatively unusual format — can have as many panels as you prefer. When it has six panels (three on each side), it's often referred to as a "Z-fold" because it looks like the letter Z. Because the panels don't fold into one another, an accordion-fold document has panels of consistent width. Accordion-fold brochures can be created with non-facing pages.

Paper Size ÷ Number of Panels = Panel Size

Double-parallel folds are commonly used for eight-panel rack brochures (such as those you often find in a hotel or travel agency). Again, the panels on the inside are 1/16" narrower than the outside panels. This type of fold uses facing pages because the margins need to line up on the front and back sides of the sheet. Double parallel-fold brochures should be created with facing pages.

Trim size ÷ 4 = Starting panel size

Outside panels = Starting panel size + 1/32"

Fold-in panels = Starting panel size – 1/32"

Barrel folds (also called **roll folds**) are perhaps the most common fold for 14 × 8.5" brochures. The two outside panels are full size, and each successive panel is 1/16" narrower than the previous one. Barrel-fold brochures should be created with facing pages.

Trim size ÷ 4 = Starting panel size

Outside panels = Starting panel size + 1/16"

Fold-in panel 1 = Starting panel size – 1/32"

Fold-in panel 2 = Starting panel size – 3/32"

On the outside of a letterfold brochure, the left panel is the fold-in panel, and it is slightly narrower than the other two panels. On the inside of the brochure, the right panel is the fold-in panel.

Because the panels for a letterfold brochure are different sizes, the inside of the brochure has to be a reflection of the outside. Illustrator does not support multiple pages in a single file, so you are going to create a separate file for each page (the inside and the outside) of the brochure.

1. **Create a new letter-size document named "Letterfold Inside" using landscape orientation with the units set to inches. Use CMYK color mode and 300-ppi resolution.**

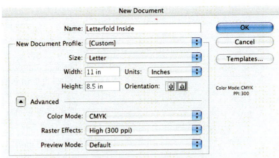

Note:

Before completing this project, copy the Estates folder from the WIP folder on your Resource CD to your WIP folder where you are saving your work. When you save files for this project, you will save them in your WIP>Estates folder.

2. **Click the Rectangle tool anywhere on the page. Using the Rectangle dialog box, create a rectangle 10.5″ wide by 8″ high.**

   This rectangle is going to act as a guide for the external margins of the brochure template. You need a 1/4″ margin on each edge of the document, so:

   11″ (document width) − 1/4″ (left margin) − 1/4″ (right margin) = 10.5″ width

   8 1/2″ (document height) − 1/4″ (top margin) − 1/4″ (bottom margin) = 8″ height

3. **Using the Align panel, activate the Align to Artboard option, and then align the center of the rectangle both vertically and horizontally.**

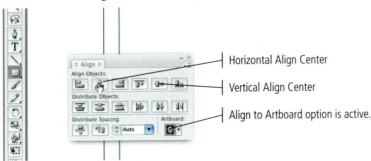

Horizontal Align Center

Vertical Align Center

Align to Artboard option is active.

4. **With the rectangle still selected, choose View>Guide>Make Guides to turn the rectangle into a guide.**

5. **Repeat the process from Steps 2–4 to create a rectangle guide that is 1/8″ larger than the page size on each side (11.25″ wide by 8.75″ high).**

   When an element is supposed to print all the way to the trim edge, that element needs to extend beyond the edge by at least 1/8″ to accommodate the mechanical variations in the trimming process; this process is called **bleeding**. The distance an element has to bleed (in this case, 1/8″) is called the **bleed allowance**.

   The rectangle guide you're creating in this step serves as the bleed guide for this layout — where elements need to extend on the press sheet before the job is trimmed and folded.

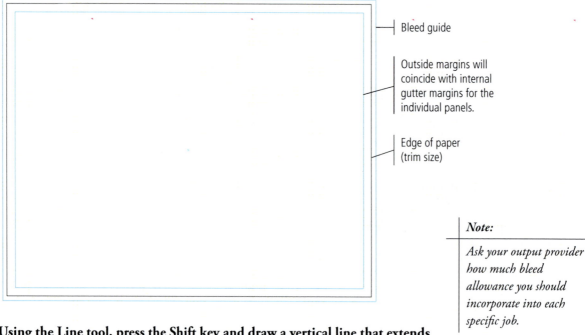

Bleed guide

Outside margins will coincide with internal gutter margins for the individual panels.

Edge of paper (trim size)

6. **Using the Line tool, press the Shift key and draw a vertical line that extends from the top bleed guide to the bottom bleed guide.**

7. **Use the Transform panel to position the line at exactly 3.687″ from the left edge of the Artboard.**

   Because this file is the inside of the brochure, the right panel is the fold-in panel. It needs to be slightly narrower than the other two panels. This line is the first of the two fold guides, positioned exactly where it needs to be in relation to the overall trim size.

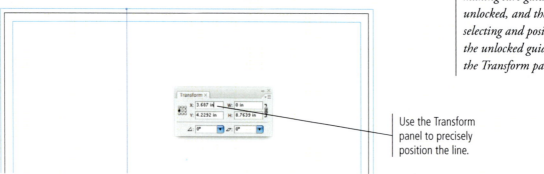

Use the Transform panel to precisely position the line.

Note:

Press Command/Control-5 to create a guide from any selected object. Add the Shift key to release all guides that have been created from objects. (This is an all-or-nothing action. You can't release a single custom guide; you have to release all of them at once.)

Note:

Ask your output provider how much bleed allowance you should incorporate into each specific job.

Note:

You could accomplish the same result by dragging guides from the ruler, making sure guides are unlocked, and then selecting and positioning the unlocked guides with the Transform panel.

8. **Clone the vertical line and position the clone at 7.375".**

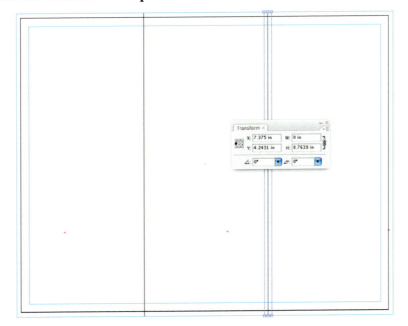

Note:

The same X and Y position fields are also available in the Control bar.

9. **Select both lines and convert them to guides.**

These two guides result in the right panel being 3.625" and the other two panels being 3.687".

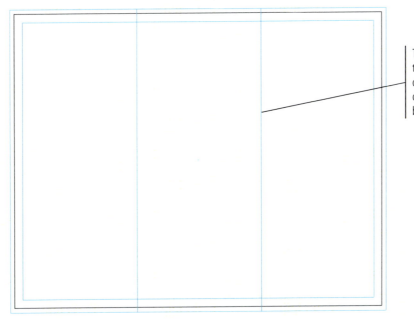

These guides mark the location of folds, defining the position of each panel in the brochure.

10. **Save the file as "Letterfold Inside.ai" in your WIP>Estates folder and continue to the next exercise.**

CREATE FOLDING MARGINS AND SLUGS

Now that you have the folds marked in the layout, you need to define margins around those folds so important design elements (specifically, text) do not get lost in the document fold. You're also going to add **slugs** (non-printing text outside the page area) that remind you which panel plays what role in the finished piece.

1. **With Letterfold Inside.ai open, make sure the rulers are visible (View> Show Rulers).**

2. **Drag the zero point from the intersection of the two rulers to the first folding guide.**

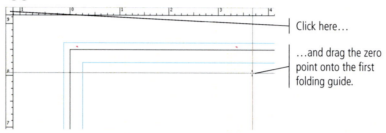

Click here...

...and drag the zero point onto the first folding guide.

When you release the mouse button, the zero point changes to reflect the new position that you defined by dragging.

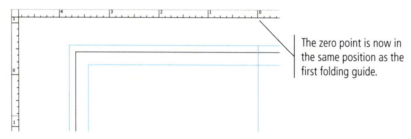

The zero point is now in the same position as the first folding guide.

3. **Click the vertical ruler and drag a guide 1/4″ to the left of the new zero point (the first folding guide).**

4. **Choose View>Guides>Lock Guides to toggle off that feature.**

If the menu command does not show a checkmark, the guides are already unlocked in your file.

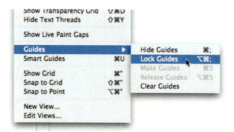

5. **Using the Selection tool, click the page guide you created in Step 3. Look at the Transform panel.**

   When guides are unlocked, you can select and modify them. The Transform panel allows you to place guides at precise positions.

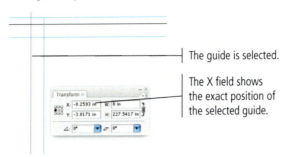

The guide is selected.

The X field shows the exact position of the selected guide.

6. **If the X position is not exactly −0.25″, highlight the field and change the guide position to X: −0.25″.**

7. **Using the same method, place a second guide exactly 1/4″ to the right of the folding guide.**

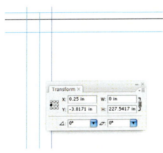

8. **Move the zero point to the second folding guide, and then place guides at 1/4″ on either side of the second folding guide.**

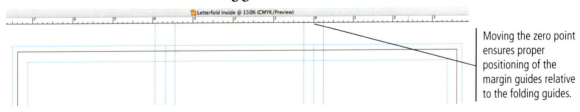

Moving the zero point ensures proper positioning of the margin guides relative to the folding guides.

9. **Double-click the zero-point (at the intersection of the two rulers) to return the zero point to its default location (the bottom-left corner of the page).**

10. **Create an area text object above the first panel (outside the bleed guide). In the text area, type "Inside Panel 1".**

These text areas are for your use while designing the piece; they will not be included in the output, and they should not interfere with the actual design area.

11. **Clone (Option/Alt-drag) the text object, and place the clone above the second panel. Change the text above the second panel to "Inside Panel 2".**

12. **Clone the text object again, and place the third copy above the right panel. Change the text to "Inside Panel 3 – fold in".**

13. **Using the Line tool, create a 1-point black dashed vertical line about 1/2" high, with 3-pt. dash and gap values. Position the line above the first folding guide, directly outside the bleed guide.**

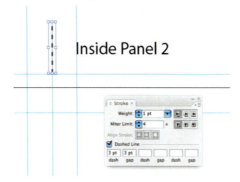

14. **Clone the fold mark and place the clone above the second folding guide.**

15. Select both dashed lines. Clone the lines and place the clones directly below the bleed guide at the bottom of the page.

If you press Shift while you clone the lines, you can drag down and the clones will be positioned exactly below the original lines (at the same X position).

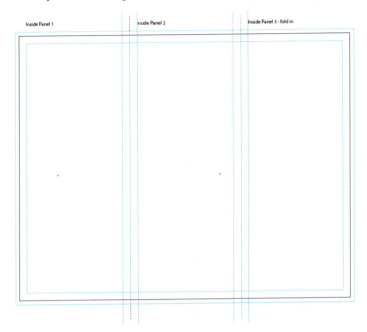

16. In the Layers panel, rename Layer 1 as "Guides" and lock the layer.

17. Choose File>Save As. With your WIP>Estates folder selected as the target, choose Illustrator Template in the Format menu, and then click Save.

Since you have taken the time to properly set up these folding guides, and because letterfolds are fairly common job formats, you are saving your work as a template so you can access these same folds whenever you need them.

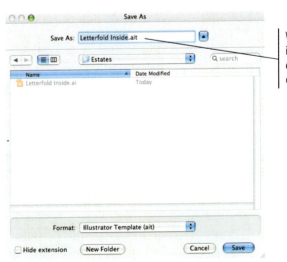

When you choose Template in the Format menu, the extension is automatically changed to ".ait."

Note:

Templates are a key time-saver when you need to create many similar files. Illustrator includes a number of pre-designed templates; look for them in the Adobe Illustrator CS3>Cool Extras>Templates folder (wherever your application is stored on your hard drive).

18. Close the file and continue to the next exercise.

If you look at a flat representation of each side of the brochure, the fold-in (short) panel is on opposite sides of the layout. Because of this positioning, the two sides of a letterfold brochure need to mirror each other — and the folding guides for the outside need to be placed such that the short panel is in the correct location relative to the short panel position on the inside of the brochure.

Inside of brochure

Outside of brochure

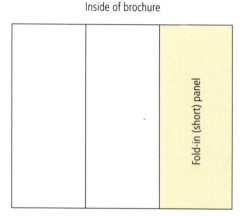

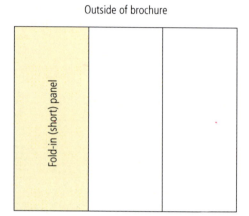

1. **Open Letterfold Inside.ait from your WIP>Estates folder.**

   When you open a template file, you are actually opening a copy of the template with the name "Untitled." This prevents you from accidentally overwriting the original template.

   The new file (created from the template) already has all of the necessary elements. You simply need to adjust their positions.

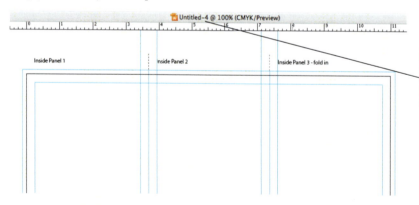

This number indicates how many new files have been created since launching the application.

2. **Unlock the Guides layer.**

   You won't be able to move the guides while they are on a locked layer.

3. **Using the Selection tool, click to select the first folding guide and the two folding marks (the dashed lines) for that guide.**

   Make sure you click each element to select it instead of dragging a selection marquee. If you drag to select the guide and folding marks, you will also select — and move — the margin and bleed guides, which you don't want to do.

Note:

You can overwrite a template by manually typing the same file name as the original template when you save the file. You will be asked to confirm that you're sure you want to replace the existing file.

4. In the Transform panel, change the X position of the selected objects to 3.625".

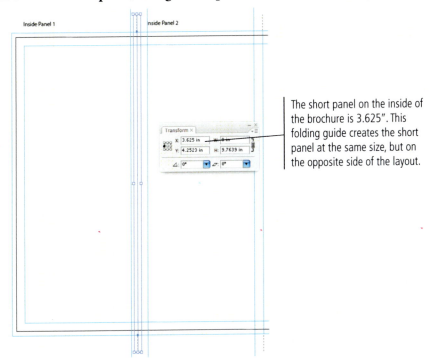

The short panel on the inside of the brochure is 3.625". This folding guide creates the short panel at the same size, but on the opposite side of the layout.

5. Change the zero point to match the repositioned folding guide, and then change the two margin guides for that fold to be exactly 1/4" from both sides of the folding guide.

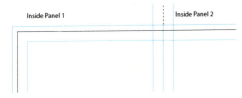

6. Restore the zero point to the default location.

7. Select the second folding guide and the associated folding marks, and then change their X position to 7.312".

8. Using the same method as in Step 5, move the margin guides for that fold to be 1/4" from both ides of the fold.

9. Restore the zero point to the default location.

10. Change the text above each panel, as shown in the following image.

11. **Lock the Guides layer.**

12. **Choose File>Save As. With your WIP>Estates folder selected as the destination, change the file name to "Letterfold Outside" and choose Illustrator Template in the Format menu.**

13. **Click Save to create the second template.**

14. **Close the file, and then continue to the next stage of the project.**

Stage 2 Managing Imported Text

Completing this project involves combining and controlling a number of client-supplied images and text files into the layouts you defined in the first stage of the project.

 ## IMPORT TEXT FOR THE INSIDE PANELS

Preparing for the text elements simply means bringing in the two text files the client gave you, and then cutting them up so you can place the correct pieces of text in the correct columns on the templates.

1. **Create a new file by opening the Letterfold Inside.ait template from your WIP>Estates folder.**

2. **Add new layers named "Text" and "Graphics" above the existing (locked) Guides layer.**

3. **With the Text layer selected, use the Type tool to draw an area text element within the margins of Inside Panel 1.**

When you use the Type tool to draw a text area, the tiny horizontal line at the bottom of the cursor is the actual starting and ending point for the resulting shape.

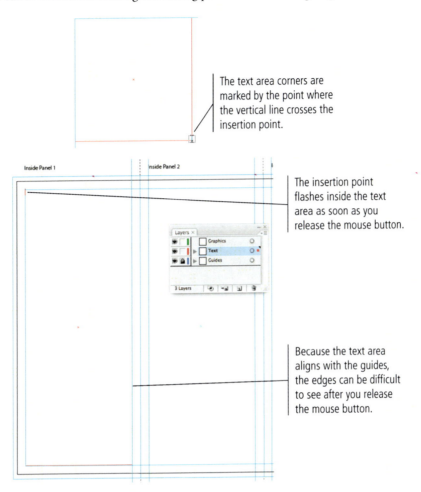

The text area corners are marked by the point where the vertical line crosses the insertion point.

The insertion point flashes inside the text area as soon as you release the mouse button.

Because the text area aligns with the guides, the edges can be difficult to see after you release the mouse button.

4. **Choose File>Place. Navigate to the file named Inside.doc in the RF_Illustrator>Estates folder and click OK.**

When you import a Microsoft Word file into Illustrator, the application asks how you want to handle the formatting saved in the file. In addition to the basic document text, you can also choose to include special options such as a table of contents, footnotes, and an index.

5. **In the Microsoft Word Options dialog box, make sure the Remove Text Formatting option is not checked and click OK.**

If the Remove Text Formatting option is checked, the imported copy will be formatted with the Illustrator default type settings only. Although you will typically reformat most imported text, it's a good idea to import the text with formatting so you can review the editorial priority of the copy (i.e., where titles and headings appear).

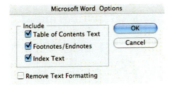

6. **Review the information in the Font Problems dialog box, and then click OK.**

For the text to display properly with the formatting that was applied in the Word file, Illustrator needs access to the same fonts that were used in the Word file. If you don't have the same fonts available on your system, you might see a Font Problems dialog box listing the missing fonts.

This dialog box appears more often than not when you import a Microsoft Word file. In many cases, you can simply dismiss it because you will replace the original fonts with ones more suited to professional graphic design.

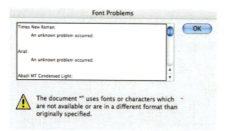

The text from the Word file flows into the text area (called a **text frame**) where the insertion point was flashing. The small red symbol at the bottom of the frame is called the **overset text icon**; this icon tells you the story includes more text than will fit in the available space.

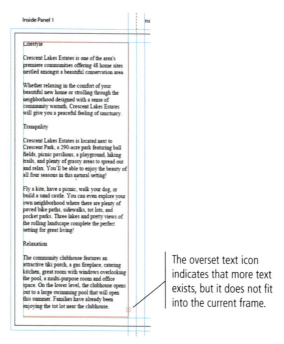

The overset text icon indicates that more text exists, but it does not fit into the current frame.

7. **Choose File>Save As. With your WIP>Estates folder as the target destination, change the file name to "Estates Inside.ai", and leave the Format menu at Adobe Illustrator Document. Click Save.**

Now that you are incorporating project-specific content, you want to save the file as a document, rather than a template.

8. **In the Illustrator Options dialog box, accept the default settings and click OK.**

9. **Continue to the next exercise.**

Using the Find Font Dialog Box

You can use the Find Font dialog box (Type>Find Font) to replace one font with another throughout a layout. The top half of the dialog box lists every font used in the file; missing fonts are surrounded by chevrons in the list.

The lower half of the dialog box defaults to show the same list as the top half. You can also choose System in the menu to list all fonts currently active on your computer.

If you click the Change or Change All button, the font selected in the top list will be replaced with the font selected in the bottom list. You can also use the Find button to locate instances of the font selected in the top list.

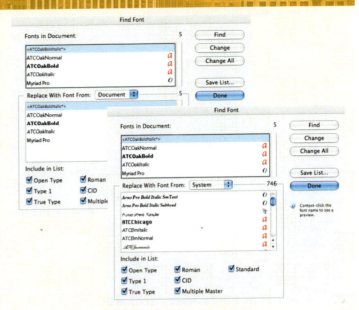

THREAD MULTIPLE TEXT FRAMES

When a story includes more text than the current frame can accommodate, you have to decide how to solve the problem. In some cases, when only one or two words are overset, minor changes in text formatting will create the additional space you need. If you have the ability to edit the text (which you usually don't), changing a word or two might also help.

When you can't edit the client-supplied text, and when you have a considerable amount of overset text (as in this project), the only solution is to add more space for the text. Here again, you have two alternatives: cut some of the text and paste it into another frame, or link the existing frame to one or more additional frames (called **threading**) so the story can flow through multiple areas.

The story you're working with in this project is intended to fill the first panel, as well as the top of the second and third panels. In this case, it's better to thread multiple text frames instead of cutting the story into multiple pieces.

1. **With Estates Inside.ai open, click the overset text icon with the Selection tool.**

   The overset text icon appears in a small rectangle, which is the **out port** of the selected text frame. By clicking the out port of a frame (regardless of whether overset text exists), you can direct the flow of text into another text frame.

   When you click an out port with an overset text icon, the cursor changes to the loaded text cursor. You can use that cursor to click any other text frame, or click and drag to create a new frame in the same thread.

Note:

You can use the frame out ports to link empty frames so when you place text into the frame, it will automatically flow from one frame to another in the chain.

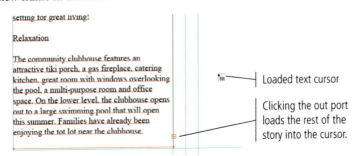

Loaded text cursor

Clicking the out port loads the rest of the story into the cursor.

2. **Using the loaded text cursor, click and drag to create a new text area in the top section of the middle panel.**

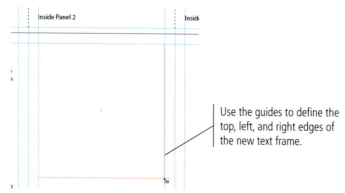

Use the guides to define the top, left, and right edges of the new text frame.

When you release the mouse button, the new frame automatically fills with text in the loaded cursor.

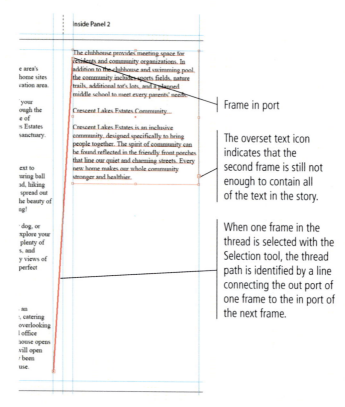

Frame in port

The overset text icon indicates that the second frame is still not enough to contain all of the text in the story.

When one frame in the thread is selected with the Selection tool, the thread path is identified by a line connecting the out port of one frame to the in port of the next frame.

Note:

If you've had prior experience with page layout software such as Adobe InDesign or QuarkXPress, you might already be familiar with the concept of threading text from one frame to another.

3. **Click the second frame's out port to load the cursor with the rest of the story, and then click and drag to create a third frame at the top of the third panel.**

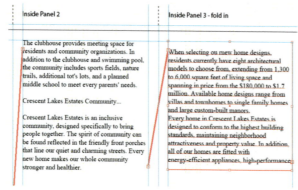

4. **Drag the bottom-center handle of the third frame down until all text in the story is visible.**

You will know the entire story is showing when the overset text icon is no longer visible in the frame's out port.

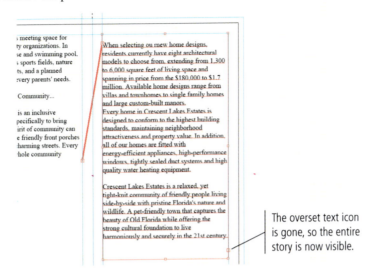

The overset text icon is gone, so the entire story is now visible.

5. **Save the file and continue to the next exercise.**

 ## WORK WITH HIDDEN CHARACTERS

Your layout now includes a story that is threaded across three separate text frames. The only obvious formatting is extra space between paragraphs. You can identify the intended headings (the short paragraphs), but the layout lacks the polish and finesse of a professional design.

1. **With Estates Inside.ai open, choose Type>Show Hidden Characters.**

Hidden characters identify spaces, paragraph returns, and other non-printing characters. It can be helpful to view these hidden characters, especially when you are working with long blocks of text.

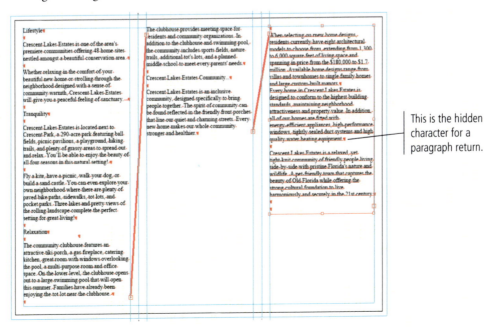

This is the hidden character for a paragraph return.

When you work with client-supplied text, you will frequently find each paragraph separated by two (or more) paragraph returns. This kind of formatting creates the visual effect of space between paragraphs, but it also adds one more element that needs to be controlled in the story. Because Illustrator's typographic controls allow you to easily change the spacing of paragraphs, these double paragraph returns are unnecessary and should be deleted.

Unfortunately, Illustrator's Find and Replace function is very limited; unlike InDesign, you can't use that utility to search for a paragraph return character. In other words, you have to manually delete the extra paragraph returns.

2. **Place the insertion point in the first empty paragraph in the left panel, and then press Delete/Backspace.**

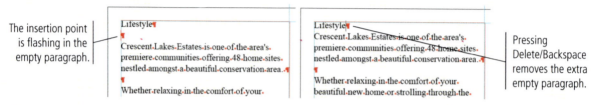

The insertion point is flashing in the empty paragraph.

Pressing Delete/Backspace removes the extra empty paragraph.

ILLUSTRATOR FOUNDATIONS

Using the Find and Replace Dialog Box

Finding and replacing text is a function common to many applications, including Illustrator. Illustrator's Find and Replace utility (Edit>Find and Replace) is fairly straightforward, offering the ability to search for and change text in a layout, including a limited number of special characters and options.

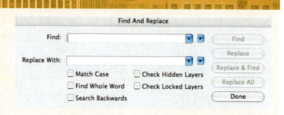

The check boxes below the Replace With field are toggles for specific types of searches:

- When **Check Hidden Layers** is active, the search includes text frames on layers that are not visible. In this case, the hidden layer remains visible until you close the Find and Replace dialog box

- When **Check Locked Layers** is active, the search locates text on locked layers.

- When **Match Case** is active, a search only finds text with the same capitalization as the text in the Find What field. For example, a search for "Illustrator" does not identify instances of "illustrator" or "ILLUSTRATOR."

- When **Find Whole Word** is active, a search only finds instances where the search text is an entire word (not part of another word). For example, a search for "old" as a whole word does not include the words "gold," "mold," or "embolden."

- When **Search Backwards** is selected, Illustrator searches from the current insertion point to the beginning of the story. (This option is irrelevant if the insertion point is not placed.)

You also have limited ability to search for and replace special characters that cannot be typed directly into the dialog box fields. The menus associated with the Find and Replace With fields list the special characters that can be identified and replaced.

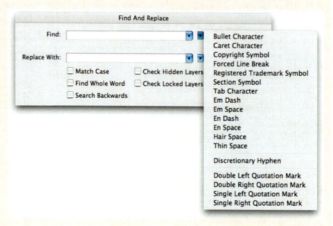

3. Using the same method, remove all of the extra empty paragraphs in the story.

In the next exercise, you will use paragraph formatting options to control the space between individual paragraphs.

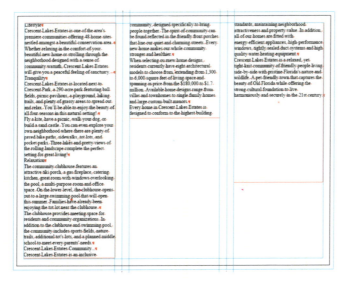

4. Save the file and continue to the next exercise.

 ## CREATE PARAGRAPH STYLES

The brochure text is currently mashed together into what appears as a long block of hard-to-read text. Using Illustrator's typographic controls, you can turn this long block of boring text into a professional-looking layout.

Of course, when you work with long blocks of text, many of the same formatting options are applied to different text elements throughout the story (such as headings). To simplify the workflow, you can use styles to store and apply multiple formatting options with a single click.

1. With Estates Inside.ai open, place the insertion point anywhere in the text and choose Edit>Select All.

When you use the Select All command, you select the entire story in all threaded frames.

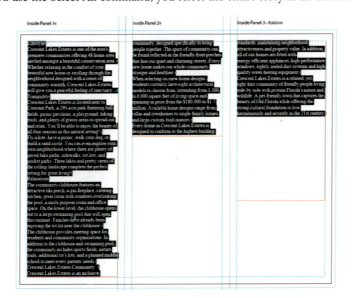

Note:

You might think that it would make more sense to start with the smaller of the two types of styles (character styles), but that doesn't really follow conventional workflows. In on-the-job situations, you will use paragraph styles far more often than character styles.

2. **Using the Character panel, change the selected text to 10-pt ATC Laurel Book with 12-pt leading.**

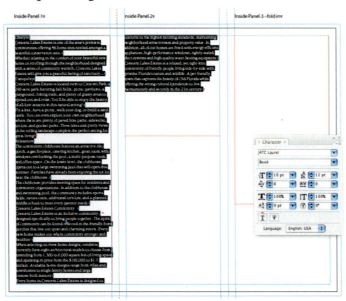

Character Formatting in Depth

Once text is in a frame, you can control a number of formatting options using the Character panel. Character formatting options apply only to the selected text.

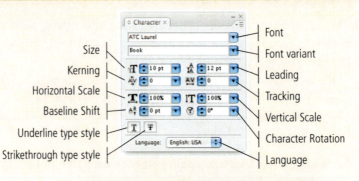

- A **font** contains all the characters (or **glyphs**) that make up the typeface, including upper- and lowercase letters, numbers, special characters, etc. (Fonts must be installed and activated on your computer to be accessible in Illustrator.)

- **Size** is the height of a typeface measured in points.

- **Leading** is the distance from one text baseline to the next. In Illustrator, leading is treated as a character attribute, so you can define different leading for different lines within a single paragraph (although this is rarely necessary).

- **Kerning** increases or decreases the space between pairs of letters. Kerning is used in cases where particular letters in specific fonts need to be brought together manually to eliminate a too-tight or too-spread-out appearance. Manual kerning is usually necessary in headlines or other large type. Many commercial fonts have built-in kerning pairs, so you won't need much hands-on intervention with kerning. Illustrator defaults to use the kerning values stored in the **font metrics**.

- **Tracking**, also known as "range kerning," refers to the overall tightness or looseness across a range of characters.

- **Vertical Scale** and **Horizontal Scale** artificially stretch or contract the selected characters. This type of scaling is a quick way of achieving condensed or expanded type if those variations of a font don't exist.

- **Baseline Shift** moves the selected type above or below the baseline by a specific number of points. Positive numbers move the characters up; negative values move the text down.

- **Character Rotation** rotates selected characters without affecting the rotation of surrounding text or the containing frame.

- **Underline** places a line below the selected characters.

- **Strikethrough** places a line through the middle of selected characters.

- **Language** defines the language dictionary used to check the grammar, spelling, and hyphenation of selected text.

3. **Using the Paragraph panel, change the Left Indent and Right Indent fields to 5 pt, change the Space After Paragraph field to 6 pt, and apply justified paragraph alignment with the last line aligned left.**

Paragraph formatting affects how your page looks and reads. Attributes that affect the entire paragraph — such as alignment, indents, and space before and after paragraphs — can be controlled in the Paragraph panel. Unlike character formatting, paragraph formatting applies to the entire paragraph in which the insertion point is placed. If text is selected, paragraph formatting applies to any paragraph that is entirely or partially selected.

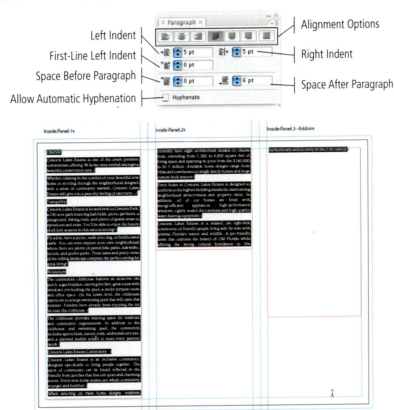

4. **With all of the text still selected, open the Paragraph Styles panel (Window>Type>Paragraph Styles).**

A **style** is a convenient method for storing and applying multiple formatting options with a single click. The Paragraph Styles panel shows two available options:

- **Normal Paragraph Style.** By default, every Illustrator file includes the Normal Paragraph Style option. The formatting applied in this style is the default formatting for new text areas created in the file. You can edit this style to change the default settings for new text areas in the existing file.

- **Normal.** This is Microsoft Word's version of Normal Paragraph Style. When you imported the Word file in an earlier exercise, you also imported the text formatting — including the Normal style applied in the Word file.

Note:

The plus sign (+) next to the Normal style name indicates that some formatting has been applied other than what is defined in the style.

The selected text is formatted with the Normal style, but some options have been modified locally, so they are different than the original style definition.

5. Click the Create New Style button in the Paragraph Styles panel.

The new style is added, based on the formatting of the selected text. However, the style has not yet been applied to the selected text.

Normal+ is still highlighted, so it is still applied to the selected text.

Create New Style button

6. In the Paragraph Styles panel, double-click the Paragraph Style 1 item.

Double-clicking a style opens the Paragraph Style Options dialog box, where you can edit the settings stored in the style.

7. Change the Style Name field to "Body Copy" and click OK.

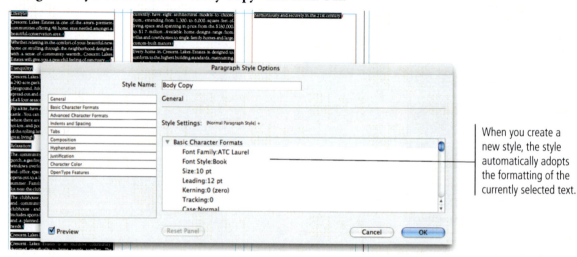

When you create a new style, the style automatically adopts the formatting of the currently selected text.

When you return to the layout, notice that the Body Copy style is now highlighted in the panel.

To apply a style, simply select the text you want to format, and then click the style name in the panel. You double-clicked the style name to edit it; the first click of that double-click applied the style to the selected text.

If you want to edit a style without applying it, make sure no text is selected in the layout before editing the style.

Note:

You can also edit a style by single-clicking it in the panel, and then choosing Paragraph Style Options in the panel options menu.

8. Select the first paragraph in the story (Lifestyle).

9. Change the selected text to 12-pt ATC Pine Heavy. Change the indents to 0 pt, and change the Space After Paragraph value to 8 pt. Using the Swatches panel, change the text color to one of the brown swatches.

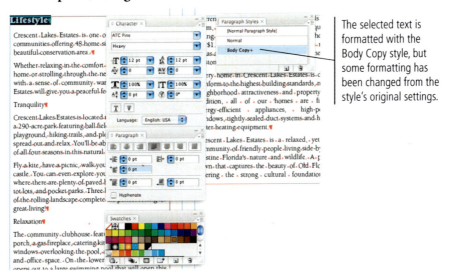

The selected text is formatted with the Body Copy style, but some formatting has been changed from the style's original settings.

10. With the heading still selected, click the Create New Style button in the Paragraph Styles panel.

11. Double-click the new Paragraph Style 2 to edit it. Change the style name to "Heading 1" and click OK.

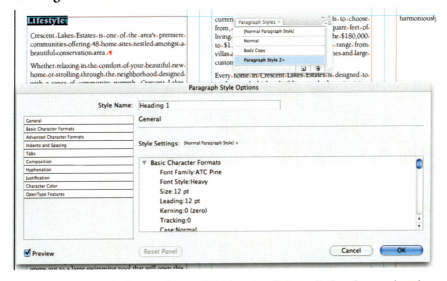

When you return to the layout, the new Heading 1 style is applied to the text, but the plus sign still suggests that local formatting is overriding the style definition. Because you just created the new style based on the selected formatting, the plus sign should not appear. In this case, this is a quirk of the software.

12. **With the text still selected, choose Clear Overrides in the Paragraph Styles panel options menu.**

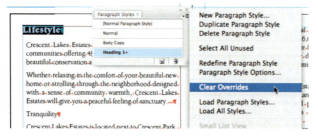

The plus sign disappears, and the selected text is now formatted properly with the Heading 1 style.

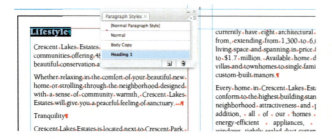

13. **Place the insertion point in the second heading (Tranquility) and click the Heading 1 style in the Paragraph Styles panel.**

Applying a paragraph style is as simple as placing the insertion point and clicking a style.

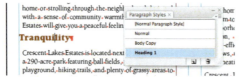

14. **Using the same method, apply the Heading 1 style to the remaining headings in the story.**

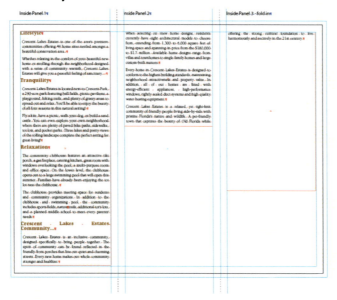

15. **Choose Type>Show Hidden Characters to toggle off their visibility.**

16. **Save the file and continue to the next exercise.**

EDIT AND DELETE STYLES

As you have seen, a style applies multiple formatting options with a single click. This makes styles very useful when applying the same formatting to different layout elements. Styles also have another benefit, which is perhaps more powerful when designing layouts.

When you change the options applied in a style, any text formatted with the style reflects the newly defined options. In other words, you can change multiple instances of non-contiguous text in one process, instead of selecting each block and making the same changes repeatedly.

1. **With Estates Inside.ai open, make sure nothing is selected in the layout.**

2. **Select Heading 1 in the Paragraph Styles panel and then choose Paragraph Style Options in the panel options menu.**

Note:

You do not have to select text to change the definition of a style. In fact, you don't even need to select a text frame for this process to work.

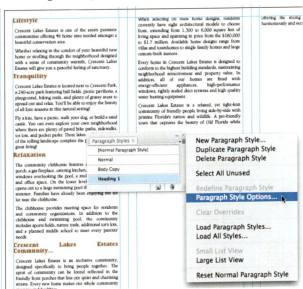

3. **Make sure the Preview option is checked in the bottom-left corner of the dialog box.**

   When the Preview option is turned on, your changes dynamically reflect in the layout (behind the dialog box). This allows you to experiment with the changes before you click OK to change the style definition.

4. **Click Indents and Spacing in the list of formatting categories.**

   Different options are available in the right side of the dialog box, depending on what is selected in the list of categories.

Note:

A paragraph style can store character formatting options as well as paragraph formatting options.

5. **Change the Space Before field to 8 pt, and change the Space After field to 0.**

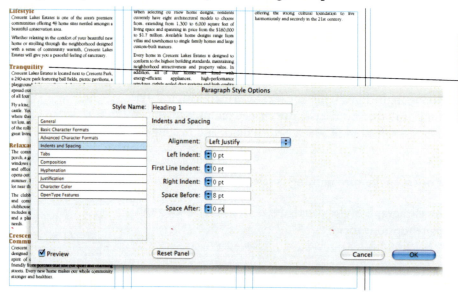

With the Preview option active, you can see the result of changing the space before and after headings before you finalize the change.

6. **Click OK to change the style definition.**

7. **Click Body Copy in the Paragraph Styles panel to select it, and then choose Paragraph Style Options in the panel options menu.**

8. **In the Indents and Spacing options, change the Left Indent to 12 pt and change the Right Indent to 0 pt.**

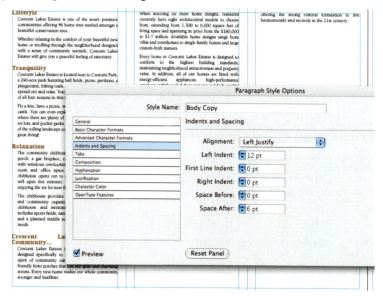

9. **Click Basic Character Formats in the list of options. Change the Size to 11 pt, and change the Leading to 13.5 pt.**

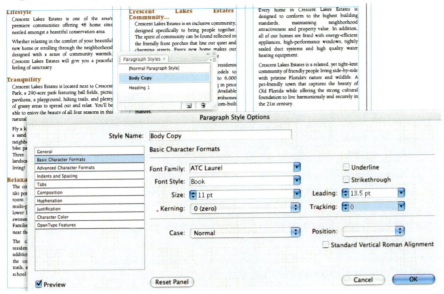

10. **Click OK to redefine the style and return to the layout.**

11. **In the Paragraph Styles panel, drag the Normal style to the Delete button.**

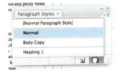

Because the Normal style is no longer used in the layout, you can delete the style. If the style had been applied, you would see a warning message asking you to confirm the deletion (although you do not have the opportunity to replace the applied style with another style, as you do in page-layout applications).

12. **Save the file and continue to the next exercise.**

 WORK WITH A CHARACTER STYLE

As with paragraph styles, a character style can be used to store and apply multiple character formatting options with a single click. The primary difference is that character styles apply to selected text only, such as italicizing a specific word in a paragraph or adding a few characters in a different font.

1. **With Estates Inside.ai open, place the insertion point at the very beginning of the story.**

2. **Type "v" and then press the Spacebar.**

v Lifestyle

Crescent Lakes Estates is one of the area's premiere communities offering 48 home sites nestled amongst a beautiful conservation area.

Whether relaxing in the comfort of your beautifu

3. **Highlight only the "v" and change the font to Zapf Dingbats or Wingdings.**

These are standard fonts on most computers, and you should have one or the other. If you don't have either, try the Webdings font, but change the "v" to a lowercase "l".

Most of the heading paragraph is formatted with one set of instructions, but a single character is formatted with a different font. This is a perfect case for using a character style.

4. **With the single alternate character selected, open the Character Styles panel (Window>Type>Character Styles).**

5. **Click the Create New Style button at the bottom of the panel.**

6. **Double-click the new Character Style 1 item in the Character Styles panel. In the Character Style Options dialog box, change the Style Name field to "Heading Bullet" and click OK.**

The process for creating a character style is essentially the same as creating a paragraph style.

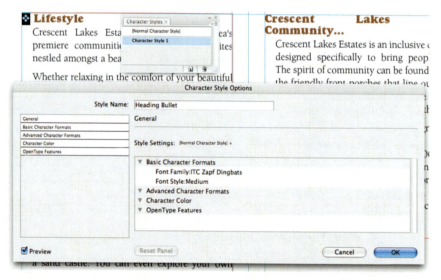

7. **If you see a plus sign next to the Heading Bullet style, choose Clear Overrides in the Character Styles panel options menu.**

As with paragraph styles, when you return to the layout, the selected character is formatted with the Heading Bullet style.

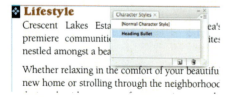

8. **Copy the bullet and the space directly after it, and then paste the copied characters at the beginning of the next two headings. Do not paste a copy at the beginning of the fourth heading (Crescent Lakes).**

9. **Deselect everything in the layout.**

10. **In the Character Styles panel, select the Heading Bullet item and choose Character Style Options in the panel options menu.**

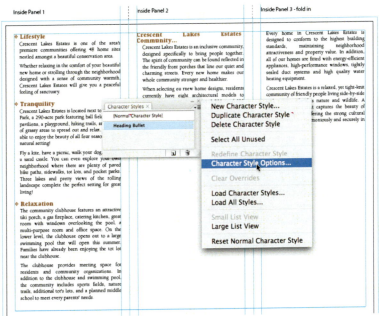

11. **Select Character Color in the list of categories. Scroll through the list of available swatches and click CMYK Blue to select it.**

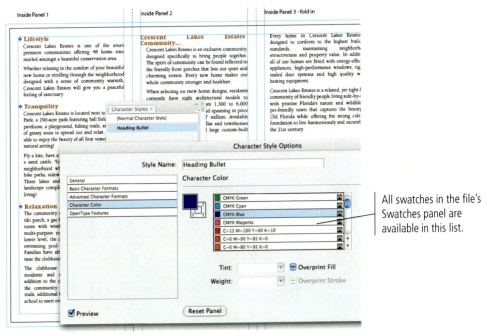

All swatches in the file's Swatches panel are available in this list.

12. **Click OK to close the dialog box and change the style definition.**

    All three bullets are now colored blue.

13. **Save the file and continue to the next exercise.**

The Glyphs Panel in Depth

ASCII is a text-based code that defines characters with a numeric value between 001 and 256. The standard alphabet and punctuation characters are mapped from 001 to 128. **Extended ASCII characters** are those with ASCII numbers higher than 128; these include symbols (copyright symbols, etc.) and some special formatting characters (en dashes, accent marks, etc.). Some of the more common extended characters can be accessed in the Type>Insert submenu.

OpenType fonts offer the ability to store more than 65,000 **glyphs** (characters) in a single font — far beyond what you could access with a keyboard (even including combinations of the different modifier keys). The large glyph storage capacity means that a single OpenType font can replace the multiple separate "Expert" fonts that contain variations of fonts (Minion Swash, for example, is no longer necessary when you can access the Swashes subset of the Minion Pro font).

Unicode fonts include two-bit characters that are common in some foreign language typesetting (e.g., Cyrillic, Japanese, and other non-Roman or pictographic fonts).

The Glyphs panel (Type>Glyphs) provides access to every glyph in a font, including basic characters in regular fonts, extended ASCII and OpenType character sets, and even pictographic characters in Unicode fonts.

Using the Glyphs panel is simple: make sure the insertion point is flashing where you want a character to appear, and then double-click the character you want to place. You can view the character set for any font by simply changing the menu at the bottom of the panel. By default, the panel shows the entire font, but you can show only specific character sets using the Show menu.

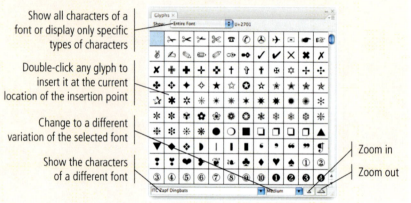

Show all characters of a font or display only specific types of characters

Double-click any glyph to insert it at the current location of the insertion point

Change to a different variation of the selected font

Show the characters of a different font

Zoom in

Zoom out

 ## Load Styles from Another File

Once styles have been defined, you can easily import those styles into another layout. This allows you to maintain consistency from one file to another without the need for tedious note-taking, copying, or pasting.

1. **Create a new file by opening the Letterfold Outside.ait template from your WIP>Estates folder.**

2. **Create two new layers in the file, named "Text" and "Graphics", located above the Guides layer in the Layers panel.**

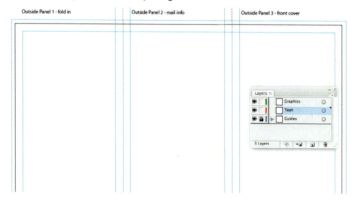

3. Make sure the Text layer is selected, and then use the Type tool to create a text frame that fills the left panel area.

4. Choose File>Place. Navigate to Outside.doc in the RF_Illustrator>Estates folder and click Place.

5. Click OK in the Microsoft Word Options dialog box to accept the default settings, and then click OK again to dismiss the Font Problems dialog box.

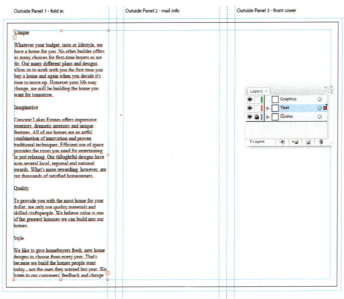

6. Show the hidden characters, and then manually delete the extra empty paragraph return characters between the existing paragraphs.

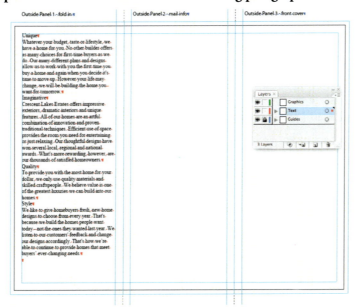

7. **In the Paragraph Styles panel, open the panel options menu and choose Load All Styles.**

   You could load paragraph styles only; however, since the inside of the brochure includes a character style, you will import all styles at one time.

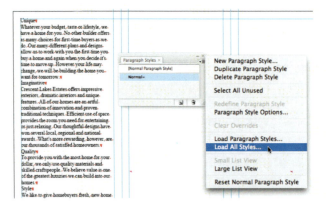

8. **Navigate to the Estates Inside.ai file (in your WIP>Estates folder) and click Open.**

   This is the file where you defined the styles you want to import.

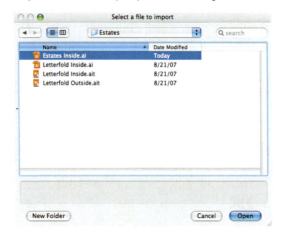

9. **Apply the imported Body Copy style to the entire story in the frame. If necessary, use the panel options menu to clear overrides in the selected text.**

10. **Apply the Heading 1 style to the four one-line paragraphs.**

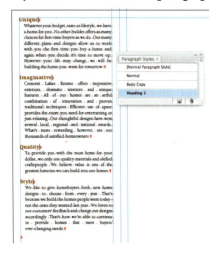

11. Type "v " (including the space character after the letter) before the first heading. Highlight the "v" and apply the Heading Bullet character style.

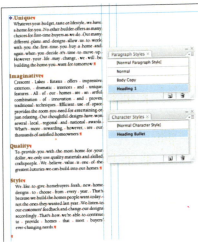

12. Add the same bullet character (and space) to the beginning of each heading in the panel.

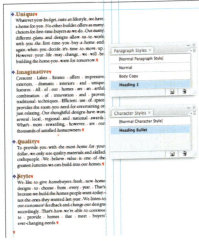

13. Save the file as "Estates Outside.ai" in your WIP>Estates folder and continue to the next stage of the project.

Stage 3 Fine-Tuning Text

For all intents and purposes, you could say that the text for inside the brochure is complete — everything is visible and the headings and body copy are formatted. There are, however, a number of typographic issues that should be addressed so the layout creates a professional, polished image instead of a "good-enough" appearance.

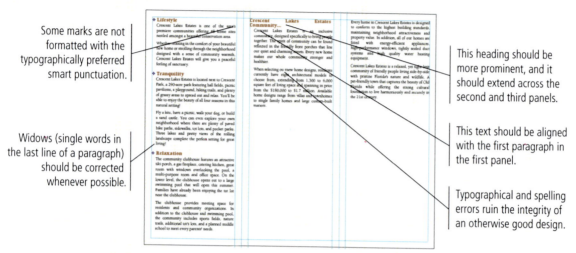

Some marks are not formatted with the typographically preferred smart punctuation.

Widows (single words in the last line of a paragraph) should be corrected whenever possible.

This heading should be more prominent, and it should extend across the second and third panels.

This text should be aligned with the first paragraph in the first panel.

Typographical and spelling errors ruin the integrity of an otherwise good design.

Some of these problems can be solved using Illustrator's built-in tools and utilities. Others will require manual adjustment to make sure the text appears exactly how and where you want it to appear.

ADJUST HEADINGS AND ALIGN BASELINES

Ranging is the misalignment from the baseline in one column to the baseline in the column or frame next to it. Ranging is most often caused by the spacing around headings and other special text elements (like bullets); you can see ranging in many different projects that have more than one adjacent column. To create a professional layout, you should fix the baseline alignment whenever possible, especially at the tops and bottoms of columns.

1. **With Estates Inside.ai open and active, select the heading at the top of the second panel and cut it (Edit>Cut).**

   In this case, the text is not likely to reflow; even if it does (for example, if the client submits a new text file), the heading content and position over the second and third panels should not change. In this situation, then, it is not necessary to keep the heading in the same text thread.

Note:

We are using the term "column" even though you are technically working with individual frames. The same concept applies whether your layout uses multiple column-like frames (as in this project) or an individual frame with multiple columns.

2. **Using the Selection tool, drag the bottom-center handle of the first frame up until the "Crescent Lakes Estates" line moves back into the second panel.**

   Illustrator does not have the orphan-control options of page-layout software such as InDesign. Moving paragraphs from one frame to another is an entirely manual process.

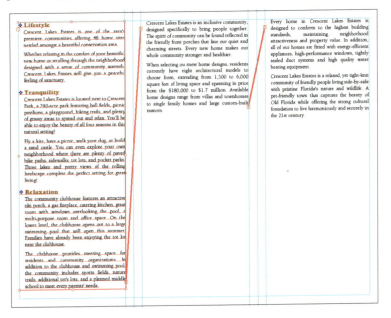

Note:

*A **widow** is a very short line — usually one or two words — at the end of a paragraph.*

*An **orphan** is the first line of a paragraph at the end of a column or the last line of a paragraph at the beginning of a column.*

3. **Using the Type tool, create a new text frame in the empty area at the bottom of the second panel.**

   If you click within an existing text frame area, you will place the insertion point in that space. To add a new frame, you have to click outside the existing frames.

4. **Paste the cut heading into the new frame.**

5. **Select the entire heading and change the formatting to 24-pt ATC Oak Bold Italic with 90% horizontal scale, and change the text color to the same CMYK Blue you used for the Heading Bullet character style.**

6. **Use the Selection tool to resize the frame to fit the width of the second and third columns (including the folding guide margins).**

7. **Drag the bottom edge of the frame up as much as possible.**

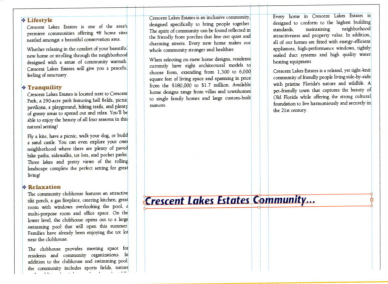

8. **Drag a horizontal guide from the top ruler, and align it with the baseline of the first heading in the left panel.**

The heading for the second and third panels, which is in its own text frame, should be positioned so the heading baseline matches the baseline of the heading in the first column. This type of multi-frame baseline alignment is only possible using manually created guides.

9. **Drag a second horizontal guide and align it with the baseline of the first line of body copy in the left panel.**

Because the body text in each panel is placed in a different frame, you must manually align the baselines across the three panels.

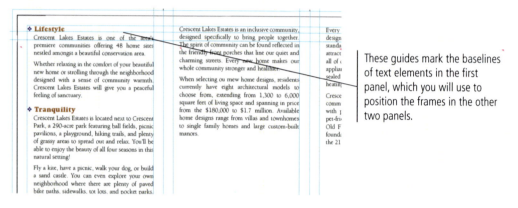

These guides mark the baselines of text elements in the first panel, which you will use to position the frames in the other two panels.

10. **Select the frame with the large blue heading. Press Shift and drag up until the baseline of the text aligns with the first horizontal page guide.**

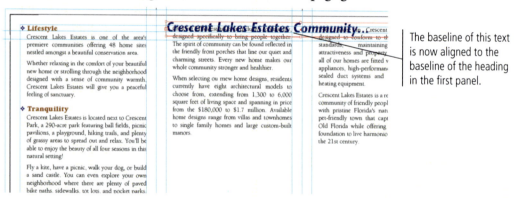

The baseline of this text is now aligned to the baseline of the heading in the first panel.

11. **Select the two text frames in the middle and right columns. Press Shift and drag down until the first-line baseline exactly aligns with the second horizontal page guide.**

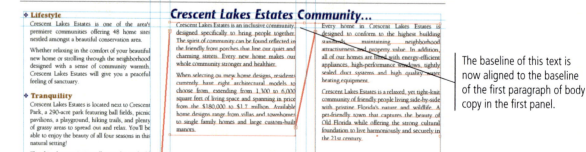

The baseline of this text is now aligned to the baseline of the first paragraph of body copy in the first panel.

12. **Delete the two horizontal page guides.**

These guides are no longer necessary, so you can remove them and avoid unnecessary clutter.

13. **Select all of the text frames on the page. Press Shift and drag down until all text is within the 1/4″ margin guides.**

Note:

Guides must be unlocked to select and delete them. If you can't select the two guides, choose View>Guides>Lock Guides to toggle off the option.

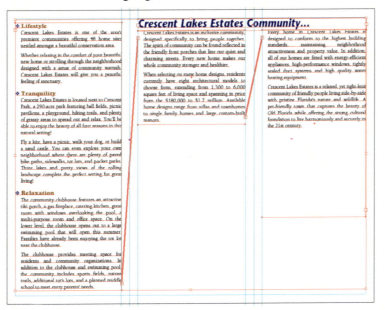

14. **Save the file and continue to the next exercise.**

 APPLY SMART PUNCTUATION

Straight double quotes are actually inch marks, and straight single quotes are foot marks. To be typographically correct, these straight marks must be converted to **smart quotes** (also called **curly quotes**).

1. **With Estates Inside.ai open, make sure nothing is selected in the layout.**

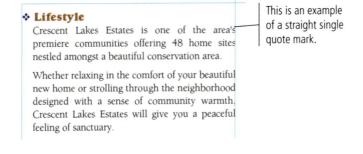

This is an example of a straight single quote mark.

2. **Choose Type>Smart Punctuation.**

   This dialog box makes it very easy to search for and change common characters into their typographically correct equivalents. You can affect selected text only, or you can affect the entire document at once.

Note:

Two spaces after a period is a common text problem; it is a relic from a time when manual typewriters placed every character in the same amount of space (called monospace type). To more clearly identify a new sentence, convention called for the typist to enter two spaces after typing a period. This convention still survives today, even though many people have never seen a manual typewriter.

   - **ff, fi, ffi Ligatures** converts these three letter combinations to the replacement ligatures.
   - **Smart Quotes** converts straight quotation marks into curly quotes (or "smart" quotes).
   - **Smart Spaces** eliminates multiple space characters after a period.
   - **En, Em Dashes** converts a double keyboard dash to an en dash and a triple keyboard dash to an em dash.
   - **Ellipses** converts three keyboard periods to a single-character ellipsis point.
   - **Expert Fractions** converts separate characters used to represent fractions to their single-character equivalents.

Note:

We do not know why the Ligatures option appears twice in the dialog box; this appears to be a bug in the software.

3. **In the Replace Punctuation area, check all options but Ellipses.**

   The actual ellipsis character is usually lighter and narrower than three sequential periods. In this project, the ellipsis in the heading should remain prominent, so you will not convert this character.

4. **Make sure the Entire Document option is selected and the Report Results box is checked, and then click OK.**

5. **Review the information in the report dialog box, and then click OK.**

❖ **Lifestyle**

Crescent Lakes Estates is one of the area's premiere communities offering 48 home sites nestled amongst a beautiful conservation area.

Whether relaxing in the comfort of your beautiful new home or strolling through the neighborhood designed with a sense of community warmth, Crescent Lakes Estates will give you a peaceful feeling of sanctuary.

The straight quote mark is now a smart or curly quote.

6. **Save the file.**

7. **Activate (or open, if necessary) the Estates Outside.ai file and apply the Smart Punctuation filter.**

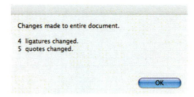

8. **Save the file and continue to the next exercise.**

The text in the second and third panels has a number of potential problems, some of which are typographically incorrect and others which are more subjective. Some problems, such as widows and orphans, should be fixed whenever possible. For other issues, you must make choices about the best way to present information, such as whether to allow hyphenation.

1. **With Estates Inside.ai open and active, select all four paragraphs in the second and third panels and change the Left Indent value to 0 pt.**

   There is no need for these paragraphs to be indented; since the indent resulted in widows at the end of three paragraphs, the logical choice is to simply remove the indent.

2. **Drag up the bottom edge of the second frame so the "Every home" line is forced into the third panel.**

   As we mentioned previously, Illustrator does not include automatic orphan control. You have to correct this problem manually by adjusting the frame size.

   The paragraphs are now in the correct frames, and the widows have been fixed. However, the right frame has one more line than the left column, which should be fixed if possible. The first paragraph in the right frame has a line with large gaps between words, which is often the result of justified paragraph alignment. You can try to fix this by changing the Justification settings or by allowing hyphenation in the affected paragraphs.

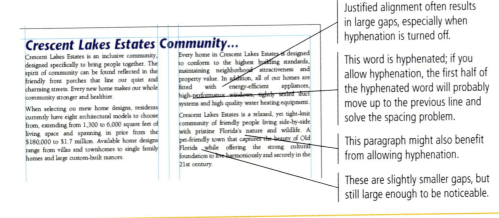

Justified alignment often results in large gaps, especially when hyphenation is turned off.

This word is hyphenated; if you allow hyphenation, the first half of the hyphenated word will probably move up to the previous line and solve the spacing problem.

This paragraph might also benefit from allowing hyphenation.

These are slightly smaller gaps, but still large enough to be noticeable.

3. **Select any part of the two paragraphs in the right frame. In the Paragraphs panel, activate the Hyphenation check box.**

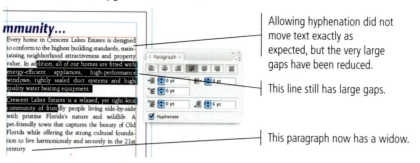

Allowing hyphenation did not move text exactly as expected, but the very large gaps have been reduced.

This line still has large gaps.

This paragraph now has a widow.

Note:

You can also apply and control hyphenation in a paragraph style definition. In this exercise, you are affecting the two selected paragraphs only (called local formatting).

4. **Select the last paragraph only. In the Paragraph panel options menu, choose Hyphenation.**

The Hyphenation options allow you to control the way Illustrator applies hyphenation.

- **Words Longer Than _ Letters** defines the minimum number of characters that must exist in a hyphenated word.

- **After First _ Letters** and **Before Last _ Letters** defines the minimum number of characters that must appear before or after a hyphen.

- **Hyphen Limit** defines the maximum number of hyphens that can appear on consecutive lines. (Remember, you are defining the limit here, so zero means there is no limit — allowing unlimited hyphens.)

- **Hyphenation Zone** defines the amount of white space allowed at the end of a line of unjustified text before hyphenation begins.

- If **Hyphenate Capitalized Words** is checked, capitalized words (proper nouns) can be hyphenated.

5. **In the Hyphenation dialog box, activate the Preview check box, and then drag the slider all the way to the left.**

This slider allows Illustrator to determine the best spacing, depending on the location of the slider. Dragging to the left allows more hyphens, but typically results in better overall line spacing. Dragging to the right reduces the number of hyphens in a paragraph, but might produce less-pleasing results in line spacing.

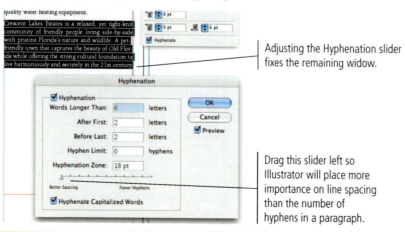

Adjusting the Hyphenation slider fixes the remaining widow.

Drag this slider left so Illustrator will place more importance on line spacing than the number of hyphens in a paragraph.

6. **Click OK to close the Hyphenation dialog box and apply the change.**

7. **Place the insertion point in the first paragraph of the frame and choose Justification in the Paragraph panel options menu.**

A paragraph does not have to be entirely selected to change the hyphenation and justification settings. Any paragraph that is partially selected — including the one where the insertion point is placed — will be affected.

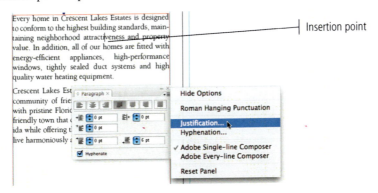

The Justification dialog box allows you to control the minimum, preferred, and maximum spacing that can be applied to create justified paragraph alignment.

- **Word Spacing** defines the space that can be applied between words (where spaces exist in the text). At 100% (the default Desired amount), no additional space is added between words.

- **Letter Spacing** defines the space that can be added between individual letters within a word. All three values default to 0%, which allows no extra space between letters; at 100%, an entire space would be allowed between characters (making the text very difficult to read).

- **Glyph Spacing** determines how much individual character glyphs can be scaled (stretched or compressed) to justify the text. At 100%, the default value for all three settings, characters are not scaled.

- In narrow columns, single words sometimes appear on a line by themselves. If the paragraph is set to full justification, a single word on a line might appear to be too stretched out. You can use the **Single Word Justification** menu to center or left-align these single words instead of leaving them fully justified.

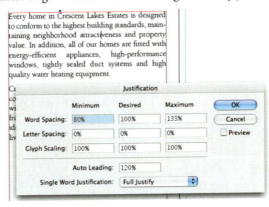

8. **Activate the Preview option, and then change the Minimum Word Spacing field to 100%.**

By enlarging the value in the Minimum Word Spacing field, the spaces between words in the second line are enlarged. Basically, you are telling Illustrator, "Do not reduce the amount of word spacing below 100% of the normal spacing that would be applied by pressing the spacebar."

This reflows the rest of the paragraph and results in larger word spaces throughout. Because the entire paragraph now has larger word spacing, however, the paragraph appears to be more balanced than when some lines had tight spacing and some had loose spacing.

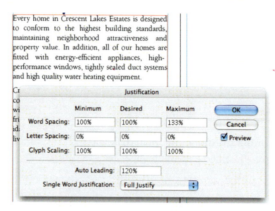

9. **Click OK to apply the change and return to the layout.**

10. **Using whichever method you prefer, fix the remaining widow in the first panel of the file.**

We activated automatic hyphenation for the paragraph, and dragged the spacing slider all the way to the left in the Hyphenation dialog box

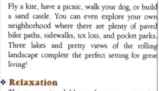

11. **Save the file and continue to the next exercise.**

CHECK SPELLING

As with most desktop applications, Illustrator allows you to check the spelling in a document. It is all too common to skip this important check; thus, spelling and typing errors remain in many jobs when they go to press. Misspellings and typos creep into virtually every job despite numerous rounds of content proofs. These errors can ruin an otherwise perfect job.

You might not (and probably won't) create the text for most design jobs, and you aren't technically responsible for the words your client supplies. However, you can be a hero if you find and fix typographical errors before a job goes to press; if you don't, you will almost certainly hear about it after it's too late to fix. Remember the cardinal rule of business: the customer is always right. You simply can't brush off a problem by saying, "That's not my job" — at least, not if you want to work with that client in the future.

1. **With Estates Inside.ai open, make sure nothing is selected in the layout.**

2. **Choose Edit>Check Spelling.**

Note:

Illustrator checks spelling based on the language defined for the text. You can change the default language in the Hyphenation pane of the Preferences dialog box, or you can assign a specific language to selected text using the Character panel.

3. **In the Check Spelling dialog box, click Start.**

   Illustrator immediately locates the single letter "v" used to add the bullet at the beginning of each heading in the left column. In this case, the single letter is not an error.

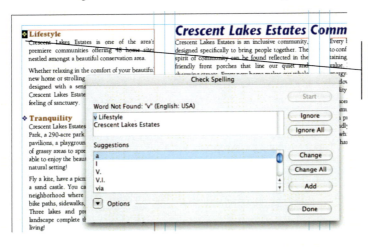

The suspect word is highlighted in the layout so you can review it in context.

4. **Click Ignore All.**

   There are three instances of the "v" bullet. If you click Ignore instead of Ignore All, the Spell Check process will identify each of the three bullets as a possible error.

5. Evaluate the next potential error.

The hyphenated phrase "290-acre" is not in the dictionary. However, this compound noun is correct in the context of the surrounding content.

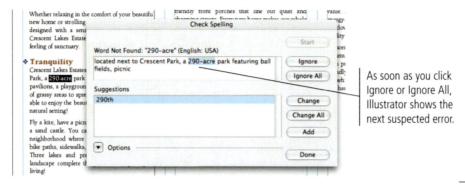

As soon as you click Ignore or Ignore All, Illustrator shows the next suspected error.

6. Click Ignore, and then evaluate the next potential problem.

The next problem is actually a typo — the client typed the space in the wrong place. Instead of "our new", the text reads "ou rnew". Fortunately, Illustrator found the problem.

7. Make sure "our" is selected in the Suggestions list and click Change.

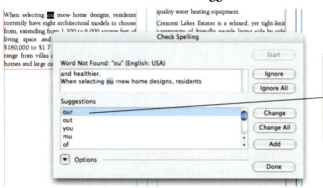

Always make sure the option you want is selected in this list. The software tries to identify the best replacement, but only you can decide if it's the right choice.

8. With the second half of the typo identified, make sure "new" is selected in the list of suggestions and click Change.

Note:

Never simply click Change when you check spelling. Carefully evaluate the suspect word in the context of the layout.

9. **Review the next suspect, and then click Ignore.**

The word "townhomes" can be a single word or two separate words. In this case, you are assuming your client typed it the way he prefers.

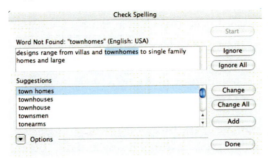

10. **Click Done to close the Check Spelling dialog box.**

When Illustrator can't find any more potential problems, the dialog box shows that the Spell Checker utility is complete.

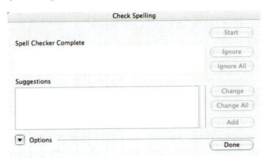

11. **Save the file.**

12. **Activate the Estates Outside.ai file and check the spelling in that layout. Make any corrections you think are necessary in the context of that layout.**

We changed the word "homebuyers" to "Home buyers", and ignored all other suspected problems.

13. **Save the file and continue to the next exercise.**

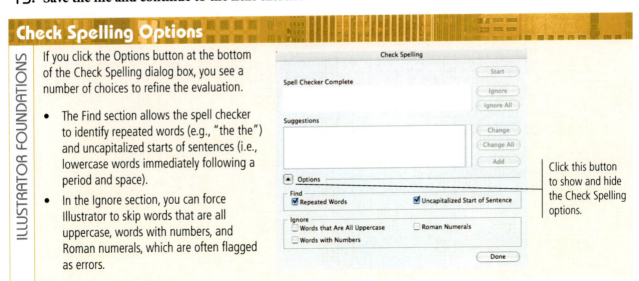

PLACE LAYOUT IMAGES

The text for both sides of the brochure is now complete. The only remaining elements to place are the images and logos. Most of this step is simply a matter of placing and positioning the external images, which you have done in every project in this book so far.

When you design a letterfold brochure, you should consider the overall design — including folds — when you place images. Consider the schematic for a letterfold brochure. The way the document folds creates an opportunity to extend a single image across the two panels that are visible after the front cover is opened.

1. **With the files for both the inside and outside of the brochure open, arrange the windows so you can see the left panel of the brochure's inside and the left panel of the brochure's outside.**

   You are going to place images in these panels so that, when the brochure cover is opened, the two halves of the image appear next to each other on the appropriate panels.

2. **In the Estates Inside.ai file, make sure the Graphics layer is selected. If necessary, drag the Graphics layer to be below the Text layer in the layer stack.**

3. **Choose File>Place. Navigate to the file Door Left.tif in the RF_Illustrator>Estates folder and click Place.**

4. **Drag the placed image so it fills the left panel, including the bleed margins.**

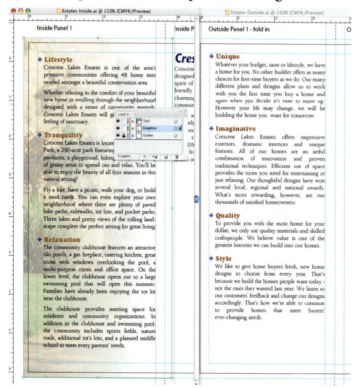

5. **Activate the Estates Outside.ai file. Using the same basic techniques, place the file Door Right.tif in the left panel of the brochure outside.**

By viewing the two layouts next to each other, you can get an idea of how the two images will meet when the job is printed and folded.

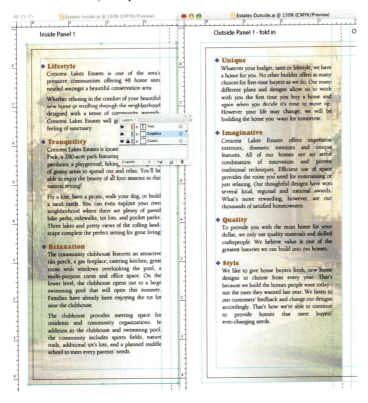

6. **Place the file Painting.tif in the empty space of the center and right panel on the inside of the brochure, just below the bottom of the two columns of text. Scale the image to fit entirely within the margin guides of the two panels.**

7. **Place the file CL Logo.ai. In the Place PDF dialog box, choose Art in the Crop To menu and click OK.**

8. **Position the logo at the bottom of the right panel of the inside of the brochure.**

9. **Below the logo, add a text area with the following text:**

   Models open daily from 10 a.m. to 4 p.m.

10. **Format the text to be consistent with the body copy in the brochure, and position the text frame as shown in the following image.**

11. **Place the file lake.tif in the right panel of the brochure's outside.**

12. **Place the file CL Logo Reverse.ai over the lake area of the image you placed in Step 11. Center the logo between the panel's margin guides.**

13. **Place the CL Logo.ai file in the center panel.**

14. **Create a text area with the following text:**

    20 Lake Loop, Tampa, FL 33456

15. **Format the text as 10-pt ATC Oak Normal, and position the text directly below the logo (as shown in the following image).**

16. **Group the logo and address elements. Scale the grouped elements to 75%, rotate them by 90° counterclockwise, and place the group in the bottom-left corner of the center panel.**

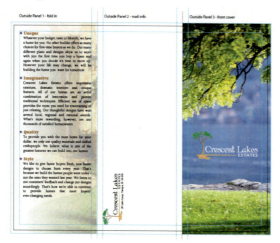

17. **Save both files and close them.**

Summary

To begin the letterfold layout, you built technically accurate folding guides for each side of the brochure, incorporating nonprinting fold guides and text frames into the slug area. To speed up the process for the next time you need to build one of these common letterfold jobs, you saved your initial work as a template.

Completing this project also required extensive work with imported text, specifically importing styles from a Microsoft Word file and controlling the flow of text from one frame to another. You also worked with several advanced text-formatting options, including paragraph and character styles and typographic fine-tuning controls.

Templates and styles are designed to let you do the majority of work once and then apply it as many times as necessary; many different projects can benefit from these tools, and you will use them extensively throughout your career as a graphic designer.

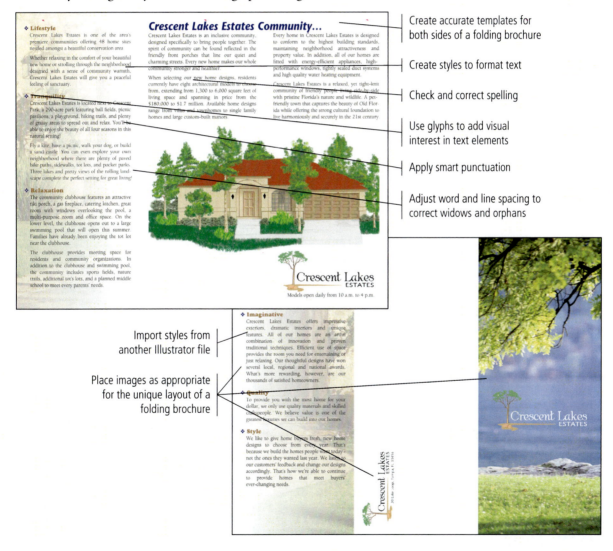

- Create accurate templates for both sides of a folding brochure
- Create styles to format text
- Check and correct spelling
- Use glyphs to add visual interest in text elements
- Apply smart punctuation
- Adjust word and line spacing to correct widows and orphans

- Import styles from another Illustrator file
- Place images as appropriate for the unique layout of a folding brochure

Portfolio Builder Project 5

The real estate developer was very pleased with your work, and has recommended your agency to a colleague at the local chamber of commerce. Your new client, Outdoor Adventures, specializes in "extreme tourism" — rock climbing, white water rafting, and similar activities

To complete this project, you should:

❏ Create a letterfold brochure to present the client's information in an aesthetically pleasing layout.

❏ Reserve the middle panel of the brochure's outside for mailing information, including only the client's logo and return address.

❏ Use any or all of the client's supplied images to support the text. All files are in the RF_Builders>Adventures folder).

"Our company caters to what we call the 'extreme tourist'. We put together tour packages for people who like to experience and challenge nature. Some of our most popular tours take people up Mount Whitney, go rafting down the Colorado River, and even hike through the Alaskan ice fields.

"Our business is doing very well with people who live on the West Coast, but we would like to extend our reach to the entire United States. We've purchased mailing lists from magazine who have a similar audience as our clients, and we want to create a brochure that we can mail to approximately 10,000 potential new clients.

"We've given you the text for the brochure — there isn't much of it, because the images tell a more dramatic story of what we do. We've given you a number of images from our previous tours, and you can use as many of them as you think are necessary. If you want to use any other images, just make sure they follow the general theme of 'outdoor adventures'."

Cereal Box Artwork

Your client, a food manufacturer, is redesigning the packaging for its primary product — a cereal targeted at the health-conscious consumer. The client hired you to build the new package. You will incorporate elements from the old design as you develop an attractive, modern packaging concept.

This project incorporates the following skills:

- ❏ Sampling colors to create custom swatches
- ❏ Placing a variety of external files in the appropriate locations to meet package design requirements
- ❏ Creating type on an irregular path
- ❏ Understanding the difference between effects and filters
- ❏ Controlling object blending modes and opacity
- ❏ Understanding and applying raster effects
- ❏ Using different methods to isolate parts of a group
- ❏ Using warp and 3D effects to add depth to artwork
- ❏ Understanding and defining document raster effect settings
- ❏ Expanding appearance attributes
- ❏ Flattening transparent effects and attributes

Client Comments

Our current package was designed about 20 years ago; it was little more than a white box with a bowl of cereal and our brightly colored logo on the front. We've conducted some focus group studies with our primary target market, women aged 25–50 with an expressed interest in eating well and living a healthy lifestyle. We've found that this group prefers a less stark appearance — they find less empty white space and softer colors more appealing than a stark white background.

The new package should incorporate the old logo, but we'd like it to be softer than it is in the basic file. It's vivid pink, which was popular in the 1980s when the old package was designed. We also want to add some color to the entire box to avoid the "sea of white space" syndrome.

We were recently endorsed by the Association for a Healthy America; the organization sent their endorsement logo, which should be included on the box. Also, incorporate the "recycled" logo in some subtle way; this wasn't a big deal in the 1980s, but it is now.

Art Director Comments

We have a template from the printer with the package structure already laid out, based on the existing die that's used to cut the flat box from the press sheet. There's no need to reinvent the wheel, so use this template to build the new cereal box artwork.

With the growing focus on breast cancer research and overall health awareness, pink has adopted a new symbolic meaning in American culture. Because the client is targeting the health-conscious female consumer, pink should play a prominent part in the design. Complement and contrast the pink with one or two other colors for different elements; the best bet is to simply pick some colors from the main image for the box cover.

The Food and Drug Administration requires certain information on any food packaging in the United States — product weight and nutrition information are not optional; they must be included on every food package that will be sold in U.S. stores. Other elements are purely decorative, but all six sides of the box should work together to create a cohesive design.

Project Objectives

To complete this project, you will:

- ❏ Create the package file from a template
- ❏ Sample colors to create custom swatches
- ❏ Place a variety of external files in the appropriate locations to meet package design requirements
- ❏ Create type on an irregular path
- ❏ Create arrowheads with effects and filters
- ❏ Change object blending modes and opacity
- ❏ Apply raster effects to vector objects and placed images
- ❏ Apply effects to pieces of a group
- ❏ Create warp and 3D effects
- ❏ Define document raster effect settings
- ❏ Expand appearance attributes
- ❏ Preview and control transparency flattening
- ❏ Flatten transparency in a PDF file

Stage 1 Building the File Structure

When you work on a package design, it's important to realize that many types of packages have a standard size and shape. If you look around your local grocery store, you'll see that similar products typically have similar size packages. Although there is something to be said for standing out in a crowd, packaging design is often governed by the space allowed on store shelves — which means you probably won't have any choice regarding the size and shape of the package.

You also need to understand that packages, especially boxes, are typically designed and printed as a single flat layout using a die-cut template to indicate edges and folds. The next time you finish a box of cereal, tear it apart (carefully) along the glue flaps to see how the package was designed. Because these types of packages are common job sizes, printers often maintain existing die-cut templates that you can use, so you don't have to re-invent the wheel for every new job.

 ## CREATE THE PACKAGE FILE FROM A TEMPLATE

The printer for this package has provided you with a template file that includes the die-cut layout and folding guides. You will use this file as the basis for the entire project.

1. **Create a new file by opening the template file named Cereal Box.ait from the RF_Illustrator>Cereal folder.**

2. **Open the Layers panel if it is not already open. Toggle the visibility of the existing layers to review their contents.**

   The file currently has three layers: one has guides that indicate the location of the folds, one has guides that define margin areas around the folds, and one has the die-cut lines for the box shape.

Note:

Before completing this project, copy the Cereal folder from the WIP folder on your Resource CD to your WIP folder wherever you are saving your work. When you save files for this project, you will save them in your WIP>Cereal folder.

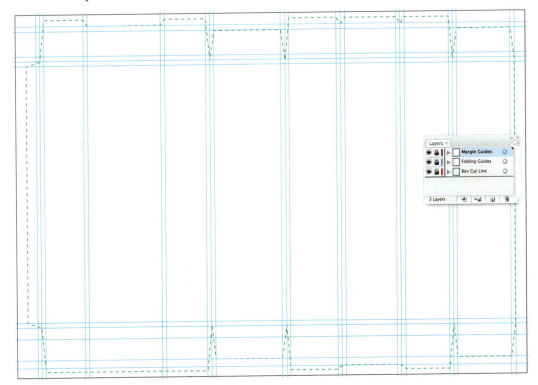

3. **Add four new layers, in the following stacking order:**

> Back Panel
>
> Jumpstart Side
>
> Front Panel
>
> Nutrition Side

Note:

Even though the panel layers are above the guide layers, guides always appear in front of artwork.

There are many ways to organize artwork; placing each panel's elements on a separate layer makes this type of complex artwork easier to manage.

4. **Drag the Box Cut Line layer to the top of the layer stack.**

Although it will not be printed, this layer needs to be visible while you create the basic package so you can clearly see the location of cut lines.

5. **Save the new file as a native Illustrator file named "HeartSmart.ai" in your WIP>Cereal folder.**

6. **Continue to the next exercise.**

 ## SAMPLE COLORS AND CREATE CUSTOM SWATCHES

Now that you have set up the basic box document and layers, you are ready to add colors that will be used throughout the design. To create a cohesive package design, you are going to select three colors directly from the image that will fill the front cover. Of course, this means you have to first place the image before you can sample its colors.

1. **With HeartSmart.ai open, select the Front Panel layer and lock the other layers. Hide the Margin Guides layer.**

In the earlier stages of package design, the folding guides are important, but the margin guides are not yet necessary.

2. **Choose File>Place. Navigate to the file Box Front.tif in the RF_Illustrator>Cereal folder and click Place.**

3. **Position the placed image so its bottom-left corner aligns with the bottom-left corner of the front panel area (as shown in the following image).**

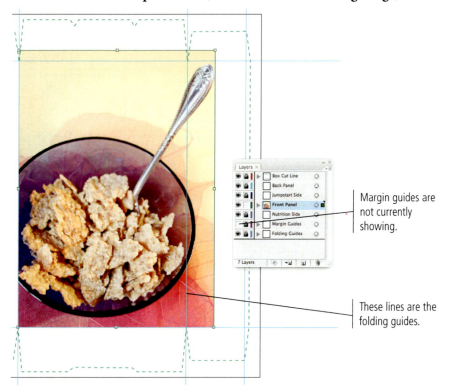

Margin guides are not currently showing.

These lines are the folding guides.

4. **Click the top-right bounding box of the image, press the Shift key, and drag down until the right edge of the image aligns with the right edge of the front panel.**

By pressing Shift before scaling the picture, you maintain the original proportions or **aspect ratio** of the placed image.

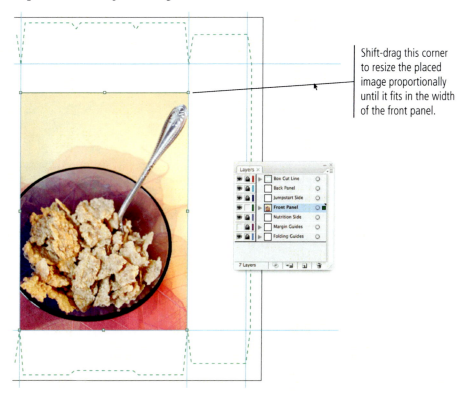

Shift-drag this corner to resize the placed image proportionally until it fits in the width of the front panel.

5. **Display the Swatches and Color panels, and then choose the Eyedropper tool in the Tools panel.**

6. **Click the Eyedropper tool in the dark purple area at the left side of the image.**

   Clicking with the Eyedropper tool changes the color in the Colors panel; this method is called **sampling** color.

Note:

If your Color and Swatches panels are docked, drag them out of the dock so you can use them both at once.

We clicked here to sample the purple color.

Eyedropper tool

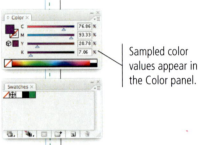

Sampled color values appear in the Color panel.

7. **Open the Color panel options menu and choose Create New Swatch.**

   This option defines a new color swatch based on the current ink percentages.

8. **In the resulting New Swatch dialog box, activate the Global check box, and then click OK to accept the default swatch name and color values.**

   The sampled color is added as a saved swatch, so you can access the exact same color again later.

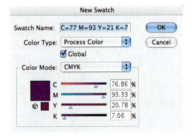

9. **Use the Eyedropper tool again to sample the light gold color in the image background, and then add the sampled color as a second custom swatch.**

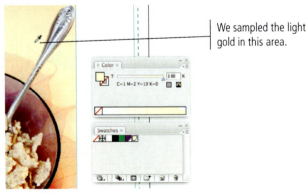

We sampled the light gold in this area.

10. **Add a third swatch by sampling the light pink color in the leaf veins below the cereal bowl.**

    You might need to zoom in to sample the color in the thin line of the leaf vein.

We sampled this leaf vein.

11. **Add a fourth swatch by sampling the dark pink color in the leaves below the cereal bowl.**

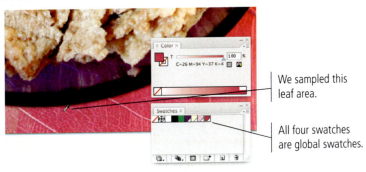

We sampled this leaf area.

All four swatches are global swatches.

12. **Save the file and continue to the next exercise.**

 ## CREATE THE BACKGROUND SHAPES

You are now ready to draw the basic background shapes for the design. Remember, the die-cut lines identify the outside edges of the box shape. The Folding Guides layer shows the location of different folds; these guides also identify the edges of the four side panels in the job. In this exercise, you use the folding guides and the die-cut template shape to create solid-colored background shapes for most of the box surface.

1. **With HeartSmart.ai open, unlock and select the Back Panel layer, and lock all other layers.**

2. **Choose the Rectangle tool from the Tools panel. Set the fill color to the light pink swatch, and set the stroke to None.**

3. **Draw a rectangle that fills the top-flap area, extending beyond the cut-line edges by at least 1/8".**

Similar to any other job where ink is supposed to print all the way to the trim edge, packaging design also requires bleed allowance. Rather than trying to meticulously match the die-cut shape, a rectangle does the job far more easily.

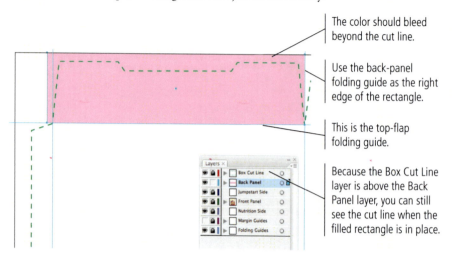

The color should bleed beyond the cut line.

Use the back-panel folding guide as the right edge of the rectangle.

This is the top-flap folding guide.

Because the Box Cut Line layer is above the Back Panel layer, you can still see the cut line when the filled rectangle is in place.

4. **Deselect the pink rectangle.**

5. **With the Rectangle tool still active, change the fill color to the light gold custom swatch.**

6. **Draw a rectangle that fills the back panel area, including the bottom flap. Make sure the bottom edge bleeds past the bottom cut line.**

7. **Show the Margin Guides layer. Extend the left edge of the gold rectangle to the margin guide on the outside glue flap.**

This flap is where the box will be glued together. The back-panel color should extend past the folding guide so there will be no white space where the side panel meets the back panel.

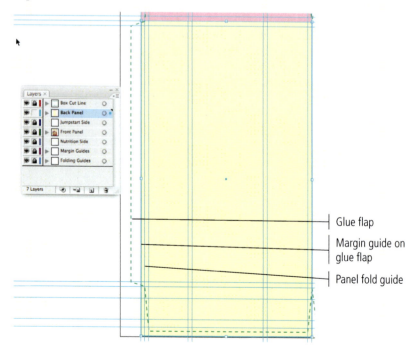

Glue flap

Margin guide on glue flap

Panel fold guide

8. Lock the Back Panel layer, and then unlock and select the Jumpstart Side layer.

9. Choose the light pink swatch as the fill color, and then use the Rectangle tool to draw the shape of the entire side panel, bleeding past the top cut line and extending to the margin guide on the bottom flap.

   The white space left at the bottom of the bottom flap will be used by the printer to add registration marks and color swatches for checking color on press.

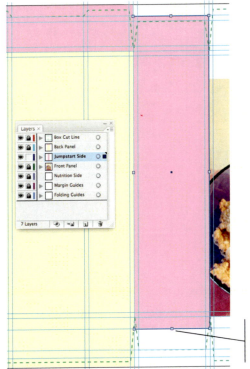

Extend the bottom of the shape to this margin guide.

10. Hide the Margin Guides layer.

11. Lock the Jumpstart Side layer, and then unlock and select the Front Panel layer.

12. Draw the top flap shape with a light pink fill, and extend its bottom edge into the front panel area. Leave a 1/8″ gap between the pink shape and the placed Box Front image.

    This white space is a common design technique called **negative space**. It can be used to add depth to an image or create the illusion of a shape. In this case, you are using it in lieu of drawing a white line.

Note:

When you are creating the background shapes, it is less confusing to show the margin guides only when necessary.

13. Draw the bottom flap shape with a light gold fill.

Note:

If you place any element on an incorrect layer, you can select it in the Layers panel and drag it to the correct layer. Just make sure that the layers involved are unlocked.

14. Bring the placed image to the front of the stacking order (Object>Arrange>Bring to Front).

15. Lock the Front Panel layer, show the Margin Guides layer, and then unlock and select the Nutrition Side layer.

16. Draw the second side panel shape with a light pink fill, extending to the same margin guide on the bottom flap as you did on the Jumpstart Side panel.

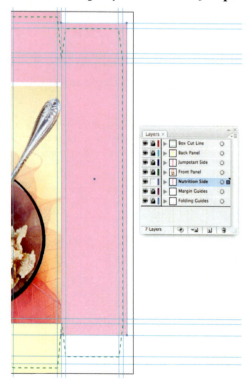

17. **Unlock all layers. If necessary, adjust the objects so the only gap between background elements is the white line on the front panel.**

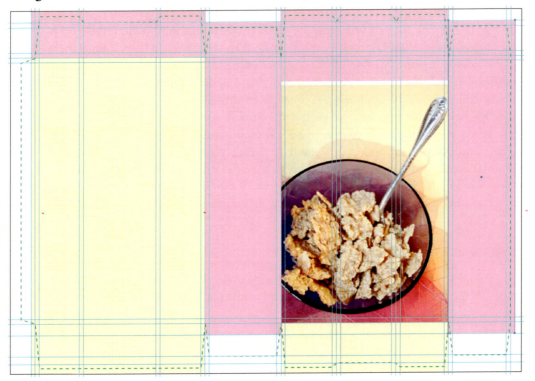

18. **Save the file and continue to the next stage of the project.**

Stage 2 Understanding Package Requirements

When you design a package, the nature of the package determines what standard elements are included in the design. In this case, a cereal box generally requires nutritional information, the package weight (in both ounces and grams), the "best by" date, and a UPC bar code label. Since the box is resealable, you should also include some simple text explaining how to open and close the box. Additionally, HeartSmart cereal is being recommended by the Association for a Healthy America; this type of product endorsement should be displayed prominently on the package.

This package design has four basic panels, and each panel combines many different elements. Most of these elements have already been created; you are going to use Illustrator to combine or **composite** the different elements into a single, unified layout. (You have already placed the primary image on the front panel, which was necessary to sample the colors that you use to build the rest of the layout.)

The most logical way to proceed is to place or create the rest of the basic design elements; you can then decide what, if anything, still needs to be done to create an attractive, finished package design.

PLACE THE NUTRITION PANEL CONTENT

When you design a complex project such as this package, it helps to decide on a logical approach to accomplish the task. Rather than jumping around across the layout, it makes more sense to work on one panel at a time.

You are going to start with the nutrition panel because it's on the right side of the page, and then work your way across to the back panel. (You could just as easily work from left to right; but for this project, we decided to start with the simplest panel.)

1. **With HeartSmart.ai open, unlock and select the Nutrition Side layer and lock all other layers.**

2. **Choose File>Place. Navigate to the RF_Illustrator>Cereal folder and select the Nutrition.ai file. Click Place, and place the file based on the Art option in the Crop To menu.**

Note:

All of the external files for this project are in the RF_Illustrator>Cereal folder.

When you place a native Illustrator file into another Illustrator file, it is contained by a bounding box that marks the outermost edges of the selected Crop To area. All of the objects in the placed file are grouped together so that you can treat the placed graphic as a single object.

3. Center the placed nutrition information in the panel area (between the margin guides), and align its top edge with the top of the cereal bowl image.

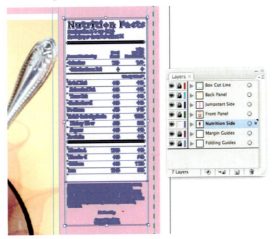

Note:

The Nutrition Facts text has been converted to outlines to ensure that the type will look exactly the same no matter where it is printed.

4. Place the file AFHA.ai into the layout using the Art bounding box as the crop area.

5. Position the placed endorsement graphic at the bottom of the panel below the nutrition information, centered between the vertical margin guides and the bottom edge, resting on the bottom margin guide.

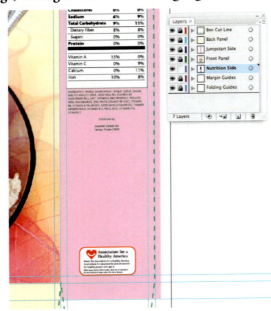

6. Save the file and continue to the next exercise.

1. With HeartSmart.ai open, lock the Nutrition Panel layer. Unlock and select the Front Panel layer.

2. Place the file Bar Code.eps, positioning it on the right side of the bottom flap. Move the bar code so the bottom corner is 1/8″ from the front flap edge, and align the bottom edge with the bottom edge of the side flap.

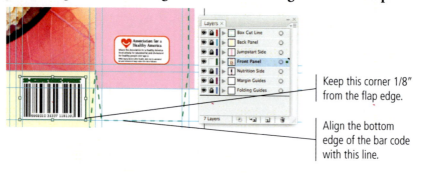

Keep this corner 1/8″ from the flap edge.

Align the bottom edge of the bar code with this line.

Note:

UPC (Universal Product Code) barcodes are symbols containing look-up numbers that uniquely identify items in the distribution and retail chain. They are specially created files that contain information about the item's name, price, and so on. These files are created by specialist companies based on specific requirements; you can't just draw a series of lines and call it a bar code.

3. Place the file HS Logo.ai (based on the Art Crop To area), positioning it in the top center of the front panel area. Align the left edge of the file with the left margin guide of the front panel area.

The crossbar of the "t" in "Heart" should overlap the line of empty white space.

4. Using the Type tool, create a point type element with the following text:

   NET WT
   20 OZ (567 g)

5. Format the text as 12-pt ATC Maple Medium with centered paragraph alignment. Change the text color to the custom purple swatch you created earlier.

6. Place the text object in the bottom-right corner of the box front area (inside the margin guides).

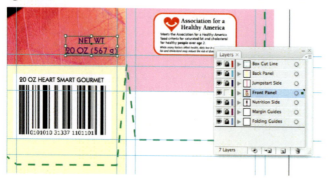

7. In the top-left section of the top flap, create a text frame and type "BETTER IF USED BY". Format the text as 11-pt ATC Maple Medium with centered paragraph alignment and a black fill.

8. Resize the area to fit the top-left flap, as marked by the guides (shown in the following image).

9. Immediately below the text frame, draw a rectangle filled with the dark pink custom swatch, fit to the rectangle created by the guides.

The sell-by date is typically stamped onto pre-printed boxes during the packaging process because every day's production has a different date. This area provides a defined space where the date will be stamped during packaging.

10. In the center section of the top flap, create a new text frame. Type the following, formatted with 10-pt ATC Maple Medium, filled with black, with centered paragraph alignment:

> To Open, Slide Finger Under
> Arrows to Left and Right

11. Clone the frame and place the clone immediately below the original. Change the text in the cloned frame to 9-pt ATC Maple Medium with a horizontal scale of 80%. Change the text in this frame to:

> TO KEEP YOUR CEREAL FRESH, REFOLD INNER BAG
> AFTER EACH USE AND CLOSE PACKAGE FLAPS.

12. Save the file and continue to the next exercise.

 PLACE THE JUMPSTART PANEL CONTENT

1. With HeartSmart.ai open, lock the Front Panel layer. Unlock and select the Jumpstart Side layer.

2. Place the file Jump Start.ai based on the Art Crop To area.

3. **Position the placed logo at the top of the panel area. Center it between the left and right panel margin guides, and align the top edge to the top margin guide.**

4. **Using the Type tool, create a text frame that fills the panel area below the placed graphic, snapping to the margin guides on the bottom and left and right sides.**

   If you click too close to the edge of the existing pink rectangle, clicking with the Type tool will convert the existing shape into a text frame. To solve this problem, click and drag to create a small text frame in the middle of the panel area, then use the Selection tool to resize the text frame to fit in the panel's margin guides.

   When you see this cursor, clicking will convert the existing shape to a text frame.

   If the cursor is far enough away from the edge of existing shapes, you can click and drag to create a new text frame.

5. **Place the file Side Copy.doc into the new text frame. Accept the default Microsoft Word options, and click OK if you get a Font Problems warning.**

   You are going to change the formatting for this text, so you don't need to worry about missing or problem fonts.

6. **Select all of the placed text and format it as 12-pt ATC Pine Normal with 21-pt leading. Change the Space After Paragraph setting to 5 pt.**

7. **Select the entire second paragraph ("The benefits of a healthy breakfast"). Change the text to 14-pt ATC Elm Italic, apply the custom purple swatch, and change the Space After Paragraph value to 0.**

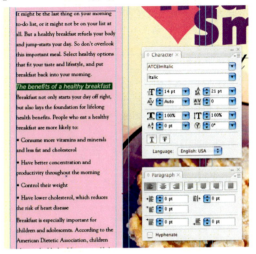

8. **Select the four bulleted paragraphs and change the leading to 17 pt. Change the Left Indent setting to 15 pt, and change the First Line Indent value to –15 pt.**

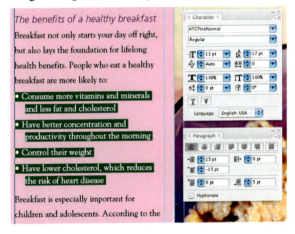

Note:

This type of negative first line indent is called a **hanging indent**.

9. **Select only the first bullet character and open the Glyphs panel (Type>Glyphs).**

10. **Search through the glyphs of different fonts to find a bullet that fits the overall product message (natural, healthy, heart-smart). When you find a glyph you like, double-click it to replace the selected character with that glyph.**

We used a leafy ornament from the Minion Pro font, but you can use whatever glyph from whatever font you prefer.

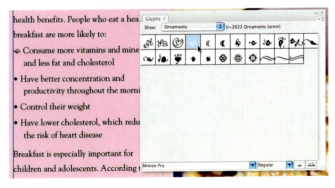

11. **Change the color of the placed glyph to the custom purple swatch.**

12. **Copy the custom glyph, and then paste it to replace the remaining three bullets.**

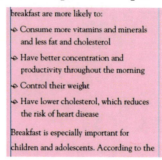

13. **Save the file and continue to the next exercise.**

 ## PLACE THE BACK PANEL CONTENT

1. **With HeartSmart.ai open, lock the Jumpstart Side layer. Unlock and select the Back Panel layer.**

2. **Place the file recycle.eps on the bottom flap of the back panel. Rotate the logo 180 degrees, and position it as shown in the following image.**

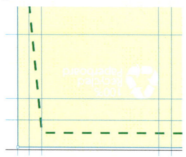

3. **Create a type area below the middle of the top flap on the back panel. Type "TO CLOSE, PUSH TAB UNDER HERE".**

4. **Format the text as 10-pt ATC Maple Medium with centered paragraph alignment.**

5. **Rotate the text frame 180 degrees, and position it as shown in the following image.**

6. **Choose File>Place. Navigate to the file Flake Heart.psd and click Place.**

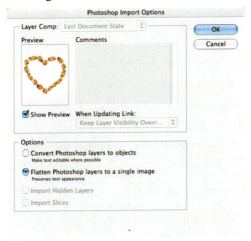

The resulting Photoshop Import Options dialog box allows you to control how Photoshop elements are translated into Illustrator:

- Use the **Layer Comp** menu to import a specific layer comp saved in the Photoshop file.

- If you link to the file instead of placing it (in the Place dialog box), you can use the **When Updating Link** menu to control what happens if you update the linked image.

- **Convert Photoshop Layers to Objects** converts Photoshop layers to Illustrator objects. This option preserves type layers as editable text objects in Illustrator, as well as masks, blending modes, transparency, and slice information. (Adjustment layers and layer effects are flattened into the placed objects.)

- **Flatten Photoshop Layers to a Single Image** combines all Photoshop layers into a single layer. The appearance of the image is preserved, but you can't edit the layers.

- **Import Hidden Layers** can be checked to include layers that are not visible in the Photoshop file.

- **Import Slices** is only available if the Photoshop file includes slices for Web layouts. If this option is checked, the slices will be maintained in the imported file.

Note:

*For more information about the different Photoshop elements, we recommend the book **Adobe Photoshop CS3: The Professional Portfolio** from Against The Clock.*

7. **Choose the Flatten Photoshop option and click OK.**

This image has only one layer, which you will not edit, so this option has the same result as converting Photoshop layers to Illustrator objects.

8. **Position the placed image in the center of the back panel area. Leave about two inches between the panel's top folding guide and the top of the placed image.**

9. **Using the Type tool, create a text frame in the area below the placed heart image, using the sides of the heart to define the frame width. Place the top edge of the frame about 1/2″ from the bottom of the heart graphic.**

10. **Place the file Back Copy.doc into the frame using the default Microsoft Word import options.**

11. **Select all of the placed text and format it as 18-pt ATC Pine Normal with 26-pt leading. Change the text color to the custom purple swatch. Apply justified paragraph alignment with the last line centered, and make sure the Hyphenate option is not checked.**

12. **Extend the bottom edge of the text frame until all of the text is visible.**

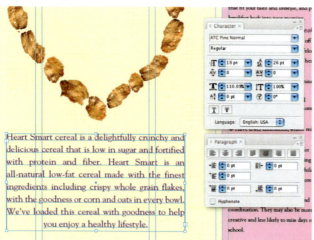

13. **Unlock the Jumpstart Side layer.**

14. **Apply the Smart Punctuation filter (Type>Smart Punctuation) and convert everything except ellipses.**

    The Smart Punctuation utility does not work on locked layers.

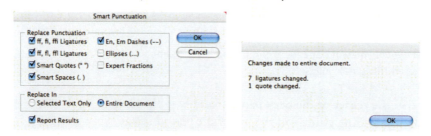

Note:

It's a good idea to include this step whenever you work with client-supplied text files.

15. **Place the insertion point in the last paragraph on the Jumpstart Side panel, and allow hyphenation in that paragraph.**

    This step fixes the widow at the end of the paragraph.

16. **Save the file and continue to the next exercise.**

CREATE TYPE ON A PATH

The last element that needs to be placed is the headline, which should appear above the heart graphic on the back panel of the box. Instead of simply flowing text into a frame, you can create unique typographic effects by flowing text onto a path. A text path can be any shape you can create in Illustrator, whether it's a simple shape created with one of the basic shape tools, a straight line you created with the Line tool, or a complex graphic you drew with the Pen tool.

1. **With HeartSmart.ai open, select the Back Panel layer and lock all other layers.**

2. **Deselect everything in the layout.**

3. **Select the Pen tool. Change the fill to None and the stroke to 1-pt black.**

4. **Draw a curve above the top of the flake heart, as shown in the following image.**

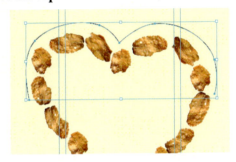

5. **Select the Type tool in the Tools panel, and then click the path you just drew.**

    Clicking an existing path with the Type tool converts the path to a type path. You could select the Type on a Path tool (nested under the Type tool), but it's not necessary because when the Type tool cursor is near an existing path, it automatically switches to the Type on a Path tool cursor.

When the Type tool cursor is near an existing path, it switches to the Type on a Path tool cursor.

After converting the path to a type path, the insertion point flashes wherever you clicked.

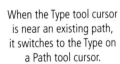 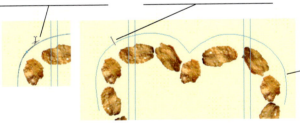

The 1-pt black stroke attribute is automatically removed when you convert the stroke to a type path.

6. **With the insertion point flashing along the path, type "A healthy start for your heart!"**

7. **Select all of the text and format it as 36-pt ATC Laurel Book with 90% horizontal scale. Change the text color to the custom purple swatch, and apply centered paragraph alignment.**

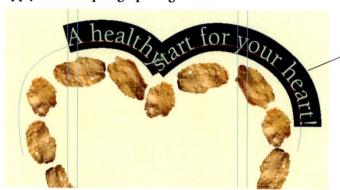

The text is centered between the location where you clicked with the Type tool and the end point of the path.

8. **Click the type path with the Direct Selection tool.**

   When you converted the path to a type path, the location where you clicked defined the starting point for text along the path. By selecting the path, you can modify the start and end points for type on the path. This is the same basic concept as changing the left and right indents for text in a regular frame.

This is the type path center point, based on the current start and end points.

This is the text start bar (basically, the left indent for the type path).

This is the text end bar (basically, the right indent for the type path).

9. **Drag the start bar to the left end of the path.**

   If you change the start or end point, the center point also changes, based on the new available space. The text is now centered, based on the entire path.

Moving the start bar to the beginning of the path repositions the center point as well.

10. **Place the insertion point and press the Spacebar enough times to separate the words "start" and "for."**

This is one of the few times when using multiple space characters is appropriate. Otherwise, the text would be unreadable where it dips into the center of the heart.

11. **Save the file and continue to the next stage of the project.**

Type on a Path Options

You can control the appearance of type on a path by choosing Type>Type on a Path>Type on a Path Options. You can apply one of five effects, change the alignment of the text to the path, flip the text to the other side of the path, and adjust the character spacing around curves (higher Spacing values remove more space around sharp curves).

- The **Rainbow** (default) effect keeps each character's baseline parallel to the path.

- The **Skew** effect maintains the vertical edges of type while skewing the horizontal edges around the path.

- The **3D Ribbon** effect maintains the horizontal edges of type while rotating the vertical edges to be perpendicular to the path.

- The **Stair Step** effect aligns the left edge of each character's baseline to the path without rotating any characters.

- The **Gravity** effect aligns the center of each character's baseline to the path, keeping vertical edges in line with the path's center.

The **Align options** determine which part of the text (baseline, ascender, descender, or center) aligns to which part of the path (top, bottom, or center).

Stage 3   Working with Effects and Filters

Illustrator includes a number of filters, effects, and other options for enhancing objects in a layout. The Filter and Effect menus are separated into two primary sections: Illustrator functions and Photoshop functions.

Note:

The Photoshop filters can be applied to rasterized objects only; the Photoshop effects, on the other hand, can be applied to both raster- and vector-based objects.

As you can see, many of the Effect options are the same as those in the Filter menu. The difference between the two appears in the result. Effects are live and non-destructive, which means they can be edited or removed from an object without destroying the original object. Filters, on the other hand, permanently change the selected object and cannot be changed once applied (although you can undo the action to "un-apply" the filter).

When you work with filters and effects, you should be aware that many of these options result in rasterized elements, even when you apply them to vector objects. For example, a drop shadow (in the Stylize submenu) creates a soft-edged shadow object that blends from the shadow color to fully transparent. To achieve this effect on output, the shadow has to be rasterized into pixels that reproduce the visual effect.

In Stage 4 of this project, you learn how to control transparent objects that need to be rasterized before they can be successfully output. In this stage, you use effects, filters, and transparency controls to add visual interest to elements of your artwork.

Note:

The Drop Shadow, Inner Glow, Outer Glow, and Feather options in the Stylize submenu all utilize some form of graded transparency, and they all result in objects that will reproduce as pixels instead of vectors.

APPLY THE ADD ARROWHEAD EFFECT

You have already placed most of the package design elements — with one exception. The text on the top flap of the front panel mentions arrows, which you haven't yet created. You could draw these shapes manually, but Illustrator's built-in effects make it easy to add symmetrical arrowheads in just one step, rather than meticulously measuring and drawing the shapes by hand.

1. **With HeartSmart.ai open, unlock and select the Front Panel layer. Lock all other layers.**

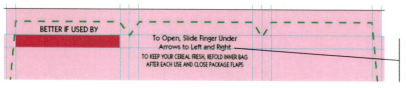

This text mentions arrows, which don't yet exist.

2. **Select the Pen tool, and then set the Fill value to None and the Stroke value to 6-pt black.**

3. **In the Artboard area above the page, draw a horizontal line approximately 1/8″ long.**

   Because this line is so short, zooming in can be very helpful for this series of steps.

4. **Press Shift, and then click above and to the right to create a second straight segment at a 45-degree angle.**

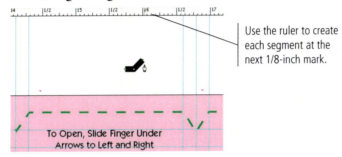

Use the ruler to create each segment at the next 1/8-inch mark.

5. **With the line selected, choose Effect>Stylize>Add Arrowheads, and then check the Preview option.**

   The Add Arrowheads effect can create arrowheads at the start (where you first clicked) and the end (where you last clicked) of a line. The dialog box defaults to the last-used settings, so yours might show different options than what you see in our screen shot.

   Illustrator offers 27 different arrowhead styles, which you can browse using the buttons below the Start and End previews. The scale defines the size of the arrowhead relative to the stroke weight.

Note:

The Add Arrowheads effect is in the Illustrator Effects Stylize menu, not the Photoshop Filters Stylize menu.

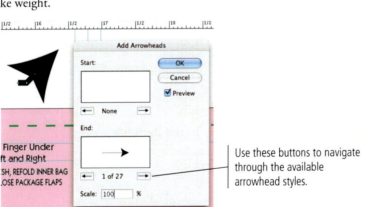

Use these buttons to navigate through the available arrowhead styles.

6. **Leave the Start arrow as None and choose 1 for the End arrow. Change the Scale field 25%.**

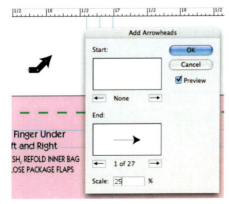

7. **Click OK to apply the arrowhead. With the line still selected, open the Appearance panel.**

Because you chose Add Arrowheads in the Effects menu, the arrowhead is applied in the same manner as a brush stroke. The Arrowhead effect is considered an attribute of the line, which means it can be changed or removed at any time, unless you choose to expand the effect.

This button toggles between New Art Has Basic Appearance (the button is highlighted) and New Art Maintains Appearance (the button is not highlighted).

Note:

To remove the effect, simply drag it to the Appearance panel's Delete button.

8. **At the bottom of the Appearance panel, make sure the New Art Maintains Appearance option is toggled on.**

When the button is not highlighted, new art will maintain the same appearance attributes (arrowheads, etc.) of the previous object. When the button is highlighted, new art will have only the basic fill and stroke appearance attributes.

This toggle button can be confusing, so you can tell which mode is selected by rolling your mouse over the button and reading the tool tip.

9. **Position the line on the top front flap, as shown in the following image.**

Because the arrowhead is an attribute of the line, it moves along with the line.

10. **Select the arrow and choose Object>Transform>Reflect. In the Reflect dialog box, choose the Vertical option, and then click Copy to create a reflected copy of the arrow.**

You won't see both arrows until you click Copy in the Reflect dialog box.

Note:

You can also open the Reflect dialog box by double-clicking the Reflect tool in the Tools panel.

11. Press Shift, and drag the reflected copy to the left side of the text.

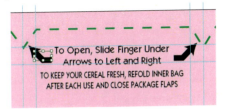

12. Save the file and continue to the next exercise.

 APPLY THE ADD ARROWHEADS FILTER

In the previous exercise, you used an effect to add an arrowhead to a line. The Filter version of the Add Arrowheads utility has exactly the same options, but creates different results.

1. With HeartSmart.ai open, unlock and select the Back Panel layer. Lock all other layers.

2. In the Artboard area above the page, use the Pen or Line tool to draw a short vertical line, from bottom to top, with a 6-pt black stroke and no fill.

If you continued directly from the previous exercise, your line will have an arrowhead pointing up, using the same style and scale settings you applied in the previous exercise.

If your line does not have an arrowhead, skip the next step (but still read the explanation of what is happening).

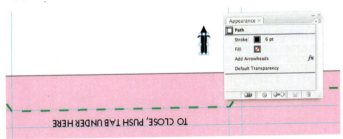

3. In the Appearance panel, click the Reduce to Basic Appearance button.

When the button at the bottom of the Appearance panel is toggled off, new objects have the same appearance attributes as the last-created object. You can change this behavior by clicking the button to toggle it on (it appears dark or outlined when toggled to the Basic Appearance mode). If you forget to check the status of this button, and a new line has unwanted appearance attributes (such as the arrowhead on this new line), you can remove the effect using the Reduce to Basic Appearance button.

Note:

The Clear Appearance button removes all attributes from the object, leaving only the shape with a fill and stroke value of None.

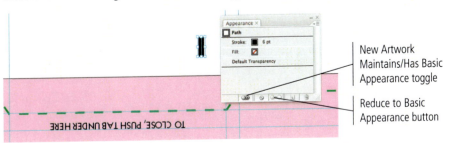

New Artwork Maintains/Has Basic Appearance toggle

Reduce to Basic Appearance button

4. **With the vertical line selected, choose Filter>Stylize>Add Arrowheads.**

This option is basically the same as the Add Arrowheads Effect option. However, filters create objects instead of attributes.

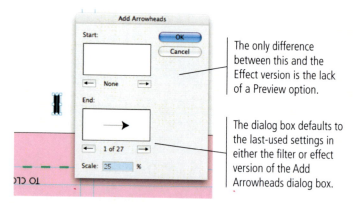

The only difference between this and the Effect version is the lack of a Preview option.

The dialog box defaults to the last-used settings in either the filter or effect version of the Add Arrowheads dialog box.

5. **Use the button below the End option to find arrowhead 11. Make sure the Scale field is set to 25%, and then click OK.**

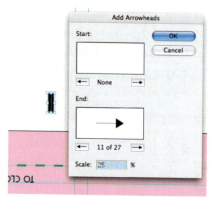

Note:

You can't preview the result of filters. You can, however, preview the result of effects.

6. **Look at the Appearance panel.**

After applying the Add Arrowhead filter, the resulting arrowhead is a separate shape, grouped with the original line.

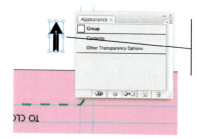

Using the filter instead of the effect, the arrowhead is an actual shape, grouped with the original line.

7. **Deselect the grouped object. Use the Direct Selection tool to select only the line. Delete the selected line.**

Because the arrowhead is an actual object instead of an appearance attribute, you can use the shape independently of the original line.

8. **Select the remaining triangle and change the fill to white and the stroke to 0.5-pt black.**

Note:

You can convert arrowhead effects into objects by choosing Object>Expand Appearance.

9. **Drag the triangle into position as shown in the following image.**

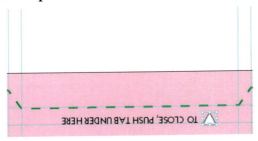

10. **Clone the triangle and move the clone horizontally to the other side of the related text.**

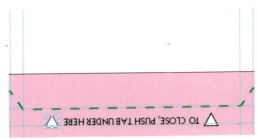

11. **Save the file and continue to the next exercise.**

 CHANGE OBJECT BLENDING MODES AND OPACITY

The effects and transparency controls in Illustrator allow you to add dimension and depth to virtually any design element. You can change the transparency of any object, apply different blending modes so objects blend smoothly into underlying objects, and apply creative effects (such as drop shadows) that incorporate transparency.

1. **With HeartSmart.ai open, unlock the four panel layers.**

2. **Select the placed Recycle logo and open the Transparency panel.**

   All parts of this graphic have a white fill. You are going to change the blending mode so the logo blends into the background color (hence the term, "blending mode").

3. Choose Soft Light in the Blending Mode menu.

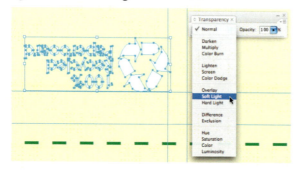

After changing the blending mode, the logo is very subtle against the underlying background color.

4. Using the Direct Selection tool, select the heart shape in the cereal name on the front panel.

5. **In the Transparency panel, change the Opacity value to 50%.**

   The Opacity option determines how much of the underlying colors show through the affected object. If an object is 75% opaque, 25% of the underlying colors will be visible.

6. **Clone the logo. Scale the clone to 35%, and position the resized version in the empty space of the nutrition panel.**

7. **In the Layers panel, drag the Selected Art icon to the Nutrition Side layer.**

   Make sure the scaled version of the logo is on the correct layer.

8. **Clone the resized logo. Place the new clone at the bottom of the Jumpstart Side panel and move the artwork to the appropriate layer.**

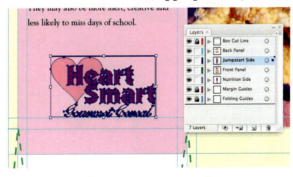

Creating an Opacity Mask

As you have seen, you can use the Transparency panel to change the blending mode and opacity of an object in Illustrator. If you choose Show Options in the panel options menu, several other choices allow you to control the behavior of transparency for more complex objects.

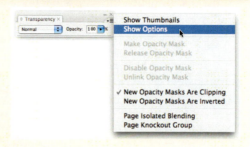

An **opacity mask** defines the transparency of selected artwork. In Illustrator, you can create an opacity mask by selecting two or more shapes and choosing Make Opacity Mask in the Transparency panel options menu. The topmost selected object (or group) becomes the **masking object**; underlying objects in the selection are the **masked artwork**.

The best way to explain the concept of opacity masks is through example. The first image shows three separate objects: the top object (the word Autumn, converted to outlines), the gradient-filled rectangle, and the black-filled rectangle.

When you define an opacity mask, shades in the masking object (in this example, the word "Autumn") determine the degree of transparency in the masked artwork (the red-gold gradient). As you can see in the second image, where the word was black, the underlying gradient is entirely transparent — the black background shape shows through those areas of the gradient. Where the masking object is white, the masked artwork is 100% opaque.

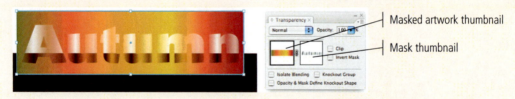

Masked artwork thumbnail

Mask thumbnail

If the **Clip** option is checked, the masking object also determines which parts of the masked artwork are visible.

If the **Invert Mask** option is checked, tones in the masking object are reversed (black becomes white and white becomes black). Transparency of the masked artwork is also effectively reversed.

By default, the masking object and the masked artwork are linked, which means you can't move one without the other. If you click the Link icon between the masked artwork and mask thumbnails, you can move the two elements independently.

Turn off the Link option to move either object independently of the other.

9. Clone the resized logo again. Rotate the new clone 180°, place it in the center of the top flap on the back panel, and move the artwork to the Back Panel layer. If necessary, scale this version so it fits entirely within the flap area.

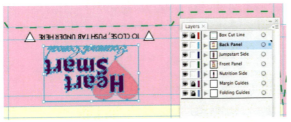

10. Save the file and continue to the next exercise.

Transparency Panel Options

Three options at the bottom of the Transparency panel allow you to control transparency settings relative to grouped objects. If **Isolate Blending** is checked, blending changes will only apply to other objects in the same group. The group effectively **knocks out** the underlying shapes.

The opacity of the purple letters has been reduced to 50%.

When Knockout Group is checked, the opacity only affects underlying objects that are not part of the grouped logo.

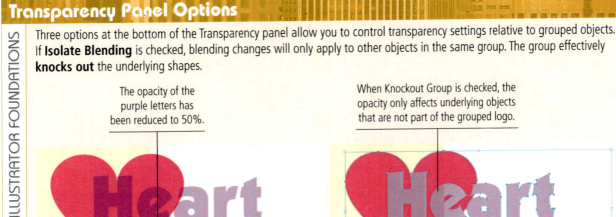

If **Knockout Group** is checked, transparency settings for elements within the group will not apply to other elements in the same group. The transparent effects are only applied to objects under the entire group. In this case, elements within the group knock out other objects in the same group.

The Hard Light blending mode is applied to the purple letters in the grouped logo.

When Isolate Blending is checked, the blending mode does not affect the underlying gold object.

If **Opacity & Mask Define Knockout Shape** is checked (at the bottom of the panel), the mask object's opacity creates a knockout effect. Where the mask is 100% opaque, the knockout effect will be strong; in areas of lower opacity, the knockout effect will be weaker.

Transparency and blending modes can help to unify different elements of a design. Other effects — specifically glows, drop shadows, and similar styles — combine graded transparency and blending modes to add depth in otherwise flat artwork.

1. **With HeartSmart.ai open, select the placed heart image on the back panel.**

2. **Choose Effect>Stylize>Outer Glow and activate the Preview check box.**

   As with the Add Arrowheads effect, we are using the Illustrator Effects Stylize menu, not the Photoshop Effects Stylize menu.

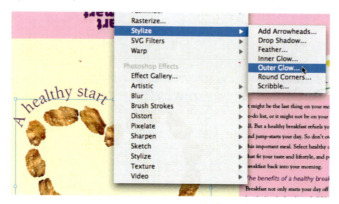

The Outer Glow effect adds a transparent effect behind the selected object. The Mode menu, color swatch, and Opacity menu determine the appearance of the glow effect. The Blur field defines the width of the apparent effect (how far the glow extends from the edges of the object).

3. **Click the color swatch to the right of the Mode menu. In the resulting Color Picker dialog box, click the Color Swatches button to show the swatches saved in the current file.**

Note:

You can use any color for the glow, but using an existing swatch helps unify the design.

4. **Choose the dark pink custom swatch and click OK.**

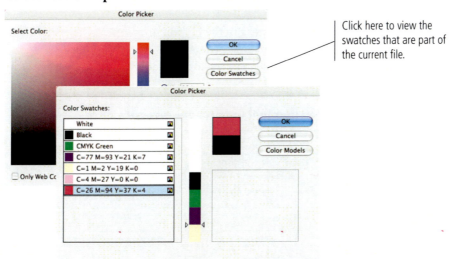

Click here to view the swatches that are part of the current file.

5. **In the Outer Glow dialog box, choose Multiply in the Mode menu and change the Blur field to 0.05".**

The Multiply blending mode combines the base color (the light gold background) with the glow color (the dark pink at 75% opacity).

6. **Click OK to apply the glow effect, and then look at the Appearance panel.**

As with the Add Arrowhead effect, the outer glow effect is an appearance attribute. You can edit the applied glow settings by double-clicking the effect in the Appearance panel, and you can remove the effect by dragging it to the Appearance panel's Delete button.

7. **Save the file and continue to the next exercise.**

APPLY EFFECTS TO PART OF A GROUP

As you know, all elements of placed graphics are grouped together in the file where they are placed. Any groupings from the original file are also maintained, often resulting in a complex series of multiple nested groups — which can make it difficult to access specific elements to make changes or apply effects.

1. **With HeartSmart.ai open, use the Direct Selection tool to select one piece of the purple man in the placed Jump Start logo.**

This icon identifies the layer where the selected object exists.

2. **In the Layers panel, click the arrow to the left of the Jumpstart Side layer.**

This shows the objects contained on the layer (called **sublayers**). You can further expand groups to show — and select — the individual elements in a group.

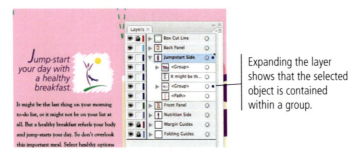

Expanding the layer shows that the selected object is contained within a group.

3. **Click the arrow to expand the group that contains the selected object.**

4. **Continue expanding groups until the group thumbnail shows the dancing man figure (with the grass and sun).**

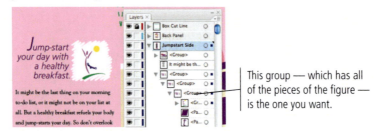

This group — which has all of the pieces of the figure — is the one you want.

5. **Click the target icon next to the small figure group to isolate it.**

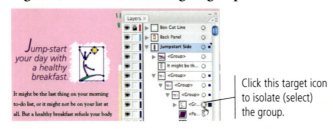

Click this target icon to isolate (select) the group.

Note:

If you can't make out the contents of the sublayer thumbnails, you can enlarge them by choosing Panel Options in the Layers panel options menu.

6. **Choose Effect>Stylize>Drop Shadow and activate the Preview check box.**

The Drop Shadow dialog box has similar options to the Outer Glow effect. The primary difference is that you can change the horizontal (X) and vertical (Y) offset values of the applied shadow.

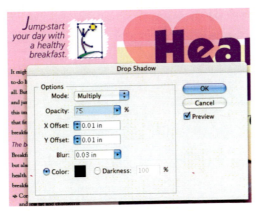

Note:

Effect dialog boxes default to the last-used settings, so your settings might be different than what you see in our screen shot.

7. **Change the drop shadow settings to the following:**

Mode:	**Multiply**
Opacity	**75%**
X Offset	**0.02″**
Y Offset	**0.02″**
Blur	**0.04″**
Color	**100% Black**

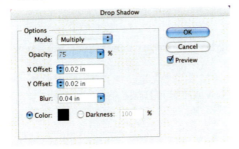

8. **Click OK to apply the drop shadow.**

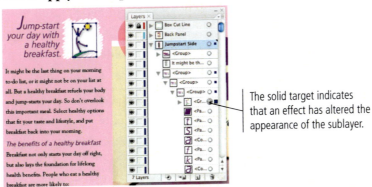

The solid target indicates that an effect has altered the appearance of the sublayer.

9. **Collapse the expanded layers in the Layers panel, and then save the file and continue to the next exercise.**

Isolating Groups

If you remember from Project 4, editing a symbol opens a separate version of the Artboard — called Symbol-Editing mode — where you make changes in the symbol contents. You also learned that you can enter symbol-editing mode in place, in which case everything but the symbol is visible, but can't be selected.

The same concept applies to editing groups. If you double-click a group with the Selection tool, you enter **Isolation mode**, in which only the group is editable. If groups are nested, you can drill deeper into the group by repeatedly double-clicking.

Click this arrow to return to the main artboard.

In Isolation mode, everything but the selected group is screened back.

Double-clicking multiple times allows you to eventually isolate the group (or element) you want.

 ## WARP DESIGN ELEMENTS

The last piece of this design is a banner across the bottom that announces a promotional premium (in this case, a recipe booklet). Rather than simply creating a flat banner, you're going to use effects to create a two-piece, three-dimensional banner that appears to wave across the box.

1. **With HeartSmart.ai open, lock everything but the Front Panel layer. Select the Front Panel layer.**

2. **In the Appearance panel, make sure the New Art Has Basic Appearance option is active.**

3. **Create a rectangle near the bottom of the front panel area that is 5.5″ wide and 1″ high. Fill the rectangle with the dark pink custom swatch.**

4. **Using the Add Anchor Point tool, add an anchor point to the right edge of the rectangle, halfway between the corners. Use the Direct Selection tool to drag the point left, creating the basic banner shape.**

5. **Using the Type tool, click to create a point text element near the center of the banner shape.**

6. **Type "Yummy! Cereal Recipes", and then format the text as 28-pt ATC Maple Ultra with 125% vertical scaling and a white fill.**

7. **Position the text relative to the banner shape (as shown in the following image).**

We added an anchor point to a basic rectangle to create the right side of the banner shape.

8. **Group the text and the banner. With the group selected, choose Effect>Warp>Arc.**

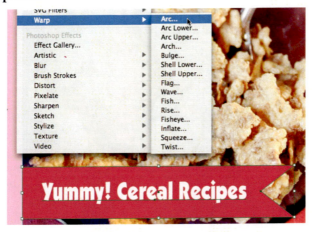

9. **In the resulting Warp Options dialog box, activate the Preview check box.**

The icon for each Warp style suggests the result that will be created.

Distortion values change the horizontal and vertical perspectives of selected objects.

The Bend value determines how much warping will be applied to the selected objects.

10. **Choose Arch in the Style menu.**

   As the Arch icon suggests, the object's left and right edges are unaffected by the warp.

Note:

You can choose from any of the 15 styles in the Style menu (these are the same as the options listed in the Effect>Warp submenu).

11. **Change the Bend value to –25% and click OK to apply the warp.**

   The Warp effect is also treated as an appearance attribute. When selected, you can see the original object shape.

The bounding box and paths reflect the actual objects without the applied appearance attributes.

Note:

Similar Warp options are available by choosing Object>Envelope Distort>Make with Warp.

12. **Create another rectangle that's 2″ wide by 1″ high, positioned on the right side of the front panel area.**

13. **Using the same method from the first banner shape, add a point to the left side of the shape, and then drag it right to create the second banner shape.**

14. **Use the Type tool to add a point text element with the words "FREE INSIDE" formatted as 20-pt ATC Maple Ultra with a white fill and a vertical scale of 125%.**

15. **Group the second banner with its text, and then apply a warp effect using the Rise style and a 50% Bend value.**

16. **Save the file and continue to the next exercise.**

 CREATE A 3D EFFECT

3D effects allow you to create three-dimensional objects from two-dimensional artwork. You can create depth by changing an object's rotation along three different axes, or use extrusion settings to basically "pull" (extrude) an object in three directions. You can also control the appearance of 3D objects with lighting, shading, and other properties.

1. **With HeartSmart.ai open, select the first banner group you created in the previous exercise.**

2. **Choose Effect>3D>Extrude & Bevel and activate the Preview option.**

   In the 3D Extrude & Bevel Options dialog box, the small preview shows the approximate position of the original object (the blue square) in relation to the object created by the settings in this dialog box.

Note:

You will work extensively with perspective and vanishing points in Project 7.

3. Click the preview icon and drag it around.

As you drag the preview, the values in the three fields change, based on how and where you drag. In the layout, the selected group also changes because the Preview option is active.

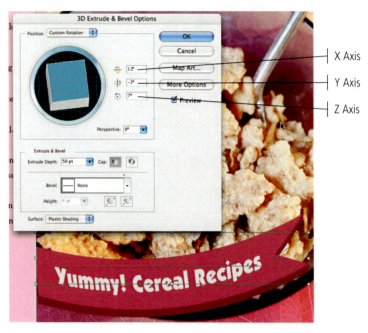

The **X Axis** value rotates an object around an invisible horizontal line.

The **Y Axis** value rotates an object around an invisible vertical line.

The **Z Axis** value rotates an object around an invisible line that moves from the front of an object to the back.

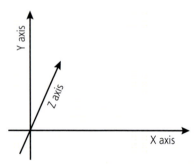

4. When you are done experimenting, specify the following values:

X Axis = 14°

Y Axis = 0°

Z Axis = 0°

5. Click OK to apply the effect.

6. **Select the small banner group and choose Effect>Apply Extrude & Bevel.**

   This top menu option shows the last-used effect. If you use this menu command, the effect will be applied using the same settings as the last time the effect was used. You will not see the effect's dialog box.

7. **Reposition the two banners across the bottom of the box, as shown in the following image.**

   Since there is some variability in banner size and text placement, you might need to adjust the placement so your banners fit in the best possible way.

8. **Save the file and continue to the next stage of the project.**

Stage 4 Preparing Complex Artwork for Output

For all intents and purposes, the box artwork is now finished. You've placed and formatted the client's text, composited a number of external graphics and images, created several design elements directly from within Illustrator, and enhanced many of the layout objects using built-in transparency controls and effects.

Whenever you design a file, however, it's important to consider the ultimate goal of the project — in other words, how will the job be output, and what needs to happen to make sure that what you see on your screen is what you get out of the printer.

For most Illustrator projects, you are probably going to use two or more formats for a completed job (depending on what you need to do with the file).

- If the file needs to be placed into Adobe InDesign, you can leave the file in its native Illustrator format. (Transparency in the file will be flattened when the InDesign document is output.)

- If the file needs to be placed into a QuarkXPress 7 document, you need to save the file using the EPS or PDF format. (QuarkXPress does not support native Illustrator files.)

- If the file needs to be placed into a QuarkXPress 6 document, you need to save PDF files to be compatible with PDF 1.3 (which does not support transparency).

- If the file needs to be placed into an earlier version of QuarkXPress (version 5 or lower), you should save the file as EPS. (Some earlier versions of QuarkXPress do not support PDF files without an extra XTension; some do not support the PDF format at all.)

When an Illustrator file is output — whether printed or exported as an EPS or PDF file — the elements in your design need to be converted to something that makes sense to an output device.

High-quality, professional output devices are driven by a **raster-image processor** (RIP) that processes the file data. Unfortunately, output devices don't understand instructions such as "put a red circle in the middle of the page." The PostScript language is used to translate visually designed elements into something the RIP can understand. The PostScript language mathematically describes each object on the page in terms of vectors and pixels.

PostScript does not have the ability to communicate information about transparency. So for transparent elements to output properly, they must be converted or **flattened** into information that can be described in the PostScript language. Flattening divides transparent artwork into the necessary vector and raster objects.

DEFINE DOCUMENT RASTER EFFECT SETTINGS

Flattening means breaking transparent elements into whatever elements are necessary to output properly. In some cases, this results in the creation of new rasterized objects (for example, where transparent text overlaps a raster image).

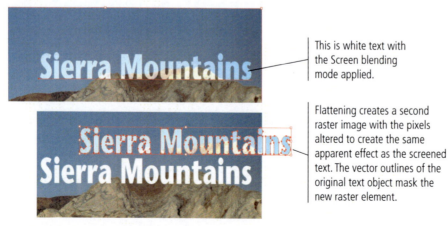

This is white text with the Screen blending mode applied.

Flattening creates a second raster image with the pixels altered to create the same apparent effect as the screened text. The vector outlines of the original text object mask the new raster element.

Some effects, such as drop shadows, create entirely new raster elements where none existed previously.

This text has a drop shadow applied.

Flattening the text with a drop shadow results in a new, separate raster object — the drop shadow.

If you are going to create raster objects — either manually or by allowing Illustrator to manage the process — you need to be able to control the resolution of those elements. For high-quality print jobs, you should use at least 300 pixels per inch.

1. **With HeartSmart.ai open, choose Effect>Document Raster Effects Settings.**

2. **Review the settings in the resulting dialog box.**

These settings are already optimized for high-quality output, applied in the printer's original document template. However, it's always a good idea to check the settings before you apply them.

The **Color Model** menu determines the mode that will be used for new rasterized objects (CMYK, Grayscale, or Bitmap for a document in CMYK mode; an RGB option replaces CMYK if the file uses the RGB color mode).

The **Resolution** options include three basic settings (72 ppi for low-resolution screen display, 150 ppi for medium-resolution desktop printers, or 300 ppi for high-resolution PostScript output). If necessary, you can also assign a custom resolution value in the Other field.

The **Background** options determine how unfilled areas of the file will be handled when placed into another file. If White is selected, underlying objects will not be visible through empty areas of the file.

In the **Options** area:

- **Anti-alias** helps to create smooth transitions, reducing stair-stepping around the edges of rasterized objects.
- **Create Clipping Mask** creates a vector mask that makes the background of the rasterized image appear transparent.
- **Add _ Around Object** creates a specific-sized border around a rasterized image. If you use the White Background option, this area will be filled with white.
- **Preserve Spot Colors** allows spot color objects to be maintained as spot colors instead of being converted to CMYK.

3. **Click OK to close the dialog box.**

4. **Save the file and continue to the next exercise.**

Note:

Note the warning at the bottom of the dialog box that says, "Changing these settings may affect the appearance of currently applied raster effects."

EXPAND APPEARANCE ATTRIBUTES

When you output a file, the RIP processes the PostScript stream to create the print. Extremely complex designs can take a long time to output (depending on the processing capability of the output device) and can even "jam the RIP" — crash the device and cause an output error. To prevent potential output problems from overly complex designs, you might want to expand appearance attributes after the design has been finalized.

1. **With HeartSmart.ai open, use the Selection tool to select the right banner shape.**

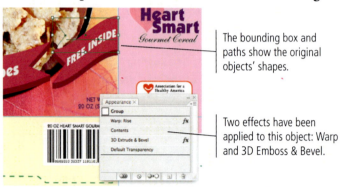

The bounding box and paths show the original objects' shapes.

Two effects have been applied to this object: Warp and 3D Emboss & Bevel.

2. **Choose Object>Expand Appearance.**

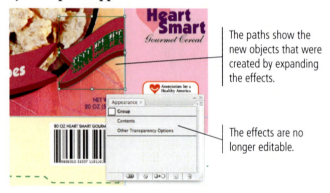

The paths show the new objects that were created by expanding the effects.

The effects are no longer editable.

3. **Using the same process, expand the appearance of the left banner.**

    Fine-tuning and optimizing a complex file for output requires a tradeoff between editability and printability. As your file currently stands, you can still change or delete any attribute of any object. After expanding effects, the file will output faster, but you won't be able to change the effect settings.

    We recommend saving the expanded version as a separate file so you can make changes if necessary.

4. **Save the file as "HeartSmart Expanded.ai" in your WIP>Cereal folder and continue to the next exercise.**

PREVIEW TRANSPARENCY FLATTENING

If you are designing with transparency, it's a good idea to know exactly what elements will be affected when the file is flattened for output. Illustrator provides a Flattener Preview panel that you can use to review the file for potential problems.

1. **With HeartSmart Expanded.ai open, choose Window>Flattener Preview.**

2. **If nothing appears in the white space of the panel, click the Refresh button.**

Drag this corner to make the panel larger, and then click Refresh to enlarge the preview image.

3. **In the Highlight menu, choose All Affected Objects.**

   The red areas in the preview show all objects that are somehow affected by transparency in the file.

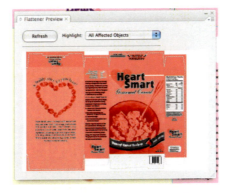

4. **In the Highlight menu, choose Transparent Objects.**

   The highlighted areas reduce to only the objects where transparency is applied.

Flattener Preview Panel Options

You can use the Flattener Preview Highlight menu to highlight different kinds of areas, allowing you to determine which flattener settings will be best for the entire file or for a specific object.

- **None (Color Preview)** displays the normal layout.

- **Rasterized Complex Regions** highlights areas that will be rasterized based on the Raster/Vector Balance defined in the applied preset.

- **Transparent Objects** highlights objects with opacity of less than 100%, blending modes, transparency effects (such as drop shadows), and/or feathering applied.

- **All Affected Objects** highlights all objects affected by transparency, including the transparent objects and the objects overlapped by transparent objects. All of these objects will be affected by flattening.

- **Affected Linked EPS Files** highlights all EPS files linked in the file but not embedded.

- **Expanded Patterns** highlights patterns that will be expanded by flattening. (Pattern effects must be expanded if they are affected by transparency; this takes place automatically when you output the file.)

- **Outlined Strokes** highlights all strokes that will be converted to filled objects when flattened. (For example, a 5-pt stroke with the Screen blending mode will be converted to a 5-pt-high rectangle filled with the underlying object when the file is flattened.)

5. **Choose Show Options in the panel options menu.**

   The options show the specific settings that will be used to flatten the artwork, based by default on a Flattener Preset.

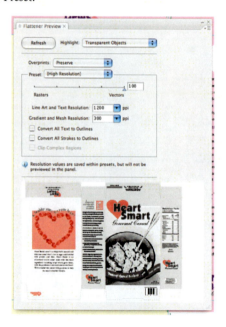

6. **Continue to the next exercise.**

FLATTEN TRANSPARENCY FOR SELECTED OBJECTS

Although flattening is typically managed for you when you output a file, you can flatten selected objects manually at any point in the process. Like expanding an object's appearance, however, flattening is a permanent action — you will no longer be able to edit any effect or setting caused by the transparency. This process should only be done at the very end of a project; again, we recommend maintaining your original file and saving a new version with the manually flattened artwork.

1. **With HeartSmart Expanded.ai open, unlock the Back Panel layer and then select the heart image on the back panel.**

2. **Choose Object>Flatten Transparency and activate the Preview option.**

3. Make sure the High Resolution option is selected in the Preset menu and the Preserve Alpha Transparency option is checked.

To produce the outer glow effect applied to this object, the color blends outward to become fully transparent at the edges. In other words, the pixels toward the outer edge of the effect are more transparent than the pixels at the inner edge of the effect. This type of effect requires a mechanism to describe the degree of transparency for each pixel. **Alpha transparency** is a type of mask that defines the degree of transparency for each pixel in the resulting raster objects.

Note:

If Preserve Alpha Transparency is not checked, the flattened artwork will have a white background; the effect will not blend into the background color.

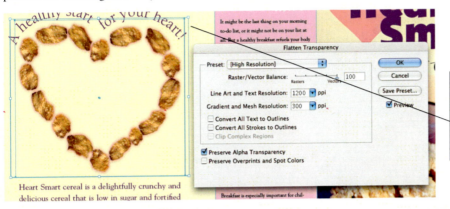

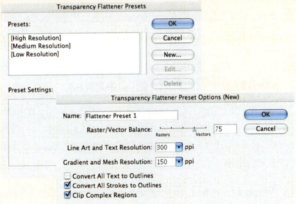

When the Preview option is checked, the file shows two bounding boxes — the result of flattening the applied outer glow effect.

Flattener Presets

Illustrator includes three default flattener presets, which are appropriate for most typical jobs:

- **Low Resolution** works for desktop proofs that will be printed on low-end black-and-white printers, and for documents that will be published on the Web.

- **Medium Resolution** works for desktop proofs and print-on-demand documents that will be printed on PostScript-compatible color printers.

- **High Resolution** works for commercial output on a printing press and for high-quality color proofs.

You can also create your own flattener presets by choosing Edit>Transparency Flattener Presets and clicking New in the resulting dialog box. In addition, you can use the Transparency Flattener Presets dialog box to load flattener presets created on another machine — such as one your service provider created for their specific output device and/or workflow.

- The preset **Name** will be listed in the related output menus. You should use names that suggest the preset's use, such as "PDF for XL Printing Company." Using meaningful names is a good idea for any asset that can have a name — from color swatches to output presets. "My Preset 12" is meaningless (possibly even to you after a few days), while "Preset for HP Indigo" tells you exactly when to use those settings.

- **Raster/Vector Balance** determines how much vector information will be preserved after flattening. This slider ranges from 0 (all information will be flattened as rasters) to 100 (maintains all vector information).

- **Line Art and Text Resolution** defines the resolution of vector elements that will be rasterized, up to 9600 ppi. For good results in commercial printing applications, this option should be at least 600–1200 ppi (ask your output provider what settings they prefer you to use).

- **Gradient and Mesh Resolution** defines the resolution for gradients that will be rasterized, up to 1200 ppi. This option is typically set to 300 ppi for most commercial printing applications.

- **Convert All Text to Outlines** converts all type to outline shapes; the text will not be editable in a PDF file.

- **Convert All Strokes to Outlines** converts all strokes to filled paths.

- **Clip Complex Regions** forces boundaries between vector objects and rasterized artwork to fall along object paths, reducing potential problems that can result when only part of an object is rasterized.

4. **Click OK to flatten the transparency of the selected object.**

5. **Using the Direct Selection tool, click one of the flakes in the image to select only the placed image file only.**

6. **Choose Object>Hide>Selection.**

   By flattening the object, a new raster object was created to reproduce the Outer Glow effect.

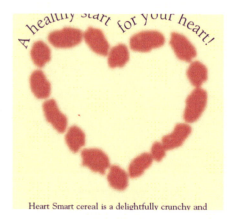

7. **Choose Object>Show All to show the heart of flakes image.**

8. **Save the file as "HeartSmart Flat.ai" in your WIP>Cereal folder and continue to the next exercise.**

 ## Export a PDF File for Proofing

Although packaging such as this box is commonly printed directly from the Illustrator file, you should still create a proof that your client can review either on screen or printed. The PDF format is ideal for this use because the client doesn't need Illustrator to open or print the proof file.

1. **With HeartSmart Flat.ai open, choose File>Save As.**

2. **Navigate to your WIP>Cereal folder as the destination and choose Adobe PDF in the Format/Save As Type menu.**

3. **Click Save.**

4. **Choose High Quality Print in the Adobe PDF Preset menu.**

   The Adobe PDF Preset menu includes six PDF presets that meet common industry output requirements.

Note:

You can manage PDF Presets by choosing File>Adobe PDF Preset>Define. The dialog box that appears lists the built-in presets, as well as any presets you have created. You can also import presets from other users, or you can export presets to send to other users.

5. **Choose Acrobat 4 (PDF 1.3) in the Compatibility menu.**

   The Compatibility menu determines which version of the PDF format you will create. Not all clients will have the latest versions of technology, so you should consider saving all proof-quality PDFs to be compatible with the earliest version of PDF possible.

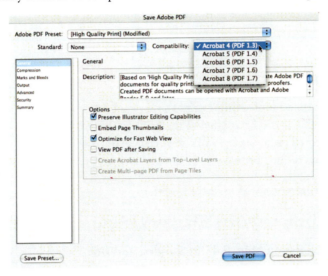

Note:

Because there are so many ways to create a PDF — and not all of those ways are optimized for the needs of commercial printing — the potential benefits of the file format are often undermined. The PDF/X specification was created to help solve some of the problems associated with bad PDF files entering the prepress workflow. PDF/X is a subset of PDF specifically designed to ensure files have the information necessary for and available to the digital prepress output process. Ask your output provider whether you should apply a PDF/X standard to your files, and if so, which version to use.

6. **Click Advanced in the list of options.**

   PDF 1.3 does not support transparency, so the file will require flattening. If you save the file to be compatible with PDF 1.4 or later, the transparency information will be maintained in the PDF file; it will have to be flattened later in the process.

7. **Choose High Resolution in the Preset menu.**

   Even though this PDF is for proofing purposes, high-resolution produces better results. If file size is not a concern, it's a good idea to use the high-resolution flattener even for proofs.

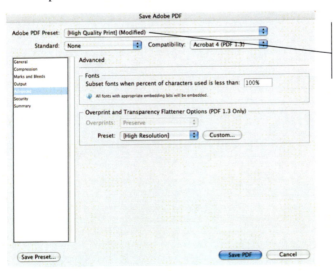

As soon as you choose a setting that is not part of the preset, the preset name shows "(Modified)".

Note:

If you need a smaller file size for proofing purposes, try applying a higher amount of compression in the Compression options.

8. **Click Save PDF to output the file.**

9. **Close the Illustrator file.**

Stage 5   Preview the Box Design in 3D

In Stage 3, you used the 3D Extrude & Bevel feature to add depth to the banners on the front of the box. This same effect can be used to create a box shape and preview your flat box artwork in three dimensions, which is especially useful for showing a client how the art will look when the final piece is printed and folded.

CREATE SYMBOLS FOR BOX PANELS

For this process to work, you first have to do a bit of set-up work. The artwork for each panel has to be saved as a symbol before it can be applied to the 3D box shape. This means that you have to do some cutting and clean up work so you have the exact shapes that you need before you create the 3D box preview.

1. **Open HeartSmart Expanded.ai from your WIP>Cereal folder.**

2. **Save the file immediately as Box Preview.ai in your WIP>Cereal folder.**

3. **Hide and lock all layers but the Nutrition Side, Folding Guides, and Box Cut Line layers.**

4. **Select the pink background shape, and use the Selection tool to drag the top and bottom edges to match the folding guides for the side panel.**

5. **Group all of the remaining objects on the layer.**

6. **Open the Symbols panel (Window>Symbols).**

7. **Drag the group into the Symbols panel.**

8. In the resulting dialog box, name the symbol "Nutrition Panel" and click OK.

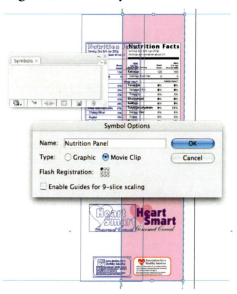

9. Repeat the same process for the Front Panel layer, Jumpstart Side layer, and Back Panel layer. If an element only exists on a flap, delete it. Name the symbols "Front Panel", "Jumpstart Panel", and "Back Panel".

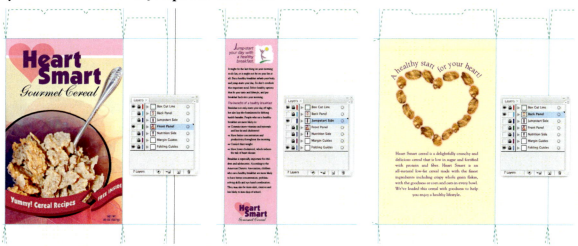

10. In the Symbols panel options menu, change the panel view to Large List View.

11. Save the file and continue to the next exercise.

APPLY THE ART TO A 3D BOX

Now that you have symbols for each side of the box, you have to create a shape that you can turn into a three-dimensional box. This shape needs to be the correct size for the existing artwork, so you will again use the panel folding guides to build this shape.

1. **With Box Preview.ai open, create a new layer named "Box Rendering". Lock and hide all other panel layers.**

2. **Using the Rectangle tool with a light gold fill and no stroke, draw a shape that fills the front panel area (excluding the flaps).**

3. **Draw a second rectangle that extends the width of the nutrition panel. Look at the Transform panel and note the width of the side panel, and then delete this rectangle.**

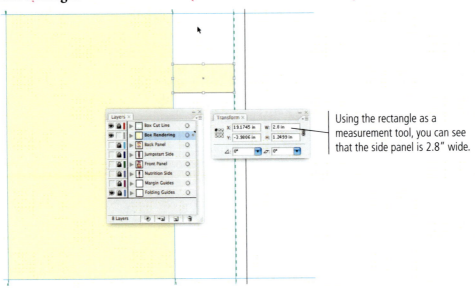

Using the rectangle as a measurement tool, you can see that the side panel is 2.8" wide.

4. **Hide the Box Cut Line and Folding Guide layers.**

5. **Select the large remaining rectangle and choose Effects>3D>Extrude & Bevel. Make sure the Preview option is unchecked.**

   An active preview slows down the application because it re-renders the artwork after every change.

6. **Fill in the following parameters:**

X axis	−3°
Y axis	32°
Z axis	−1°
Perspective	50°
Extrude Depth	Width of the side panel (from Step 3)

7. **Check the Preview box and review the shape in the layout.**

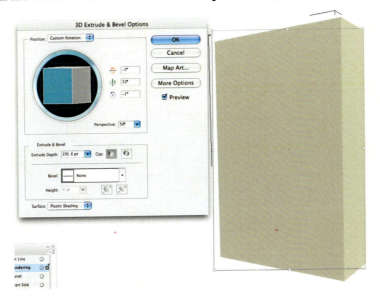

8. **Turn the preview back off.**

9. **Click Map Art in the 3D Extrude & Bevel Options dialog box.**

When the Map Art dialog box is open, the object in the layout displays as a 3D wireframe preview even when the Preview option is unchecked. The red line around the preview shows which side (surface) of the shape is being mapped.

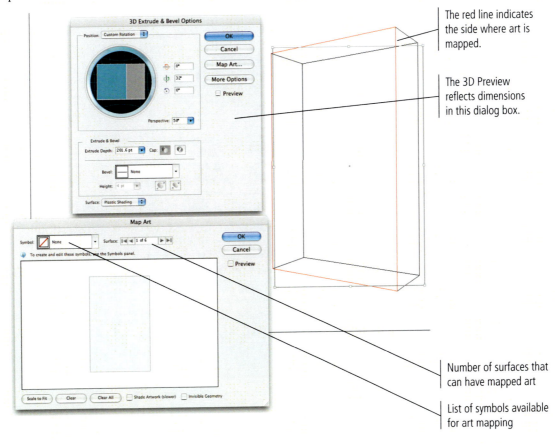

The red line indicates the side where art is mapped.

The 3D Preview reflects dimensions in this dialog box.

Number of surfaces that can have mapped art

List of symbols available for art mapping

10. **Choose Front Panel in the Symbol pop-up menu.**

The picture of the front of the box is placed on the page, but you need to adjust it so that it exactly fits the page outline; otherwise, there will be gray areas when you render the picture.

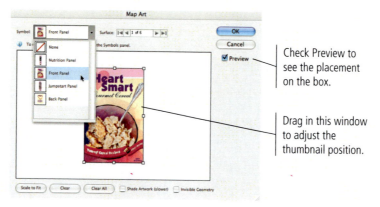

Check Preview to see the placement on the box.

Drag in this window to adjust the thumbnail position.

11. **Check the Preview option.**

Illustrator renders a preview of the symbol on the 3D box shape (this might take a few minutes).

Note that the white stripe indicated by negative space shows a gray background, instead of the white in the design. To work around this, you will edit the symbol and create an actual white stripe in the symbol art.

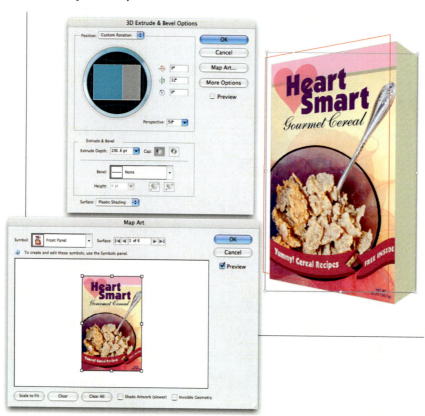

12. **Click the right Surface arrow until you are looking at surface 3, and then choose Nutrition Panel in the Symbol menu.**

The thumbnail is placed in the wrong orientation, so you need to rotate it. You can click an object in the Map Art preview and drag to move the symbol artwork, or use the bounding box handles to resize or rotate the symbol so it fits the gray surface shape.

13. Click the symbol artwork in the preview and drag down so you can see the top bounding-box handles.

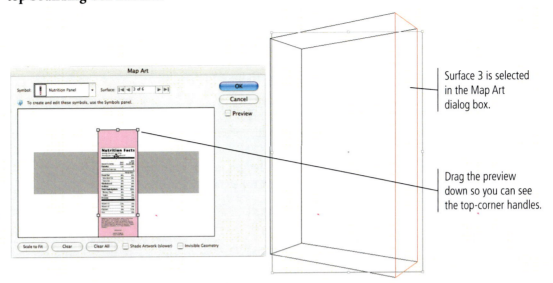

Surface 3 is selected in the Map Art dialog box.

Drag the preview down so you can see the top-corner handles.

14. Place the cursor near one of the top corner handles, press Shift, and drag around to rotate the artwork 90° counterclockwise.

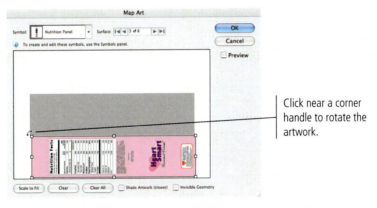

Click near a corner handle to rotate the artwork.

15. Drag the rotated art in the preview until it aligns with the gray surface shape.

16. Check the Preview option and review the results.

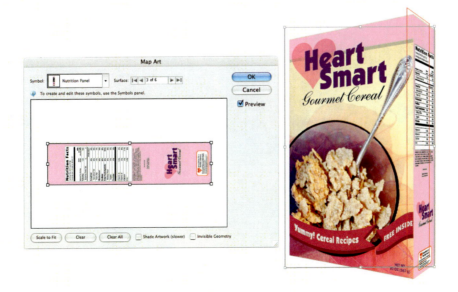

17. Click OK to close the Map Art dialog box, and then click OK again to finalize the 3D box preview.

18. In the Symbols panel, double-click the Front Panel symbol to enter Symbol Editing Mode.

19. In the Appearance panel, click the New Artwork Maintains Appearance button to turn this option off.

3D Extrude & Bevel is an effect; if you don't turn off the Maintain Appearance option, the shape you're about to draw will be beveled and filled with the two symbols.

20. In the area of the empty white space, draw a white-filled rectangle the same width as the symbol artwork and send it to the back of the stacking order.

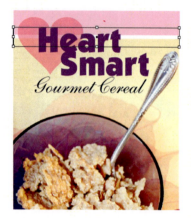

21. Click the arrow button in the top-left corner of the document window to exit Symbol Editing Mode.

Note:

Once art has been mapped, you can view the 3D virtual effect from different angles by changing the settings in the 3D Extrude & Bevel Options dialog box.

22. Save the file and close it.

Summary

The large Artboard size and layer controls, coupled with the extensive set of creative tools, make Illustrator ideally suited to meet the complex needs of packaging design. You can design sophisticated artwork that can be wrapped or folded into virtually any shape to package virtually any product.

This project combined the technical requirements of packaging design — specifically using a custom die-cut supplied by the output provider — with the artistic capabilities necessary to create the final design for a standard-size cereal box. You composited a number of existing elements and created others, then used a number of features to modify artwork — adding interest and depth to unify the different pieces into a single, cohesive design.

Create artwork to fit a printer-supplied die-cut template

Place external elements as necessary for package design

Create type on a custom path

Use effects and filters to add design elements like arrowheads

Use transparency to unify artwork components

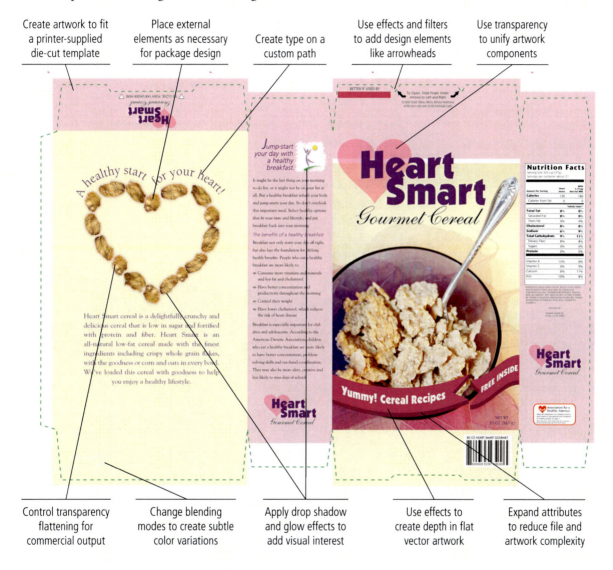

Control transparency flattening for commercial output

Change blending modes to create subtle color variations

Apply drop shadow and glow effects to add visual interest

Use effects to create depth in flat vector artwork

Expand attributes to reduce file and artwork complexity

Portfolio Builder Project 6

Your agency has been hired to develop packaging for a new video game called *Eye of Horus*, which is an adventure game set in Egypt when the pyramids were being built.

To complete this project, you should:

❏ Disassemble (flatten) an existing game box and measure the different elements. Create a die-cut template in Illustrator using those measurements.

❏ Design box artwork for the new video game, using images or creating illustrations that support the general theme of the product.

❏ Incorporate the product name on all sides of the box.

"The new game is a typical action adventure game with a historical context. The goal is to the navigate a labyrinth inside one of the pyramids to find the Pharaoh's treasure without being captured by the various beasties that protect the hidden chamber.

"One side panel needs to list the system requirements for the game, which haven't yet been finalized. We know that the game will work on both Mac and Windows, but we're still trying to work out the bugs on the latest system releases so we haven't finalized that information yet.

"For now, we'd like you to create placeholder bullets that say something like 'requirement listing'. That way we can see the formatting you choose even though the actual text isn't ready yet. We'll also have to incorporate the Apple and Windows logos, so make sure you leave space for those logos on the same panel.

"The back of the box will incorporate some screen captures, which we'll provide as soon as the development is finalized. For now, just leave placeholders to mark the space where those will be placed.

"Finally, make sure you build a space on either the back or one side of the box for a bar code."

Financial Infographics

As the illustrator for a magazine publisher, it's your job to create interesting graphics for articles in a variety of magazines. Next month's feature article is about trends in consumer spending and debt. You need to create a graphic that will accompany the article, presenting five different sets of data in a friendly, easy-to-understand format.

This project incorporates the following skills:

❑ Creating graphs to present data in a visual format

❑ Editing graph data to change the appearance of a graph

❑ Importing data from an external file

❑ Managing fills, legends, and labels to create aesthetically pleasing, technically accurate graphs

❑ Defining a perspective grid for complex, three-dimensional artwork

❑ Using different constrain angles to create objects on alternate horizontal planes

❑ Using the Free Transform tool to put objects into the correct perspective

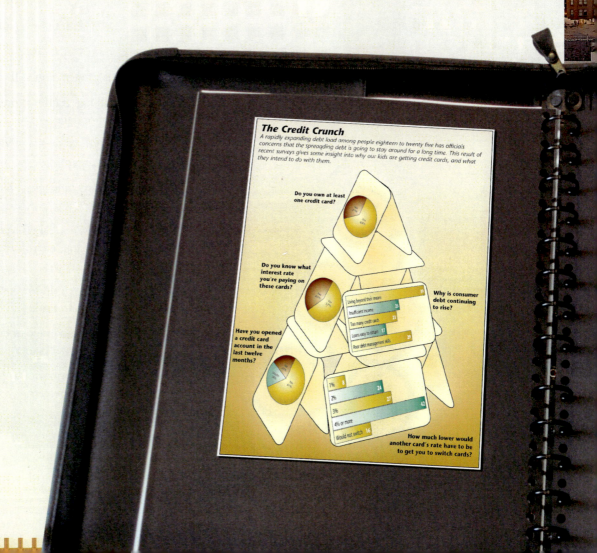

Client Comments

The feature article in next month's personal finance magazine is an investigation into the spending habits and debt load of the average 20-something American consumer. We conducted a survey through our Web site, and we have some interesting data that we want to include in support of the article text.

Since this is a general-interest consumer magazine, and not a cut-and-dry financial report, I'd like something more than just a set of plain graphs. I'd like you to put the graphs into some kind of context or overall illustration to make the presentation more interesting.

Art Director Comments

Before you start creating the graphs, you should evaluate the kinds of data you have. That way, you can determine which type of graph will best suit the data. Illustrator's graphing tools support many different graph types, but you probably won't need more than a few. Bars and pies are the most common types, but the others have important uses too.

You might want to look at some other consumer and personal financial magazines to see how different kinds of graphs and charts are typically used — and how they are incorporated into illustrations to make the data appear more attractive and interesting.

I sketched a "house of cards" idea that I think will be good container for the five different graphs (of course, we're talking about credit cards and not playing cards). I'll also send you the color library that we typically use for this magazine — it has a series of "money" colored gradients that work well for financial infographics.

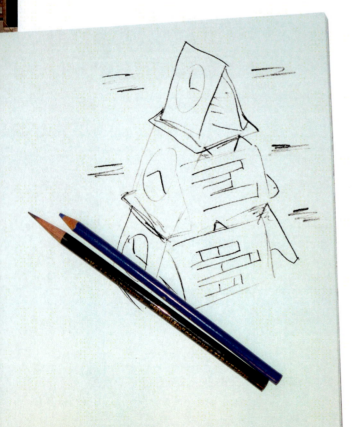

Project Objectives

To complete this project, you will:

- ❏ Create pie and bar graphs to present different types of data

- ❏ Edit live graph data to change the segment breakdown in a graph

- ❏ Import data from an external file to create a graph

- ❏ Edit fills, legends, and labels to create aesthetically pleasing, technically accurate graphs

- ❏ Create a perspective grid for complex, three-dimensional artwork

- ❏ Change the constrain angle to create objects on alternate horizontal planes

- ❏ Use the Free Transform tool to put objects into the correct perspective

- ❏ Ungroup graphs so they can be placed in perspective

Stage 1 Creating Charts and Graphs

The first stage of this project revolves around one of the most powerful but least-used functions in Illustrator — the ability to generate graphics based on variable data. **Information graphics** (referred to as infographics) are illustrations that deliver information; bar graphs, pie charts, and area charts are all examples of information provided in a visual format that makes it easier to understand.

Successfully designing infographics requires knowing which kind of chart best shows which types of information. Once you know what kind of chart you need, Illustrator provides the tools and functionality to generate the chart.

Distinguishing Types of Graphs

You can create a wide variety of graphs in Illustrator.

Column graphs compare values using vertical columns.

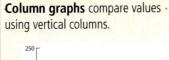
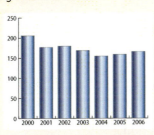

Bar graphs compare values using horizontal columns.

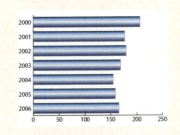

Line graphs plot a series of points across the graph, connecting those points with a line. These graphs show a progressive change in values, such as different prices over time.

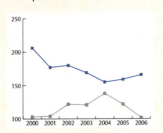

Stacked column graphs break each column into segments to show the relationship between pieces of the total value.

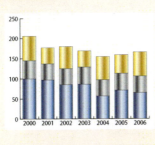

Stacked bar graphs are horizontal versions of stacked column graphs.

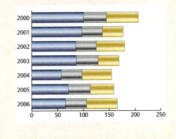

Area graphs are modified line graphs; the space below the line is filled to emphasize the plotted values.

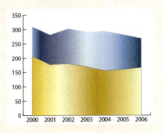

Scatter graphs plot multiple data points along the horizontal and vertical axes. These graphs are used to show trends or clusters in the data points.

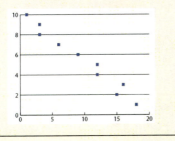

Pie graphs show values as a percentage of the whole.

Radar graphs compare sets of values in a circular format.

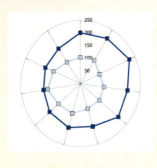

CREATE A PIE GRAPH

This project involves five different graphs, based on data from a survey of a specific number of people:

- The number of people who have at least one credit card

- The number of people who know the interest rate of their credit card(s)

- The number of people who would switch to a 0% rate for one year, regardless of the eventual rate

- The point at which consumers say they would switch to a lower-rate credit card

- The perceived reasons for the overall increase in consumer debt

For the first three sets of data (and the resulting graphs), each person surveyed was allowed only a single answer. For the last two sets of data, respondents were allowed to check more than one option from a defined list.

Using this information, you can determine the best type of graph to represent each set of data. Because each person gave a single response to the first three questions, the combined percentages of responses will equal 100%. A pie graph is the best way to show values as a percentage of the whole, so you will use pie graphs to visually represent the first three sets of data.

1. **Create a new file using a letter-size page with inches as the default unit of measurement and portrait orientation. Use the CMYK color mode and the High (300 ppi) Raster Effects setting.**

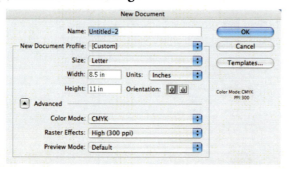

Note:

When you create graphs in Illustrator, you can either type the graph data directly into a table or import data from an external text file. You will use both methods to complete this project.

Note:

Before completing this project, copy the Cards folder from the WIP folder on your Resource CD to your WIP folder where you are saving your work. When you save files for this project, you will save them in your WIP>Cards folder.

InfoGraphics Aren't Just for Wall Street

We've been lucky to work with one of the country's most respected information artists, Scott MacNeil, whose amusing presentations are among the best you'll see. The image shown here includes an example of using pie charts to show eating trends (notice how the green pie slice grows from 16% to 35% as the target audience gets older). Infographics are used to make data more interesting and attractive.

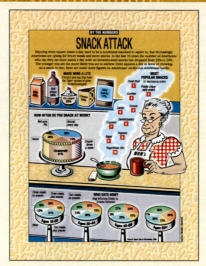

ILLUSTRATOR FOUNDATIONS

2. **With the new file open, change the font to ATC Oak Normal in the Character panel.**

By changing the font with nothing selected, you are changing the default font of any new type elements in the file — including the legends that will be attached to the different graphs.

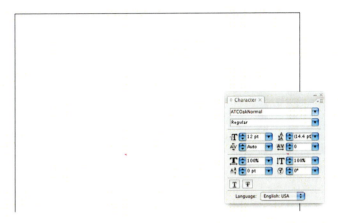

3. **In the Tools panel, choose the Pie Graph tool (it might be nested under one of the other graph tools).**

When you choose a specific graph tool, it becomes the default tool in the Tools panel. Depending on what was done in your version of the application before now, your default graph tool might be different than ours.

4. **Click once anywhere in the page.**

Like single-clicking a basic shape tool, this method opens a dialog box where you can define the dimensions of the new object (in this case, the graph).

5. **In the Graph dialog box, change both the Width and Height values to 2″ and click OK.**

When you create a new graph, a window opens with what appears to be a spreadsheet. This **Data panel** is where you enter (or import) the data that will make up your graph.

6. **Type "Yes" (without the quotation marks) in the first cell.**

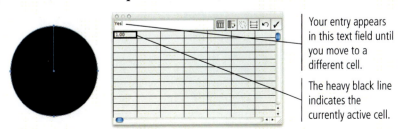

Your entry appears in this text field until you move to a different cell.

The heavy black line indicates the currently active cell.

Note:

The size you define here represents the size of the graph shape only; it does not include the legend or axis labels. If you know the amount of space available for the entire graph (including labels and legend), you should define a smaller graph size so the labels and legend will fit within the available space.

Using Quotes in the Data Panel

Quotation marks have a specific use in the Data panel. By default, Illustrator's Data panel treats all numbers as parts of the data. In some cases, however, the first row or column of numbers might actually be labels for the data, such as years included in the data set. To prevent Illustrator from treating these numbers as data, you can enclose them in quotation marks in the Data panel.

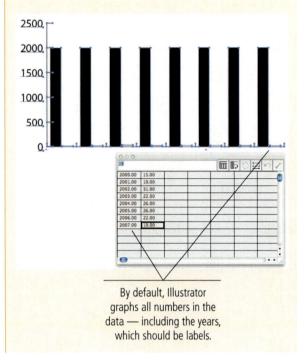

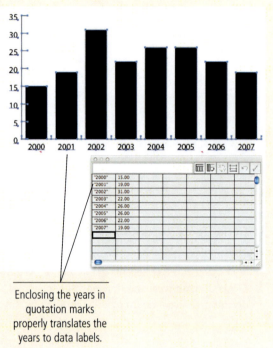

By default, Illustrator graphs all numbers in the data — including the years, which should be labels.

Enclosing the years in quotation marks properly translates the years to data labels.

7. **Press Tab to move to the next cell in the row, and then type "No" in the selected cell.**

   Pressing Tab moves to the next cell in the row. Pressing Return/Enter moves to the next cell down in the column. You can also use the Arrow keys to move through the different cells in the chart.

   The first row of the chart can be used to add labels to each set of data. If you don't want to include data labels, you can simply type the data in the first row.

8. **Click the first cell in the second row to select it, and then type "63".**

9. **In the second cell of the second row, type "37".**

   On the Artboard, the graph is still a solid black dot.

Note:

You can create more than one pie graph by entering additional sets of values in subsequent rows.

10. **Click the Apply button at the top of the Data panel.**

The pie graph is now split into sections, based on the data you defined and applied. The total of the two data values is 100, so each wedge occupies a percentage of the graph that is the same as the related data.

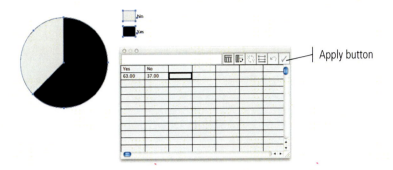

Apply button

11. **Click the Data panel Close button to close the panel.**

12. **Save the file as "credit.ai" in your WIP>Cards folder and continue to the next exercise.**

Whole Numbers or Percentage?

ILLUSTRATOR FOUNDATIONS

Data is sometimes provided as actual numbers instead of percentages. Pie graphs, however, always present those numbers as percentages of the whole. For example, let's say you have a set of data that shows how many people prefer dogs and how many people prefer cats. You can enter those numbers into the Data panel rather than manually calculating the percentage of each number; Illustrator automatically calculates the percentages to generate the appropriate pie graph wedges.

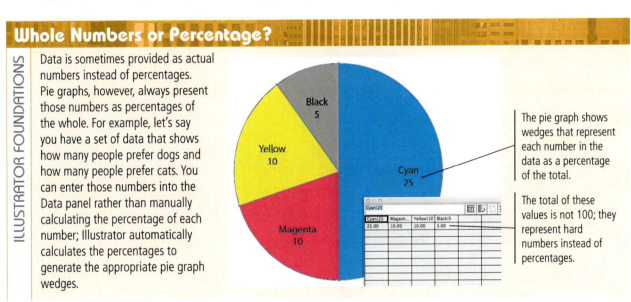

The pie graph shows wedges that represent each number in the data as a percentage of the total.

The total of these values is not 100; they represent hard numbers instead of percentages.

When you create a graph in Illustrator, the graph, labels, and legend (if used) are grouped together as a single object. As long as the object remains grouped, you can edit the related data, which changes the graph as necessary.

1. **With credit.ai open, use the Selection tool to drag the existing graph to the top-left corner of the Artboard.**

2. **Press Option/Alt-Shift, and then drag the graph down to clone a second pie graph.**

3. **Press Command/Control-D to repeat the last transformation (the cloning movement) and create a third version of the pie graph.**

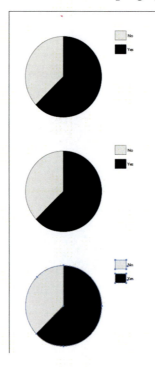

4. **Using the Selection tool, click the second graph and choose Object>Graph>Data to reopen the Data panel.**

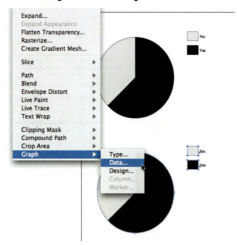

5. Change the Yes value to "57" and the No value to "43", and then click the Apply button.

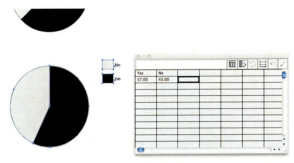

Note:

Pressing the Enter key on your numeric keypad has the same effect as clicking the Apply button.

6. Click the third graph to select it and show the related data in the Data panel.

7. In the Data panel, drag to select the two fields in the second column.

8. Choose Edit>Cut (Command/Control-X) to cut the data to the clipboard.

9. Click the first cell in the third column and choose Edit>Paste (Command/Control-V).

Unlike traditional spreadsheet applications, you can't drag data cells to a new location. You can, however, cut cells and paste them into a new position if you need to add new data in between existing data.

10. Select the first cell in the second column and type "Maybe".

11. Select the second cell in the second column and type "18".

12. Change the Yes value to "61" and change the No value to "21", and then click the Apply button.

Note:

The Cell Style button in the Data panel allows you to control the number of decimal points included in each cell, as well as the cell width in the Data panel.

Cell Style button

13. Click the Data panel Close button to close the panel.

14. Save the file and continue to the next exercise.

When the first row of your data defines labels for each set, the graph automatically includes a legend with a small block of the wedge color and the related label. You can change the type or position of legend, or you can remove it completely by editing the graph type settings.

1. **With credit.ai open, use the Direct Selection tool to select the black wedge in each graph.**

    The Direct Selection tool allows you to change individual pieces of the graph without ungrouping the graph object.

    Don't worry about the Yes blocks in the legends; those blocks will be removed when you change the legend type later in this exercise.

2. **Change the fill of the selected shapes to 25% black.**

    This color change allows you to see the black text when you change the legend type.

Note:

As we stated earlier, all elements of the graph object — including the legend — are grouped into a single object; as long as the group remains a group, you can edit the related data. If you try to select the legend elements and delete them from the Artboard, however, you'll see a warning that you can't delete the objects as long as the graph object remains grouped.

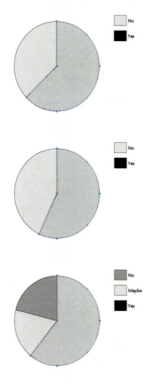

3. **Deselect all the objects, and then use the Selection tool to select the top graph.**

4. **Choose Object>Graph>Type.**

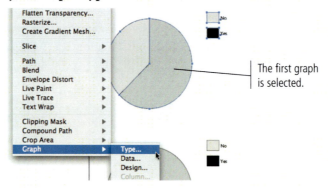

The first graph is selected.

5. In the Options area, choose Legends in Wedges in the Legend menu.

This dialog box has different available options, depending on the type of graph you are working with. For a pie graph, you can use the Legend menu to remove the legend completely, create a standard stacked legend (the default), or place the legend labels inside the associated wedges.

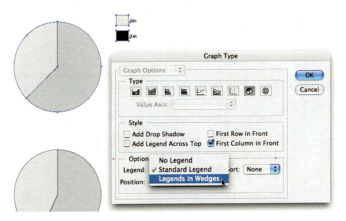

Note:

If you check Add Legend Across Top when the Standard Legend option is selected, the legend is added in a row above the graph.

6. Click OK to close the Graph Type dialog box.

The legend text is now placed inside each wedge.

Illustrator automatically reduces the label text size as necessary to fit.

7. Click the graph with the Selection tool and choose Object>Graph>Data.

8. In the Data panel, select the first label field.

9. In the field at the top of the Data panel, place the insertion point at the end of the existing label (Yes).

10. Type "|63%" (excluding the quotes).

The pipe character (Shift-Backslash on your keyboard) is used to create a new line in the graph label.

11. Using the same method, add the appropriate percentage to the No label.

The labels now reflect the actual data that was used to create the graph wedge. The point of infographics is to make data easy to view and understand; these enhanced labels are far more informative than the basic Yes/No labels.

12. **Click the Apply button, and then close the Data panel.**

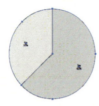

13. **With the graph still selected, change the Font Size menu in the Character panel to 10 pt.**

Even though you defined the default type size in the first exercise, legend type is automatically scaled to some smaller size to fit the graph. Because the type elements are part of the larger graph group, you have to use the Direct Selection tool to select (and change) only the type elements.

14. **Repeat this process for the two remaining graphs: move the legend text into the wedges, add the actual data value to the label text, and then change the label text to 10 pt.**

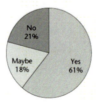

15. **Save the file and continue to the next exercise.**

COLOR GRAPH COMPONENTS

One of the advantages of building graphs in Illustrator is the ability to use the extensive artistic tool set to decorate the graphs. Rather than relying solely on the default shades-of-gray fills, you can fill the wedges with swatches — colors, gradients, patterns — to make the data more visually appealing.

1. **With credit.ai open, choose Window>Swatch Libraries>Other Library.**

2. **Navigate to the file Money Colors.ai in the RF_Illustrator>Cards folder and click Open.**

    This is a custom library of swatches that your magazine frequently uses to illustrate financial concepts. You're going to use these gradients to fill the different elements of the graphs.

3. **Using the panel options menu, display the Money Colors library panel in List view (either small or large, whichever you prefer).**

4. **Deselect everything on the Artboard.**

5. **Using the Direct Selection tool, Shift-click the Yes wedge in each graph.**

6. **Click the Gold Radial swatch in the Money Colors library.**

    If you completed Project 4, you should know that radial gradients are automatically applied from the center of the object, as determined by the outermost edges of the selected shape. For a gradient to be centered in the entire graph area instead of just the wedge shape, you have to use the Gradient tool to reposition the gradient center.

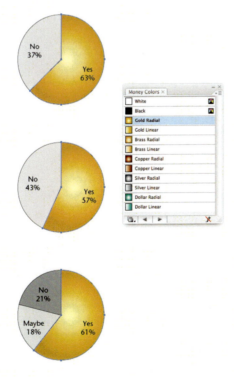

7. **Deselect the three wedges, and then use the Direct Selection tool to select the Yes wedge in only the first graph.**

8. **Choose the Gradient tool in the Tools panel.**

9. **Click the center point of the graph and drag to the outer edge of the wedge.**

This action repositions the gradient so it radiates from the graph center instead of the wedge center.

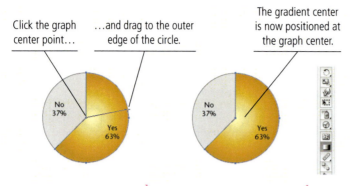

Click the graph center point...   ...and drag to the outer edge of the circle.   The gradient center is now positioned at the graph center.

10. **Repeat this process so the gradients in all three wedges radiate from the respective graph centers.**

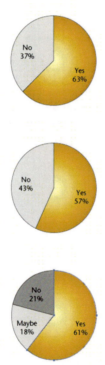

Filling Wedges with Gradients

If a pie graph wedge is 75% or more of the graph area, a radial gradient will be correctly centered in the graph area because the outermost edges of the wedge are the same as the outermost edges of the entire graph. In the following images, the dashed lines show the outer dimensions of the cyan wedge; you can see the gradient center (the white spot) move as the wedge shape changes.

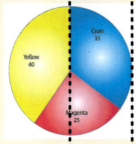

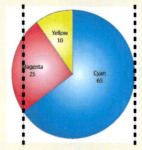

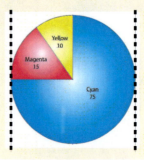

11. Select the No wedges of all three graphs and apply the Copper Radial gradient swatch. Use the Gradient tool to reposition the gradients to radiate from the graph centers.

12. Apply the Dollar Radial gradient to the Maybe wedge in the third graph, radiating from the graph center.

13. Using the Direct Selection tool, reposition the label elements closer to the centers of the graphs.

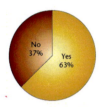

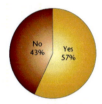

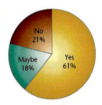

14. Save the file and continue to the next exercise.

 ## CREATE A BAR GRAPH WITH IMPORTED DATA

In this exercise, you create two additional graphs to show how many survey respondents selected specific answers to a posed question. Respondents were allowed to select more than one answer, so the data does not reflect percentages of a total — in other words, a pie graph is inappropriate for presenting this type of data. Bar and column charts, on the other hand, are well suited for showing this type of data.

Orientation is the only real difference between a bar graph and a column graph. Bar graphs represent each data set as a horizontal bar, while column graphs use vertical columns. These two graphs need to be horizontally oriented (as you'll see when you get to Stage 2 of the project), so you will use bar graphs for the last two sets of data.

1. With credit.ai open, choose the Bar Graph tool (nested under the Pie Graph tool) from the Tools panel.

2. Click in the right side of the Artboard to open the Graph dialog box. Define the new graph to be 4″ wide by 2″ high and click OK.

3. In the Data panel, click the Import Data button.

4. Navigate to the file rates.txt in the RF_Illustrator>Cards folder and click Open.

This data was originally a Microsoft Excel file, but it was exported as a tab-delimited text-only file.

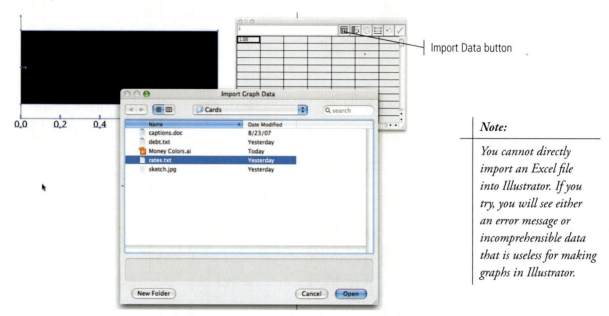

Import Data button

Note:

You cannot directly import an Excel file into Illustrator. If you try, you will see either an error message or incomprehensible data that is useless for making graphs in Illustrator.

5. Click the Apply button, and then close the Data panel.

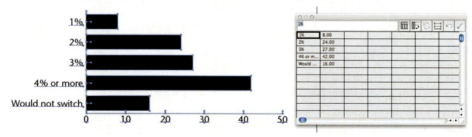

6. With all of the graph elements selected, use the Character panel to change the type size to 10 pt.

7. **Choose Object>Graph>Type. In the Graph Type dialog box, choose Value Axis in the top menu.**

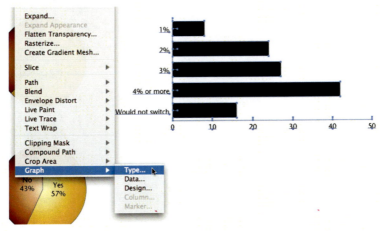

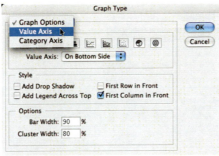

8. **Check the Override Calculated Values box. Type "42" in the Max field (the highest number in the data set) and type "1" in the Divisions field.**

By default, Illustrator uses a range beginning with 0 and extending in increments as necessary to show the defined data. You can use the Min and Max fields to define a specific value axis, such as always extending to 100 instead of ending at 70 or some other lower value. The Divisions field determines how many tick marks and labels are added to the value axis (the horizontal axis for this bar graph).

Because you changed the Max field to the largest number in the data set, the bar for that data field will extend the entire width of the graph.

9. **Choose None in the Tick Marks Length menu.**

By default, tick marks are short lines on the inside of the graph area. You can also choose Full Width to extend the tick marks the full range of the graph, or you can choose None to effectively turn off the value axis divisions.

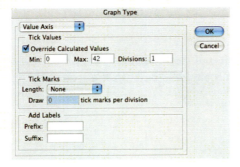

Note:

If you are including divisions in your graph, you can add subdivisions using the Draw _ Tick Marks Per Division option.

Note:

The Prefix and Suffix fields can be used to add specific characters in front of or at the end of defined value labels.

10. **Choose Category Axis in the top menu and change this Tick Marks menu to None.**

   Similar to the value axis, categories are also separated by tick marks by default. In the case of a bar graph, tick marks are usually unnecessary.

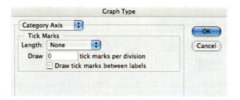

11. **Click OK to close the Graph Type dialog box and apply your changes.**

Note:

Unfortunately, the Graph Type dialog box does not include a Preview check box. You can't see the results of your choices until you click OK. As long as the graph object remains a graph object, you can always make changes.

12. **Save the file and continue to the next exercise.**

 EDIT AND FORMAT GRAPH LABELS

When it comes to labeling graph elements for bar graphs, you can change the appearance and position of labels, and you can edit the label text by changing the fields in the Data panel. You cannot, however, add multiple labels to the same data.

   In the pie graphs you created earlier, you modified the data labels to include the actual values of the wedges. You could use this same technique for bar graphs, but in some cases it's better to simply add new text elements as secondary labels.

1. **With credit.ai open, use the Direct Selection tool to select the first, third, and fifth bars, and then apply the Gold Linear gradient.**

   Remember, every part of the graph must remain grouped if you want to be able to edit the associated data. The Direct Selection tool allows you to access individual pieces of the graph group.

2. **Apply the Dollar Linear gradient to the second and fourth bars.**

3. **Use the Direct Selection tool to select all five text elements on the left side of the graph.**

4. **Apply left paragraph alignment to the selected elements, and then Shift-drag the labels right so they are positioned within the related bars (in the graph).**

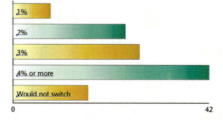

5. **With the same five elements selected, choose Edit>Copy.**

6. **Choose Edit>Paste to create copies of the selected objects.**

   When you paste these objects, they are no longer considered part of the graph group.

   In this case, you cannot use the Option/Alt-drag cloning method or the Paste in Place command to make the secondary labels. Both of these methods result in duplicate labels that are still part of the graph, which will cause problems if you update the graph data or edit the graph type.

7. **Change the pasted text objects to ATC Oak Bold filled with white, and then position each secondary label at the right end of the associated bar. For the bottom label, make sure that at least the W is visible in the bar (as shown in the image after Step 8).**

8. **Select the graph object with the Selection tool, display the Data panel (Object>Graph>Data), write down the five values, and then close the Data panel.**

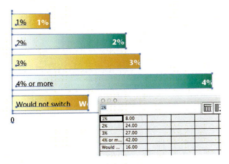

9. **Change each of the bold text elements to show the actual value for that bar, and then fine-tune the position of the modified elements so they align close to the right ends of the associated bars.**

10. **Select the graph and the five extra text elements and group them.**

11. **Press Option/Alt-Shift and drag down to clone the group that contains the bar graph.**

12. **Double-click the second bar graph to enter into Isolation mode.**

   In Isolation mode, you can access the graph group (and its Data panel) without ungrouping the graph and the secondary label-text objects.

13. In Isolation mode, click the graph object and choose Object>Graph>Data.

In Group Isolation mode, you can select the graph object without affecting the other text elements grouped with the graph.

14. In the Data panel, click the Import Data button. Navigate to the file debt.txt (in the RF_Illustrator>Cards folder) and click Open.

15. Write down the five values, click the Apply button, and then close the Data panel.

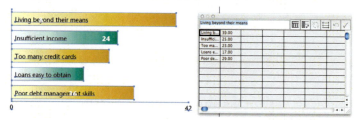

16. With the graph object selected, choose Object>Graph>Type. In the Value Axis options, change the Max field to match the largest number in the data set.

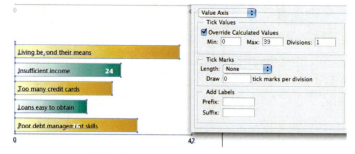

17. Click OK to close the Graph Type dialog box.

When you edit the graph type, changes to the label formatting will be restored to the defaults — in this case, restored to right paragraph alignment.

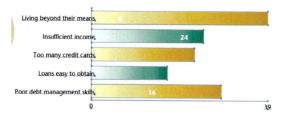

18. Use the Direct Selection tool to select the five primary label elements and reapply left paragraph alignment.

19. Change the secondary text labels to match the new data, place them at the ends of the bars, and then exit Group Isolation mode.

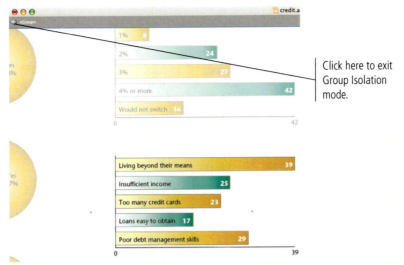

Click here to exit Group Isolation mode.

20. Save the file and continue to the next stage of the project.

Stage 2   Drawing in Perspective

The second half of the word "infographics" means adding visual elements that make the data seem more attractive and accessible to users. Although the graphs are already visual representations of data, true infographics typically refer to something more than just graphs — some type of visual context for containing the graphs.

The graphs that you built for this project are all related to trends in consumer credit and debt. Following the theme of the data, you are going to create a stacked "house of credit cards" illustration, and then place the data on the visible faces of the stacked cards.

CREATE PERSPECTIVE GUIDES

In this series of exercises, you create the artwork for this project based on a pencil sketch. As you will see in the sketch, stacked cards create a three-dimensional object. To recreate this effect using two-dimensional drawing tools, you need to understand the basic artistic principle of perspective.

The concept of perspective means that all lines on the same surface (or **plane**) eventually meet at a single point, called the **vanishing point**. Lines move closer together as they get closer to the vanishing point, creating the illusion of depth.

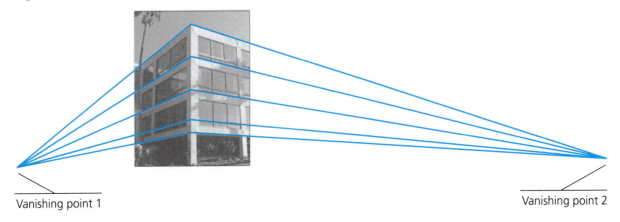

Vanishing point 1

Vanishing point 2

1. **With credit.ai open, rename Layer 1 as "Graphs", and then hide and lock the layer.**

2. **Create a new layer named "Sketch". Place the file sketch.jpg into the Sketch layer, center the image horizontally and vertically to the Artboard, and then lock the layer.**

   The sketch shows that the artwork has four primary surfaces; each of those surfaces has two vanishing points (called **two-point perspective**). You need to define two-point perspective guides for each surface in the artwork so you can more easily draw and transform the card shapes.

Note:

Artists using traditional media typically create perspective lines using tracing paper. You will use layers to build the digital equivalent of perspective guides.

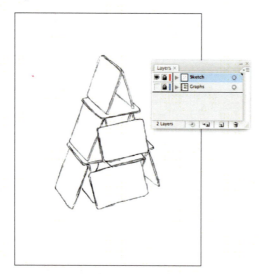

3. **Create a new layer named "Left Face Guides" and select it as the active layer.**

4. **Using the Line tool with a 1-pt black stroke and no fill, draw a line along the left side of the cards on the left side of the stack. Extend the top edge of the line past the top edge of the Artboard.**

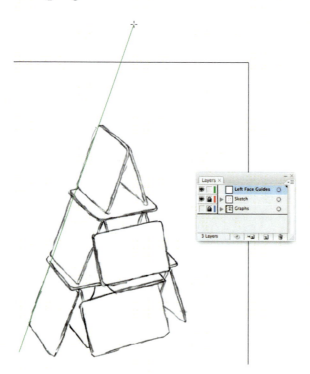

5. Draw a second line along the right edge of the same cards.

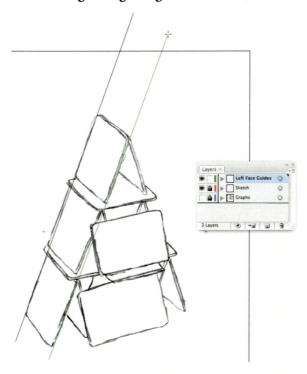

6. Using the Direct Selection tool, select the top anchor points of both lines.

7. Choose Object>Path>Average. Average the selected points based on both axes, and then click OK.

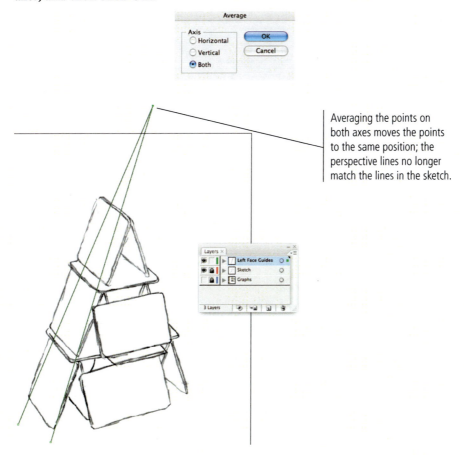

Averaging the points on both axes moves the points to the same position; the perspective lines no longer match the lines in the sketch.

8. **Choose Object>Path>Join. Join the selected points as a corner point and click OK.**

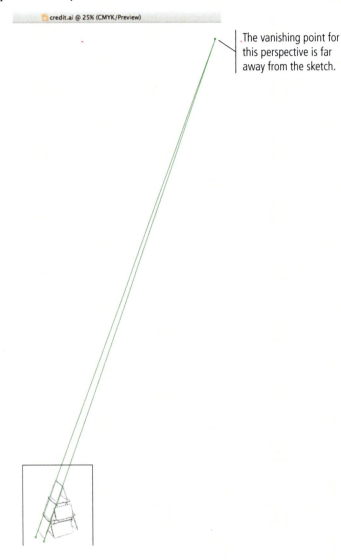

Note:

It's not mandatory that you join the two points, but it's easier to manage a single point than trying to control multiple points at the same location.

9. **Zoom out to a 25% view. Using the Direct Selection tool, drag the joined point away from the sketch until the lines match the card edges in the sketch.**

Depending on your monitor size and resolution, you might have to zoom out farther than 25% view to match the perspective lines to the sketch. However, 25% is a good starting point because you can still make out the lines in the sketch.

The vanishing point for this perspective is far away from the sketch.

10. **Zoom back in to 100% and check the accuracy of the lines relative to the cards in the sketch.**

If the lines don't match the sketch, the vanishing point is either too close or too far away.

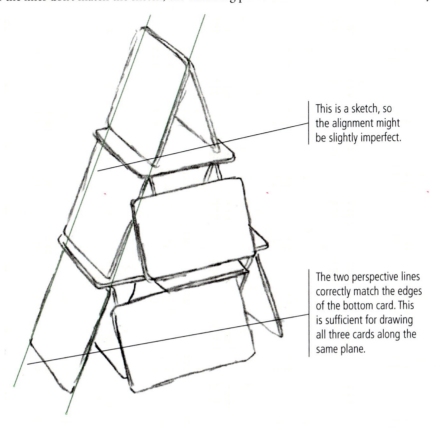

This is a sketch, so the alignment might be slightly imperfect.

The two perspective lines correctly match the edges of the bottom card. This is sufficient for drawing all three cards along the same plane.

11. **Adjust the location of the vanishing point (if necessary) until the perspective lines align correctly on the cards.**

12. **Using the same basic technique, create a vanishing point and perspective lines for the second perspective of the cards on the left side of the stack.**

13. **Use the Selection tool to select both lines of the second perspective point.**

14. **Choose Edit>Copy, and then choose Edit>Paste in Front to paste a copy of the perspective lines in the exact same spot.**

15. Deselect everything, and then use the Direct Selection tool to drag the right end points of the lines so the two new lines mark the bottoms of the top and middle cards (as shown in the following image).

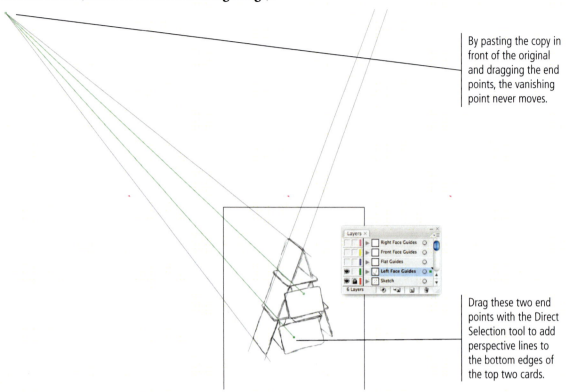

By pasting the copy in front of the original and dragging the end points, the vanishing point never moves.

Drag these two end points with the Direct Selection tool to add perspective lines to the bottom edges of the top two cards.

16. Select all six lines on the layer and convert them to guides (View>Guides> Make Guides).

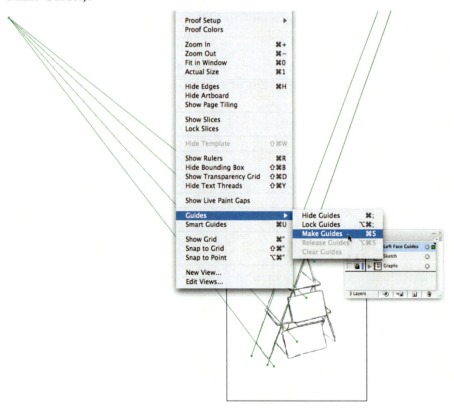

17. Save the file and keep it open for the next exercise.

IDENTIFY AND CREATE ADDITIONAL PLANES

The process for creating a vanishing point is fairly simple, as you saw in the previous exercise. The most complicated part of drawing in perspective is identifying the different planes that you need to map with perspective lines.

As we said at the beginning of this series of exercises, this sketch contains four basic planes:

- The cards that face out on the left side of the stack

- The cards that face forward

- The cards that face out to the right side of the stack

- The cards that lay flat (the "support" cards for the upright cards)

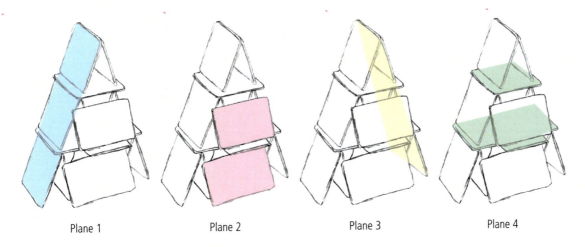

Plane 1   Plane 2   Plane 3   Plane 4

The cards on the inside of the stack also need to be created, but they will follow the same basic perspective as the outer cards. Because most of these cards are hidden, their perspective is not as critical as the primary planes.

1. **With credit.ai open, hide and lock the Left Face Guides layer.**

2. **Create three new layers, with the following names:**

    Right Face Guides

    Front Face Guides

    Flat Guides

    Because this is going to be a very complex file, you are placing the guides for each plane on a separate layer; doing so allows you to show only the guides you need when you are creating specific cards.

3. Using the same techniques as in the previous exercise, create two-point perspective guides for each of the three planes. Make sure the lines are on the appropriate layers, and then convert each set of lines to guides.

It will help to hide other layers as you define each new set of perspective guides.

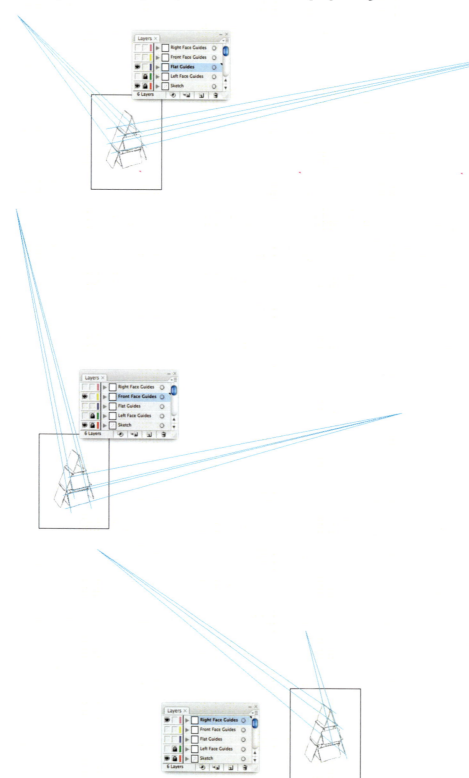

4. Save the file and continue to the next exercise.

CHANGE THE DEFAULT CONSTRAIN ANGLE

Now that you have four sets of perspective guides, it's time to start drawing the cards. There are many elements to draw, but they all require the same basic technique.

Because you are looking at the sketch from an angle, "horizontal" lines — where the card edges sit on a surface — are not really horizontal. Instead, they are at the angle necessary to create the depth effect of the related vanishing point.

If you know the angle of that implied horizon, you can use it as the basis of drawing the objects that will make up the artwork.

1. **With credit.ai open, lock and hide all but the Sketch and Front Face Guides layers.**

2. **Lock the Sketch and Front Face Guides layers. Create a new layer named "Front Cards" at the top of the layer stack, and select that layer.**

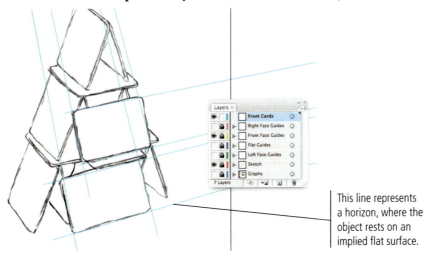

This line represents a horizon, where the object rests on an implied flat surface.

3. **Select the Measure tool (nested under the Eyedropper tool in the Tools panel).**

4. **Make sure the Info panel is visible (Window>Info).**

5. **Click with the Measure tool near the left edge of the bottom-front perspective guide, and then drag along the line.**

The angle is approximately 15.5°. If this were a technical illustration, "approximately" would be unacceptable. For the sake of this illustration, however, you can use "close enough" numbers.

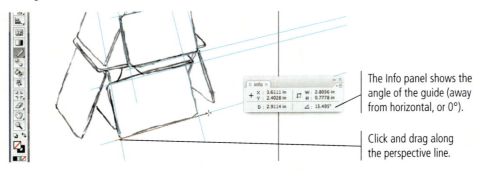

The Info panel shows the angle of the guide (away from horizontal, or 0°).

Click and drag along the perspective line.

6. **Open the General panel of the Preferences dialog box.**

Remember, Macintosh preferences are accessed in the Illustrator menu; Windows preferences are accessed in the Edit menu.

7. Change the Constrain angle to 15.5°.

This option resets the X axis to the newly defined angle (instead of perfectly horizontal).

8. Set the Corner Radius to 0.2".

This is the default corner radius for corner effects on basic shapes, such as the rounded rectangles you create next.

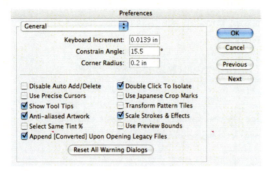

9. Click OK to apply the change and return to the open document.

10. Choose the Rounded Rectangle tool. Set the stroke to 2-pt Magenta and the fill to None.

This bright stroke allows you to see the shape more easily against the sketched image.

11. Click at the bottom corner of the lower front-facing card, and then drag to create a new rounded rectangle. Use the intersections of perspective lines to mark the start and end of the shape.

As you draw the shape, notice that the bottom edge is angled based on the new constrain angle — i.e., the new "horizon" or X axis.

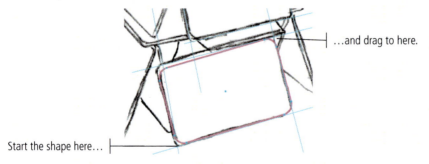

...and drag to here.

Start the shape here...

12. Choose the Free Transform tool from the Tools panel.

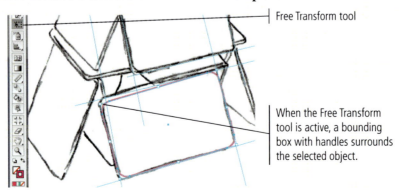

Free Transform tool

When the Free Transform tool is active, a bounding box with handles surrounds the selected object.

Free Transform Options

The Free Transform tool allows you to change the shape of selected objects by dragging the bounding box handles. Depending on where you click and whether you press any of the modifier keys, you can use this tool to stretch, shrink, rotate, distort, and skew a selection.

Click a center handle to stretch or shrink the selection in one direction.

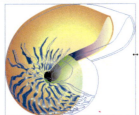

Click a corner handle to stretch or shrink the selection horizontally and vertically at the same time.

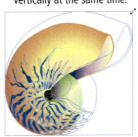

Click slightly outside a corner handle to rotate the selection.

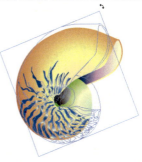

Click a center handle, then press Command/Control to skew the selection.

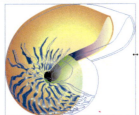

Click a corner handle, and then press Command/Control to distort the selection.

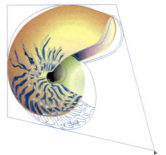

Click a corner handle, then press Command-Option-Shift/Control-Alt-Shift to alter the perspective of the selection.

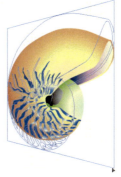

Press Option/Alt while making any free transformation to apply it equally on both sides of the selection center.

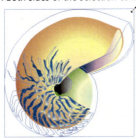

Press Shift and drag a handle to constrain the related transformation. For example, press Shift while dragging a corner handle to scale the selection at the same proportional height and width (below left) rather than scaling disproportionately (below right).

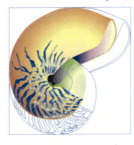
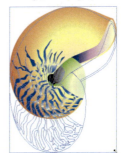

13. **Click the top-left bounding box handle of the shape, press Command/Control, and then drag the handle to the intersection of the two perspective lines.**

By pressing the Command/Control modifier key after you click the corner handle, you can reposition one corner of the object without affecting the other corners.

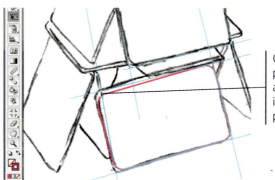

Click the corner handle, press Command/Control, and then drag to the intersection of the perspective guides.

Note:

*You must click the object's handle **before** pressing the Command/Control key. If you press the modifier key before clicking the handle, this process won't work.*

14. **Deselect the object and review the results.**

The drawing does not match the sketch, but it does match the perspective guides. When the sketch is removed from the artwork, the card will appear in the correct perspective.

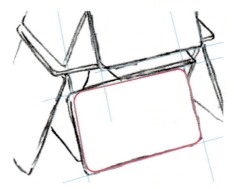

15. **Save the file and continue to the next exercise.**

CREATE CARDS ON DIFFERENT PERSPECTIVE PLANES

The rest of this perspective drawing is more of the same — measure the apparent horizon, change the constrain angle, draw the rounded rectangle based on the perspective guides, and then use the Free Transform tool to drag the shape's corners into the correct perspective.

After all the cards have been created, you will need to change the stacking order of every card so the cards appear as they would in a real "house of cards". The easiest way to accomplish this is to either create each card on its own layer, or create all cards on the same layer so you can rearrange the sublayers. This choice is mostly a matter of personal preference, but we find it easier to manage individual layers rather than trying to organize sublayers.

Some cards are at least partially hidden by other cards. You will have to make an educated guess about the correct positions and shapes of these elements. The best way to create these implied elements is to clone existing shapes and make adjustments as necessary.

1. **With credit.ai open, create a new layer named "Front Card 2" and select it as the active layer.**

2. Draw the second front-facing card using the Rounded Rectangle tool.

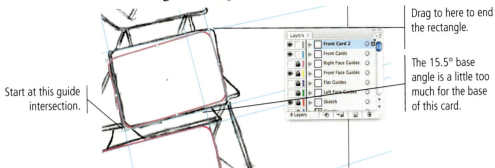

Start at this guide intersection.

Drag to here to end the rectangle.

The 15.5° base angle is a little too much for the base of this card.

3. Using the Free Transform tool, adjust the top-left and bottom-right corners of the card to fit the perspective guides.

Remember, you have to click the handle first, then press Command/Control and drag to reshape the corner.

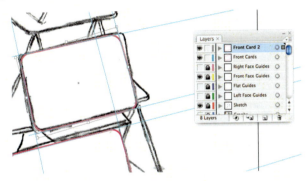

4. Hide the two Front Card layers and the Front Face Guides layer, and then show the Left Face Guides layer.

5. Open the General pane of the Preferences dialog box and reset the Constrain Angle value to 0°. Click OK to close the Preferences dialog box.

You need to find the base angle of the left-facing cards, but you need to find this angle from the actual horizontal X axis. If you don't change the constrain angle back to 0°, the next measurement will be from the altered horizon (15.5° instead of the original 0°).

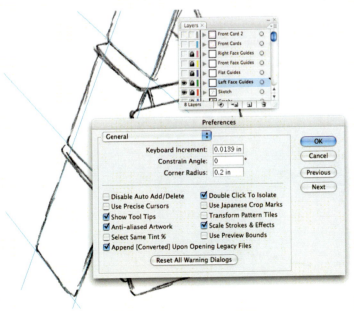

6. Use the Measure tool to determine the angle of the bottom card edge.

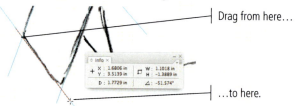

Drag from here…

…to here.

7. In the General pane of the Preferences dialog box, change the Constrain Angle value to match the angle value from the Info panel in Step 6.

8. Create a new layer named "Left Card 1" and select that layer.

9. Draw a rounded rectangle based on the bottom perspective line.

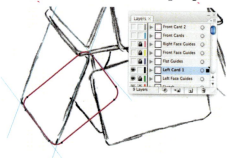

10. Use the Free Transform tool to drag the rectangle's corners to match the perspective lines (as shown in the following image).

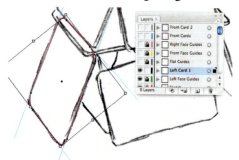

11. Create the remaining two left-facing cards, placing each card on its own layer.

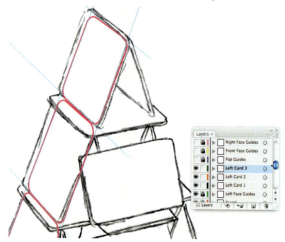

12. Hide the three left-facing card layers and the Left Face Guides layer.

13. Show the Flat Guides layer. Create two new layers for the flat cards, named "Flat Card 1" and "Flat Card 2".

14. Draw the flat cards on two separate layers.

    - Reset the constrain angle, and then measure the base angle for the flat cards using the front edge of the bottom flat card. (We found the required angle to be 13.2°.)

    - Draw a single rounded rectangle for the lower flat card, and then transform the corners to match the perspective guides.

    - Draw a second rounded rectangle on the same layer for the perpendicular card that sticks out from the lower flat card layer.

    - Draw a single rounded rectangle for the upper flat card, and transform the corners.

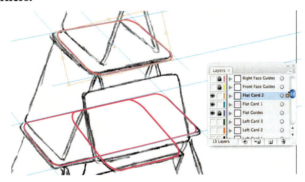

15. Hide the two Flat Card layers and the Flat Guides layer, and then show the Right Face Guides layer.

16. Draw the right-facing cards, each on its own layer, starting with a 0-degree constrain angle.

    - Create the top card first because more of that card is visible than the other two.

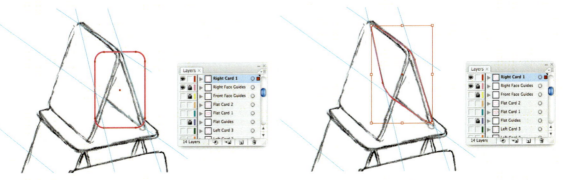

- **Clone the top card two times, drag each clone to a separate layer, and make adjustments as necessary based on the perspective guides.**

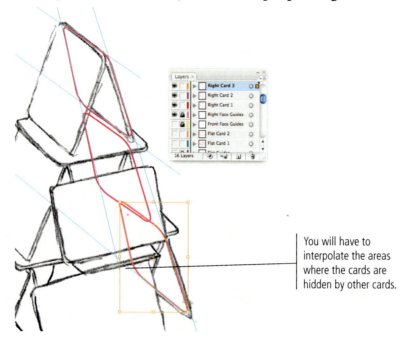

You will have to interpolate the areas where the cards are hidden by other cards.

17. **Create a final layer named "Hidden Cards".**

- **Clone one of the right-facing cards and move it to the Hidden Cards layer.**

- **Show the Left Card 1 layer, clone the shape on that layer, and move it to the Hidden Cards layer.**

- **Hide all the card and guide layers, and lock everything except the Hidden Cards layer.**

- **Adjust the cloned objects and create additional clones as necessary to create the partially hidden cards. If a card is entirely hidden in the sketch, you can leave it out of your drawing.**

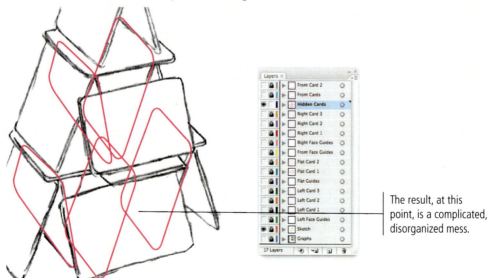

The result, at this point, is a complicated, disorganized mess.

18. **Save the file and continue to the next exercise.**

You currently have a large number of layers, including one layer with five shapes in no apparent order. The last step in building this artwork is arranging the different shapes to appear as they would in real life.

1. **With credit.ai open, drag all the guide layers to the bottom of the stack; hide and lock these layers.**

2. **Hide the Sketch layer, and then drag the Hidden Cards layer directly above the Sketch layer.**

3. **Show and unlock all card layers.**

Note:

You could delete the sketch and guide layers at this point, but we prefer to leave that step for the very end of the process.

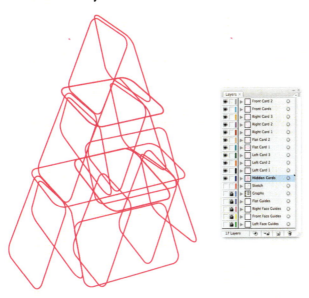

4. **Using the Selection tool, select all the card shapes, and then click the Default Fill and Stroke button in the Tools panel.**

   When the card shapes are filled, you can begin to see why reordering is necessary — and why managing cards on individual layers is a better option than placing multiple cards on a single layer.

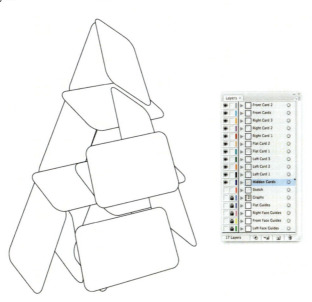

5. **Hide everything but the Hidden Cards layer.**

6. **Drag the Hidden Cards layer to the Create New Layer button.**

   This creates an exact copy of the Hidden Cards layer.

7. **Hide the original Hidden Cards layer. With the Hidden Cards copy layer selected, delete the three shapes in the bottom row.**

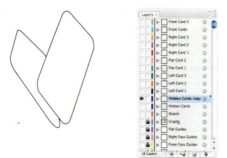

8. **Hide the Hidden Cards copy layer and show the original Hidden Cards layer. With the Hidden Cards layer selected, delete the two shapes in the top row.**

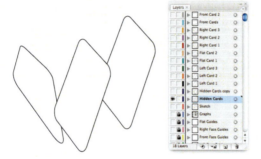

9. **Show all the card layers except the two Front Card layers.**

10. **Rearrange the layers as necessary to reproduce the realistic stacking order of a house of cards.**

    - **Cards in the bottom row should be below the Flat Card 1 layer.**
    - **Cards in the middle row should be above the Flat Card 1 layer and below the Flat Card 2 layer.**
    - **Left-facing cards should be above right-facing cards in the layer stack.**

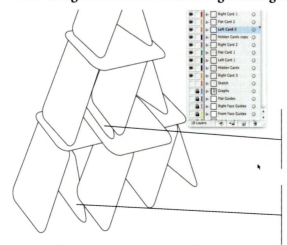

This card should be higher in the layer stack than the other card on the Hidden Cards copy layer.

This card should be higher in the layer stack than the other cards on the Hidden Cards layer.

11. Rearrange the objects on the Hidden Cards layer so the objects on the left are higher in the layer stack than objects on the right.

12. Show the two Front Card layers, and then make any necessary adjustments to fine-tune the house of cards.

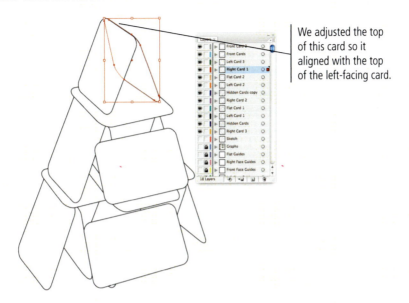

We adjusted the top of this card so it aligned with the top of the left-facing card.

13. Select all objects on the page and fill them with a radial gradient that blends from C=0 M=15 Y=50 K=0 to C=0 M=0 Y=15 K=0.

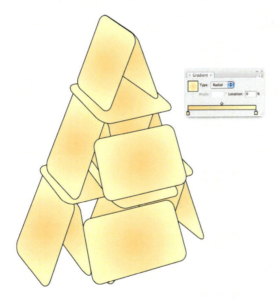

14. Select all of the card layers in the Layers panel and choose Merge Selected from the Layers panel options menu.

15. Rename the new merged layer "Cards".

16. Save the file and continue to the next exercise.

You have several choices for transforming the perspective of graphs to match the stacked cards. If you need to maintain the live link to the graph data, you can use the 3D Extrude & Bevel filter to apply a transformation effect to the graph object. This filter is complex, however, and can be particularly difficult to manage when you apply it to a text element.

If you don't need to maintain the live data link in the Illustrator graphs, you can use the same transformation options you used to transform the card shapes. In this case, you have to ungroup the graph object before you can transform it.

Because the data will no longer be editable after you transform it, we recommend saving a working back-up copy of the illustration before you ungroup the graphs.

1. **With credit.ai open, lock the Cards layer and choose File>Save As.**

2. **Save the file as "credit transformed.ai" in your WIP>Cards folder.**

3. **Show and unlock the Graphs layer, and then drag it to the top of the layer stack.**

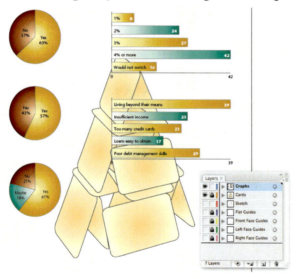

4. **Select all but the top pie graph and choose Object>Hide>Selection.**

    The card shapes are on the locked layer, so they will remain visible. Step 4 is only affecting the graphs on the visible and unlocked layer.

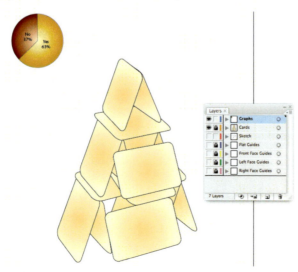

5. **Select the remaining graph and choose Object>Ungroup.**

6. **Read the resulting warning, and then click OK.**

   After you ungroup the graph, you won't be able to edit the graph type or data.

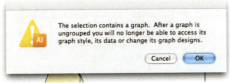

7. **With the resulting objects selected, choose Object>Group.**

   You have to ungroup the graph to convert it into regular vector objects. Regrouping the resulting vector objects allows you to maintain them as a single object, even when they are no longer technically a graph.

8. **Scale the group to 50%, drag it onto the top left-facing card, and rotate it clockwise to match the approximate angle of the card.**

9. **Use the Free Transform tool to adjust the corners of the group bounding box, placing the graph into the same approximate perspective as the card upon which it sits.**

10. **Lock the grouped object to the Artboard (Object>Lock>Selection).**

Note:

The text elements in the group will not be transformed. You would have to convert them to outlines if you wanted to free-transform the text elements.

11. **Repeat this process to transform the remaining pie graphs onto the left-facing cards.**

   - **Show the remaining hidden graphs (Object>Show All).**

   - **Select all but one of the graphs and hide them.**

   - **Ungroup and then transform the visible graph to fit one of the left-facing cards.**

12. **Show the remaining hidden graphs (the bar graphs).**

- Hide one of the remaining graphs while you transform the other.

- Enter into Group Isolation mode, select the graph object (without the group of secondary labels), and ungroup it.

- After the graph is ungrouped, delete the axis lines and axis labels.

- Using the Direct Selection tool, move each bar (and the related labels) to leave only a small gap between the bars.

- While in Group Isolation mode, select all objects and convert the type to outlines (Type>Create Outlines).

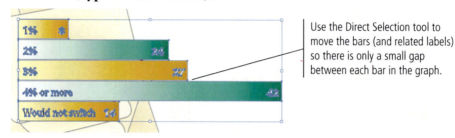

Use the Direct Selection tool to move the bars (and related labels) so there is only a small gap between each bar in the graph.

- Return to the main Artboard. Rotate, scale, and transform the group to fit one of the front-facing cards.

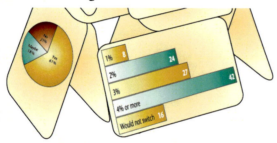

13. **Repeat Step 12 for the final bar graph, placing it on the other front-facing card.**

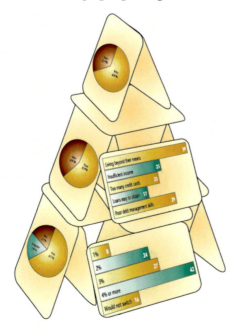

14. **Save the file and continue to the next exercise.**

FINISH THE DESIGN

Infographics aren't very informative without something to tell the viewer what the different graphs represent. Illustrator does not include a caption function, so you have to create those elements manually.

1. With credit transformed.ai open, create a new layer named "Background" directly below the Cards layer.

2. Create a rectangle 6″ wide by 8″ high. Fill the rectangle with the Brass Linear gradient (from the Money Colors library) with a –90° angle, and change the rectangle stroke to 1-pt black.

3. Center the rectangle horizontally behind the stack of cards, and leave half an inch between the bottom of the rectangle and the bottom of the cards.

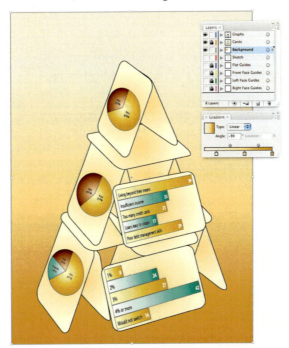

4. Deselect everything in the layout, and then choose File>Place. Place the file captions.doc (from the RF_Illustrator>Cards folder) into the file using the default options. Click OK if you get a Font Problems dialog box.

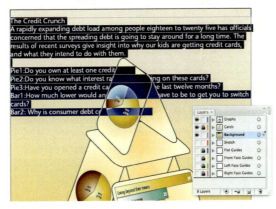

5. Adjust the top, left, and right edges of the text frame so it sits 1/8″ from the edges of the gradient-filled rectangle.

6. **Change the first paragraph of imported text to 18-pt ATC Oak Bold Italic.**

7. **Change the second paragraph to 11-pt ATC Oak Italic.**

8. **Change all the remaining paragraphs to 10-pt ATC Oak Bold with 90% horizontal scaling.**

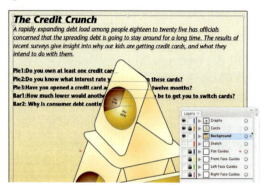

9. **Cut each caption from the main text frame and paste it into its own text frame. Position the caption frames as indicated by the text at the beginning of each line.**

   Make sure the captions match the cards where you placed each graph. In our example, we placed the rates bar graph on the lower front-facing card, so we had to place the correct caption (Bar1) next to the lower front-facing card.

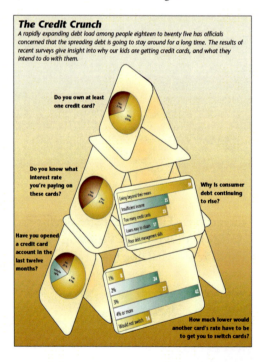

10. **Duplicate the Cards layer, and then hide the new Cards copy layer.**

    The duplicate layer — named Cards copy by default — automatically appears above the original Cards layer. Because the original is lower in the layer stack, you are going to combine the shapes on that lower layer.

11. **Unlock the Cards layer. Select all the card shapes on the original Cards layer and use the Pathfinder panel to combine the selected shapes into a single object.**

    Use the Add to Shape Area option, and then expand the resulting shape.

12. **With the combined object selected, apply the Outer Glow Stylize effect using white as the color and a large Blur value (we used 0.35″).**

By combining the cards into a single object, you can apply the effect to the overall shape rather than to individual cards.

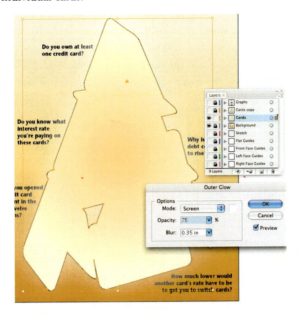

13. **If you hid the Cards copy and/or Graph layers while you completed Steps 11–12, show the hidden layer(s) now.**

14. **Create a new layer named "Captions" at the top of the layer stack, and move all the text elements to the Captions layer.**

This prevents the cards' glow from affecting the text.

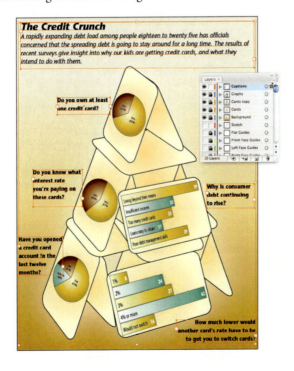

15. **Save the file and close it.**

Summary

Information graphics like the one you created in this project are frequently used in newspapers, magazines, and presentations to visually represent complex statistics or other numerical data. Information graphics range from simple pie charts and line graphs to elaborate full-color images.

When you create this type of illustration, keep in mind that "information" is the first word in information graphics. Also notice that this category of illustration work is not called "information decorating" — the information or data being presented is always the priority. Although aesthetic appeal is a primary concern of most graphic designers, the integrity of the information is the most important aspect of creating information graphics.

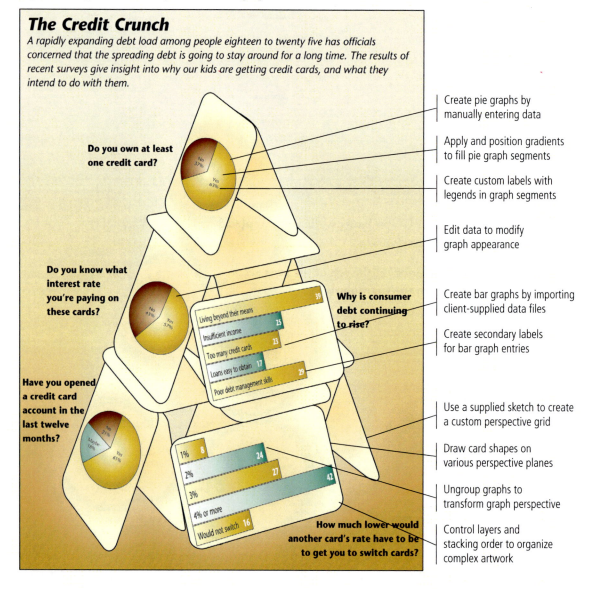

The Credit Crunch

A rapidly expanding debt load among people eighteen to twenty five has officials concerned that the spreading debt is going to stay around for a long time. The results of recent surveys give insight into why our kids are getting credit cards, and what they intend to do with them.

Create pie graphs by manually entering data

Apply and position gradients to fill pie graph segments

Create custom labels with legends in graph segments

Edit data to modify graph appearance

Create bar graphs by importing client-supplied data files

Create secondary labels for bar graph entries

Use a supplied sketch to create a custom perspective grid

Draw card shapes on various perspective planes

Ungroup graphs to transform graph perspective

Control layers and stacking order to organize complex artwork

Portfolio Builder Project 7

The main theme for next month's magazine is "Living Green". The main articles all focus on some aspect of environmental conservation, such as renewable energy, recycling strategies, and landfill reduction. Your job is to create information graphics for data that will accompany the cover story.

To complete this project, you should:

❏ Use the supplied data (in the RF_Builders>Info folder) to create three information graphics that present the data in some visually interesting way.

❏ Create illustrations for each set of data that support the overall theme of the article.

"The main focus of next month's cover story is the growing energy shortage in some areas in the country, and different methods that are being explored to supply affordable electricity to an ever-growing number of people in large metropolitan areas such as New York City and Los Angeles.

"The author has compiled three different sets of data about renewable energy — wind power, water power, and so on — that will support the ideas and facts in the article. We need some type of illustrated graph for each of these data sets.

"We want our readers to see the graphs even if they only flip through and skim the article. Create a compelling illustration for each one so they are more than just graphs. However, keep in mind that the data is the most important element — it needs to be clear and understandable.

"Use a consistent color scheme in all three graphs; green should play a prominent role because people naturally associate that color with environmentalism and natural resources."

Web Site Interface

Your client is a corporate training services company that specializes in in-house computer and technology training. Your agency was hired to build the company's Web site. The basic site has already been created; your job is to make the client's requested changes, place the content for one of the pages as a sample, and slice the page into pieces that can be reassembled in a Web design application.

This project incorporates the following skills:

❏ Using gradient meshes to create realistic illustrations with complex color blending, including highlights and shadows to add depth in the illustration

❏ Using Live Trace to create complex illustrations based on the pixels in a photograph

❏ Slicing a page into pieces and defining settings for individual slices

❏ Saving images and pages in appropriate format for display on the Web

Client Comments

We're happy with the overall look of the site, except for the boring banner at the top of the page. We would like to replace the red-and-white blend with an image of the Tampa skyline (since we're based in Tampa).

We were also thinking of adding an apple image into the banner somehow, but we don't know how that would work. Is there any way you can take a photograph of an apple and turn it into an illustration? We want it to look realistic, but not *too* realistic.

We also want to see what the different employee photos are going to look like in the placeholder boxes. I sent you a photo of Patrice, the customer service manager, who will appear on the Support page. Like the apple, we want all of these images to be somewhere between cartoon illustrations and photographs.

Finally, we want something to indicate that the buttons in the green bar are actually buttons. Can you add some kind of shadow or glow to the over state of the buttons?

Art Director Comments

Before you start on the Web site, you should create the two illustrations from their photographs. The apple has come up several times in various conversations with the client, so I think we'll be using that again in some other jobs — for both print and the Web. Make sure you create the apple so it will work on either type of job, and save it as a separate file that an be easily accessed. Patrice will only be used on the Web, so you can set up that file with Web color and resolution.

When you get to the site interface, build a graphic style for what the button looks like when the mouse rolls over — the "over state". You're going to export the same interface several times (once for each page), but each one will only show the over state of a single button. A style will make it far easier to apply and remove the special formatting wherever and whenever it's needed.

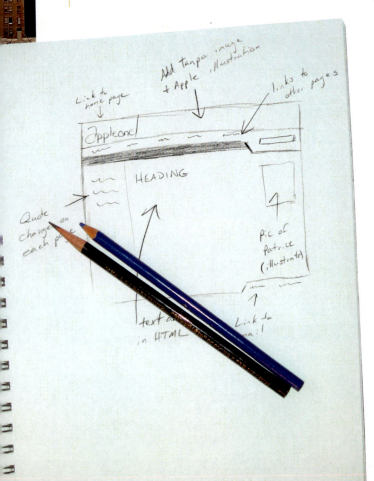

Project Objectives

To complete this project, you will:

- ❏ Create a gradient mesh
- ❏ Use Smart Guides to manage a gradient mesh
- ❏ Use filters to add object highlights
- ❏ Use Live Trace to create complex images
- ❏ Use a mask to create a custom banner image
- ❏ Create a graphic style for button over states
- ❏ Create slices from selections
- ❏ Create manual slices
- ❏ Divide slices
- ❏ Optimize image settings and export HTML

Stage 1 Working with Gradient Meshes

The first half of this project requires creating two illustrations based on objects in photographs. If you completed the earlier projects in this book, you've already used photographs as templates for drawing line art. For this project, however, you are going to go one step further. Rather than drawing only the outline of the objects, you're going to use the colors in the photographs to create complex blends that mimic those colors. These gradient meshes will add realistic depth to the vector artwork, resulting in a more realistic illustration than simply filling shapes with flat color.

 ## SET UP THE WORKSPACE

A significant amount of illustration work requires adding an element of depth to vector graphics. In Project 7 you created depth by drawing a perspective grid and transforming objects to match the guidelines. You can also add depth by varying shades and blending colors to create the appearance of three dimensions in a flat vector element. Gradient meshes — an extremely powerful Illustrator function — are perfectly suited for achieving this goal. Depending on the type of illustration you are building, you can create a gradient mesh from scratch, or you can use a photograph as a template for both the object shape and the colors in the mesh.

1. **Choose File>New and type "Apple" in the Name field. Choose RGB in the Color Mode menu and choose Screen (72 ppi) in the Raster Effects menu.**

   When you use the Web document profile, the other settings automatically change to reflect the standard settings for files that will be distributed on the Internet: pixels as the unit of measurement, RGB color mode, and 72 ppi raster effects.

   You are using this file as a drawing board only, so you can leave the page size and units options at the default values.

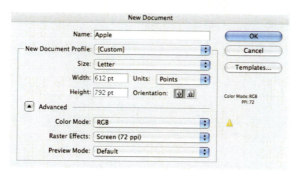

2. **Click OK to create the new file.**

3. **Place the file Apple.jpg from the RF_Illustrator>AppleOne folder into the document. Center the photo to the horizontal and vertical center of the Artboard.**

4. **Choose View>Hide Artboard.**

   As we mentioned, you are using this file as a drawing surface only. You are hiding the Artboard edges so they aren't distracting while you draw the artwork.

5. **Rename Layer 1 "Template Image".**

> **Note:**
>
> *Before completing this project, copy the AppleOne folder from the WIP folder on your Resource CD to the WIP folder where you are saving your work. You will save your files for this project in your WIP>AppleOne folder.*

6. **In the Layers panel, drag the Template Image layer to the Create New Layer button at the bottom of the panel.**

   This makes a duplicate of the selected layer.

Create New Layer button

7. **Select the image on the Template Image copy layer and drag it to the left.**

   You are going to draw on other layers, and then delete these image layers when your apple artwork is complete.

   For most of the process, you're going to use the original Template Image photo as the basis of your artwork. When you get to a certain point, however, you will need a copy of the photo because your artwork will obscure the placed photograph.

8. **Lock both Template Image layers, and hide the Template Image copy layer.**

   You will use the copy layer as a reference later, but for now you should hide it to avoid confusion.

9. **Create a new layer at the top of the layer stack and rename it "Apple Front".**

10. **Using the Pen tool with a 1-point black stroke and no fill, draw the outline for the front part of the apple. Follow the shape of the apple as it curves in front of the stem.**

    We started our contour line at the bottom part of the apple where there is a sharp corner because starting and stopping a contour line on a curve often creates less than perfect results. You can start your outline wherever you feel the most comfortable.

11. **If necessary, use the Direct Selection tool to adjust your anchor points and handles so the outline shape matches the shape of the apple.**

12. **Create another new layer and rename it "Apple Back". In the Layers panel, drag this layer below the Apple Front layer.**

13. **On the Apple Back layer, use the Pen tool to draw the shape of the back part of the apple (where the apple curves behind the stem).**

Be sure to overlap this shape with the Apple Front shape so no blank space will show between the two elements later.

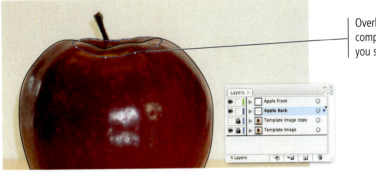

Overlap this line to ensure complete coverage when you start adding color.

14. **Create a new layer and rename it "Stem".**

Since you were just using the Apple Back layer, this new layer should automatically reside between the Apple Front and Apple Back layers in the Layers panel. If not, drag the Stem layer to the correct position before continuing.

15. Draw the shape of the stem on the active Stem layer. Again, overlap the bottom of the stem shape with the Apple Front shape.

You now have all the outlines for the apple, each on its own layer. When you start adding gradient meshes in the next stage of the project, you will see how important it is to use a different layer for each element.

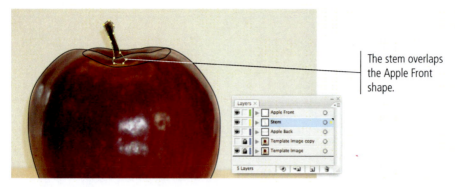

The stem overlaps the Apple Front shape.

16. Save the file as "Apple.ai" in your WIP>AppleOne folder and continue to the next exercise.

 CREATE A GRADIENT MESH

A gradient mesh is basically a special type of fill. Each point in the mesh can have a different color value; the colors of adjacent mesh points determine the colors in the gradient between the two points. When you paint objects with a mesh, it's similar to painting with ink or watercolor. It takes considerable practice to become proficient with gradient meshes.

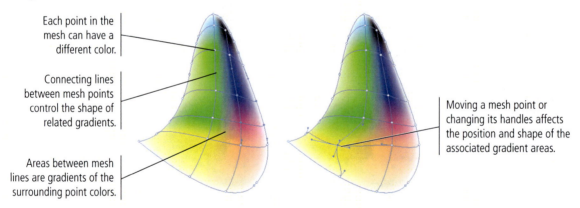

Each point in the mesh can have a different color.

Connecting lines between mesh points control the shape of related gradients.

Areas between mesh lines are gradients of the surrounding point colors.

Moving a mesh point or changing its handles affects the position and shape of the associated gradient areas.

One of the techniques you apply in this project is Illustrator's Outline Mode. Outline mode allows you to see the points and paths of an object without the colors and fills. This mode can be very useful when you need to adjust anchor points of one shape while viewing the underlying objects.

1. With Apple.ai open from your WIP>AppleOne folder, select the Apple Front layer, and then lock and hide the Apple Back and Stem layers.

2. Using the Selection tool, select the outline shape on the Apple Front layer.

3. **Using the Eyedropper tool, click a medium red color in the apple image to fill the selected apple shape with the sampled color.**

   You can add a gradient mesh to a path without filling it with color first; but if you don't choose a color, the mesh will automatically fill with white. It is easier to create a good mesh if you start with a fill that colors most of the object.

4. **Choose Object>Create Gradient Mesh and make sure the Preview option is checked.**

5. **In the Create Gradient Mesh dialog box, set the Rows value to 8 and the Columns value to 9, and make sure the Appearance menu is set to Flat.**

The Rows and Columns settings determine how many lines will make up the resulting mesh.

Note:

When you convert a path to a mesh, the shape is no longer a path. You cannot apply a stroke attribute to a gradient mesh object.

Gradient Mesh Options

When creating a gradient mesh, the numbers of rows and columns you create is dependent on the size and shape of the object you want to create. You might want to experiment with these settings before you click OK and create the mesh. If you add too many mesh points, the colors blend incorrectly and take a long time to paint; if you add too few mesh lines, it can be difficult — if not impossible — to add enough depth to the illustration. (Even though you can use the Mesh tool to add and delete mesh lines later, it's more efficient to create a mesh as close as possible to what you need as the end result.)

The Appearance option in the Create Gradient Mesh dialog box determines how colors affect the mesh you create:

- The **Flat** option spreads a single color to all points in the mesh. If you don't fill the shape with a color before creating the mesh, the mesh object will fill with solid white.

- The **To Center** option creates a white highlight at the center of the mesh, and gradually spreads highlight color outward toward the edges of the object. The Highlight (%) field controls the strength of the white highlight in the resulting mesh.

- The **To Edge** option is essentially the opposite of the To Center option; the white highlight appears around the edges of the mesh, blending to the solid color in the center of the mesh object.

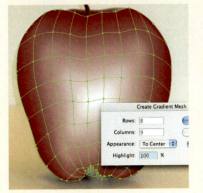
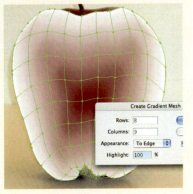

6. Click OK to create the mesh.

7. Choose View>Outline.

In Outline mode, you see only the **wireframes** that make up the objects in the file.

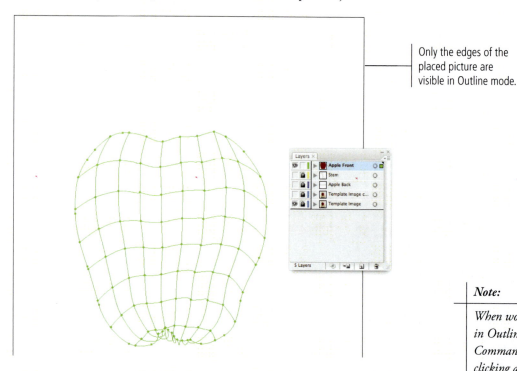

Only the edges of the placed picture are visible in Outline mode.

Note:

When working in Outline mode, Command/Control-clicking a layer's visibility icon turns only that layer back to Preview mode.

8. Command/Control-click the eye icon next to the Template Image layer to set it back to Preview viewing mode.

You're going to paint the mesh points using colors sampled directly from the apple image. You can now see the mesh wireframe and the actual pixels of the apple image, which makes this process possible.

The iris in the icon is hollow when a layer displays in Outline mode.

Note:

Using the View menu commands, you can't go directly from partial Outline mode back to the regular Preview mode. You have to first return all layers to Outline mode and then return to Preview mode.

9. **Using the Direct Selection tool, click the top-left point on the inside of the mesh object to select only that mesh point.**

   Don't select one of the mesh points on the edge of the shape.

10. **With the mesh point selected, choose the Eyedropper tool in the Tools panel and click next to the selected mesh point to sample the color from the apple photo.**

    Because the mesh object is still displayed in Outline mode, you can't yet see the effect of the color sampling.

Selected anchor point

Use the Eyedropper tool to sample color next to the anchor point.

11. **Press Command/Control to temporarily access the Direct Selection tool, and then click the next mesh point down on the same mesh line.**

12. **Release the Command/Control key to return to the Eyedropper tool, and then sample the color next to the selected mesh point.**

Selected anchor point

13. **Continue this process to change the color of the mesh points in the first three columns of the mesh.**

14. **Choose View>Outline to return all layers to Outline mode, and then choose View>Preview to see the actual content of the visible layers.**

15. Deselect everything on the page and review your progress.

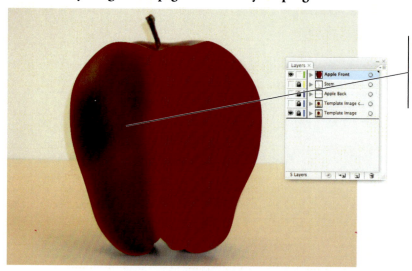

After painting only three columns of the mesh, you can already see how the shadows and highlights are starting to blend naturally.

16. Command/Control-click the eye icon for the Apple Front layer to change only that layer to Outline mode.

17. Using the same technique as in the previous steps, finish painting all the mesh points in the mesh object.

Ignore the bright highlights for now; you will add the proper highlights to your apple in a later exercise.

This might seem tedious because there are so many points in the mesh. With this process, though, you can create realistic depth in a flat vector object in a matter of minutes — using manual techniques, it would require many hours and a high degree of artistic skill to accomplish the same result.

18. Command/Control-click the Apple Front layer eye icon to return the layer to Preview mode, and then deselect the mesh object and review your results.

19. Save the file and continue to the next exercise.

WORK WITH A MESH USING SMART GUIDES

It is difficult (at best) to select and manipulate points in a mesh in Preview mode because you can't see the actual mesh lines and points until the mesh object is selected. You could move your cursor around until you locate the exact mesh point you want to work with, or you could continue switching back and forth between Preview and Outline modes, but both methods can be time consuming (and frustrating).

Fortunately, Smart Guides solve this problem. Using Smart Guides, you can see the entire mesh wireframe as soon as your cursor touches any part of the object — basically providing a temporary outline/preview combination.

1. **With Apple.ai open, choose View>Smart Guides.**

2. **Make sure the Snap to Point option is toggled off in the View menu.**

Note:

When using Smart Guides, make sure the Snap to Point option is toggled off. If Snap to Point is active, Smart Guides will not work (even if you have the command selected in the menu).

Using Smart Guides

ILLUSTRATOR FOUNDATIONS

In addition to being the best tool to view and select gradient mesh points, Smart Guides are also temporary snap-to guides that help you create, align, and transform objects relative to other objects.

This anchor is being dragged with the Direct Selection tool.

The Smart Guide shows that the anchor is being moved at a 45-degree angle from the original position.

Smart Guides show you when the cursor is at a precise angle relative to the original position of the object or point you're moving. When a Smart Guide is visible, it acts as a temporary snap-to guide so you can more easily maintain the correct angle (such as exactly horizontal, vertical, or 45 degrees from the origin).

You can change the appearance and behavior of Smart Guides in the Smart Guides & Slices pane of the Preferences dialog box. The Display options determine what is visible when Smart Guides are active:

- When **Text Label Hints** is active, Smart Guides include text labels that show the element (path or anchor) under the insertion point, the angle of movement, and other useful information.

- When **Construction Guides** is active, Smart Guides display when you move or change objects in the file.

- When **Transform Tools** is active, Smart Guides display when you scale, rotate, or shear objects.

- When **Object Highlighting** is active, moving the mouse over any part of an unselected object shows the anchors and paths that make up the object. If this option is turned off, Smart Guides show only the exact element (path or point) where the cursor is positioned.

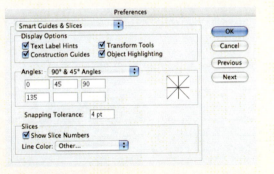

By default, Smart Guides show 45-degree intervals from the origin point (0 degrees, 45 degrees, 90 degrees, and 135 degrees). You can change or add to the guide angles using the Angles options; a number of options are built into the Angles menu, or you can type up to six specific angles in the available fields.

3. Make sure everything in the file is deselected, and then roll the Direct Selection tool over the apple shape.

You can now see the mesh points and lines, as well as what part of the mesh you are hovering your tool over.

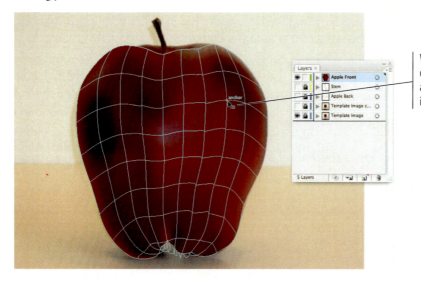

With Smart Guides turned on you can easily view and select specific anchors in the mesh.

4. Using the Eyedropper tool, sample the highlight color in the top-left side of the apple shape.

You are going to use the Mesh tool to create the rest of this highlight. By choosing a color from the existing highlight on your mesh object, rather than taking a sample from the photo, the highlight you create will blend more naturally with the highlight already in the top part of your mesh object.

Sample the color from this highlight.

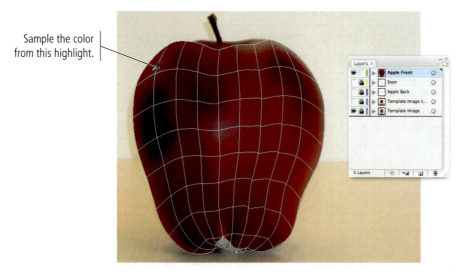

5. Choose the Mesh tool from the Tools panel.

The Mesh tool adds new gridlines to an existing mesh, or it creates a mesh if you click inside a basic shape that doesn't currently have a mesh.

6. **Click the third horizontal mesh line, between the first and second vertical lines, to create a new vertical mesh line (as shown in the following image).**

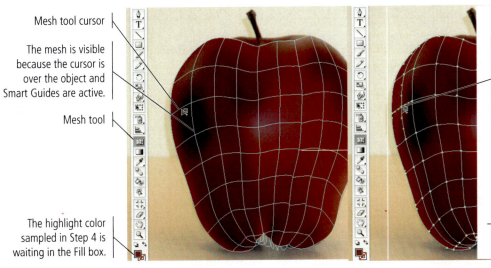

Mesh tool cursor

The mesh is visible because the cursor is over the object and Smart Guides are active.

Mesh tool

The highlight color sampled in Step 4 is waiting in the Fill box.

Clicking this horizontal mesh line with the Mesh tool adds a new vertical mesh path, already colored with the highlight color you sampled in the previous step.

Note:

Clicking a horizontal mesh path with the Mesh tool creates a new vertical mesh line. To add a horizontal mesh line, click the Mesh tool on a vertical mesh line.

7. **Using the Selection or Direct Selection tool, click away from the mesh object to deselect all points on the mesh.**

8. **Show the Template Image copy layer.**

9. **Using the Eyedropper tool, sample the highlight along the top curve of the apple on the Template Image copy layer.**

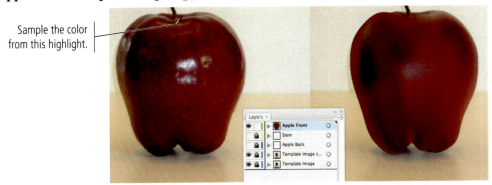

Sample the color from this highlight.

10. **Select the Mesh tool and click twice on the vertical mesh line directly below the stem to add two horizontal mesh lines between the first two rows of the existing mesh.**

It might be helpful to deselect the mesh after adding the first new mesh line, and then click again to add the second mesh line.

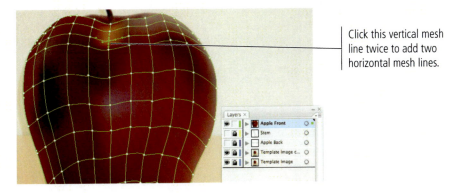

Click this vertical mesh line twice to add two horizontal mesh lines.

11. **Using the Direct Selection tool, select the point on the second horizontal gridline directly below the stem.**

This is one of the gridlines that you created with the Mesh tool in the previous step.

12. **With the mesh point selected, use the Eyedropper tool to sample a medium red of the apple to change the color of this point.**

When you change the color of a mesh point, you change the way surrounding colors blend into that point's color. By changing this point to a medium red, you reduce the distance over which the highlight color (in the lower point) can blend — effectively shortening the highlight area.

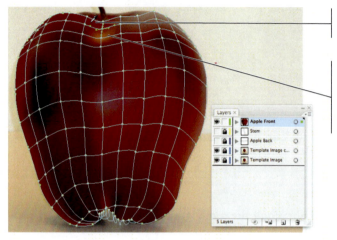

We sampled the red in this area.

Changing this anchor to medium red shortens the highlight area, more closely matching the highlight in the original image.

13. **Command/Control-click to select the mesh point to the immediate right of the point where you placed the highlight.**

Remember, pressing Command/Control temporarily accesses the Direct Selection tool.

14. **Release the mouse button to return to the Eyedropper tool, and then sample the highlight color again to spread the highlight horizontally across the apple.**

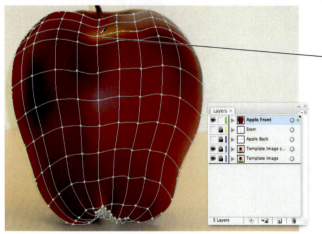

By filling this anchor with the highlight color of the point to the left, you are extending the highlight horizontally along the gridline.

15. Repeat Steps 13–14 for the mesh point to the immediate left of the point where you first placed the highlight.

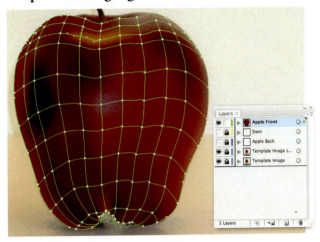

16. Deselect the mesh object and review the results.

The highlight is adding more depth, but it is spreading a bit too far (compared to the original image).

17. Using the Direct Selection tool, drag up the three mesh points immediately below the highlight points.

Reducing the distance between the points shortens the distance of the blended highlight-colored area.

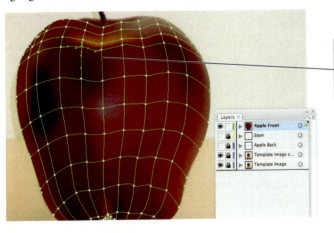

Moving the anchors below the highlight shortens the height of the blended highlight.

18. **Continue adjusting the color of the mesh points until you are satisfied with the results. Ignore the brightest highlight in the front for now; you'll use another technique to create that highlight later.**

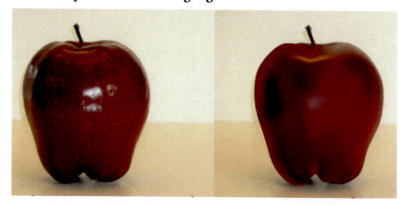

19. **Choose View>Smart Guides to toggle off the Smart Guides.**

20. **Save the file and continue to the next exercise.**

 ## COLORIZE THE REMAINING OBJECTS

Building and coloring the shape for the apple's front should have given you a good idea of how mesh points control color blending from one point to another. Because you set up the file using layers for the individual shapes that make up the apple, it will be fairly easy to create additional meshes for the remaining pieces of the apple.

1. **With Apple.ai open, lock and hide the Apple Front layer, and then show and unlock the Apple Back layer.**

2. **Using the Selection tool, select the shape on the Apple Back layer.**

3. **Using the Eyedropper tool, click a darker part of the apple to fill the selected shape with the sampled color.**

4. **Choose Object>Create Gradient Mesh and add a 3-row, 5-column mesh with the Appearance menu set to Flat.**

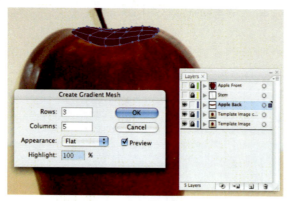

5. **Using the same method you used to color the mesh for the apple front shape, color the mesh points for the apple back shape.**

6. **Switch the mesh object to Outline mode, and then use the Eyedropper tool to sample colors from the photo for each point in the mesh.**

7. Show the Apple Front and Stem layers and review your work.

8. Lock the Apple Back layer and unlock the Stem layer.

9. Select the stem shape and fill it with a color sampled from the lightest color near the top of the stem.

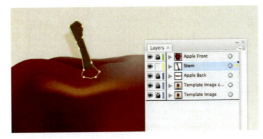

10. Change the Stem layer to Outline mode.

11. Deselect all objects, and then use the Eyedropper tool to sample the dark color of the stem.

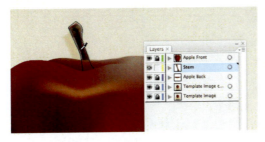

12. Return the Stem layer to Preview mode.

13. Using the Mesh tool, click in the middle of the stem shape to create a mesh, and then add a mesh point of the darker color.

Clicking with the Mesh tool converts the stem shape to a mesh object and adds a point (and the associated lines) where you click.

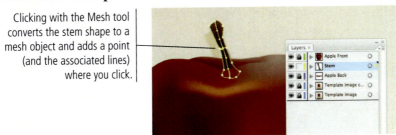

14. Save the file and continue to the next exercise.

USE FILTERS TO ADD OBJECT HIGHLIGHTS

As with any illustration, painting, or drawing, the details separate good work from great work. In this exercise, you add the highlights on the front and left sides of the apple to finish the illustration.

1. **With Apple.ai open, hide and lock the Apple Front, Apple Back, and Stem layers.**

2. **Create a new layer named "Apple Highlights" and move this new layer to the top of the Layers panel.**

3. **Using the Pen tool with a 1-point black stroke and no fill, create the shapes of the highlights on the front and left side of the apple.**

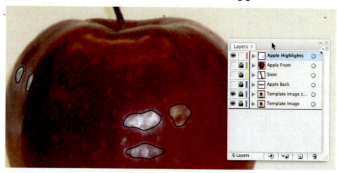

4. **Select all the highlight shapes you drew in Step 3 and fill them with a color sampled from the highlights in the photo.**

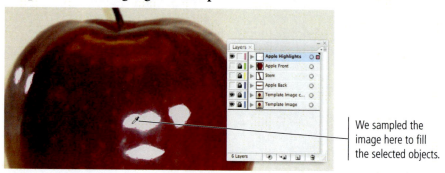

We sampled the image here to fill the selected objects.

5. **Deselect all objects. Select one of the larger highlight shapes and choose Effect>Stylize>Feather.**

6. **Activate the Preview option in the Feather dialog box, and then set the Feather Radius to 0.2".**

   The Feather effect softens the edges of the shape, blending from fully opaque to fully transparent. A higher Feather Radius value extends the distance from opaque to transparent color in the effect.

It is difficult to evaluate the actual results while the Apple Front layer is hidden.

7. **Click OK, and then show the Apple Front layer.**

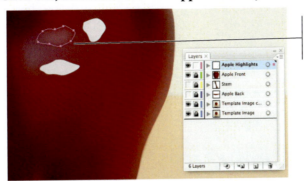

With the Apple Front layer showing, the large feather radius appears weak.

8. **With the feathered object selected, open the Appearance panel.**

   If you remember from Project 7, effects are applied as appearance attributes. You can edit the settings that create these attributes until you are satisfied with the results.

9. **Double-click the Feather effect in the Appearance panel to open the dialog box for that appearance attribute.**

10. **Make sure the Preview option is checked, and then experiment with the Feather Radius setting until you are satisfied with the highlight.**

11. **Zoom out so you can see both the Template Image copy layer and the apple you're drawing.**

12. **Apply the Feather effect to all the highlight areas, changing the Feather Radius value as appropriate for each object. Use the visible image copy to create highlights that approximate the original image.**

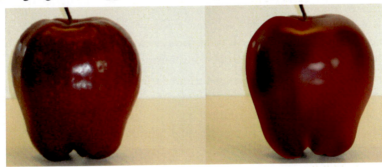

13. Delete both Template Image layers and show all remaining layers.

14. Open the Nature symbol library (Window>Symbol Libraries>Nature) and display the panel in Large List view.

As a finishing touch for your apple illustration, you're going to take a bit of artistic license and add a leaf to the apple. Instead of drawing one from scratch, you can use an existing Illustrator symbol.

15. Find the Leaf 3 symbol and drag it onto the page. Move the leaf so the stem of the leaf touches the stem of the apple, and then rotate and resize the leaf until you are satisfied with its position.

Note:

You worked extensively with symbols in Project 4, so you should be familiar with these libraries. If not, refer to Project 4 for complete explanations and instructions.

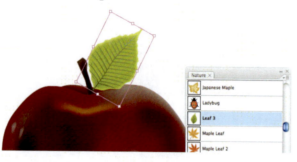

16. Control/right-click the leaf on the page and choose Break Link to Symbol from the contextual menu.

17. Save file and close it, and then continue to the next exercise.

 ## USE LIVE TRACE TO CREATE COMPLEX IMAGES

Once you've learned to use a gradient mesh, you will be able to create a very wide array of objects in Illustrator. However, hand-painting a mesh to recreate an extremely complex object (such as a face) from an image can be a very time-consuming process.

To illustrate a face, which you need to do for this project, you could create individual gradient mesh objects for all the different elements of the image — hair, skin, nose, eyes, teeth, lips, and so on. This could take many hours, if not days, to complete. If you don't have days (and you usually won't) to create a single illustration, you can use Illustrator's Live Trace function to automatically create the necessary vectors to reproduce a complex object.

1. Create a new letter-size document using the RGB color mode and 72 ppi raster effects.

2. Save the new file as "Patrice.ai" in your WIP>AppleOne folder.

3. **Place the file Patrice.tif (from the RF_Illustrator>AppleOne folder) into the document, centered horizontally and vertically on the Artboard.**

4. **Choose Object>Live Trace>Tracing Options.**

   If you use the command Object>Live Trace>Make, Illustrator automatically traces the image using the last-applied settings. If you (or anyone else) haven't used this function before now, the tracing defaults to black and white.

5. **Make sure the Preview check box is selected in the Tracing Options dialog box.**

6. **Click the Preset menu and choose the Photo High Fidelity option.**

   Illustrator includes a number of Live Trace presets that you can apply to any photo. Because the Preview option is checked, you can see the results of the preset as soon as the application finishes processing the command.

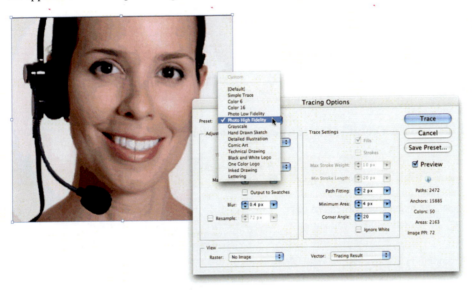

7. **In the dialog box, change the Max Colors field to 125.**

   By allowing more colors, you are allowing Illustrator to create more objects of different solid colors — ultimately increasing the range of tones available in the resulting illustration and making the drawing appear less choppy.

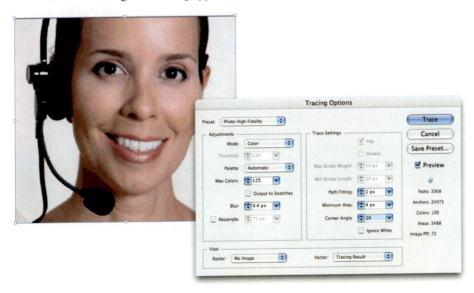

8. Click Trace to accept these settings and illustrate the photo.

The original photo disappears and your new tracing appears its place. The traced paths are not yet visible or editable. You need to expand the tracing so Illustrator can create editable anchors and paths, in case you need them in the future.

9. Select Object>Expand. Make sure the Object and Fill options are checked, and then click OK.

The individual paths are only accessible after expanding the Live Trace operation.

10. Save and close the file, and then continue to the next stage of the project.

Live Trace Options

With all of its different options and sliders, the Live Trace Options panel might seem a bit intimidating at first. As with any tool, it's easier to get the desired results if you know what each option does.

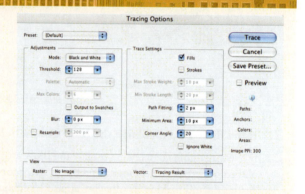

- **Mode** defines the color mode (color, grayscale, or black and white) of the resulting vector illustration.

- **Threshold**, which is only available when the mode is set to black and white, defines the maximum tonal value that will remain white before an area is filled with black.

- **Palette** defines the specific colors that can be used in a live trace; the default Automatic option allows Illustrator to use an unlimited palette as necessary to reproduce the image.

- **Max Colors** defines the maximum number of colors Illustrator can use to create the illustration. More colors create more depth, but also increase the complexity and number of points in the resulting illustration.

- **Output to Swatches** creates individual swatches from the colors in the traced illustration.

- **Blur** adjusts the amount of blur applied to the original image before tracing. Higher values can help eliminate artifacts and noise in the photo.

- **Resample** changes the resolution of a source image prior to tracing.

- **Fills**, when checked, results in solid-filled paths.

- **Strokes**, when checked, results in paths with an applied stroke color and weight.

- **Max Stroke Weight** defines the maximum stroke weight (when the Strokes option is checked) that can be applied before a stroke will be recreated as a fill object.

- **Min Stroke Length** defines the shortest allowable stroke (when the Strokes option is checked).

- **Path Fitting** adjusts how closely traced paths will follow the pixels of the original image.

- **Minimum Area** adjusts the smallest color area (in pixels) that can be drawn as a path.

- **Corner Angle** defines the minimum angle that can be traced as a sharp corner instead of a smooth curve. (By default, Live Trace by attempts to create smooth curves.)

Stage 2 Creating Web Site Graphics

It is very common to create the look and feel of a Web site in Illustrator, and then hand off the pieces to a programmer to assemble in a Web application such as Dreamweaver. That is exactly what you will do in the second half of this project.

To complete this project, you are going to modify a Web layout that has already been created, and then cut the page into pieces that can be reassembled and programmed later. For the client presentation, you will create the five different pages of the site, place images in the home page and customer service page to represent "finished" samples, and create the rollover appearance of navigation buttons.

Note:

To build a Web page in Illustrator, you can use built-in Web page sizes by choosing Web in the New Document Profile menu. A number of standard screen/monitor sizes are built into the Size menu, or you can define a custom width and height, as you can for a print layout.

Use a Mask to Create a Custom Banner Image

Your client is pleased with the overall site design, but would like to replace a plain gradient banner with an image of the Tampa skyline and the apple illustration floating over the city. Because the gradient is already filling a rectangle, you can use that existing shape to create the image-based banner.

1. **Open the file AppleOne_Web.ai from your RF_Illustrator>AppleOne folder.**

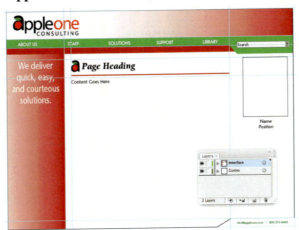

2. **Place the file Tampa.jpg from your RF_Illustrator>AppleOne folder into the Interface layer. Drag the image so it completely covers the white-to-red gradient at the top of the page.**

3. **Place the file Apple.ai (use the Art option in the Crop To dialog box). If you get a warning that some objects will be reinterpreted, click OK.**

4. **Drag the illustration so it overlaps the area where the banner rectangle exists.**

5. Select the placed image and the apple illustration, and then choose
   Object>Arrange>Send to Back.

6. Select only the skyline image and scale it to fit horizontally in the gradient-
   filled area to the right of the logo.

7. Select only the apple illustration and scale it to 75% horizontally and vertically.
   Make sure part of the illustration is behind the gradient-filled rectangle.

8. Using the Selection tool, choose the apple illustration, the skyline image,
   and the gradient-filled rectangle.

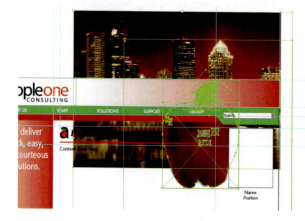

9. **Choose Object>Clipping Mask>Make.**

   The top selected object becomes a mask shape; anything outside the mask object boundaries becomes invisible.

Note:

Objects that aren't selected when you create the mask are unaffected by the mask.

10. **Double-click the mask area to enter Isolation mode for the mask group.**

    When you create a clipping mask, the mask object and the masked objects are automatically grouped. In this case, the apple illustration is already a very complex series of groups, so Isolation mode is the easiest way to manage the masked objects.

11. **Using the Selection tool, drag the skyline image until you are satisfied with the area that remains visible in the mask object.**

    One advantage to using masks is that you can drag masked objects to change the portion that is visible in the mask.

12. **Drag the apple image so the top area of the apple is visible, and the stem and leaf extend beyond the top edge of the mask shape.**

13. **Exit Isolation mode, save the file, and continue to the next exercise.**

 ## CREATE MOUSEOVER STYLES

The five text elements in the green bar will become navigation buttons. You will slice these elements and define targets for them in a later exercise. It is common practice to change the appearance of buttons when the mouse rolls over the button (called a Mouseover). Because of the way Illustrator manages page slicing, you need to be able to apply and remove the altered appearance from text elements used in mouseovers—and graphic styles enable you to do so.

1. **With AppleOne_Web.ai open, use the Selection tool to select the About Us text element in the green bar.**

2. **Choose Effects>Stylize>Drop Shadow.**

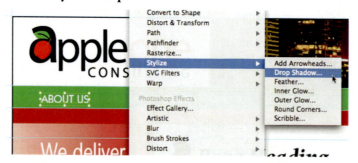

3. **Apply a small drop shadow with a small Blur value, using the Multiply blending mode and black as the shadow color. Click OK to apply the drop shadow.**

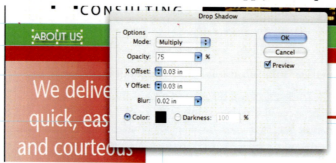

4. **Choose Effects>Stylize>Drop Shadow again.**

5. **When you see the warning message, click Apply New Effect.**

   You can apply multiple effects to a single object, including multiple instances of the same effect.

6. **Change the blending mode to Soft Light and the color to white. Change the X Offset and Y Offset fields to the inverse of the drop shadow from Step 3. Click OK to apply the second drop shadow to the text object.**

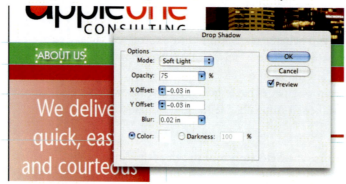

7. **Choose Window>Graphic Styles.**

   Graphic styles are managed in much the same way as the swatches and other libraries you used in Project 4.

8. With the shadowed text object selected, click the New Graphic Style button at the bottom of the Graphic Styles panel.

9. With the new style selected in the panel, choose Graphic Style Options from the panel options menu.

Delete Graphic Style

New Graphic Style

Break Link to Graphic Style

Graphic Styles Libraries Menu

10. Name the new style "Button Over State" and click OK.

This graphic style contains all of the effects and attributes applied in the first text object (the one that was selected when you created the style). You can now use the style button to apply multiple effects with a single click.

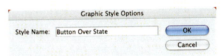

Note:

Illustrator includes a number of built-in style libraries, which you can access from the Window>Graphic Style Libraries menu, or by clicking the Graphic Styles Libraries Menu button at the bottom of the Graphic Styles panel.

11. With the About Us text element selected, click the Reduce to Basic Appearance button at the bottom of the Appearance panel.

The style is made of two effects, which you can remove in the Appearance panel.

12. Select the Support element, and then click the Button Over State option in the Graphic Styles panel.

Because you are going to present the final Support page, you should apply the over state style to that button text instead of the About Us button text.

13. Save the file and continue to the next exercise.

CREATE SLICES FROM SELECTIONS

The next step is to cut the file into pieces (called **slices**) that can work properly on a Web page. To present a finished page to the client, you also need to define hyperlink destinations for the main links. At the very least, each element that needs to link to a different location should become a slice, as should any element that requires unique output options (such as file format).

When you export the page, Illustrator can create an HTML file with the necessary information for assembling the slices into a functional Web page — which is useful for previewing your work. However, Illustrator is not a Web design application. You can create functional HTML for client review, but the final slices will be handed off to a programmer to reassemble in Dreamweaver using the appropriate structure and code.

Illustrator includes three options for creating slices: based on guides, based on a selection, and based on a manually defined area.

1. **With AppleOne_Web.ai open from your WIP>AppleOne folder, make sure the guides are visible (View>Guides>Show Guides).**

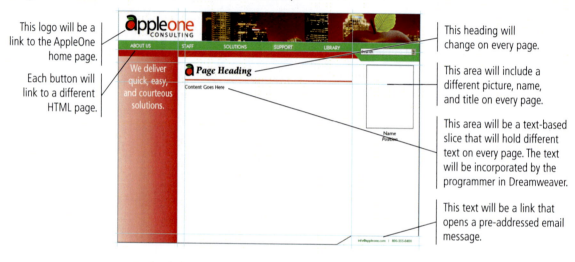

2. **Using the Selection tool, click the white space behind the AppleOne logo (in the top-left corner of the file).**

3. **Choose Object>Slice>Create from Selection.**

Slices are identified by a small number and icon in the top-left corner. When you create a slice, Illustrator automatically creates other slices as necessary — called automatic slices — to keep the ones you create in the proper positions.

Automatic slice

User slice

These slices, which are outside the design area, are created based on the outer edges of the objects in the banner clipping mask. They will be thrown away when the page is assembled in Dreamweaver, but they are necessary for Illustrator to maintain the proper slice alignment.

Note:

Automatic slices are identified with a grayed-out slice number and icon.

4. **With Slice 02 selected, choose Object>Slice>Slice Options.**

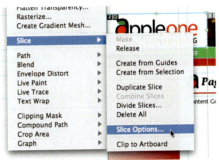

For every slice, you can define a number of settings:

- **Name** is the file name that will be used when you save the page or slice for the Web.

- **URL** is the page or file that opens if a users clicks the slice. (Slices don't have to be links; if you don't want a slice to link to something, simply leave the URL field blank.)

- **Target** is the location where the URL opens when you click the slice. Although there are other options available in full-scale HTML development applications such as Dreamweaver, you will primarily use "_self" to open the link in the same window or "_blank" to open the link in a new window.

- **Message Text** appears in the browser's status bar. If you don't type a specific message, the URL link will display.

- **Alt Tag** appears in place of an image when image display is disabled in the browser, or when a Web page is being read by screen-reader software for a visually impaired user.

Note:

You can also change the slice background type and color if the slice contains areas of transparency.

5. **Define the following settings for the slice, and then click OK:**

Name: **ao_logo**

URL: **index.html**

Target: **_self**

Alt text: **Welcome to AppleOne Consulting**

6. **Click OK to close the Slice Options dialog box.**

When you return to the document window, the slices seem to jump and renumber themselves. This is a bug in the software.

Slice 02, for which you just defined options, now incorrectly shows as Slice 03.

7. **Click away from Slice 02 to deselect it.**

The slices return to the correct positions and numbering.

After clicking away from the selected slice, the slices return to their correct positions and numbering.

8. **With the Selection tool active, click the search bar.**

When you try to select the Search bar, you will only access the hidden part of the apple illustration (and, because you're using the Selection tool, the group to which it belongs).

9. **With the apple illustration selected, choose Object>Lock>Selection.**

   You don't want to rearrange the stacking order, so you have to lock the clipping mask group to be able to select the Search bar.

10. **Click the search bar and choose Object>Slice>Create from Selection.**

    Because the clipping mask group is locked, you are able to select the group of objects that make up the search bar.

More automatic slices are added as necessary to support the user-defined slice.

11. **With the new slice selected, choose Object>Slice>Slice Options.**

12. **Change the Name field to "search_bar".**

    For any particular slice, you can define as many or as few of the slice options as you prefer. You don't have to define all options for all slices.

Note:

Search bars such as this one are entirely created and implemented in Dreamweaver. You are including this one only as a placeholder so the client can see the overall page layout for approval.

13. **Click OK to close the Slice Options dialog box, and then click away from the search bar slice.**

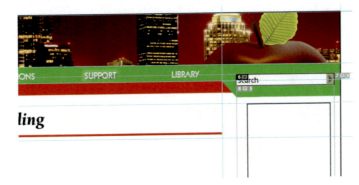

14. **Save the file and continue to the next exercise.**

CREATE MANUAL SLICES

Although some slices can be created based on an object's boundaries, other slices will be easier to manage by simply drawing them manually. The Slice tool, nested under the Crop Area tool in the Tools panel, allows you to create custom slices for any area of the page.

1. **With AppleOne_Web.ai open from your WIP>AppleOne folder, choose the Slice tool in the Tools panel (nested under the Crop Area tool).**

   You have already defined two user slices, and a number of automatic slices were also created to support the positioning of the ones you defined.

   When you export the page, the automatic slices will be named with sequential numbers based on the page name. If you want to be able to define a custom file name, link, or other option for a slice, you have to create a user slice in place of an automatic slice.

Slice tool cursor

Slice tool

2. **Using the Slice tool, draw a rectangle over the banner area. Start drawing the slice at the top-right corner of the logo slice and snap to the page guides on the right and bottom edges.**

   When you release the mouse button, the new slice becomes Slice 03 because slices are numbered by rows from top to bottom and left to right.

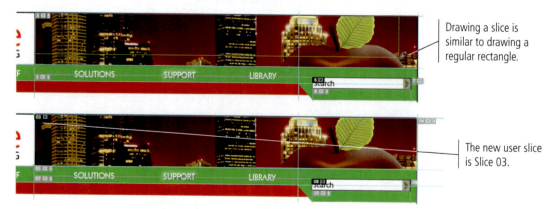

Drawing a slice is similar to drawing a regular rectangle.

The new user slice is Slice 03.

3. **Open the Slice Options dialog box for this slice and name the file "ao_banner". Leave all other fields empty and click OK.**

The slice you just created is still selected.

4. **Using the Slice tool, create additional slices as indicated by the semi-transparent rectangles in the following image.**

   For now, simply create the slices; you will change the options for those slices in the next steps.

5. **Choose the Slice Select tool (nested under the Slice tool) in the Tools panel.**

6. **Click to select the slice on the left side of the page where the "We deliver…" text appears (Slice 13 in our screen shot).**

7. **Choose Object>Slice>Slice Options.**

Selected slice

Slice Select tool

8. **Name the slice "support_message" and type the message text in the Alt field.**

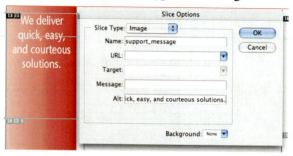

9. **Click OK to apply the options to the selected slice.**

10. **Using the same method, change the slice name for the page heading to "support_head", and change the slice name for the picture placeholder slice to "support_rep".**

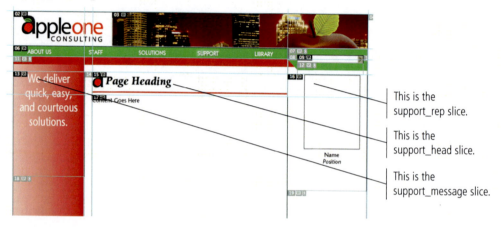

This is the support_rep slice.

This is the support_head slice.

This is the support_message slice.

11. **Select the slice below the support_head slice and open the Slice Options dialog box.**

12. **In the Slice Options dialog box, choose No Image in the Slice Type menu.**

The No Image slice type is useful if you want to create a slice to contain editable HTML text instead of a graphic representation of text.

13. **In the Text Displayed in Cell field, type "Support content goes here."**

When No Image is selected in the Slice Type menu, you can type the text that will appear in the slice after the page is exported. This text won't appear anywhere in Illustrator, except within the Slice Options dialog box.

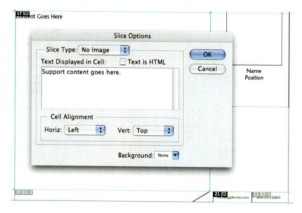

Note:

You can change the text alignment within the slice using the Cell Alignment menus. These alignment options function in the same way as aligning text within a regular text frame. The word "cell" is used in this case because the exported text area is actually a table cell, not an image slice.

14. **Click OK to close the Slice Options dialog box.**

15. **Select the slice that contains the email address and open the Slice Options dialog box.**

16. **Name the slice "email_link", and type "mailto:info@appleone.com" in the URL field.**

    The mailto: URL is the proper code format for creating an email link. Do not add a space between the colon and the email address.

17. **Click OK to change the slice options.**

18. **Save the file and continue to the next exercise.**

 ## DIVIDE SLICES

The buttons are the last bit of required slicing. Rather than trying to manually create the buttons with the Slice tool, you're going to divide the existing slice into equal pieces.

1. **With AppleOne_Web.ai open, use the Slice Select tool to click the button bar slice.**

2. **Choose Object>Slice>Divide Slices.**

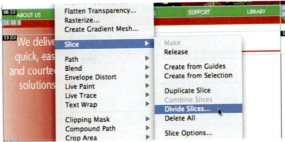

3. **Activate the Preview option in the Divide Slice dialog box and uncheck the Divide Horizontally option.**

    This bar includes five buttons that are distributed horizontally, which means you need to add vertical slices to separate the buttons.

4. **In the Divide Vertically section, type "5" in the Slices Across field.**

With the Preview option selected, you can see the five slices that will be created.

5. **Click OK to create the new slices.**

6. **Click away from the selected slices to deselect them.**

   You can't change the options for more than one slice at a time.

Note:

You can also create slices of a specific size using the Pixels Per Slice option.

7. **Using the Slice Select tool, click the first button slice, and then open the Slice Options dialog box.**

8. **Define the following options for the slice:**

   Name: about_button

   URL: about.html

   Target: _self

   Alt: Link to About Us Page

9. **Click OK to apply the slice options.**

10. **Using the same method, change the options for each of the remaining buttons:**

   Staff button

   Name: staff_button

   URL: staff.html

   Target: _self

   Alt: Link to Staff Listings

   Solutions button

   Name: solutions_button

   URL: solutions.html

   Target: _self

   Alt: Link to Custom Solutions Information

   Support button

   Name: support_over

   URL: support.html

   Target: _self

   Alt: Link to Customer Support

   Library button

   Name: library_button

   URL: library.html

   Target: _self

   Alt: Link to Resource Library

11. **Save the file and continue to the next exercise.**

Note:

You are using the "over" name for the support button because that button has the over state style applied. You will create the default state in a later exercise. The buttons' default and over states will be coded in Dreamweaver to function as rollovers.

All slices are now defined. As you might have guessed, however, you need to export six different pages for this site. The page content currently includes all of the elements that are visible on all pages. You still need to place the actual content for the support page, as well as create sample pages for the rest of the site so your client can preview the link functionality.

When you export a page to HTML, only visible content will be included in the resulting slices. The easiest way to manage object visibility is layers, so you are going to create a separate layer for each page in the site. You can then export each page, changing individual slice options as necessary for the page you're currently exporting.

1. **With AppleOne_Web.ai open, drag the Interface layer to the Create New Layer button.**

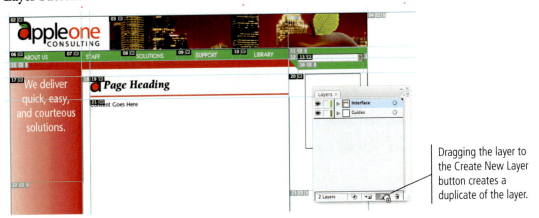

Dragging the layer to the Create New Layer button creates a duplicate of the layer.

2. **Repeat this process four more times so you have six copies of the Interface layer.**

Each of these layers will hold the content for a different page in the site.

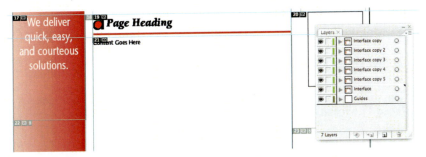

3. **Rename the layers as follows:**

> **Home Page**
>
> **About Us Page**
>
> **Staff Page**
>
> **Solutions Page**
>
> **Support Page**
>
> **Library Page**

The important point here is that each page has its own layer. It isn't necessary to use the same stacking order in this case, because only one layer will be visible at a time when you export the pages. We simply find a linear approach in layer ordering more easy to manage than random layer ordering.

4. **Hide all layers but the Support Page layer.**

   We're starting with this page because it will be the "completed" sample, and because you defined slice names based on the support page in previous exercises.

5. **Choose View>Hide Slices to turn off the slice numbers and icons.**

   If you need to work on the actual content, the slice indicators can be distracting. You can easily turn slice numbers and icons back on by choosing View>Show Slices.

6. **With the Support Page layer selected, use the Type tool to change the words "Page Heading" to "Customer Service".**

7. **Change the message text from "We deliver..." to "24/7 support, online and on target."**

   We also placed a soft return between the words "and" and "on" to create a more aesthetically pleasing text balance.

8. **Place the file Patrice.ai (from your WIP>AppleOne folder) in the page, using the Art crop-to option in the Place PDF dialog box.**

9. **Scale the placed artwork to approximately fit the area marked with the empty frame on the right side of the page, and align the bottom edge of the placed artwork to the bottom edge of the empty rectangle.**

10. **Select the rectangle placeholder shape and choose Object>Arrange> Bring to Front.**

11. **Press Shift and add the placed Patrice artwork to the selection, then choose Object>Clipping Mask>Make.**

12. **Below the placed artwork, change the word "Name" to "Patrice", and change the word "Position" to "Service Manager".**

13. **Save the file and continue to the next exercise.**

OPTIMIZE IMAGE SETTINGS AND EXPORT HTML

Once all the content has been placed and the slices have been defined, you can safely export the page and create all of the necessary image files for the Web. Before exporting, however, you should define the file formats, compression method, and color settings that will work best for each slice. This process is made easier using the File>Save For Web command.

1. **With AppleOne_Web.ai open from your WIP>AppleOne folder, choose File>Save For Web & Devices.**

   The Save For Web dialog box defaults to show the optimized version of the image. You can use the tabs at the top of the preview to show the original image or split the window into two or four panes (each pane can have different settings for experimentation).

2. **Using the Slice Select tool, click the top-left slice (Slice 02) where the AppleOne logotype appears.**

   Illustrator defaults to export slices using the GIF format, which is appropriate for vector art with areas of flat color (such as this logo). If you review the optimization settings, you can see the optimized file will download in 4 seconds over a 28.8-K modem.

Note:

Don't assume that all users have high-speed Internet access. Many people, especially in the general consumer and international markets, still use dial-up modems. If your target audience is one of these, you should optimize your files for slower download speeds.

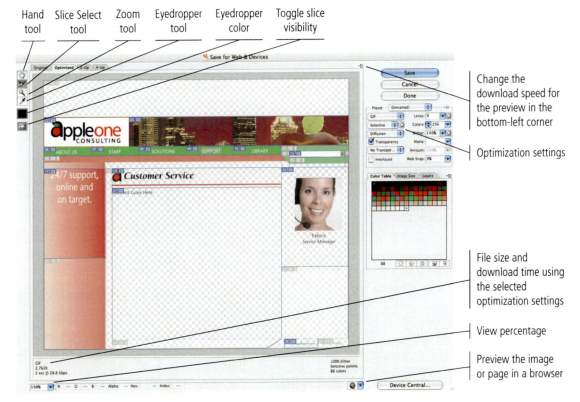

The large space at the top of the file is the result of Illustrator's auto-slicing, based on masked areas of visible objects. This slice will be removed in the Web programming application when the final pages are assembled.

3. **Select the banner slice and review the optimization settings.**

   Because this is a photograph, the JPEG format is a better choice than the default GIF.

When optimizing files for the Web, the format you use will affect the display of the colors in the exported file, as well as compression and transparency capabilities. The Save For Web dialog box allows you to save images or slices in one of five formats (JPEG, GIF, PNG-8, PNG-24, or WBMP), and then define options specific to the format you choose.

JPEG

JPEG is the format of choice for continuous-tone images (such as photos) since it can store up to 24-bit color. The JPEG format compresses information using lossy compression, which means information is lost in the resulting file. It is not well suited for text or graphics, since its compression method introduces a blurring effect to the images.

You can choose a predefined compression level (Low, Medium, High, Very High, or Maximum) or define a specific quality percentage. These choices refer to the quality of the resulting image, not the amount of compression applied; the higher quality you want, the less compression you should apply.

- The **Optimized** check box creates an enhanced JPEG with a slightly smaller file size. Some older browsers don't support this feature.
- The **Progressive** option allows the image to appear in stages as more data downloads; this option is only available if the Optimized check box is selected.
- The **Blur** option applies a Gaussian blur to the exported image, which allows higher compression without destroying the image.
- The **ICC Profile** preserves the profile of the image in the exported file.
- The **Matte** option defines a color for any pixels that were transparent in the original image. The JPEG format does not support transparency.

PNG-8 and PNG-24

PNG is another format used for Web graphics and images. Two versions of the format — PNG-8 and PNG-24 — support 8-bit and 24-bit color respectively. For the PNG-8 format, the options are the same as for the GIF format, except that PNG-8 files cannot be compressed. PNG-24 can support continuous-tone color as well as transparency.

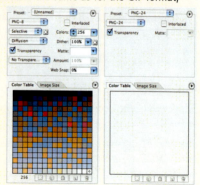

GIF

GIF is an 8-bit format typically used for graphics and artwork that don't have a large range of color. It is ideally suited for files with large areas of solid color, but it is ill suited for continuous-tone images that have subtle color variations.

When you save a file in the GIF format, all the colors are mapped to a color table (called **indexed color**). Indexed color is an 8-bit color model in which the specific 256 values are based on the colors in the image. You can remap the indexed colors using a number of options:

- **Perceptual** gives priority to colors to which the human eye is more sensitive.
- **Selective** is similar to Perceptual, but favors broad areas of color. This usually produces the best results.
- **Adaptive** samples colors appearing most commonly in the image.
- **Restrictive (Web)** uses a standard 216-color Web-safe color table. This option can result in drastic color shift.

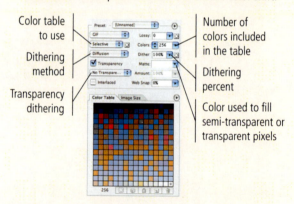

The **Lossy** option reduces file size by selectively discarding data; higher settings result in more data being discarded.

The **Dithering Method** option applies **dithering**, which blends two available colors to simulate additional colors. A higher dithering percentage creates the appearance of more colors and more detail, but can also increase the file size.

The **Transparency** and **Matte** options determine how transparent pixels are treated. If Transparency is checked, semi-transparent pixels blend into the defined Matte color.

The **Transparency Dithering** option allows you to dither transparency in a similar manner as dithering colors.

The **Interlace** option allows the image to display in stages as more data downloads (similar to progressive JPEG files).

The **Web Snap** option specifies a tolerance level for shifting colors to the closest Web palette equivalents.

4. **Click the Format menu, choose JPEG, and then review the Optimization settings.**

Using the High compression option, the image will download in 4 seconds on a 28.8-K modem. This is an acceptable download time, and the image preview shows that the quality will be fine for a small image like this one.

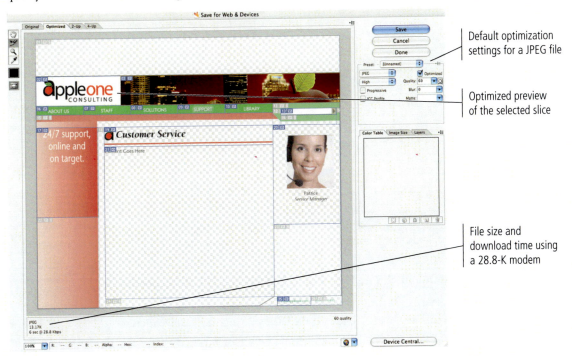

Default optimization settings for a JPEG file

Optimized preview of the selected slice

File size and download time using a 28.8-K modem

5. **Select the slice with Patrice's face and change the slice to export as a JPEG file.**

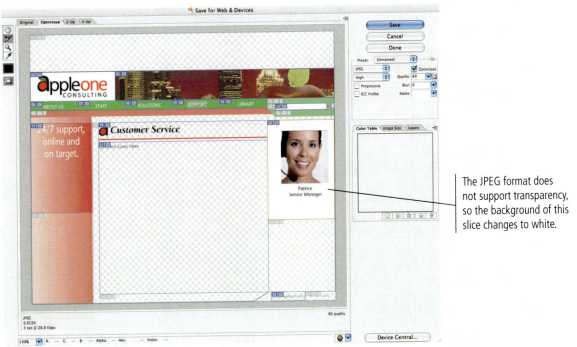

The JPEG format does not support transparency, so the background of this slice changes to white.

6. **Click the Save button and navigate to your WIP>AppleOne folder as the location for saving.**

7. **Change the file name to "support.html".**

Note:

Clicking Done closes the Save For Web dialog box and saves your slice Optimization settings.

Clicking Cancel simply closes the dialog box; your choices are not saved.

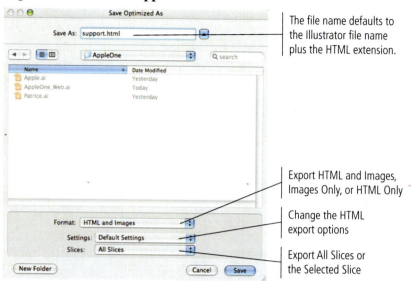

The file name defaults to the Illustrator file name plus the HTML extension.

Export HTML and Images, Images Only, or HTML Only

Change the HTML export options

Export All Slices or the Selected Slice

8. **Click the Settings menu and choose Other to define custom HTML export options.**

By default, auto slices export with names following the "filename_number" convention. You are going to export six different pages, however, and the automatic slices are exactly the same for all six pages. Rather than export six versions of the same slice (one for each page), you are going to change the naming structure for these slices so all six pages will use the same automatic slice images.

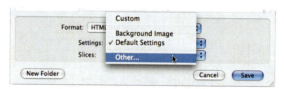

9. **In the Output Settings dialog box, choose Slices in the menu below the Settings heading.**

10. **In the first Default Slice Naming field, type "ao".**

11. **Click the menu to the right of the second field and choose underscore.**

12. **Click the menu to the right of the third field and choose slice no. (01, 02, 03 …).**

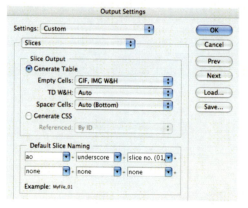

13. Click the Save button.

Rather than changing these settings for each of the six pages you need to output, you are saving the settings so you can easily call them again later.

14. Change the file name to "AO slices.iros" and click Save to create the custom output settings file.

15. Click OK to return to the Save Optimized As dialog box.

16. Make sure HTML and Images is selected in the Format menu and All Slices is selected in the Slices menu.

17. Click Save to export the HTML page and all of the necessary slices. If you receive a warning about file names, click OK to allow the export.

18. On your desktop, open your WIP>AppleOne folder and double-click the file support.html to open it in a browser window.

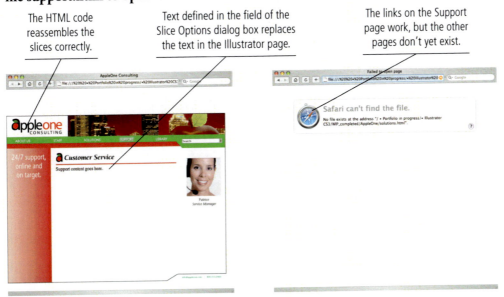

The HTML code reassembles the slices correctly.

Text defined in the field of the Slice Options dialog box replaces the text in the Illustrator page.

The links on the Support page work, but the other pages don't yet exist.

19. Close the browser and return to Illustrator.

20. Save the file and continue to the next exercise.

Using the Save For Web dialog box does not save your work in the native Illustrator file. You have to save the Illustrator file separately after the HTML and images have been exported.

HTML Output Options

When you use the Save For Web dialog box to output HTML, you can change the options for the resulting HTML by choosing Other in the Settings menu of the Save Optimized As dialog box. (Background Image, Default Settings, and XHTML are saved sets that you can call without opening the Output Settings dialog box.)

The Output Settings dialog box has four panes, which are accessed in the menu below the Settings menu. Most of these options require a good understanding of HTML, CSS, and Web design structure; if you don't understand these concepts, you can safely use the default settings for most basic Web pages that you design in Photoshop.

Background Options

The **View Document As** option defines a specific image or color to use as the Web page background. If Image is selected, the page displays an image or color as the background behind the image or page you are exporting. If Background is selected, the page will display the optimized image as a tiled background.

In the **Background Image** field, you can define an image to use as the page background. The background image will be tiled behind the optimized image on the Web page.

The **Color** field and menu allow you to define a color that will be used as the background of the exported page.

Saving Files Options

The **File Naming** options change the default file naming conventions for files created when you export an image or page for the Web. These options are similar to those that you used to assign names to batch-processed files.

The **Filename Compatibility** options make the filename compatible with Windows, Mac OS, or UNIX servers.

The **Put Images In Folder** option defaults to "images", which is a standard convention for Web site folder structure. If a folder named "images" does not exist where you save the optimized file, the images folder will be created for you.

The **Copy Background Image When Saving** option preserves a defined background image as a single image.

The **Include XMP** option preserves any defined metadata that was added to the document. (**Metadata** is information about a file such as author name, copyright, and keywords.)

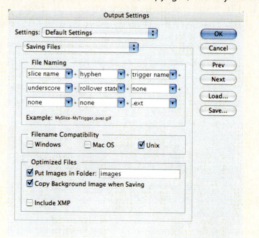

HTML Options

The **Output XHTML** option creates Web pages that meet the XHTML standard. This option disables options that might conflict with this standard; when this is selected, the Tags Case and Attribute Case options are automatically set.

The **Formatting** options determine how the resulting HTML code will be formatted:

- **Tags Case** defines the capitalization for tags.
- **Attribute Case** defines the capitalization for attributes.
- **Indent** defines a method for indenting lines of code.
- **Line Endings** defines the platform for line ending compatibility.
- **Encoding** defines the default character encoding for the page.

The **Coding** options determine what will be included in the resulting code:

- **Include Comments** adds explanatory comments to the HTML code.
- **Always Add Alt Attribute** adds the ALT attribute to images to comply with Web accessibility standards.
- **Always Quote Attributes** places quotation marks around tag attributes, which is required for compatibility with some older browsers.
- **Close All Tags** adds closing tags for all HTML elements in the file for XHTML compliance.
- **Include Zero Margins On Body Tag** removes default internal margins in a browser window, and adds margin tags with zero values to the body tag.

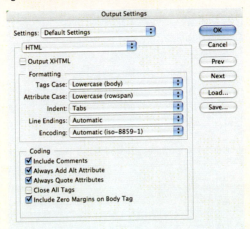

Slices Options

The **Generate Table** option creates an HTML table to reassemble the slices in the exported Web page.

- **Empty Cells** defines how empty slices are converted to table cells.
- **TD W&H** defines when to include width and height attributes for table data.
- **Spacer Cells** defines when to add empty spacer cells around the generated table.

The **Generate CSS** option creates a cascading style sheet to reassemble the slices in the exported page. The **Referenced** menu defines how slice positions are referenced in the HTML file (By ID, Inline, or By Class).

The **Default Slice Naming** options are, again, like the options that you used to name batch-processed files.

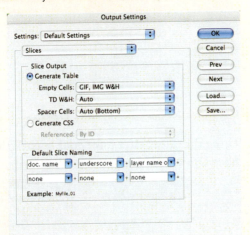

CREATE THE REMAINING PAGES

For all intents and purposes, the main work for this project is done. The final step is to create the other five "placeholder pages" so the client can click through the samples and review the overall functionality. Completing this exercise will be somewhat repetitive, but it is required to get the job done.

1. **With AppleOne_Web.ai open, hide the Support Page layer and show the Home Page layer.**

2. **Using the Selection tool, select the Support button text and click the Reduce to Basic Appearance button at the bottom of the Appearance panel.**

3. **Change the words "Page Heading" to "Welcome to AppleOne Consulting".**

4. **Choose File>Save For Web & Devices.**

5. **Using the Slice Select tool, double-click the support button slice to open the Slice Options dialog box.**

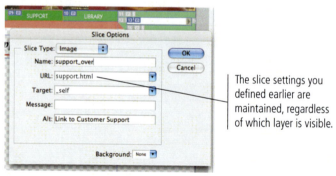

The slice settings you defined earlier are maintained, regardless of which layer is visible.

6. **In the Name field, change the word "over" to "button".**

Because you removed the over state style, you can now change this slice name to create the default button state image.

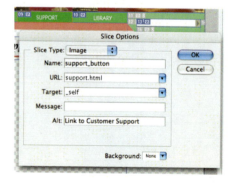

7. **Click OK to apply the updated options.**

8. **Double-click the slice containing the "We deliver…" quote.**

    Four slices have different content on each page: the quote on the left side, the page heading, the content area, and the headshot/title on the right. You need to change the name of each of these four slices for every page you export.

9. **In the Name field, change the word "support" to "home" and click OK.**

10. **Using the same method, change the names of the heading and headshot slices to indicate the home page instead of the support page.**

11. **Double-click the text area slice. In the text field, change the word "Support" to "Home page". Click OK to close the Slice Options dialog box.**

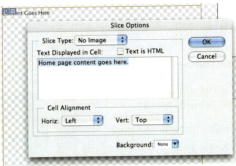

12. **Click Save.**

13. **Navigate to the WIP>AppleOne folder as the target location and change the file name to "index.html".**

14. Choose AO slices in the Settings menu and click Save.

15. When you see the Replace Files dialog box, click Replace.

This dialog box shows that some slices already exist in the location where you are saving the files — these are the slices you created when you exported the Support page. Because those slices haven't changed, you can safely overwrite the original slices with the new versions.

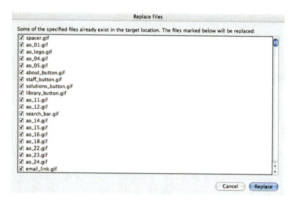

16. When you return to the Illustrator file, export the remaining four pages (and the associated slices) using the techniques you have already learned.

For the About Us page:

- Apply the Button Over State graphic style to the About button text. Change the slice name to "about_over".

- Restore the Support button text to the basic appearance. Change the support button slice name to "support_button".

- Change the page heading to "About AppleOne Consulting". Change the slice name to "about_head".

- Change the sidebar message to "AppleOne is the NumberOne Source." Change the slice name to "about_message".

- Change the headshot slice name to "about_rep".

- Change the no-image slice text to "About Us content goes here." (Remember, this text won't appear in the Illustrator file; it will only appear in the exported page.)

- Export the page as "about.html" (the name that you defined earlier as the link for the About Us button).

For the Staff page:

- Apply the Button Over State graphic style to the Staff button text. Change the slice name to "staff_over".

- Restore the Support button text to the basic appearance.

- Change the page heading to "AppleOne Staff Directory". Change the slice name to "staff_head".

- Change the sidebar message to "AppleOne experts are in your corner." Change the slice name to "staff_message".

- Change the headshot slice name to "staff_rep".

- Change the no-image slice text to "Staff Directory content goes here."

- Export the page as "staff.html" (the name that you defined earlier as the link target for the Staff button).

For the Solutions page:

- Apply the Button Over State graphic style to the Solutions button text. Change the slice name to "solutions_over".

- Restore the Support button text to the basic appearance.

- Change the page heading to "Custom Training Solutions". Change the slice name to "solutions_head".

- Change the sidebar message to "Custom solutions can solve all our customers' problems." Change the slice name to "solutions_message".

- Change the headshot slice name to "solutions_rep".

- Change the no-image slice text to "Custom Solutions content goes here."

- Export the page as "solutions.html" (the name that you defined earlier as the link for the Solutions button).

For the Library page:

- Apply the Button Over State graphic style to the Library button text. Change the slice name to "library_over".

- Restore the Support button text to the basic appearance.

- Change the page heading to "AppleOne Resource Library". Change the slice name to "library_head".

- Change the sidebar message to "The definitive source for management solutions." Change the slice name to "library_message".

- Change the headshot slice name to "library_rep".

- Change the no-image slice text to "Library content goes here."

- Export the page as "support.html" (the name that you defined earlier as the link target for the Support button).

17. Save the native Illustrator file and close it.

Summary

The gradient mesh functionality extends Illustrator's basic drawing tools, allowing you to create complex vector graphics with a degree of depth that would be difficult — if not impossible — to create otherwise. The apple that you created manually is as close to a photograph as possible, while still maintaining the flexibility of vector artwork; the artwork of the Patrice illustration combines photo realism with illustration techniques to create a unique artistic effect.

Although many developers use dedicated Web design software like Adobe Dreamweaver to build sophisticated Web sites, the images for those sites have to come from somewhere. It is very common for a designer to build the "look and feel" of a site in Illustrator, then slice and export the pieces so the developer can reassemble them in the Web design application. And as you saw by completing this project, Illustrator can be used to create complete (although basic) pages.

Use a gradient mesh to create depth in a vector-based illustration

Combine images and illustrations using a clipping mask

Use Live Trace to create complex illustrations from photographic pixels

Create a graphic style for button over states

Slice a page into pieces for HTML export

Define hyperlink destinations for various layout elements

Portfolio Builder Project 8

Every professional designer needs a portfolio of their work. If you've completed the projects in this book, you should now have a number of different examples to show off your skills using Illustrator CS3.

The eight projects in this book were specifically designed to include a broad range of *types* of projects; your portfolio should use the same principle.

Using the following suggestions, gather your best work and create printed and digital versions of your portfolio:

❏ Include as many different types of work as possible.

❏ Print clean copies of each finished piece that you want to include.

❏ For each example in your portfolio, write a brief (one or two paragraph) synopsis of the project. Explain the purpose of the piece, as well as your role in the creative and production process.

❏ Design a personal promotion brochure — create a layout that highlights your technical skills and reflects your personal style.

❏ Create a PDF version of your portfolio so you can send your portfolio via email, post it on job sites, and keep with you on a CD at all times — you never know when you might meet a potential employer.